JUSUUR 1
BEGINNING COMMUNICATIVE ARABIC

Jusuur 1

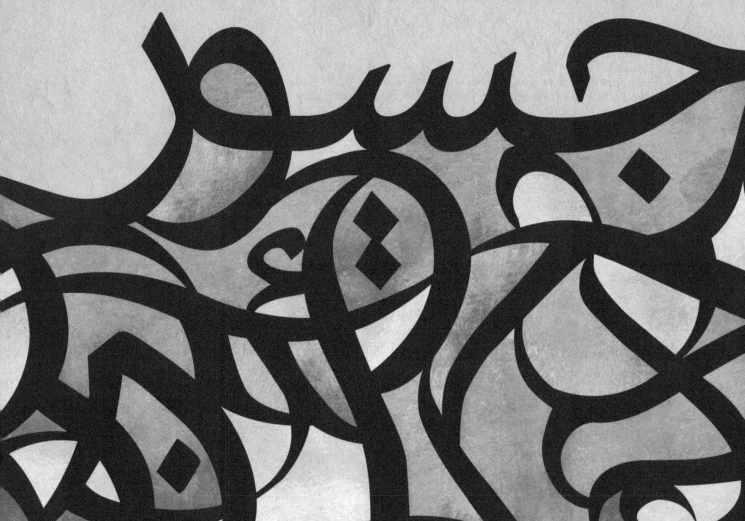

BEGINNING COMMUNICATIVE ARABIC

Sarah Standish | Richard Cozzens | Rana Abdul-Aziz

Georgetown University Press | Washington, DC

The publisher is not responsible for third-party websites or their content. URL links were active at time of publication.

Library of Congress Cataloging-in-Publication Data

Names: Standish, Sarah, author. | Cozzens, Richard, author. | Abdul-Aziz, Rana, author.
Title: Jusuur 1: Beginning Communicative Arabic / Sarah Standish, Richard Cozzens, Rana Abdul-Aziz.
Description: Washington, DC: Georgetown University Press, 2022. | Includes index.
Identifiers: LCCN 2021047320 | ISBN 9781647120207 (paperback) |
    ISBN 9781647120191 (hardcover) | ISBN 9781647120221 (paperback)
Subjects: LCSH: Arabic language—Textbooks for foreign speakers—English. |
    Arabic language—Conversation and phrase books—English.
Classification: LCC PJ6307 .S73 2022 | DDC 492.7/82421—dc23/eng/20211122
LC record available at https://lccn.loc.gov/2021047320

∞ This paper meets the requirements of ANSI/NISO Z39.48-1992 (Permanence of Paper).

23 22   9 8 7 6 5 4 3 2   First printing

Printed in the United States of America

Cover design by Martha Madrid
Interior design by Matthew Williams, click! Publishing Services

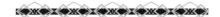

Dedicated to those teaching Arabic as a world language—your hard work
is our inspiration. A textbook is nothing without a committed, hardworking,
and talented teacher. Thank you for bringing Arabic to life for your students.

Table of Contents

المحتويات

Acknowledgments

الشكر والتقدير

As the Arab saying goes, "one hand can't clap alone." There were many helping hands offering the advice, support, expertise, and feedback that brought this book into fruition. We would like to express our sincere thanks to the following people:

We would like to thank the staff at Georgetown University Press. They have worked tirelessly to bring our vision to life, and this textbook is a testament to their flexibility and creative problem-solving abilities.

We also thank Mahmoud Al-Batal for his mentorship and ongoing encouragement throughout the entire process. Mahmoud regularly took time out of his incredibly busy schedule to advise us on the book, especially the video scripts.

We are grateful to Qatar Foundation International for its pivotal support, both of K–12 Arabic language education broadly speaking and specifically on this project. In particular, Maggie Mitchell Salem, Carine Allaf, and Kelly Doffing have given indefatigable support to ensure a high-quality final product.

Several talented and innovative K–12 Arabic teachers were willing to offer themselves as pilot teachers, using our draft textbook and homemade pilot videos and audio recordings over an entire academic year. Many thanks to Annie Hasan (Shawnee Mission South High School), Katie Quackenbush (Boston Latin Academy), George Kimson (Hendrickson High School and Pflugerville High School), Kwame Larson (E.L.-Haynes Public Charter School), Ruth McDonough (American School of London), and Rachid Rhenifel (OneWorld Now!). We greatly appreciate the valuable input from them and their students.

Our film crew in Amman was exemplary for their hard work and professionalism throughout, with special thanks to Producer Ibraheem Shaheen, Director Lina Al-Haj, and the many cast and crew members including Yara Takriti, Leanne Katchuda, Mohammad Abdulraheem, Farah al-Nasser, and Khalid Al-Damin. For the pilot audio and visual materials, we are also grateful to seven newly arrived Syrian and Palestinian refugees in Cyprus who acted in our pilot videos and recorded audio files for the schools' use, especially Khawla, Retaaj, and Jehad. Additionally, we want to thank Udai AbuLteaf for his pilot audio recordings.

Our reviewers' input was extremely valuable as the book took shape, and we extend our sincere thanks to Ruth McDonough, Samar Moushabak, Lucy Thiboutot, Iman Hashem, Alaa El Gibali, Katie Quackenbush, and Alaa Razeq.

We are grateful for the sharp eyes of Paul Wulfsberg and Jackie Compton who proofread early drafts of the manuscript. A special thanks goes to Keegan Terek for his comprehensive review of the manuscript. His comments and suggestions helped us improve all aspects of the manuscript, from fixing spelling to clarifying concepts. Any remaining errors are our own responsibility.

As lifelong students of Arabic, we were all fortunate to have professors and mentors who stimulated our love for the Arabic language and inspired us to make our own

contribution to the Arabic teaching community such as Amira El-Zein, Mohammad Alwan, Kristen Brustad, Cathy Keatley, Dora Johnson, Steven Berbeco, Taoufiq Ben-Amor, Carl Sharif El-Tobgui, Hussein Maxos, and too many others to name here.

Thank you to our own students who inspire us with their work ethic and drive to learn and explore a new language and culture and who keep us on our toes to be more effective guides on their journey.

Each of us must also thank the people who have personally supported us in this journey.

Sarah: This project would never have begun, much less been completed, without the encouragement of my husband, John Compton. John's practical advice and continuous moral support helped me make a project I had dreamed of into a reality and kept me going along the way. Many thanks as well to my parents, Emily and Myles Standish, for opening up to the world of Arabic and the Middle East along with me when I began studying Arabic as a freshman in college. My many Arabic professors in college, on my study abroad trips, and at the Center for Arabic Study Abroad pushed me to learn more than I would have thought possible. Dr. Steven Berbeco and Peyton Chapman believed in me as a teacher, hired me for teaching jobs that challenged me, and gave me the freedom to create my own curricula and teaching materials without which I never would have conceived of a textbook.

Richard: Many thanks to my colleagues and students at Roland Park Country School in Baltimore and the STARTALK Arabic Summer Academy in Boston. Teachers and students alike supported my developing practice of teaching Arabic and inspired me to keep exploring, learning, and trying new things. Thanks to the confidantes and supporters who encouraged me: Carla Childs, Bill Cozzens, Ian Cozzens, Dan Cozzens, Josh Neff, and Chelsea Saltos, among many others. Finally, I would like to express my deep gratitude to my co-authors Rana and Sarah for their constancy and companionship over the course of this journey.

Rana: Thank you to my parents, Emad Abdul-Aziz and Maha Hamza, for keeping Baghdad alive in a Boston suburb. Many thanks as well to my children, Reema and Zade, who I hope will always find their identity and home through their language, and to my husband, Paul Wulfsberg, for encouragement and endless support. I also wish to express my gratitude to my students and colleagues at Tufts University, especially Souhad Zendah and Fadi Jajji.

Introduction

المقدمة

Ahlan wa-sahlan! Welcome to Arabic and welcome to the *Jusuur* curriculum. This is the first part of a two-textbook series, *Jusuur 1* and *Jusuur 2*, that will teach you to communicate in Arabic about yourself and your life, while learning the letters and sounds of the Arabic alphabet.

Why are you learning Arabic? What are your goals in learning the language? It is important to identify and write these down somewhere, so you can remind yourself occasionally of why you started this journey!

The *Jusuur 1* curriculum consists of the following:

- This textbook, which is organized in thematic units filled with activities to help develop your skills in speaking, listening, reading, and writing. It includes vocabulary lists, short and simple grammar explanations to help you use the language in a specific context, along with images, graphs, and lots of rich cultural information.
- An alphabet workbook focused on the Arabic alphabet. You or your teacher may choose to learn the letters and sounds with a different book.
- Extensive audio-visual material to help you learn Arabic. Throughout *Jusuur* you will find audio recordings accompanying vocabulary lists and listening exercises. When you see the icon , you will know that there is a recording that goes with the activity. There are also videos featuring conversational scenes of everyday life filmed on location in Jordan. When you see the icon , you will know that there is a video that goes with the activity. These audio and video materials can be found by visiting the *Jusuur* website (http://JusuurTextbook.com).

Listen to a recording on the Jusuur website.

Watch a video on the Jusuur website.

Challenge yourself with this task.

Teachers: Find a printable sheet for this activity on the Jusuur website.

GETTING THE MOST OUT OF YOUR LANGUAGE LEARNING EXPERIENCE

Learning a new language is an exciting endeavor. We understand that for some, this might be your first experience, so we want to offer a few tips below using some Arabic proverbs.

AS-Sabr jamiil "*patience is beautiful*"

الصبر جميل

Learning a language takes time and dedication. Initially, as you encounter new sounds and combination of sounds, it is useful to realize that you will not be able to master them overnight. Do not get down on yourself. Producing new sounds requires locating and activating muscles you may not have used before. Similarly, patience is required as you first learn to sound out letters to read words and then move on to sentences and texts. Writing and connecting letters will also be slow at first but will later become quick and automatic for you, with practice. New vocabulary will be challenging to remember at first. If you study and practice enough, you will be able to access those new words easily. Your brain needs time to absorb and internalize the new content and material, so try to dedicate a little time every day to studying Arabic. Practicing Arabic at home for ten minutes a day, six days a week will go a lot further than cramming for one hour once a week.

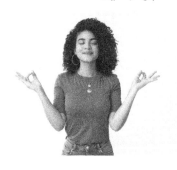

Man jadda wajada wa man zaraᶜ HaSada "*one who searches will find and one who plants will harvest*"

من جد وجد ومن زرع حصد

Learning a new language does not occur by osmosis alone; it requires hard work. Babies and small children take years to start forming sentences in their first language. Anyone can acquire a new language much faster than children can by working actively and deliberately. You cannot expect to merely glance at a vocabulary list to learn it or to hear a word or phrase once to memorize it. Be an active and engaged learner! Listen to the audio recordings over and over again, write out words in a special practice notebook, create flashcards and use them to practice outside of class. In the textbook, you will see some questions marked with the icon 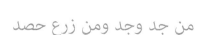. These questions are especially challenging or are a task that goes above and beyond. Challenge yourself to take on as many of these questions and tasks as you can throughout the year. By pushing yourself, you will learn both what you are good at and what you need to focus more on.

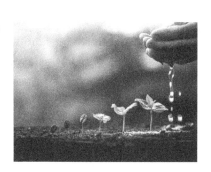

Learning a language goes beyond memorizing and repeating words. By understanding patterns and how you can create meaning with the words and phrases you have learned, you will truly begin to become an Arabic speaker. Ask your teacher about apps you can use to help you quiz yourself and study on your own or in groups. Look for ways to engage with and use Arabic within your community. See if you can find cultural activities or meet Arabic-speaking members of the community, either physically or virtually, and ask them to talk with you in Arabic. You may be surprised by how delighted they are to find someone learning their language.

Jammid qalbak "freeze your heart" ("*tough it out*")

جمّد قلبك

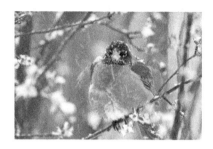

Your teacher and sometimes your classmates will correct you when you make mistakes. These corrections are designed to keep you on the right path and help you internalize the right sounds and patterns. Understand that this process is an essential part of learning a language. Think of your teacher and peers as your coaches in sports or directors in a play. Everyone will make mistakes when learning a language. Work with your classmates to create a learning environment where everyone is supported, and no one is quiet out of the fear of making a mistake. One of the hallmarks of successful language learners is their willingness to practice—in class and outside of it.

This book is designed in such a way that all students will need to participate actively by speaking aloud in every single class. There is no room to be silent. It is crucial not to be self-conscious about the mistakes or corrections. If you struggle with this, try taking on a different personality in class, such as by adopting a new name. It is normal that some of us feel more comfortable expressing ourselves in different ways, so challenge yourself to develop a new strength. If you are a confident speaker, you may have to push yourself to improve your writing. If writing comes more easily to you than speaking, push yourself to express yourself in speech.

Good luck!
Bit-tawfiiq!
بالتوفيق!

Greetings and Introductions

التحيات والتعارف

UNIT ONE GOALS— HOW IS YOUR ARABIC?

أهداف الوحدة الأولى— كيف عربيتك؟

This section lists the unit objectives. While you are working through the lessons in this unit, refer to this list and keep track of your progress toward each objective as you go. By the end of each lesson, you should be able to do the following in Arabic:

Lesson 1

الدرس الأول

- Ask how to say something
- Ask the meaning of a word
- Ask your teacher or classmate to repeat what they said
- Respond to a yes or no question

Lesson 2

الدرس الثاني

- Greet others politely in Arabic
- Use polite body language for greeting others in Arab cultural contexts
- Ask and respond to questions about how you are doing
- Take leave of someone else and say goodbye to someone who is leaving

Lesson 3

الدرس الثالث

- Ask and respond to questions about where you are from
- Ask and respond to questions about your age

Lesson 4

الدرس الرابع

- Introduce a friend to others
- Tell others what your family background is
- Tell what others' family backgrounds are, such as friends and famous people

Lesson 5

الدرس الخامس

- Write down your own or someone else's phone number in Eastern Arabic numerals
- Ask someone else for their email address and phone number
- Respond to requests for your email address and phone number

1

Classroom Talk:
How do we say … ?

الدرس الأول

كلام الصفّ:
كيف نقول...؟

LESSON ONE GOALS

أهداف الدرس الأول

By the end of this lesson, you should be able to do the following in Arabic:

- Ask how to say something
- Ask the meaning of a word
- Ask your teacher or classmate to repeat what they said
- Respond to a yes or no question

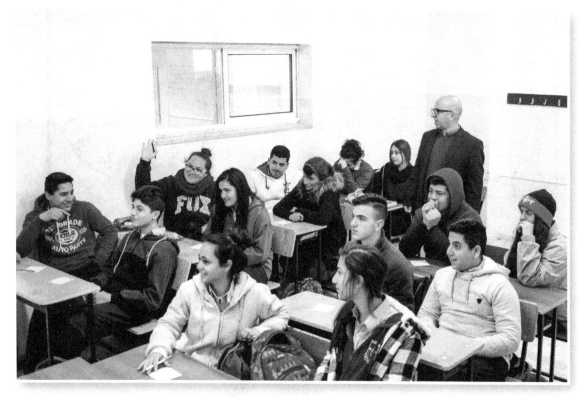

Each unit begins with a lesson called "Classroom Talk." In these lessons, you will learn words and phrases that are essential for using Arabic in class. In this lesson, you will learn how to use Arabic to ask basic questions about the meaning of words in Arabic and English.

HOW DO WE SAY...?

How do I read the vocabulary lists?

كيف نقول...؟
كيف أقرأ لائحات المفردات؟

Whenever you see a vocabulary list, you will notice three columns:

المعنى	العاميّة الشاميّة	الفصحى
yes	آه	نَعَم

The right and middle columns represent the two varieties of Arabic that appear in this book. Why two varieties? What is the difference between them? This is where Arabic is a little different from English.

The middle column presents vocabulary in العاميّة الشاميّة *al-ᶜaammiyya al-shaamiyya*, or the Levantine variety of informal Arabic. This is the everyday, informal language primarily used in speech on the street, in homes, and at work by Arabic speakers in the Levant region (Jordan, Syria, Palestine, Israel, and Lebanon [colored blue in the map]), and it is widely understood across the Arab world. There are many varieties of informal Arabic (also known as dialects) used throughout the Arab world; some are spoken throughout a region, and some are specific to a town or smaller area. The further away you get from the Levant region, the more likely it is that the informal variety you encounter will be different from

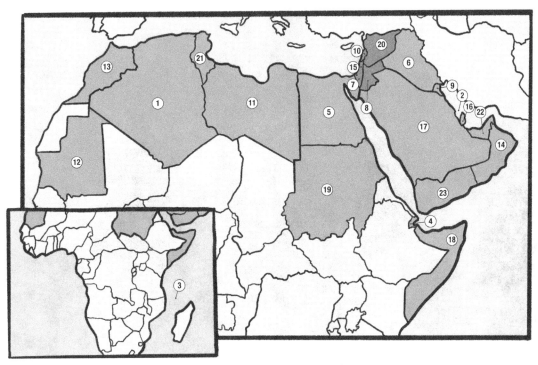

1. Algeria	6. Iraq	11. Libya	16. Qatar	21. Tunisia
2. Bahrain	7. Israel*	12. Mauritania	17. Saudi Arabia	22. United Arab Emirates
3. Comoros	8. Jordan	13. Morocco	18. Somalia	23. Yemen
4. Djibouti	9. Kuwait	14. Oman	19. Sudan	
5. Egypt	10. Lebanon	15. Palestine	20. Syria	

*Israel is not a member of the Arab League, although Arabic was formerly an official language.

al-ᶜaammiyya al-shaamiyya. It is possible for the informal varieties to be different enough that when you speak to someone from a different region you will have to work a little harder to understand one another.

Similar things happen in English, though in different ways and to different degrees. Have you ever had trouble understanding people who speak English differently than you do? It might simply be the case that a person has a different accent from you, but they may also use different words or different common phrases. For instance, an English speaker from America may have trouble understanding an English speaker from England if she uses expressions or slang that are common in England but not in the United States. The differences between informal Arabic varieties include all of those factors, in addition to differences in grammar.

If you are chatting with friends, buying groceries, or bargaining for a souvenir in Arabic, you will speak in *al-ᶜaammiyya*. It is like the everyday English you use all the time without even thinking about it. Now imagine that you are from Boston and you are talking to a friend from Houston. You may notice some regional differences in pronunciation and vocabulary yet still be able to understand each other almost all the time. If you talk to other native English speakers from Ireland, India, or Australia, however, there may be a lot of things you completely miss even though you are speaking varieties of the same language. The same can be true for speakers of different varieties of informal Arabic. For example, if a Kuwaiti tourist is listening to two Tunisian street vendors joking with one another, she will probably not understand the jokes, even if she is able to understand the topic.

The right-hand column contains words or phrases in الفصحى *al-fuSHaa* (pronounced so that the "H" is heard at the beginning of a syllable and not as part of "sh"), which is often referred to as Modern Standard Arabic (MSA). *Al-fuSHaa* is the same wherever you go—people from Morocco to Iraq learn it at school and understand it, but rarely speak it in daily life. So why doesn't everyone just speak *al-fuSHaa* all the time? Well, for many Arabic speakers, *al-fuSHaa* is too formal because it is not exactly how they would speak at home. Imagine if instead of saying, "Mom, I'm gonna go to the mall," you were to say, "Mother, I shall go to the shopping center."

Al-fuSHaa is used most often in writing and in formal contexts—in newspapers, news broadcasts, academic settings, and religious sermons. Most literature is still written predominantly in *al-fuSHaa*, although it is becoming more common to see dialogue passages or entire books written in a variety of *al-ᶜaammiyya*. *Al-fuSHaa* is the link to understanding a remarkably rich culture and history, which is written in a similar, older form of Arabic called Classical Arabic. In English, anything earlier than Shakespeare is virtually incomprehensible to us today, while an educated Arabic speaker can understand and enjoy Arabic poetry from the 500s CE.

Al-fuSHaa and the many varieties of *al-ᶜaammiyya* are all part of the Arabic language, and Arabic speakers draw on both, mixing them to get their point across. For example, on Arabic news talk shows, guests might discuss abstract topics like the economy primarily using *al-fuSHaa* but still mix in *ᶜaammiyya* pronunciation and grammatical structures, like verb conjugations.

In the vocabulary list you will see that many *fuSHaa* words are in blue, many *shaami* words (those in *al-ᶜaammiyya al-shaamiyya*) are in purple, and all English meanings are in

black. Sometimes you will see that both the *shaami* and *fuSHaa* columns have words in the same color, black. This indicates that *al-fuSHaa* and *al-ᶜaammiyya al-shaamiyya* use the same word or phrase for the given English meaning. This will help you start to build an understanding of what is shared between the different varieties. But be careful! Even when words are in black, you still need to pay attention to how each word is pronounced in the audio because there will often be differences between the *fuSHaa* and *ᶜaammiyya shaamiyya* pronunciations.

المعنى	العاميّة الشاميّة	الفصحى
no	لا	لا

You will focus primarily on the column of vocabulary words in the variety you study, *al-fuSHaa* or *al-ᶜaammiyya al-shaamiyya*. It is good practice, however, to read and listen to material in the variety of Arabic you are *not* studying, as well. When you listen for familiar words in an unfamiliar variety of Arabic and focus on what you can understand, you will use some of the same processes that native speakers of Arabic use to understand varieties that are different from their own.

Vocabulary

المفردات

Vocabulary lists in this book will usually appear at the beginning of sections. You will use them to learn the relevant words and phrases as well as for reference and review. While there will be activities after each list for activating and polishing your skills with the vocabulary, start by studying on your own to begin the process of learning and internalizing the vocabulary. It may take some time to figure out the best ways of studying that work for you. Here are some suggestions to get you started:

- Listen to the audio recording of the vocabulary lists and say the words and phrases aloud.
- Create flashcards and talk with your classmates and teacher about how best to use them.
- Study with your classmates, quizzing each other.
- Ask your teacher to lead more practice activities in class.

المعنى	العاميّة الشاميّة	الفصحى
I have a question.	عِنْدي سُؤال.	عِنْدي سُؤال.
How do we say ___ in Arabic?	كَيف مِنْقول ___ بِالعَرَبي؟	كَيْفَ نَقول ___ بِالعَرَبيّة؟
What does "salaam" mean in English?	شو يَعْني "سَلام" بِالإنْكْليزي؟	ما مَعْنى "سَلام" بِالإنْكْليزيّة؟

المعنى	العاميّة الشاميّة	الفصحى
One more time? *(used to ask for something to be repeated)*	مَرّة ثانية؟	مَرّة ثانية؟
yes	آه	نَعَم
no	لا	لا
I do not know.	ما بَعْرَف.	لا أعْرِف.
How do we say ____?	كيف مِنْقول ____؟	كَيْفَ نَقول ____؟
What does ____ mean?	شو يَعْني ____؟	ما مَعْنى ____؟
in Arabic	بالعَرَبي	بالعَرَبيّة
in English	بالإِنْكْليزي	بالإِنْكْليزيّة

Activity 1 Conversation: What does your name mean?	محادثة: ما معنى اسمك؟ نشاط ١

First names in Arabic are very often common nouns that have everyday meanings. For instance, the Arabic word أمَل *amal* means "hope" and is a popular female name, the same way that "Hope" is in English and "Esperanza" is in Spanish. What does your name mean?

Your teacher will provide you with a list of the names of the students in your class. Walk around your classroom and talk with your classmates one by one. Introduce yourselves to one another and then ask each person what their name means, using these model sentences in Arabic:

I have a question: what does ____ mean?	عِنْدي سُؤال: شو يَعْني ____؟	عِنْدي سُؤال: ما مَعْنى ____؟
My name means ____.	اِسْمي يَعْني ____.	اِسْمي يَعْني ____.

Write down the meanings of as many names as you can in the time your teacher gives you. (If you are not sure what your name means, you can define what it means to you or say "I do not know" in Arabic.)

محادثة: مفردات تشبه
الإنكليزية

نشاط ٢

In this activity, you will ask a classmate about the meanings of words that sound similar in
Arabic and English and mean the same thing. Some of these words came from Arabic to
English (usually via a European language), while others came from another language (such
as Greek or Persian) to both languages separately. You should be able to find the correct
match from your paper. Say to your classmate in Arabic "I have a question," and then ask
how to say each word in Arabic or English, depending on the blank spaces on your paper.

Activity 2   Conversation: Words that
             resemble English

Hello!

الدرس الثاني

مرحباً!

LESSON TWO GOALS

أهداف الدرس الثاني

By the end of this lesson, you should be able to do the following:

- Greet others politely in Arabic
- Use polite body language for greeting others in Arab cultural contexts
- Ask and respond to questions about how you are doing
- Take leave of someone else and say goodbye to someone who is leaving

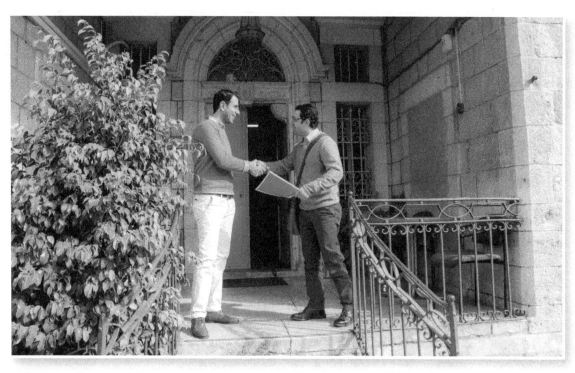

At the beginning of each lesson you will find some questions to get you thinking about the upcoming topic. Write some notes and discuss your ideas with a classmate to activate your prior knowledge!

- What does it mean to greet someone politely in your culture?
- How do you say goodbye to someone politely in your culture?

MY NAME IS . . .

Vocabulary 1

اسمي...

مفردات ١

Remember to start learning the words in each vocabulary section with a variety of study strategies before starting the in-class activities:

- Listen to the audio recording of the vocabulary lists and say the words and phrases aloud.
- Create flashcards and talk with your classmates and teacher about how best to use them.
- Study with your classmates, quizzing each other.
- Ask your teacher to lead more practice activities in class.

المعنى	العاميّة الشاميّة	الفصحى
My name is ____.	اِسْمي ____.	اِسْمي ____.
I am . . .	أنا...	أنا...
What is your name? (m.)	شو اِسْمَك؟	ما اسْمُكَ؟
What is your name? (f.)	شو اِسْمِك؟	ما اسْمُكِ؟
Nice to meet you.	تْشَرَّفْنا.	تَشَرَّفْنا.

Levantine Arabic in videos

العاميّة الشاميّة في الفيديوهات

The video you are about to watch and the majority of the videos in this book are in the Levantine dialect of informal Arabic (العاميّة الشاميّة *al-ᶜaammiyya al-shaamiyya*) instead of Modern Standard Arabic (الفصحى *al-fuSHaa*). For each video, we decided whether العاميّة الشاميّة *al-ᶜaammiyya al-shaamiyya* or الفصحى *al-fuSHaa* would more likely be used by native speakers in the depicted context. As nearly all of the videos involve dialogues within the context of daily living situations, العاميّة الشاميّة *al-ᶜaammiyya al-shaamiyya* was usually more appropriate and authentic to how native Arabic speakers would use the language.

More specifically, the videos are in the Jordanian variety of the Levantine dialect. This is because they were filmed in Amman, Jordan's capital. While other speakers from the Levant region—Palestinians, Lebanese, and Syrians—share the same broad dialect of Arabic, some of the language and pronunciation here is specific to the Jordanians in Amman. You may notice that certain pronunciations differ slightly from those of your instructor, other speakers, or authentic materials you will be using in your class and throughout the book.

There will be several occasions where you will notice both عامية شامية *ᶜaammiyya shaamiyya* and فصحى *fuSHaa* versions of a video available. These videos are monologues of people talking about certain aspects of their lives, such as their eating preferences or their favorite hobbies. In the Arab world, documentaries and introductions to contestants for various television shows or lifestyle segments will often feature the person talking about their life in الفصحى *al-fuSHaa*.

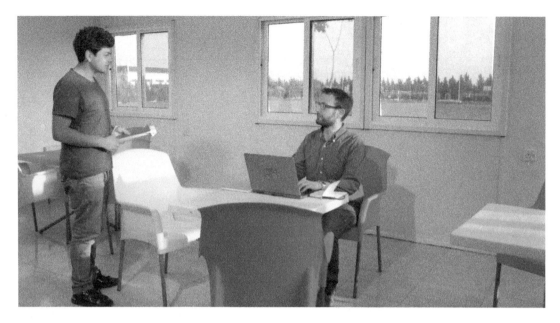

| **Activity 1**   Listening: "What's your name?" | استماع: "شو اسمك؟" | نشاط ١ |

In this activity, you will have the chance to practice recognizing common phrases in a real-life context.

Listening   الاستماع

As you watch the video, write down the names of as many of the characters as you can for each of the three scenes on a separate piece of paper. The characters in these videos will reoccur throughout the book, so it will help you to remember their names later on!

After listening   بعد الاستماع

Work together with a classmate. Watch the video with the sound turned off and create a new dialogue for the video with your classmate. You do not need to say the exact same words as the characters in the video, but you must accomplish the same task of introducing yourselves.

HELLO!   مرحباً!

Vocabulary 2   مفردات ٢

المعنى	العاميّة الشاميّة	الفصحى
hello	مَرْحَبا	مَرْحَباً
(response to "marHaban")	أَهْلَين	أَهْلاً
hello peace be upon you (Islamic greeting)	السَّلامُ عَلَيْكُم	السَّلامُ عَلَيْكُم

المعنى	العاميّة الشاميّة	الفصحى
(response to "as-salaamu ᶜalaykum")	وعَلَيْكُم السَّلام	وعَلَيْكُم السَّلام
hello welcome	أَهْلا وْسَهْلا	أَهْلاً وَسَهْلاً
(response to "ahlan wa-sah-lan") (m.)	أَهْلَين فيك	أَهْلاً بِكَ
(response to "ahlan wa-sah-lan") (f.)	أَهْلَين فيكِ	أَهْلاً بِكِ

نشاط ٢   استماع: "السلام عليكم"   Activity 2   Listening: "As-salaamu ᶜalaykum"

Music videos are a very popular form of entertainment in Arab countries. The video your teacher is about to show you is from one of the most popular music video channels for kids, called طُيور الجَنّة *Tuyuur al-janna*, which is also the name of the kids' musical group that usually performs on the channel. Ashraf Yusuf, a Palestinian-Jordanian singer, sings the song "السلام عليكم" "*As-salaamu ᶜalaykum*."

Listening   الاستماع

Watch the music video a few times. You will see at least three scenes depicted. For each scene listed below, write down on a separate piece of paper: What is happening? What motions do people use as they greet each other? What other details do you notice?

1. Buying a sandwich from a street vendor and riding a carriage
2. Playing a soccer game
3. Attending a wedding

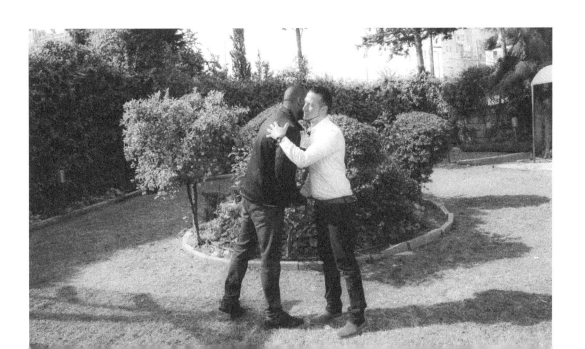

The greeting السلام عليكم *as-salaamu ᶜalaykum* is different from أهلاً وسهلاً *ahlan wa-sahlan* and مرحباً *marHaban* because it can have an Islamic religious connotation. In more observant communities in the Arab world, السلام عليكم *as-salaamu ᶜalaykum* is the default greeting. In some non-Muslim or more secular communities, people use other greetings more frequently.

After listening

بعد الاستماع

Find a classmate and greet them with السلام عليكم *as-salaamu ᶜalaykum*, accompanied by appropriate body language. Then, switch classmates and repeat.

Activity 3   Listening: "Ahlan wa-sahlan!"

نشاط ٣   استماع: "أهلاً وسهلاً!"

The phrase أهلاً وسهلاً *ahlan wa-sahlan* is often translated as meaning "welcome" in English, and it does have the meaning of welcoming someone formally to a new place. أهلاً وسهلاً *ahlan wa-sahlan* is very commonly used in Arabic, more than the phrase "welcome" is in English. In العاميّة الشاميّة *al-ᶜaammiyya al-shaamiyya* it is often pronounced in a shortened form: أهلا وسهلا *ahla w-sahla*. It is a good example of a word in Arabic that does not have a single exact equivalent word in English. It is also used in a slightly different way than English speakers may use "welcome." Rather than being said just once when you see someone for the first time, Arabic speakers say أهلاً وسهلاً *ahlan wa-sahlan* repeatedly throughout a conversation to make the other person really feel welcome.

Listening

الاستماع

Watch the video and use your observation skills to learn about how and when the phrase أهلاً وسهلاً *ahlan wa-sahlan* is used in the following situations. On a separate piece of paper, write some notes about each of the situations listed below. Be sure to include: who says the phrase, in what context is it said, what responses you hear, and how many times the phrase is repeated in each scene.

- A friend visits someone's home
- A customer and a salesperson interact
- A customer and a waiter interact

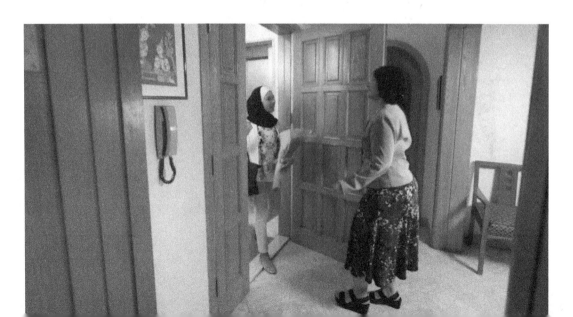

After listening   بعد الاستماع

Get into groups of two or three with your classmates. Create a few different mini skits, based on the video clips, using this greeting and its response phrase appropriately in different settings. Remember to use the appropriate gestures that you observed!

HOW ARE YOU?   كيف حالك؟

Vocabulary 3   مفردات ٣

المعنى	العاميّة الشاميّة	الفصحى
How are you? (m.)	كَيف حالَك؟	كَيْفَ حالُكَ؟
How are you? (f.)	كَيف حالِك؟	كَيْفَ حالُكِ؟
How are you? (m.) (casual)	كَيفَك؟	
How are you? (f.) (casual)	كَيفِك؟	
How is your family?	كَيف الأهْل؟	كَيْفَ الأهْل؟
Praise God!	الحَمْدُ لله!	الحَمْدُ لله!

Activity 4   Listening: "al-Hamdulillaah,"   استماع: "الحمد لله،" أغنية   نشاط ٤
              song by Charbel Rouhana   لشربل روحانا

The phrase الحمد لله *al-Hamdulillaah* has a religious meaning, "praise God," but it is also used to show your satisfaction with your current state, whatever it is. This phrase has

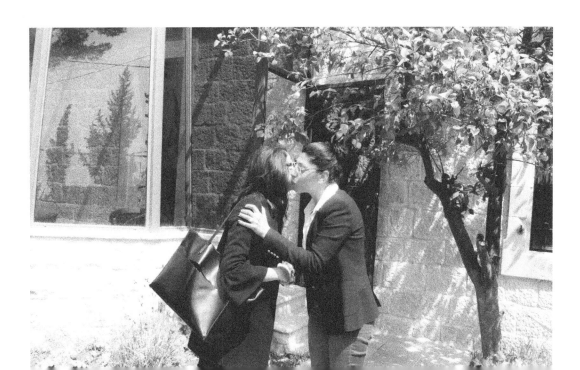

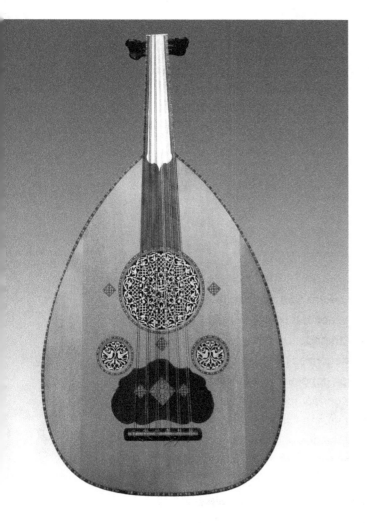

an Islamic origin, but Arabic speakers from multiple religious communities use *al-Hamdulillaah* with this meaning. In this way, the way this phrase is used similarly to how the phrase "bless you" (or "God bless you") is used in English after someone sneezes. It is a polite and formulaic phrase and is often used regardless of how religious the speaker is.

Search for and listen to the song *"al-Hamdulillaah"* by Charbel Rouhana, a contemporary Lebanese singer and *oud* player. The *oud* is a distinctive stringed instrument, similar to the lute, that is typical of traditional Arab music.

You are not expected to understand any of the lyrics of this song except for the expression *al-Hamdulillaah*, which is the chorus. At the beginning of the song, the singer is happy to have gotten a visa to the United States and sings *al-Hamdulillaah* in gratitude. By the end of the song, after returning to Lebanon, he sings *al-Hamdulillaah* in appreciation of life in his home country.

Listen carefully to identify the places where Charbel Rouhana sings *al-Hamdulillaah*. Try to identify when you hear its Standard Arabic pronunciation and when you hear the shortened pronunciation in the Lebanese variety of the Levantine dialect. Sing along with the chorus and then practice saying both pronunciation varieties aloud with your classmates.

Vocabulary 4

In this list, the word أَنا appears in parentheses. This is because the word is optional when responding to the question "how are you?" in everyday conversation—just as English speakers may only say "good" instead of "I am good" when responding to that question.

مفردات ٤

المعنى	العاميّة الشاميّة	الفصحى
(I am) good. (I am) well. *(m.)*	(أَنا) مْنيح.	(أَنا) جَيِّد.
(I am) good. (I am) well. *(f.)*	(أَنا) مْنيحة.	(أَنا) جَيِّدة.

المعنى	العاميّة الشاميّة	الفصحى
(I am) excellent. *(m.)*	(أنا) مُمْتاز.	(أنا) مُمْتاز.
(I am) excellent. *(f.)*	(أنا) مُمْتازة.	(أنا) مُمْتازة.
(I am) well. (I am) in good health.	(أنا) بِخَيْر.	(أنا) بِخَيْر.
Things are OK.	ماشي الحال	
Everything is good.	تَمام	

Grammar: Masculine and feminine   القواعد: المذكر والمؤنث

All varieties of the Arabic language include many words that are marked by grammatical gender. Grammatical gender in language overlaps with, but is not identical to, human gender identity. In Arabic, for example, while words referring to people change according to gender identity, even nouns referring to objects are categorized as "masculine" or "feminine." The words "masculine" and "feminine" in this book generally refer to grammatical gender, but these concepts have implications for human gender identity as well. The conventions of Arabic communication ask those who converse in the language to identify the gender category of themselves and others. Talk with your teacher if you are concerned about how to best express your gender identity in the Arabic classroom.

Listen again to the words in Vocabulary 4 to identify the pattern of how the adjectives change. When someone asks you how you are doing, you must respond appropriately and follow this pattern to describe yourself. With your classmates, practice how to say "I am good" and "I am excellent" as appropriate for you.

Activity 5   Grammar: Masculine and feminine adjectives   نشاط ٥   قواعد: صفات بالمذكر والمؤنث

To complete this activity, listen again to the words and phrases in Vocabulary 4.

Listening to words   الاستماع إلى الكلمات

Based on what you hear in the recordings of Vocabulary 4, finish these sentences to describe the pattern of adjectives that you notice:

1. When Arabic adjectives describe a woman . . .
2. When adjectives describe a man, however . . .

Challenge yourself: Scan the Arabic words in Vocabulary 4 in both columns. Even though you may not have learned all of the Arabic alphabet yet, try to identify the letter at the end of words that refers to women. The letter has two possible shapes. Write them on a separate sheet of paper.

Listening to differentiate between
masculine and feminine forms

الاستماع للتمييز بين المذكر والمؤنث

Listen to the recording (or to your teacher) and you will hear people express how they are doing. Point to the picture that matches each phrase that you hear.

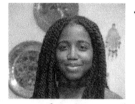

.٢

أنا مُمْتاز

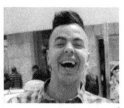

.١

أنا جَيِّدة   أنا مْنيحة

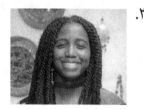

.٤

أنا جَيِّد   أنا مْنيح

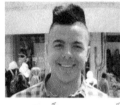

.٣

أنا مُمْتازة

Activity 6   Conversation: How are you?

نشاط ٦   محادثة: كيفك؟

After you have practiced and learned the different forms of the adjectives, try to use them. Find a classmate and take turns asking each other "how are you doing?" Don't forget to do the following:

- Change the phrase "how are you?" according to the gender of the person with whom you are speaking.
- Use *al-Hamdulillaah* as part of your response, even if you are combining it with other adjectives or phrases.
- Change the adjectives you use to describe yourself according to your own gender.

Challenge yourself: Begin each interaction with an appropriate greeting and response, using a different greeting each time you have a new partner!

Activity 7   Listening: "How are you, everybody?"

نشاط ٧   استماع: "كيف حالكم يا جماعة؟"

In any culture, being polite involves using the right body language—not just the right words.

Before listening

قبل الاستماع

Before watching this video, talk about your own culture and other cultures you know with your classmates: What physical actions and movements do you do or make when you greet strangers? What about those you use when greeting your friends and family members? When do you shake hands and when do you not? When do you hug people? Do you ever kiss people when greeting them? How would others react if you did?

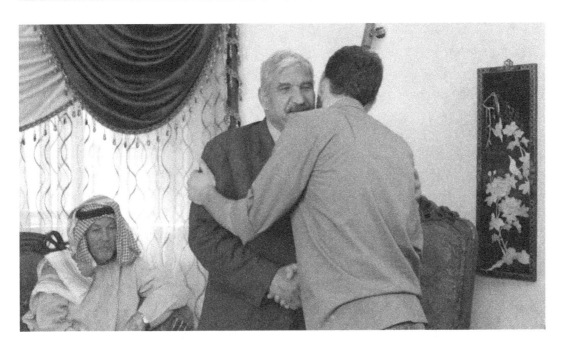

Listening for general understanding   الاستماع للفهم العام

Watch the video and listen to the people greeting each other. Write some reasoned guesses:

- Where does this take place?
- Who are these people?
- What are their relationships to each other?

Close listening   الاستماع الدقيق

While watching the video, listen for the greetings and questions that the characters ask one another. Listen for words and phrases that you have already learned.

Look at what is physically happening in the video. What specific movements and actions do you observe? What do you guess makes the different ways of physically interacting appropriate? On a separate piece of paper, draw pictures of at least three different culturally significant actions or gestures from the video. For each one, write a guess about the meaning or reason behind it.

After listening   بعد الاستماع

With a group of classmates, act out a scene in which you use the greetings and phrases you have learned, and put into practice the movements and gestures that you observed in the video. Use as many different phrases and gestures as possible.

Culture: Body language   الثقافة: لغة الجسد

One way to get to know another culture is to pay attention to and learn about the body language its community uses to give unspoken messages.

Personal space

Imagine you are standing next to a close friend, a teacher, or someone you just met. What is a comfortable distance between you and them? You can act this out in class, taking note of the differences. What are some factors that play a role in determining this distance for you personally? In English, discuss as a class and make a list.

This distance is called personal space. Social scientists have conducted studies like what you did in class to help draw conclusions about how personal space is defined. For many Arabs, this distance may be smaller than what many Americans are used to, especially for acquaintances of the same gender. However, this may be different for some individuals and sub-cultures in the United States and the Arab world.

Physical contact

What kind of physical contact do you use with your friends? Are there contexts in which it is more or less appropriate? How are your habits different from or similar to others in the communities you belong to?

Like in the United States, friends in the Arab world commonly use physical gestures to express affection for one another, although they tend to be more prevalent among friends of the same gender. The gestures might differ from what you are accustomed to. When you shake hands with someone of the same gender, you might notice that the handshake can turn into holding hands as you continue to talk. Holding hands with a friend of the same gender, while walking together or having a conversation, is common in Arab culture. Likewise, cheek-kissing when greeting someone of the same gender is very common. Cheek-kissing always starts with leaning left giving them the right cheek. The number of kisses varies from region to region—ask your teacher for more information.

In public, physical contact between those of different genders, especially people who are not related, is less common and is sometimes considered inappropriate. If you are being introduced to someone of the opposite gender, it is polite to let that person make the first move to shake hands. If they prefer to not shake hands, you can smile, nod, and place your hand over your heart.

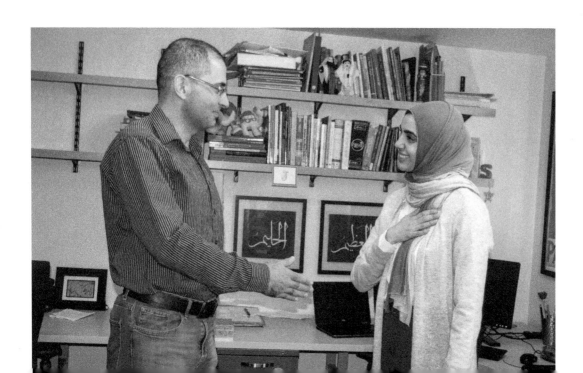

Respecting your elders

Many cultures stress the importance of showing respect to one's elders and we see this in various social interactions. What does this look like in your household and community? As you saw in the video you just watched, if you are seated and someone significantly older than you enters the room, you should stand up as they come by to greet you.

Activity 8 Listening: "Elhamdella," song by Fares Karam	استماع: "الحمد لله،" أغنية نشاط ٨ لفارس كرم

Your instructor will search for and show you the song "الحمد لله" "*Elhamdella*" (*al-Hamdulillaah*) by Lebanese pop star فارس كَرَم Fares Karam. He is famous for singing a modernized, pop version of الدَبْكة *ad-dabke* music. الدَبْكة *Ad-dabke* is also the name of the dance that accompanies this type of music. This type of dance and music is most prevalent in the Levant, or the eastern part of the Arab world, comprising Syria, Lebanon, Jordan, and Israel and the Palestinian Territories.

Listen to the first verse of this song. It consists entirely of greetings and responses that people use when they meet someone or see someone they know. Listen for the following words and phrases in Levantine dialect. How many times do you hear each?

- Good—مْنيح
- Things are okay—ماشي الحال
- Praise God—الحَمْدُ لله

GOODBYE!   مع السلامة!

Vocabulary 5   مفردات ٥

المعنى	العاميّة الشاميّة	الفصحى
with your permission (m.) (used when leaving)	عَن إذْنَك	عَن إذْنَكَ
with your permission (f.) (used when leaving)	عَن إذْنِك	عَن إذْنِكِ
go safely goodbye (usually said by the person staying)	مَع السَّلامة	مَعَ السَّلامة

Activity 9   Listening: "With your permission!"   استماع: "عن إذنك!"   نشاط ٩

Saying goodbye in Arabic is different depending on whether you are the person leaving or the person staying. The person leaving asks permission to leave, and then the person staying wishes the person who is leaving well. If both people are leaving the place they are in, then the person who initiates the goodbye can start the exchange.

Listening   الاستماع

Watch the video and listen to the goodbye exchanges between people. You are not expected to understand everything that they say. For each of the five scenes, write down on a separate sheet of paper (a) who is leaving and (b) who wishes the other to leave well. You can write the names, if you are able to, or a simple description of the person.

Challenge yourself: What response do you hear in the videos to عن إذنك *ᶜan iznak?*

After listening   بعد الاستماع

Watch the video again with the sound turned off and recreate the dialogue from the scenes with a classmate. Switch roles so that everyone gets to practice each phrase.

Then, in groups of two or three, create your own short skits of people saying goodbye to one another. What different scenarios could your scenes be set in? Create multiple scenes so that every group member can practice taking leave of the others. Present your skits in front of your classmates.

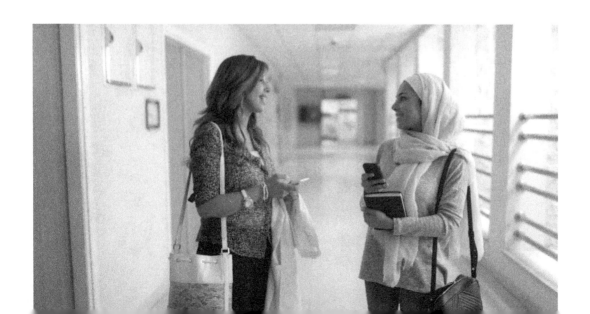

Where are you from?

من أين أنت؟

LESSON THREE GOALS

By the end of this lesson, you should be able to do the following:

أهداف الدرس الثالث

- Ask and respond to questions about where you are from
- Ask and respond to questions about your age

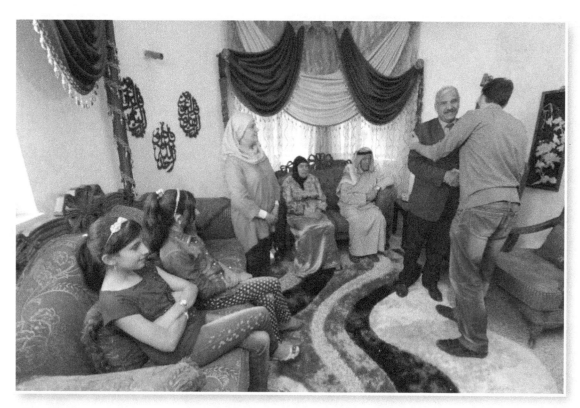

- When might you greet someone the way the men are greeting each other in the picture?
- What are some possible greetings that might have been used in this situation?
- How many countries can you name in the Arab world?
- Do you know in which countries people might wear the traditional Arab dress depicted in the picture?

23

WHERE ARE YOU FROM?

Vocabulary 1

من أين أنت؟

مفردات ١

المعنى	العاميّة الشاميّة	الفصحى
Where are you from? (m.)	مِن وَين اِنْتَ؟	مِن أَيْنَ أَنْتَ؟
Where are you from? (f.)	مِن وَين اِنْتِ؟	مِن أَيْنَ أَنْتِ؟
I am from the city of ____ in the state of ____.	أنا مِن مَدينة ____ في وِلاية ____.	أنا مِن مَدينة ____ في وِلاية ____.
Welcome (to you)! *(said after someone says where they are from)*	أهْلا وسَهْلا!	أَهْلاً وَسَهْلاً!
from	مِن	مِن
Where . . . ?	وَين...؟	أَيْنَ...؟
you You are . . . (m.)	اِنْتَ	أَنْتَ
you You are . . . (f.)	اِنْتِ	أَنْتِ
I I am . . .	أنا	أنا
the city of ____	مَدينة ____	مَدينة ____
the state of ____ *(i.e., state in the US)*	وِلاية ____	وِلاية ____
and	و	وَ
in	في بِ*	في بِ*

* Both of these words mean "in" and also can carry other meanings depending on the context. In al-ᶜaammiyya al-shaamiyya, بِ is used more commonly than في to mean "in." Choose a word that you will memorize and use but be prepared to recognize both.

Activity 1   Conversation: Where is this city?   نشاط ١   محادثة: أين هذه المدينة؟

How well do you know US states and cities? In this activity, you will give the names of states where certain cities are located.

Before speaking   قبل المحادثة

Before you start, review the list below, taking turns with a classmate saying the names of each city using the structure, "the city of ____," in Arabic.

1. Detroit	7. Tallahassee
2. Houston	8. Las Vegas
3. Tucson	9. Sacramento
4. Jefferson City	10. Boston
5. Providence	11. Santa Fe
6. Saint Paul	12. Albany

Speaking   المحادثة

Take turns with your classmate asking and answering questions about where the cities on the list are located using the example below. Write down your answers on a separate sheet of paper.

Question: Where is the city of Chicago?	وَين مَدينة شيكاغو؟	أَيْنَ مَدينة شيكاغو؟
Answer 1: In the state of Illinois	في وِلاية إلينوي	في وِلاية إلينوي
Answer 2: I don't know.	ما بَعْرَف.	لا أعْرِف.

If you are done early, think of some more cities to test your classmate's knowledge of geography!

Activity 2   Listening: "Who's learning Arabic?"   نشاط ٢   استماع: "من يتعلّم العربية؟"

In this activity, you will hear some American students introducing themselves in Arabic. The video includes two rounds of the same people introducing themselves, giving different information each time.

Before listening   قبل الاستماع

Look at the list of cities on the next page. Do you know in which state they are located? Tell a classmate your guess for each city using words from Vocabulary 1.

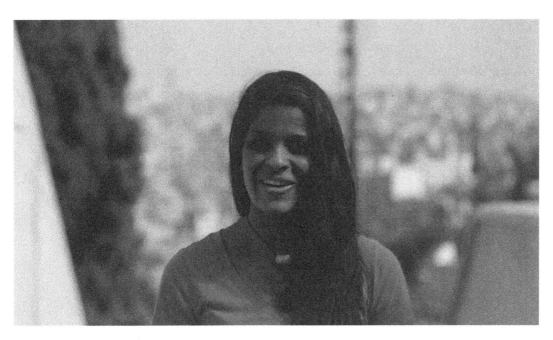

Listening for general understanding   الاستماع للفهم العام

Number a separate sheet of paper from 1 to 9. Listen to part (1) of the video (0:00–0:48).
For each person, write down the matching letter of the city they are from.

اسم Name	المدينة City
1. Keegan	a. Kingwood
2. Sarah	b. Los Angeles
3. Ali	c. Johnstown
4. Katy	d. Lakeville
5. Sam	e. Wayland
6. Mohammad	f. St. Louis
7. Ritchie	g. Shelburne Falls
8. Rosi	h. Philadelphia
9. Chris	i. Minneapolis

Close listening   الاستماع الدقيق

Listen to part (2) of the video (0:49–end). This time, the speakers will also provide the
names of their states. For each person, write down the state they are from.

After listening   بعد الاستماع

With a classmate, take turns pretending to be one of the individuals from the videos.
In your conversation, include the following elements:

- Greet each other
- Ask the other person's name
- Tell where you are from
- Excuse yourself/say good-bye

Activity 3   Listening: "Yasmine and   نشاط ٣   استماع: "ياسمين وتغريد"
Taghreed"

In this video, you will watch two people meet for the first time. You have already seen parts
of this video in various activities in Lesson 2.

Before listening   قبل الاستماع

Brainstorm some phrases in Arabic you might hear in a conversation between two people
who have just met.

Listening for general understanding   الاستماع للفهم العام

Note some of the basic information you hear about each character including their name
and where they are from.

Close listening   الاستماع الدقيق

You previously learned the phrase أهلا وسهلا *ahla w-sahla*. Remember that unlike the
word "welcome" in English, Arabs say this phrase repeatedly to show that someone is truly
welcome.

1. How many times do you hear this phrase throughout the entire scene?
2. What are some of the phrases that Yasmine says that Taghreed responds to with
   أهلا وسهلا *ahla w-sahla*?

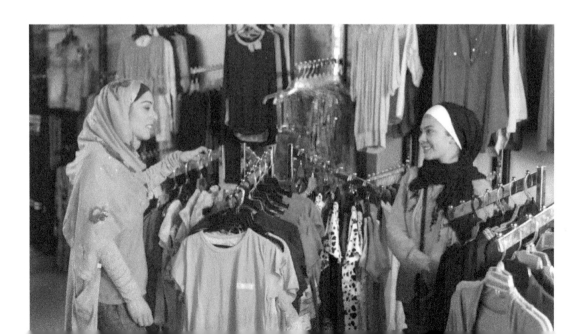

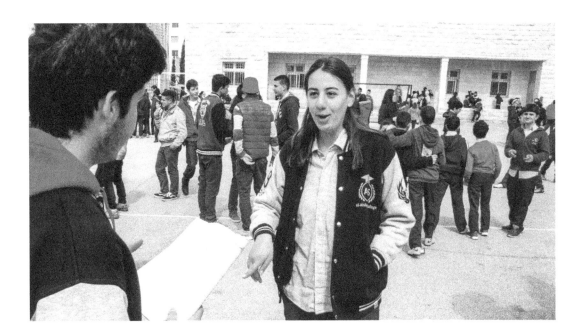

After listening   بعد الاستماع

With a classmate, act out a scene of two people meeting for the first time. Be sure to do the following:

- Use polite greetings.
- Ask where the other person is from.
- Use the phrase أهلا وسهلا *ahla w-sahla* an appropriate number of times to show that the other person is welcome.

Activity 4   Listening: Who's talking?   نشاط ٤   استماع: من يتكلم؟

It can be confusing for English speakers to learn a language where you must address people differently depending on their gender. In the following exercise, you will practice differentiating between statements where people are talking about themselves, addressing a man, and addressing a woman.

Before listening   قبل الاستماع

Brainstorm some of the Arabic phrases you know that you can use:

1. To address a man
2. To address a woman
3. When speaking to someone of any gender
4. When talking about yourself

Listening   الاستماع

On a separate piece of paper, make a chart like the one below. Listen to the eight statements in the audio. For each one, mark whether the speaker is talking about themselves, addressing a man, or addressing a woman.

Addressing a man	Addressing a woman	Talking about themselves	
			.1
			.2
			.3
			.4
			.5
			.6
			.7
			.8

After listening   بعد الاستماع

From the phrases that you have learned so far, how do you say the following?

1. I _____
2. You (*m.*) _____
3. You (*f.*) _____
4. My _____
5. Your (*m.*) _____
6. Your (*f.*) _____

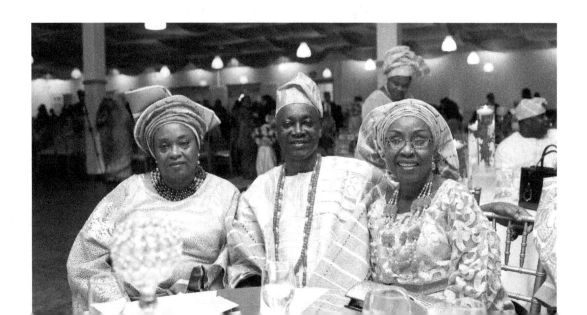

Activity 5   Conversation: Where are you from?   نشاط ٥   محادثة: من أين أنت؟

For this activity, you will pretend to be someone else and talk about where you are from.

Before speaking   قبل المحادثة

Who are you going to be? Choose a new name and place that you are from. Write on a separate piece of paper the following information about yourself:

- Name—الاسْم
- City—المَدينة
- State—الوِلاية

Speaking   المحادثة

With a classmate, create a skit to present to the class in which you greet another person and ask where they are from. Pay attention to the gender of the person you are addressing in your questions and answers. Make sure you include the following elements:

- Greeting
- How are you?
- Exchange names
- Exchange cities, states, and/or countries
- Excuse yourself/say goodbye

LET'S COUNT TO TEN!   دعونا نعدّ إلى عشرة!

Vocabulary 2   مفردات ٢

Remember that *fuSHaa* and *ᶜaammiyya* words that are in black are shared words, though the pronunciation may differ.

المعنى	العاميّة الشاميّة	الفصحى
0	صِفِر	صِفْر
1	واحِد	واحِد
2	إِثْنَين	إِثْنان
3	ثَلاثة	ثَلاثة
4	أَرْبَعة	أَرْبَعة
5	خَمْسة	خَمْسة
6	سِتّة	سِتّة

المعنى	العاميّة الشاميّة	الفصحى
7	سَبْعة	سَبْعة
8	ثَمانْية	ثَمانِية
9	تِسْعة	تِسْعة
10	عَشَرة	عَشَرة

Activity 6   Listening: Emergency numbers نشاط ٦   استماع: أرقام الطوارئ

What would you do if you were traveling in the Arab world and you had an emergency? Who would you call? In this listening activity, you will find out the emergency numbers of various countries in the Arab world.

Before listening قبل الاستماع

On a separate piece of paper, write down three phone numbers of institutions or people you would call if you had an emergency. Unlike words, phone numbers are written from left to right in Arabic. Share these phone numbers in Arabic with your classmate by reading each digit out loud. Who are you calling?

Listening الاستماع

Number a separate sheet of paper from one to twelve. As you listen to the audio, write down the emergency telephone number that corresponds with each country.

رقم الطوارئ Emergency number	Country	البلد
	1. *al-imaaraat*	١. الإمارات
	2. *al-baHrayn*	٢. البحرين
	3. *tuunis*	٣. تونس

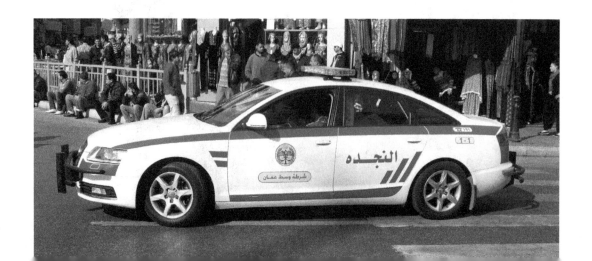

رقم الطوارئ Emergency number	Country	البلد
	4. *al-urdunn*	٤. الأردنّ
	5. *as-sa^cuudiyya*	٥. السعودية
	6. *^cumaan*	٦. عُمان
	7. *qatar*	٧. قطر
	8. *al-kuwayt*	٨. الكويت
	9. *lubnaan*	٩. لبنان
	10. *miSr*	١٠. مصر
	11. *al-maghrib*	١١. المغرب
	12. *liibiyaa*	١٢. ليبيا

After listening   بعد الاستماع

Without looking at each other's papers, speak in Arabic to compare the phone numbers you wrote down.

HOW OLD ARE YOU?

كم عمرك؟

Vocabulary 3

مفردات ٣

Learn the numbers eleven through twenty when talking about ages by listening to the audio in the variety you are learning. Listen for how these numbers differ from numbers one through ten. The rules for pronouncing numbers in Arabic are complex and change depending on what you are counting and quantifying. Ask your teacher if you want more information.

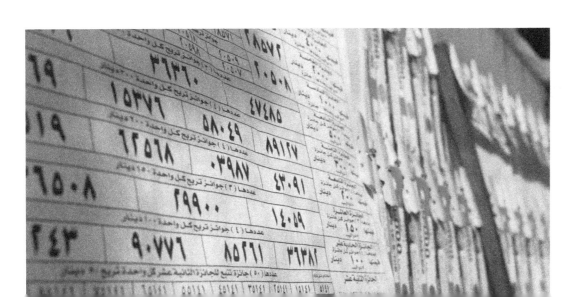

المعنى	العاميّة الشاميّة	الفصحى
How old are you? *(m.)*	كَم عُمْرَك؟	كَم عُمْرُكَ؟
How old are you? *(f.)*	كَم عُمْرِك؟	كَم عُمْرُكِ؟
My age is . . .	عُمْري...	عُمْري...
I am 11 years old.	عُمْري ١١ سَنة.	عُمْري ١١ سَنة.
I am 12 years old.	عُمْري ١٢ سَنة.	عُمْري ١٢ سَنة.
I am 13 years old.	عُمْري ١٣ سَنة.	عُمْري ١٣ سَنة.
I am 14 years old.	عُمْري ١٤ سَنة.	عُمْري ١٤ سَنة.
I am 15 years old.	عُمْري ١٥ سَنة.	عُمْري ١٥ سَنة.
I am 16 years old.	عُمْري ١٦ سَنة.	عُمْري ١٦ سَنة.
I am 17 years old.	عُمْري ١٧ سَنة.	عُمْري ١٧ سَنة.
I am 18 years old.	عُمْري ١٨ سَنة.	عُمْري ١٨ سَنة.
I am 19 years old.	عُمْري ١٩ سَنة.	عُمْري ١٩ سَنة.
I am 20 years old.	عُمْري ٢٠ سَنة.	عُمْري ٢٠ سَنة.

| Activity 7   Listening: Driving ages around the world | نشاط ٧   استماع: عمر القيادة حول العالم |

How old do you have to be to legally drive where you live? In this listening activity, you will hear the minimum age to obtain a driver's license in some US States and in some countries around the world.

| Before listening | قبل الاستماع |

Review the list of places you will hear about by reading the table below. Are you familiar with the driving age in any of these states and countries? If you are, use Arabic to tell a classmate the age in Arabic.

| Listening for general understanding | الاستماع للفهم العام |

As you listen, keep a tally of the number of times you hear each age.

14 ____   15 ____   16 ____   17 ____   18 ____   19 ____

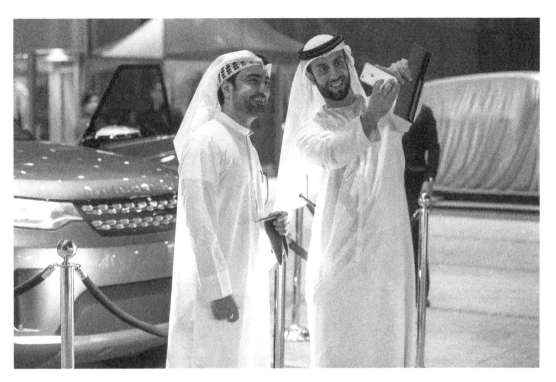

Close listening   الاستماع الدقيق

Number a separate piece of paper from one to seventeen. Write down the age that corresponds with each country or US state based on what you hear.

عمر القيادة Driving age	Country or state	البلد أو الولاية الأمريكية
	1. *al-maghrib*	١. المغرب
	2. *hunghaariyaa*	٢. هنغاريا
	3. *ghaanaa*	٣. غانا
	4. *as-salfaaduur*	٤. السلفادور
	5. *al-kaamiiruun*	٥. الكاميرون
	6. *wilaayat nyuujiirsii*	٦. ولاية نيوجيرسي
	7. *nyuuziilandaa*	٧. نيوزيلندا
	8. *tuunis*	٨. تونس
	9. *al-mamlaka al-muttaHida*	٩. المملكة المتّحدة
	10. *isbaaniyaa*	١٠. إسبانيا

عمر القيادة Driving age	Country or state	البلد أو الولاية الأمريكية
	11. *wilaayat muuntaanaa*	١١. ولاية مونتانا
	12. *usturaaliyaa*	١٢. أستراليا
	13. *wilaayat aydaahuu*	١٣. ولاية أيداهو
	14. *al-baraaziil*	١٤. البرازيل
	15. *ithyuubiyaa*	١٥. إثيوبيا
	16. *maaliiziyaa*	١٦. ماليزيا
	17. *aS-Siin*	١٧. الصين

After listening　　　　　　　　　　　　　　　　بعد الاستماع

With a classmate, review the ages you wrote down in the prior section. For each place and age, tell your classmate نعم، ممتاز if you agree that this is the right age to get a driver's license, or لا if you disagree and think that this is not the right age to get a driver's license.

Activity 8　　Listening: "How old are you?"　　استماع: "كم عمرك؟"　　نشاط ٨

In this video, you will see two people meeting for the first time.

Before listening　　　　　　　　　　　　　　　قبل الاستماع

Fast forward a few seconds into the video and look at the characters. How old do you think each person is? Say the age in Arabic that represents your guess; you do not have to use a full sentence.

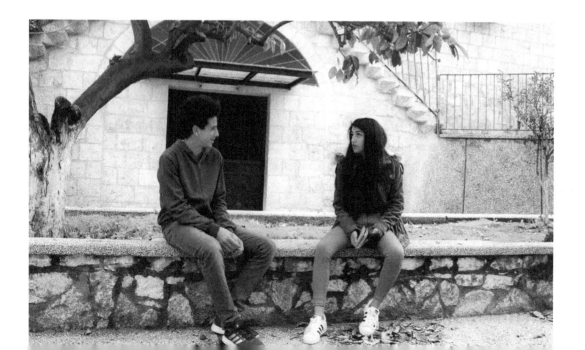

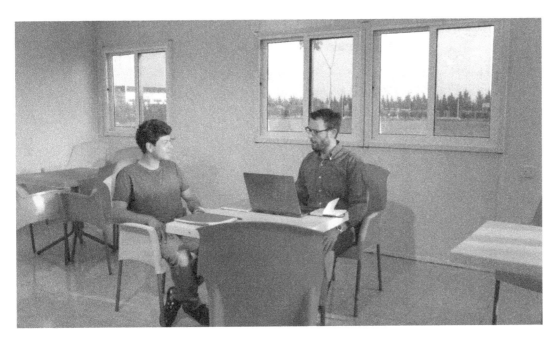

Listening

الاستماع

In the video, you will see two people meet for the first time. Write down the information you can understand.

1. العمر—age: _____
   من—from: _____
   الاسم—name: _____
2. العمر—age: _____
   من—from: _____
   الاسم—name: _____

Close listening

الاستماع الدقيق

At 0:32 in the video, one character comments on the other character's name. What does he say?

Challenge yourself: What response do you hear one character give when the other says تشرّفنا *tsharrafnaa*?

Activity 9   Conversation: At what age...?

نشاط ٩   محادثة: في أي عمر...؟

Families within the same culture often have different beliefs about when children and teen-agers should be allowed to do different activities on their own. At the same time, you may find broad cultural trends in these beliefs if you get to know many people from the same culture. Looking at the list of activities on the next page, at what age do you think you should be allowed to do each activity alone?

Before speaking   قبل المحادثة

Number lines on a separate sheet of paper from one to nine. Next to each number, write down what you think is the age when people should be allowed to do each of the activities listed below alone.

1. Babysit
2. Go to the movies
3. Get a job other than babysitting
4. Own a cellphone
5. Sleep over at a friend's house

6. Go to the mall
7. Go to a concert
8. Stay home without adult supervision
9. Ride public transportation

Speaking   المحادثة

Ask your classmates, while you point to the number of the activity listed:

At which age is this?	بِأَيّ عُمْر هٰذا؟	في أَيّ عُمْر هٰذا؟

Respond by saying:

This is at the age of ____.	هاذا بِعُمْر ____.	هٰذا في عُمْر ____.

As is customary in Arab culture when speaking to someone, do not forget to greet your classmate and ask how they are doing before asking your question. Be sure to say good-bye before moving on to someone else.

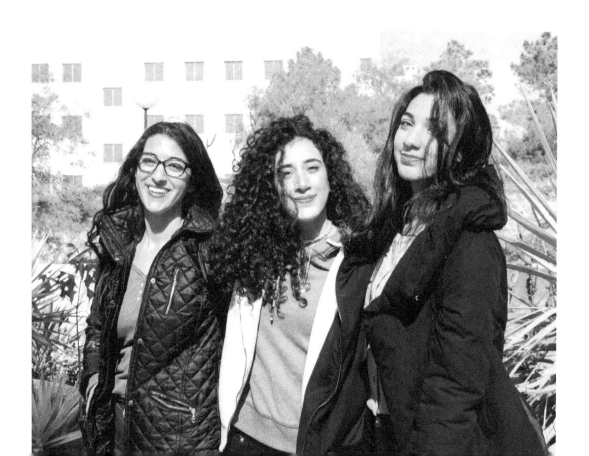

| Activity 10 Conversation: Who is the same age as you? | نشاط ١٠ محادثة: من من نفس عمرك؟ |

On orientation day for a new program, your instructors ask you to get in groups with students of your same age.

Before speaking   قبل المحادثة

Your teacher will give you a fake identity. Look over your identity and practice making statements about yourself in Arabic that include the information you have been given. Do not share the details with your classmates at first.

Speaking   المحادثة

Find the classmates who are the same age as you by asking questions! Remember to always use a greeting and excuse yourself before moving on to speak to someone else.

Because the person with whom you are speaking does not know your name or your gender, offer a gentle correction if they are addressing you with the wrong pronoun by saying أنتَ or أنتِ.

On a separate piece of paper, write down the names of all the people in your age group.

| Activity 11 Reading and writing: I am ... | نشاط ١١ قراءة وكتابة: أنا... |

What can you understand of the following? Can you fill in any information?

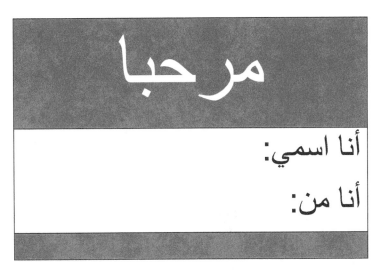

This is my friend

الدرس الرابع

هذا صديقي

أهداف الدرس الرابع

By the end of this lesson, you should be able to do the following:

- Introduce a friend to others
- Tell others what your family background is
- Tell what others' family backgrounds are, such as friends and famous people

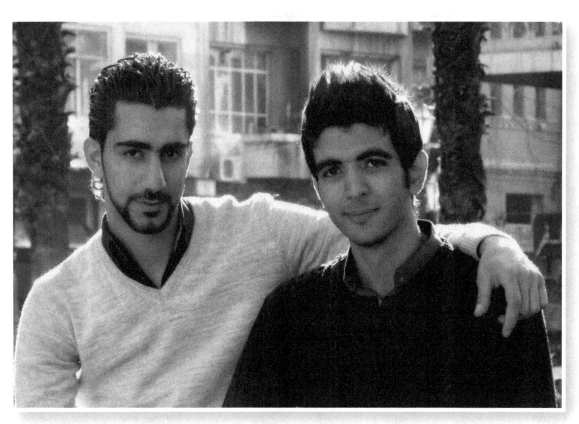

Close friends of the same gender often embrace and hold hands in the Arab World.

- What do you know about how friendship differs across cultures?

WHO IS HE?
Vocabulary 1

من هو؟
مفردات ١

المعنى	العاميّة الشاميّة	الفصحى
This is my friend. (m.)	هاذا صاحْبي.	هٰذا صَديقي.
This is my friend. (f.)	هاي صاحِبْتي.	هٰذِهِ صَديقَتي.
He is from ____.	هُوِّ مِن ____.	هُوَ مِن ____.
She is from ____.	هِيِّ مِن ____.	هِيَ مِن ____.
His name is ____.	اِسْمُهْ ____.	اِسْمُهُ ____.
Her name is ____.	اِسْمْها ____.	اِسْمُها ____.
he He is . . .	هُوِّ	هُوَ
she She is . . .	هِيِّ	هِيَ
friend (m.)	صاحِب	صَديق
friend (f.)	صاحْبة	صَديقة

When you learn a new language, it can be difficult to know whether first names in that language are generally given to men or to women. In this audio you will hear someone looking at pictures of her friends and introducing them. Listen to the way she introduces them, thinking about the clues you have learned, to learn whether each name is used as a man's name or a woman's name in the recording.

Before listening   قبل الاستماع

Imagine that you are introducing two friends to someone else who speaks only Arabic. With a classmate, brainstorm Arabic phrases you could use for each person below:

- Isabel
- Noah

Listening   الاستماع

Listen to the audio. Next to each name, write M or F according to whether you hear the person being referred to as a man or a woman. The names are listed in the order they will be mentioned.

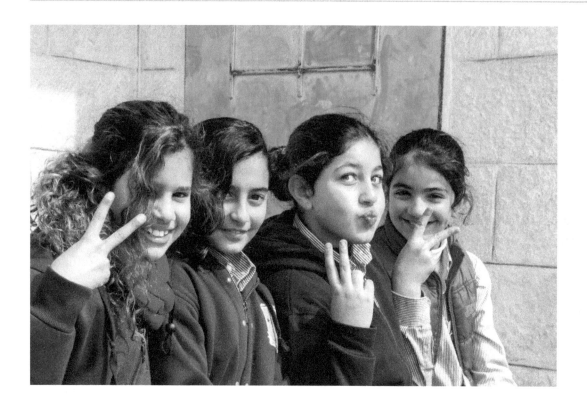

Name, in Latin script	الاسم بالحروف العربية	M. or F.?
ashraf	أَشرَف	
manaar	مَنار	
amiina	أَمينة	
tamaam	تَمام	
amal	أَمَل	
anwar	أَنوَر	
bilaal	بِلال	
nuur	نور	
amiin	أَمين	

Sketch a picture of three or four people and give each one an Arabic name from the list you just heard. Introduce them to a classmate.

Activity 2   Listening: Which picture?   نشاط ٢   استماع: أي صورة؟

You will hear a series of statements introducing people. Which pictures go with which of
the statements?

Before listening   قبل الاستماع

Look over the pictures below. With a classmate, try to say at least one Arabic word that
could go with each picture.

Listening   الاستماع

On a separate sheet of paper, write numbers from one to nine. Listen to the statements in
the audio; there are nine total. Next to the number corresponding to each statement, write
the letter of the picture that best illustrates that statement.

a. 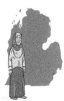   b. 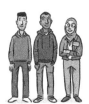   c.

d. 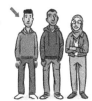   e. 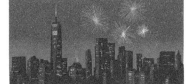   f.

g. 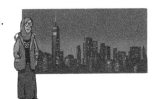   h. 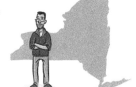   i.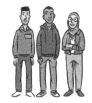

Grammar: Simple questions in Arabic   القواعد: أسئلة بسيطة بالعربية

In this activity, you will learn the basics about asking yes-or-no questions in Arabic.

المعنى	العامّية الشاميّة	الفصحى
(used to ask a yes-or-no question)		هَل

   If you are studying Modern Standard Arabic: You can easily turn a statement into
a yes-or-no question by adding the word هل to the beginning of the statement and pronouncing the resulting phrase with rising intonation. Look at the examples on the following
page.

If you are studying Levantine Arabic: To ask a yes-or-no question, just pronounce a statement you already know with rising, question-like intonation. No additional word or change in word order is needed. Look at the examples below.

He is from New York.	هُوِّ مِن نْيويورْك.	هُوَ مِنْ نْيويورْك.
Is he from New York?	هُوِّ مِن نْيويورْك؟	هَل هُوَ مِنْ نْيويورْك؟
Her name is Sally.	اِسِمْها سالي.	اِسْمُها سالي.
Is her name Sally?	اِسِمْها سالي؟	هَل اِسْمُها سالي؟

Activity 3   Conversation: Guess who …   نشاط ٣   محادثة: احزر من...

Use what you have learned to ask and answer questions about your classmates.

Before speaking   قبل المحادثة

Brainstorm five yes-or-no questions in Arabic that you could ask your classmates about another person in the class. It is okay if your questions are somewhat repetitive.

Speaking   المحادثة

Play a game of "ten questions" with your classmates:

1. Pick a person to be "it." That person should think of one of their classmates but not tell anyone whom they are thinking of.
2. Everyone else who is not "it" can ask yes or no questions of that person to try to figure out who they are thinking of.
3. If you are "it," be sure to respond by saying "yes" or "no" in Arabic!

Activity 4   Conversation: This is my friend   نشاط ٤   محادثة: هذا صديقي

In this activity, you will assume a new, secret identity and introduce yourself to others.

Before speaking   قبل المحادثة

Create a new name for yourself and a new place you are from and write it down on a separate sheet of paper.

You will need to work with a classmate for this activity. When you find a partner, decide who will be Partner أ and who will be Partner ب. Then, introduce yourself with your secret identity to your partner. Memorize each other's identities before starting the activity!

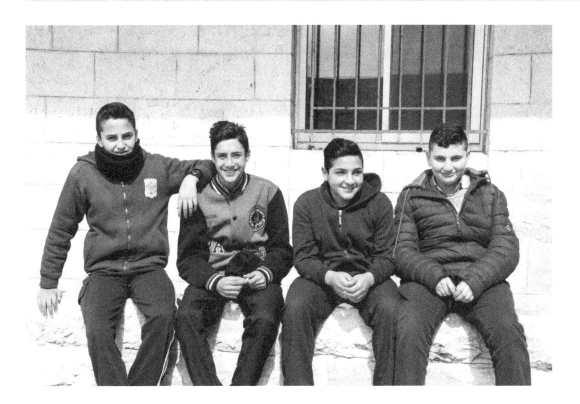

Speaking   المحادثة

With your partner, circulate around the classroom and greet the other pairs of students. You and your partner will take turns introducing each other, using your secret identities:

- The first time you meet another pair, Partner أ is responsible for introducing themselves *and* their partner.
- The second time you meet another pair, Partner ب is responsible for introducing themselves *and* their partner.
- The third time you meet another pair, Partner أ is responsible once again, and so on.

Don't forget to use polite greetings and to say goodbye politely as well. Record the identities of the people you meet—their names and where they are from—on a separate sheet of paper.

Activity 5   Listening: Are you talking to me?   استماع: هل تتكلّم معي؟   نشاط ٥

A common mistake new Arabic students make is using the wrong pronouns when they are talking to someone—for example, saying "he" or "she" instead of "you" or using "my" instead of "your." You have learned some ways to talk about yourself, some ways to talk to someone, and some ways to about someone else. In this activity, you will review the difference between talking to someone, talking about them, and talking about yourself.

Think of at least one example of each of the following that you have learned:

1. A phrase someone uses when talking about themselves (often saying "I" or "my")
2. A phrase someone uses when talking about someone else (often saying "he," "she," "his," or "her")
3. A phrase someone uses when talking directly to someone (often saying "you" or "your")

Listen to the ten statements in the audio. For each one, mark whether the speaker is talking about themselves, talking about someone else, or addressing someone directly.

Talking about themselves	Talking or asking about someone else	Addressing someone directly	
			.1
			.2
			.3
			.4
			.5
			.6
			.7
			.8
			.9
			.10

Reflect on the statements and questions you just heard. When you hear someone speaking in Arabic, what are some specific words or parts of words that tell you that a person is

talking about themselves? About someone else? Directly to someone? Brainstorm as many as you can think of from the audio you just heard, focusing on words or parts of words.

- Talking about themselves: _____
- Talking about someone else: _____
- Talking directly to someone: _____

Vocabulary 2 مفردات ٢

You have already learned five personal pronouns in different contexts; review them here.

المعنى	العاميّة الشاميّة	الفصحى
I	أَنا	أَنا
you (m.)	إِنْتَ	أَنْتَ
you (f.)	إِنْتِ	أَنْتِ
he	هُوِّ	هُوَ
she	هِيِّ	هِيَ

Activity 6   Conversation: What's his name? نشاط ٦   محادثة: ما اسمه؟

Using what you have learned so far, practice asking your classmates about their friends.

Before speaking قبل المحادثة

In this activity, you will show your classmates pictures of some of your friends. Draw a picture of three to five friends (real or imagined) on a separate piece of paper or bring in pictures from home. Think back over the Arabic words and phrases you have learned that will help you talk about your friends. How do you say the following questions?

1. What is your name?
2. Where are you from?

Now see if you can figure out how to say these questions:

3. What is his name?
4. What is her name?
5. Where is he from?
6. Where is she from?

You will need these phrases for the activity.

Speaking
المحادثة

Speak with your classmates one by one and ask them the names of the people in their photos and where they are from. Be sure to ask each classmate about at least two of the people they show you. When your classmates ask you questions about your picture, try to answer in complete sentences.

SHE IS OF ARAB ORIGIN

هي من أصل عربيّ

Culture: Identity and origin
الثقافة: الهوية والأصل

Though seemingly straightforward, the question "where are you from?" can prompt nuanced discussion about identity and different ways to think about it. Prepare for this discussion by reflecting on your own thoughts; write a reflective paragraph in which you respond to the following questions:

- If someone asks you where you are from, how do you answer? What does it mean to you to be "from" somewhere? Do you have multiple ways you could answer this question? If so, how do you decide which answer to give?
- How do you define your family's origin? If you have multiple possible answers, how do you decide which one to give?
- How do you feel when someone asks you questions about where you are from or about your family's origin?
- What words do you use to define your identity? Imagine a few different situations: talking with close friends, talking with family, discussing something in class, visiting another country, or filling out a form. How do you define your identity differently in different situations?

Discuss your responses with your teacher and classmates. Issues of identity and origin are complex in cultures across the world, and this includes Arabic-speaking communities.

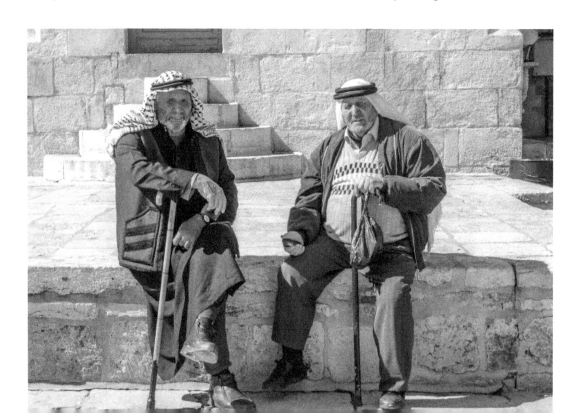

In Arabic, the question "من وين انت؟" "min ayna anta?" or "من أين أنت؟" "min wayn inta?" can refer to different things in different contexts. It could carry the connotation of "where did you grow up?" or the connotation of "where is your family from?" In some places, such as the United States, this question may be considered rude or presumptuous. It is a very common introductory question in many Arabic-speaking contexts.

In the coming lesson, you will learn the word أصْل *aSl*, which literally means "origin." In Arabic, the phrase "أنا من أصل ____" "*ana min aSl* ____" is used to mean "I am of ____ origin." Speakers may use this phrase to share their families' cultural or ethnic origins, including in contexts where immigration and naturalization are common, such as the United States. For example, you will hear Yasmine say, "أنا أمريكية من أصل عربي"—"I am American of Arab origin."

As you continue to learn Arabic and talk with more Arabic speakers, notice the different ways that they define their identities and origins. In the Arabic classroom, talk with your teacher to learn any words and expressions you need to discuss your own identity in a way that is comfortable for you.

Vocabulary 3 مفردات ٣

المعنى	العامّيّة الشاميّة	الفصحى
I am from America, and I am also of Arab origin.	أنا مِن أَمْريكا وأنا مِن أَصْل عَرَبي كَمان.	أنا مِن أَمْريكا وَأَنا مِن أَصْل عَرَبيّ أَيْضاً.
I am from Spain, but I am of Syrian origin.	أنا مِن إِسْبانيا بَس مِن أَصْل سوري.	أنا مِن إِسْبانيا وَلْكِن مِن أَصْل سوريّ.
of ____ origin	مِن أَصْل ____	مِن أَصْل ____
America*	أَمْريكا	أَمْريكا
Arab	عَرَبي	عَرَبيّ
and also	كَمان	أَيْضاً
but	بَس	وَلْكِن

*As in English, the meaning and usage of the word أمريكا (sometimes pronounced أميرْكا) in Arabic varies with context. People often use the word to refer specifically to the United States, but it can also be used to refer collectively to the continents of North and South America.

Activity 7   Listening: What's his origin?   نشاط ٧   استماع: من أي أصل هو؟

Many famous people are immigrants or children of immigrants and have origins outside of the location they called home. You will hear statements about famous people; match them to the country or countries that their families came from.

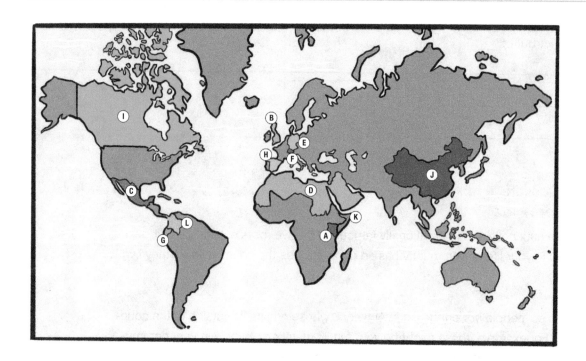

Before listening   قبل الاستماع

Label a separate piece of paper with numbers from one to ten.

Listening   الاستماع

First, listen to the ten statements by different people and write the name of the famous person that you hear discussed. (Use English if you do not know all of the letters yet.)

Listen again and indicate each person's place of origin by writing the letter of the country next to the number and their name. Some countries on the map may be mentioned more than once, and others may not be used at all. Focus only on the person's origin, not where they live right now.

Many adjectives for national origin closely resemble those you hear in English; practice listening closely to recognize words to which you have not been formally introduced yet.

After listening   بعد الاستماع

Check your answers with a classmate by stating what you heard in your own words. Use the phrases in the Vocabulary 2 list and the words that appear in this activity to describe each of the people mentioned, taking turns making a sentence about each number. Here are some phrases to get you started:

| He is from ____, and of ____ origin also. | هَوَّ مِن ____ ومِن أَصْل ____ كَمان. | هُوَ مِن ____ وَمِن أَصْل ____ أَيْضاً. |
| She is from ____, and of ____ origin also. | هِيِّ مِن ____ ومِن أَصْل ____ كَمان. | هِيَ مِن ____ وَمِن أَصْل ____ أَيْضاً. |

He is from ____, but of ____ origin.	هَوِّ مِن ____ بَس مِن أَصْل ____.	هُوَ مِن ____ وَلٰكِن مِن أَصْل ____.
She is from ____, but of ____ origin.	هِيِّ مِن ____ بَس مِن أَصْل ____.	هِيَ مِن ____ وَلٰكِن مِن أَصْل ____.

Activity 8   Conversation: He has roots in . . .

نشاط ٨   محادثة: هو من أصل...

It is not just the nationally and internationally famous who have roots outside of their own countries. Who in your life or community has an origin outside the country where they live?

Before speaking

قبل المحادثة

Think of four to six people *not* on the list in Activity 7 whose origins lie outside of the country they live in. For example, these might be your family members; people in your community, city, or state; or famous authors, musicians, or sports stars.

If you do not know how to express your origin in Arabic yet, ask your teacher. Practice these new vocabulary words by yourself until you can say them smoothly.

If you would like to talk about someone who is indigenous, rather than of immigrant origin, you can say:

He / she is indigenous.	هُوَّ \ هِيِّ مِن السُّكان الأَصْليين	هُوَ \ هِيَ مِن السُّكان الأَصْليين

Bring in or draw pictures of the people on your list to share with your classmates and teacher. Be ready to say where they are from and what their origin or their family's origin is.

Speaking

المحادثة

Find a partner. Present the four to six people you have chosen to one of your classmates. Then choose a new classmate and repeat.

Continue speaking

واصلوا المحادثة

Working independently, figure out how to ask yes-or-no questions about someone's origin. If you are not sure how, review the grammar section in this lesson. Talk with a classmate you have not spoken with yet in this activity and ask them two or three yes-or-no questions about the origins of the people in their pictures.

Activity 9   Listening: "A new friend"

نشاط ٩   استماع: "صاحبة جديدة"

In the video, Raya introduces her cousin Yasmine to a friend. For this activity, you only need to watch the first half of the video—until about 0:55.

Before listening   قبل الاستماع

In Arabic, tell a classmate what you remember about Yasmine from previous videos. Where is Yasmine from?

Listening   الاستماع

Watch and listen carefully for some new information about Yasmine:

1. What is her origin?
2. Where is her mother from?
3. Where is her father from?

After listening   بعد الاستماع

Tell a classmate about where *your* parents' families are originally from, using the same phrasing as Yasmine. You can use your real parents or create a fake identity for yourself.

Activity 10 Conversation: Where is your family from?   نشاط ١٠   محادثة: من أي أصل أنت؟

In this activity, you will find out where your classmates' families are from.

Before speaking   قبل المحادثة

Prepare to tell your classmates where your family is from. If you do not feel like talking about your own family, you can adopt a fake identity—for example, you could use one of the people you researched earlier for your presentation on community members or adopt a celebrity identity. Be sure that your fake identity includes a city, state or country, and the person's origin.

Speaking   المحادثة

When someone asks you where you are from, tell them not only the city, state, or country you are from, but also what your origin is—whether you are talking about yourself or using another identity. For example, you could say, "I'm from Detroit, Michigan, and I'm of Arab origin." Write down on your own paper what you learn about your classmates' origins,

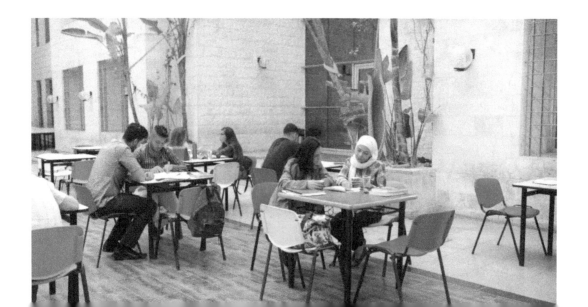

or the characters they have adopted. Be sure to ask what your classmates' names are, as well—they may be using a fake or celebrity identity!

After speaking   بعد المحادثة

Choose someone you talked to during this exercise and introduce them to another person in Arabic. Include their name and their origin. Speak in complete sentences as much as possible.

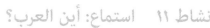

Activity 11 Listening: Where are the Arabs?   نشاط ١١   استماع: أين العرب؟

You will listen to a short passage about people of Arab descent living outside of the Arab world.

Before listening   قبل الاستماع

What are some places you expect to hear mentioned? Brainstorm with a classmate.

Listening for general understanding   الاستماع للفهم العام

Jot down the names of countries you recognize from the listening passage. Listen for the words مِلْيون *milyuun* and مَلايين *malaayiin*. What do you guess they mean?

Close listening   الاستماع الدقيق

For each country you identified in the immediately prior section, try to write down the number of people of Arab descent in each country (numbers are not precise but have been rounded).

After listening   بعد الاستماع

What did you hear that surprised you? Look at some of the numbers that you wrote down. Point to one that surprised you and use an expression of surprise to tell a classmate:

Really?	عَنْ جَدّ؟	حَقّاً؟

Activity 12 Reading: The biggest groups of immigrants to the United States   نشاط ١٢   قراءة: أكبر مجموعات من المهاجرين إلى الولايات المتّحدة

The following tables show the top three largest groups of immigrants by national origin to the United States in particular years over the past several decades.[1]

Skim the headings of the tables and the format of the entries. What information can you understand? What words can you guess?

السنة: 1960		
العدد	النسبة	الأصل
1,257 مليون	12.9%	إيطاليّ
0,990 مليون	10.2%	ألمانيّ
0,953 مليون	9.8%	كنديّ

السنة: 1970		
العدد	النسبة	الأصل
4,298 مليون	21.7%	مكسيكيّ
0,913 مليون	4.6%	فلبّينيّ
0,745 مليون	3.8%	كنديّ

السنة: 1980		
العدد	النسبة	الأصل
2,199 مليون	15.6%	مكسيكيّ
0,849 مليون	6.0%	ألمانيّ
0,843 مليون	6.0%	كنديّ

السنة: 1990		
العدد	النسبة	الأصل
4,298 مليون	21.7%	مكسيكيّ
0,913 مليون	4.6%	فلبّينيّ
0,745 مليون	3.8%	كنديّ

العدد	النسبة	الأصل
السنة: 2000		
9,177 مليون	29.5%	مكسيكيّ
1,369 مليون	4.4%	فلبّينيّ
1,023 مليون	3.3%	هنديّ

العدد	النسبة	ألأصل
السنة: 2010		
11,711 مليون	29.3%	مكسيكيّ
1,780 مليون	4.5%	هنديّ
1,778 مليون	4.4%	فلبّينيّ

What's your phone number?

الدرس الخامس

ما رقم هاتفك؟

LESSON FIVE GOALS

أهداف الدرس الخامس

By the end of this lesson, you should be able to do the following:

- Write down your own or someone else's phone number in Eastern Arabic numerals
- Ask someone else for their email address and phone number
- Respond to requests for your email address and phone number

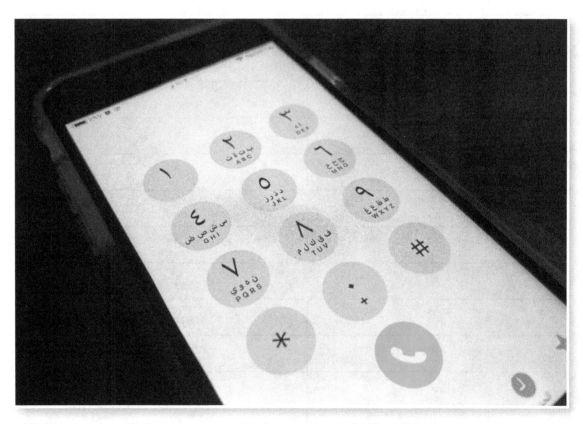

- Which numerals on the keypad correspond to the ones you are familiar with?
- Why do you think some of these numerals look so similar to those you are familiar with?

HOW DO I WRITE EASTERN ARABIC NUMERALS?

كيف أكتب الأرقام العربيّة الشرقيّة؟

Eastern Arabic Numerals

الأرقام العربيّة الشرقيّة

In this lesson, you will learn how to exchange phone numbers with someone you meet. Before you do that, do you know how to write your phone number in Arabic?

There are two sets of numerals used in the Arab world. In general, the Arab countries of North Africa primarily use the numerals you are familiar with from European languages like English, Spanish, French, and others (1, 2, 3, etc.). These are actually called "Arabic numerals" because they were developed in the Arab world at a time when Europe was still using Roman Numerals (I, II, III, IV, etc.). The Arab countries in the Persian Gulf and the Levant (the eastern part of the Arab world), however, use a different set of numerals called "Eastern Arabic numerals" because they were originally developed in India but quickly became widely used in the Middle East. In this lesson, you will practice using Eastern Arabic numerals to write a variety of items you may see in the Arab world, including phone numbers.

In the table below, you will see the two ways of writing the numerals presented side-by-side. Look over the table. What do you notice? Which numerals are similar and which are different? Which numerals may be confusing? As you know, Arabic words are written and read from right to left. Based on the information in the table, what can you learn about the direction in which Eastern Arabic numerals are written and read?

Writing numbers with Arabic numerals	Writing numbers with Eastern Arabic numerals
0	٠
1	١
2	٢
3	٣
4	٤
5	٥
6	٦
7	٧
8	٨
9	٩
10	١٠

Writing numbers with Arabic numerals	Writing numbers with Eastern Arabic numerals
11	١١
12	١٢

نشاط ١   تدريب على كتابة الأرقام

Activity 1   Writing numerals practice

Train your hand to form the Eastern Arabic numerals by practicing writing each number several times over on a separate piece of paper after studying them in the table above. Note that the numbers ٢ and ٣ appear slightly different in handwriting. Practice each:

- The number ٢ is written in handwriting with a flat line across the top: ٱ

- The number ٣ is written in handwriting with a single dip: ٢

نشاط ٢   قراءة وكتابة: في السوق

Activity 2   Reading and writing: In the market

Use your knowledge of numbers to go shopping in السوق *as-suuq*, or the market!

القراءة

Reading

Look at the examples of money from Jordan. What do you notice? What denominations are these bills (called "dinars") and coins (called "qirsh")? Look in particular at the denominations of ten and above. What order are the numbers written in?

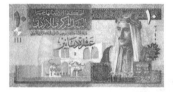
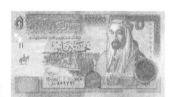
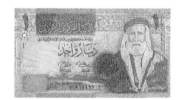

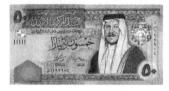
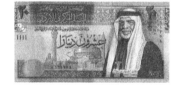

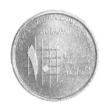
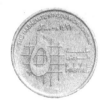

Writing   الكتابة

Imagine that you want to buy some of the following items from السوق *as-suuq* in Amman, Jordan. Look at the price tags. For each item, draw on a separate sheet of paper a combination of bills and coins you could use to pay for this item.

   Example:

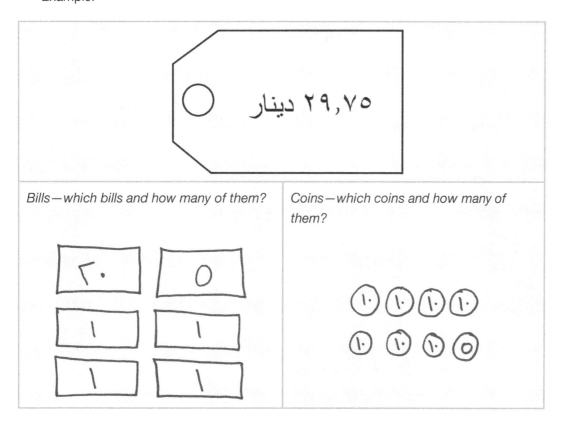

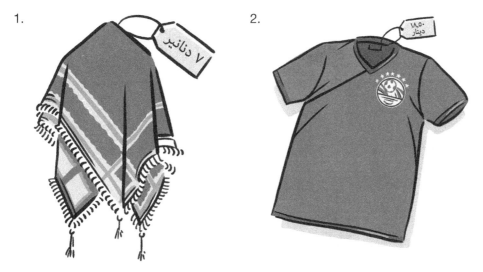

1.

2.

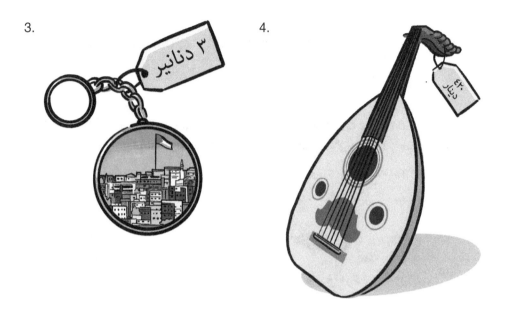

3.

4.

Challenge yourself: Look up the exchange rate for Jordanian dinars. Do these items seem expensive or cheap to you?

Activity 3   Reading and writing: Numbers in math class   نشاط ٣   قراءة وكتابة: الأرقام في صف الرياضيات

Children in the Levant use Eastern Arabic numerals in their math classes. Practice using Eastern Arabic numerals to solve these math problems. Be sure to write the answer using Eastern Arabic numerals, too.

٢) ١٠ + ٧ = _____   ١) ١٠ + ٦ = _____
٤) ٦ + ٤ = _____   ٣) ٥ + ٣ = _____
٦) ٧ + ٤ = _____   ٥) ٨ + ٣ = _____

١٠) ٤٦   ٩) ١٨   ٨) ١٥   ٧) ٣٦
    + ٢٤   + ٢٥   + ١٥   + ٢٦

١٤) ٢٨   ١٣) ٢٣   ١٢) ٣٥   ١١) ٧٤
     ١٦   ٨   + ٢٨   + ١٨
    + ٥١   + ٢٦

١٨) ٢٥   ١٧) ٤٧   ١٦) ١٨   ١٥) ٣٩
     ٢٥   ٣٦   ٢١   ١٠
    + ٣٤   + ١٥   + ٥٣   + ٣٩

Numerals are also used in writing the date. Use what you know about numbers to read and write dates in Arabic.

Before reading   قبل القراءة

Imagine that you work at a library. Someone has just donated a big pile of Iraqi newspapers to your archive. Before you can put them in the right place, you need to organize them by date.

1. Look at this large view of the heading. Find the date.

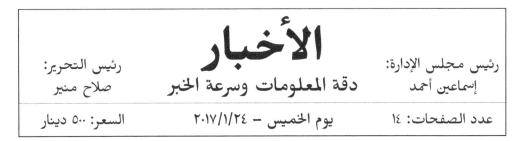

2. What do you notice about the date? What order are the day, month, and year written in?

Reading   القراءة

These newspapers are completely out of order. Check the date of each one and then number them from oldest to newest on your own sheet of paper.

a.

رئيس مجلس الإدارة:
إسماعين أحمد

الأخبار

رئيس التحرير:
صلاح منير

دقة المعلومات وسرعة الخبر

عدد الصفحات: ١٤   يوم الأربعاء—٢٠١٥/٥/٢٠   السعر: ٥٠٠ دينار

b.

رئيس مجلس الإدارة:
إسماعين أحمد

الأخبار

رئيس التحرير:
صلاح منير

دقة المعلومات وسرعة الخبر

عدد الصفحات: ١٤   يوم الأربعاء—٢٠١٣/٢/٦   السعر: ٥٠٠ دينار

c.

رئيس مجلس الإدارة:
إسماعين أحمد

الأخبار

رئيس التحرير:
صلاح منير

دقة المعلومات وسرعة الخبر

عدد الصفحات: ١٤   يوم الثلاثاء—٢٠١٢/٧/٣١   السعر: ٥٠٠ دينار

d.

الأخبار
دقة المعلومات وسرعة الخبر

رئيس التحرير: صلاح منير		رئيس مجلس الإدارة: إسماعين أحمد
السعر: ٥٠٠ دينار	يوم الاثنين—٢٠١٣/٢/٤	عدد الصفحات: ١٤

e.

الأخبار
دقة المعلومات وسرعة الخبر

رئيس التحرير: صلاح منير		رئيس مجلس الإدارة: إسماعين أحمد
السعر: ٥٠٠ دينار	يوم الخميس—٢٠١٣/٥/٣٠	عدد الصفحات: ١٤

f.

الأخبار
دقة المعلومات وسرعة الخبر

رئيس التحرير: صلاح منير		رئيس مجلس الإدارة: إسماعين أحمد
السعر: ٥٠٠ دينار	يوم الاثنين—٢٠١٣/١٠/١٤	عدد الصفحات: ١٤

g.

الأخبار
دقة المعلومات وسرعة الخبر

رئيس التحرير: صلاح منير		رئيس مجلس الإدارة: إسماعين أحمد
السعر: ٥٠٠ دينار	يوم الاثنين—٢٠١٣/٣/١٨	عدد الصفحات: ١٤

h.

الأخبار
دقة المعلومات وسرعة الخبر

رئيس التحرير: صلاح منير		رئيس مجلس الإدارة: إسماعين أحمد
السعر: ٥٠٠ دينار	يوم الاثنين—٢٠١٣/١٢/٩	عدد الصفحات: ١٤

After reading   بعد القراءة

Write today's date using Eastern Arabic numerals and in the correct Arabic order. Then, write your birth date using Eastern Arabic numerals and in the correct Arabic order.

Source: Newspaper headers are from http://libguides.aucegypt.edu/content.php?pid=574389&sid=4774255

WHAT'S YOUR PHONE NUMBER?   ما رقم هاتفك؟

Vocabulary   المفردات

المعنى	العاميّة الشاميّة	الفصحى
What is your email address? (m.)	شو إيمَيلَك؟	ما عُنْوان بَريدِكَ الإِلِكْترونيّ؟
What is your email address? (f.)	شو إيمَيلِك؟	ما عُنْوان بَريدِكِ الإِلِكْترونيّ؟
My email address is ____.	إيمَيلي ____.	عُنْوان بَريدي الإِلِكْترونيّ ____.
What is your phone number? (m.)	شو رَقْم تَلِفونَك؟	ما رَقْم هاتِفَك؟
What is your phone number? (f.)	شو رَقْم تَلِفونِك؟	ما رَقْم هاتِفِك؟
My phone number is ____.	رَقْم تَلِفوني ____.	رَقْم هاتِفي ____.

Activity 5   **Listening: "University registration"**   استماع: "التسجيل في الجامعة"   نشاط ٥

In this video, you will see someone registering for an Arabic class at a university.

Before listening   قبل الاستماع

Brainstorm some questions you might hear if you were trying to register for a class in the Arab world. Share them with a classmate or write them down.

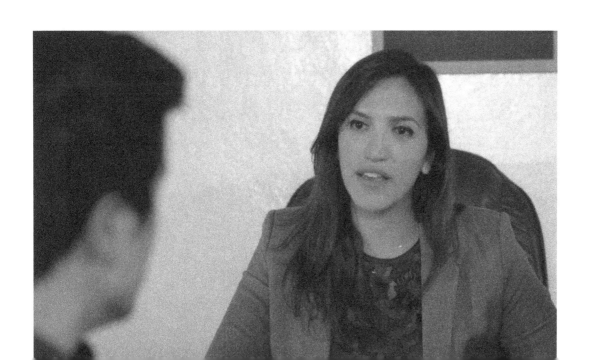

Listening   الاستماع

Imagine that you are taking notes for the registrar, the person registering students for courses. Write down as much information as you can from the student who is registering for classes. Try to catch the following details:

1. The student's name
2. Where he is from
3. His age
4. His email address
5. His phone number

After listening   بعد الاستماع

With a classmate, take turns acting out a similar scene. One person should play the role of the registrar, while the other should play the role of the student. When you are done, switch roles.

**Activity 6   Listening: "What's your   استماع: "شو رقم تلفونك؟"   نشاط ٦
telephone number?"**

You will watch a video in which two people greet each other and exchange some information.

Listening for general understanding   الاستماع للفهم العام

Watch the first few seconds of the video and pay attention to the characters' body language and the things they say. Take a guess about the relationship between these two people. Are they meeting for the first time, or do they know each other? Write down the name and phone number for each person on a separate piece of paper.

Close listening   الاستماع الدقيق

The young women in the video used some shorter versions of the question "شو رقم تلفونك؟". What phrases do you hear?

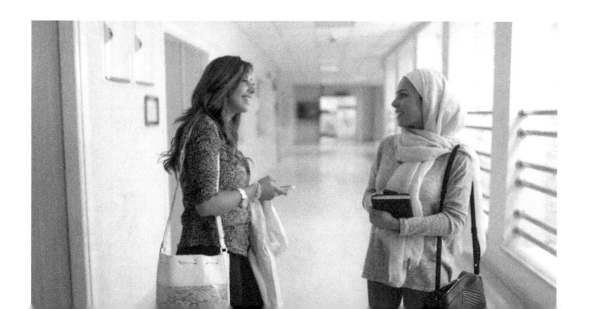

After listening   بعد الاستماع

Find out a classmate's phone number using at least one of the phrases you heard in the video.

Activity 7   Listening: Who are you   استماع: مع من تتكلّم؟   نشاط ٧
                  talking to?

One important part of speaking correctly in Arabic is being able to address men and women with the appropriate grammatical forms. Some phrases change depend on who you are talking to and some do not. In this activity, you will practice these phrases.

Before listening   قبل الاستماع

Can you think of some examples of phrases in Arabic that you use when speaking to a woman, to a man, and some that you could use to address either?

Listening   الاستماع

Listen to the questions and statements in this audio, taken from this lesson and from previous lessons. For each phrase, mark whether the speaker is specifically addressing a man, a woman, or could be speaking to either. Listen to the list twice if you need to.

M.	F.	M. or F.	
			١.
			٢.
			٣.
			٤.
			٥.
			٦.
			٧.
			٨.
			٩.
			١٠.
			١١.
			١٢.

M.	F.	M. or F.	
			١٣.
			١٤.
			١٥.

After listening

بعد الاستماع

Think back to the phrases you just heard. What patterns did you notice, either during this listening activity or while studying the past few lessons?

Activity 8   Conversation: A telephone directory

نشاط ٨   محادثة: دليل أرقام الهاتف

You have listened to others give their contact information. Now, prepare to give your contact information to your classmates.

Before speaking

قبل المحادثة

If you do not feel comfortable giving out your real contact information, make up a fake phone number and email address. Write them down if you need to on a separate piece of paper so that you can remember them.

Speaking

المحادثة

You want to create a contact list for your class. Ask as many classmates as you can for their email addresses and phone numbers, and share yours when asked. On your own paper, write down the information you hear in Arabic—and be sure to use Eastern Arabic numerals for the phone numbers.

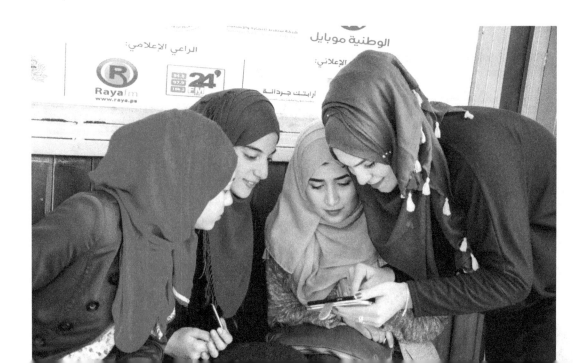

Continue speaking   واصلوا المحادثة

If you notice you are missing some classmates' phone numbers or email addresses, ask a classmate who was able to record them. You will have to change your phrasing slightly, as in the examples below. Note that the phrasing here is the same when speaking to a person of any gender.

What is Sarah's email address?	شو إيمَيل سارة؟	ما عُنْوان بَريِد سارة الإلِكْترونيّ؟
What is Sarah's phone number?	شو رَقْم تَلِفون سارة؟	ما رَقْم هاتِف سارة؟

Activity 9   Conversation: What is McDonald's phone number?   نشاط ٩   محادثة وكتابة: ما رقم هاتف ماكدونالدز؟

Ordering food delivery, even from fast food restaurants, is extremely popular in Egypt.

Before speaking   قبل المحادثة

Work with a classmate to compile a list of some of Egypt's fast-food restaurants and their phone numbers. To ask for the phone number of a restaurant, you will have to use the same sentence structure you used in the final section of Activity 8:

What is McDonald's phone number?	شو رَقْم تَلِفون ماكُدونالْدْز؟	ما رَقْم هاتِف ماكُدونالْدْز؟
McDonald's phone number is ____.	رَقْم تَلِفون ماكُدونالْدْز ____.	رَقْم هاتِف ماكُدونالْدْز ____.

Challenge yourself: How would you ask about another restaurant's phone number, such as Sherri's?

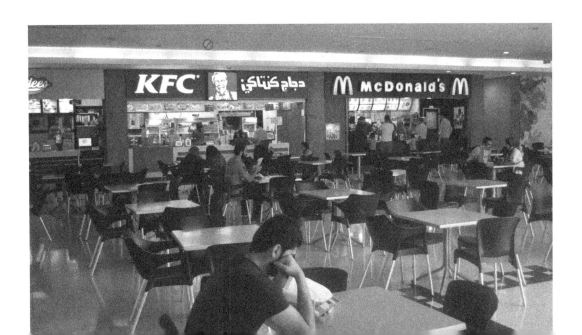

Your teacher will give you a sheet of paper with the phone numbers of some of the restaurants listed below. Ask your classmate about the restaurants whose phone numbers you do *not* have. Note that some of the numbers look different because they are in different parts of Egypt, just as different American cities have different area codes.

Activity 10 Reading: Business cards   نشاط ١٠   قراءة: بطاقات العمل

Look over these business cards from the Middle East. What is the phone number to reach each business? What other information can you identify?

المسافر

كافة أنواع الحقائب والماركات العالمية

عمان – وسط البلد – شارع جامعة الدول العربية – بجانب مطعم هارديز

خلوي ٠٧٩٧٢٩٧٢٢٤
أرضي ٣٩٠١٤٨٦

مصنع المفروشات

فرشات هارموني – فرشات طبية – فرشة سعودية

عمان وسط البلد – شارع الأمير محمد

أرضي: ٠٦٤٨٢٠١٧٤
علي: ٠٧٩١٨٤٧٤٥٦ – ٠٧٩٣١١٩٩٨٩

مكتب الشروق للتصميم الجرافيكي

مواد دعائية – دروع كرستال – نحاسيات

أبو محمد ٠٧٩٧٣٦٤٥٣٦

عمان
وسط البلد
مقابل مطعم الخليل

maktabshuruuq@yahoo.com

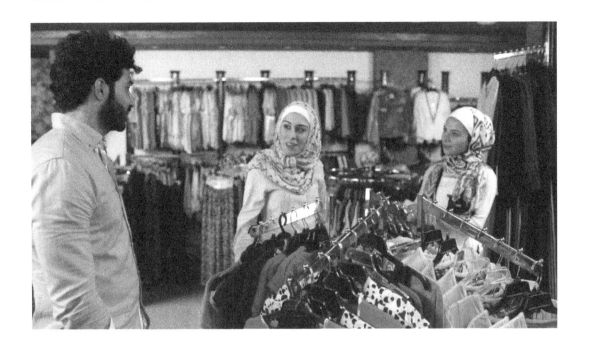

Activity 11 Listening and Conversation: استماع ومحادثة: "صاحبتي من   **نشاط ١١**
                "My friend is of Arab origin"   أصل عربي"

In this activity, you will see a video with some familiar characters and one new character.

Before listening   قبل الاستماع

Watch a few seconds of the video "صاحبتي من أصل عربي" without the sound and look at the characters who appear in it. In Arabic, tell a classmate as much information as you can remember about the character you already know. Use as many complete sentences as you can.

Listening   الاستماع

Watch the video with sound and answer the following questions:

1. What is the name of the new character you meet in this video?
2. What phone numbers do you hear in the video, and whose phone numbers are they?

Challenge yourself: At about 0:28, the new character expresses surprise that Yasmine is from the US. What does he say to explain his surprise?

Before speaking   قبل المحادثة

Think back over everything you have learned in this chapter. You should be able to greet someone, introduce yourself and give some background information about yourself, introduce a friend, tell where your family is originally from, and exchange contact information with someone else. What do you know how to do well? What do you still need to study and practice?

Speaking   المحادثة

In small groups, create a skit about your first day at a new school in the Arab world. You will need to create a new identity for some or all of your group members. Through your skit, review the new vocabulary you have gained. Be sure to include the following components:

- Greetings
- Introductions
- Some background about yourselves (where you are from, your family origin, your age)
- Introducing someone else to your new classmate
- Exchanging contact information

As you prepare, think about the video you just watched. Try to model some of your greetings and other sentences on the video, and imitate the actors' way of speaking as much as possible.

Prepare to present your skit either to another small group or to your whole class. Be ready to present without using any written notes or script. If you want, you can draw some pictures that will remind you of what you want to say.

Activity 12   Reading and writing: Student information   نشاط ١٢   قراءة وكتابة: معلومات الطالب

You want to register for Arabic classes at an institute in the Middle East. Look over the student registration form. What can you understand on this form? How much information can you fill out about yourself?

معلومات الطالب
الاسم: _____
العمر: _____
من: _____
البريد الإلكتروني: _____
رقم الهاتف: _____
رقم الموبايل: _____

Unit One
Vocabulary

مفردات الوحدة الأولى

Core vocabulary

الدرس الأوّل
المفردات الأساسيّة

المعنى	العاميّة الشاميّة	الفصحى
I have a question.	عِنْدي سُؤال.	عِنْدي سُؤال.
How do we say ____ in Arabic?	كَيْف مِنْقول ____ بِالعَرَبي؟	كَيْفَ نَقول ____ بِالعَرَبِيّة؟
What does "salaam" mean in English?	شو يَعْني "سَلام" بِالإِنْكْليزي؟	ما مَعْنى "سَلام" بِالإِنْكْليزِيّة؟
One more time? *(used to ask for something to be repeated)*	مَرّة ثانية؟	مَرّة ثانِية؟
yes	آه	نَعَم
no	لا	لا
I do not know.	ما بَعْرَف.	لا أَعْرِف.
How do we say ____?	كيف مِنْقول ____؟	كَيْفَ نَقول ____؟
What does ____ mean?	شو يَعْني ____؟	ما مَعْنى ____؟
in Arabic	بِالعَرَبي	بِالعَرَبِيّة
in English	بِالإِنْكْليزي	بِالإِنْكْليزِيّة

71

Extra vocabulary		المفردات الإضافيّة
I have a question: what does ____ mean?	عِنْدي سُؤال: شو يَعْني ____؟	عِنْدي سُؤال: ما مَعْنى ____؟
My name means ____.	اِسْمي يَعْني ____.	اِسْمي يَعْني ____.

LESSON TWO
Core vocabulary

الدرس الثاني
المفردات الأساسيّة

المعنى	العاميّة الشاميّة	الفصحى
My name is ____.	اِسْمي ____.	اِسْمي ____.
I am ...	أنا...	أنا...
What is your name? *(m.)*	شو اِسْمَك؟	ما اسْمُكَ؟
What is your name? *(f.)*	شو اِسْمِك؟	ما اسْمُكِ؟
Nice to meet you.	تْشَرَّفْنا.	تَشَرَّفْنا.
hello	مَرْحَبا	مَرْحَباً
(response to "marHaban")	أَهْلَين	أَهْلاً
hello *(Islamic greeting)*	السَّلامُ عَلَيْكُم	السَّلامُ عَلَيْكُم
(response to "as-salaamu ᶜalaykum")	وَعَلَيْكُم السَّلام	وعَلَيْكُم السَّلام
hello welcome	أَهْلا وْسَهْلا	أَهْلاً وَسَهْلاً
(response to "ahlan wa-sahlan") (m.)	أَهْلَين فيك	أَهْلاً بِكَ
(response to "ahlan wa-sahlan") (f.)	أَهْلَين فيكِ	أَهْلاً بكِ
How are you? *(m.)*	كَيف حالَك؟	كَيْفَ حالُكَ؟
How are you? *(f.)*	كَيف حالِك؟	كَيْفَ حالُكِ؟
How are you? *(casual) (m.)*	كَيفَك؟	

المعنى	العاميّة الشاميّة	الفصحى
How are you? (casual) (f.)	كِيفِك؟	
How is your family?	كَيف الأَهْل؟	كَيْفَ الأَهْل؟
Praise God!	الحَمْدُ لله!	الحَمْدُ لله!
(I am) good. (I am) well. (m.)	(أَنا) مْنيح.	(أَنا) جَيِّد.
(I am) good. (I am) well. (f.)	(أَنا) مْنيحة.	(أَنا) جَيِّدة.
(I am) excellent. (m.)	(أَنا) مُمْتاز.	(أَنا) مُمْتاز.
(I am) excellent. (f.)	(أَنا) مُمْتازة.	(أَنا) مُمْتازة.
(I am) well. (I am) in good health.	(أَنا) بِخَير.	(أَنا) بِخَير.
Things are OK.	ماشي الحال	
Everything is good.	تَمام	
with your permission (used when leaving) (m.)	عَن إذْنَك	عَن إذْنَك
with your permission (used when leaving) (f.)	عَن إذْنِك	عَن إذْنِك
go safely goodbye (usually said by the person staying)	مَع السَّلامة	مَع السَّلامة

LESSON THREE

Core vocabulary

الدرس الثالث
المفردات الأساسيّة

المعنى	العاميّة الشاميّة	الفصحى
Where are you from? (m.)	مِن وَين اِنْتَ؟	مِن أَيْنَ أَنْتَ؟
Where are you from? (f.)	مِن وَين اِنْتِ؟	مِن أَيْنَ أَنْتِ؟

المعنى	العاميّة الشاميّة	الفصحى
I am from the city of ____ in the state of ____.	أنا مِن مَدينة ____ في وِلاية ____.	أنا مِن مَدينة ____ في وِلاية ____.
Welcome (to you)! *(said after someone says where they are from)*	أَهلا وسَهلا!	أَهْلاً وَسَهْلاً!
from	مِن	مِن
Where . . . ?	وَين...؟	أَيْنَ...؟
you You are . . . *(m.)*	إنْتَ	أَنْتَ
you You are . . . *(f.)*	إنْتِ	أَنْتِ
I I am . . .	أَنا	أَنا
the city of ____	مَدينة ____	مَدينة ____
the state of ____ *(i.e., state in the US)*	وِلاية ____	وِلاية ____
and	وَ	وَ
in	في بـ	في بـ
0	صِفْر	صِفْر
1	واحِد	واحِد
2	إثْنَين	اثْنان
3	ثَلاثة	ثَلاثة
4	أَرْبَعة	أَرْبَعة
5	خَمْسة	خَمْسة
6	سِتّة	سِتّة

المعنى	العاميّة الشاميّة	الفصحى
7	سَبْعة	سَبْعة
8	ثَمانْية	ثَمانِية
9	تِسْعة	تِسْعة
10	عَشَرة	عَشَرة
How old are you? *(m.)*	كَم عُمْرَك؟	كَم عُمْرَك؟
How old are you? *(f.)*	كَم عُمْرِك؟	كَم عُمْرُكِ؟
My age is . . .	عُمْري...	عُمْري...
I am 11 years old.	عُمْري 11 سَنة.	عُمْري 11 سَنة.
I am 12 years old.	عُمْري 12 سَنة.	عُمْري 12 سَنة.
I am 13 years old.	عُمْري 13 سَنة.	عُمْري 13 سَنة.
I am 14 years old.	عُمْري 14 سَنة.	عُمْري 14 سَنة.
I am 15 years old.	عُمْري 15 سَنة.	عُمْري 15 سَنة.
I am 16 years old.	عُمْري 16 سَنة.	عُمْري 16 سَنة.
I am 17 years old.	عُمْري 17 سَنة.	عُمْري 17 سَنة.
I am 18 years old.	عُمْري 18 سَنة.	عُمْري 18 سَنة.
I am 19 years old.	عُمْري 19 سَنة.	عُمْري 19 سَنة.
I am 20 years old.	عُمْري 20 سَنة.	عُمْري 20 سَنة.

Extra vocabulary   المفردات الإضافيّة

Where is the city of Chicago?	وَين مَدينة شيكاغو؟	أَيْنَ مَدينة شيكاغو؟
In the State of Illinois	في وِلاية إلينوي	في وِلاية إلينوي
At which age is this?	بِأَيّ عُمْر هاذا؟	في أَيّ عُمْر هٰذا؟
This is at the age of ____.	هاذا بِعُمْر ____.	هٰذا في عُمْر ____.

LESSON FOUR
Core vocabulary

الدرس الرابع
المفردات الأساسيّة

المعنى	العاميّة الشاميّة	الفصحى
This is my friend. (m.)	هاذا صاحْبي.	هٰذا صَديقي.
This is my friend. (f.)	هاي صاحْبتي.	هٰذِه صَديقَتي.
He is from ____.	هُوِّ مِن ____.	هُوَ مِن ____.
She is from ____.	هِيِّ مِن ____.	هِيَ مِن ____.
His name is ____.	اِسْمُهْ ____.	اِسْمُهُ ____.
Her name is ____.	اِسْمْها ____.	اِسْمُها ____.
he He is . . .	هُوِّ	هُوَ
she She is . . .	هِيِّ	هِيَ
friend (m.)	صاحِب	صَديق
friend (f.)	صاحْبة	صَديقة
(used to ask a yes-or-no question)		هَل
she	هِيِّ	هِيَ
I am from America, and I am also of Arab origin.	أنا مِن أَمْريكا وأنا مِن أَصْل عَرَبيّ كَمان.	أنا مِن أَمْريكا وأَنا مِن أَصْل عَرَبيّ أَيْضاً.
I am from Spain, but I am of Syrian origin.	أنا مِن إِسْبانيا بَس مِن أَصْل سوري.	أنا مِن إِسْبانيا وَلٰكِن مِن أَصْل سوريّ.
of ____ origin	مِن أَصْل ____	مِن أَصْل ____
America	أَمْريكا	أَمْريكا
Arab	عَرَبي	عَرَبيّ
and also	كَمان	أَيْضاً
but	بَس	وَلٰكِن

Extra vocabulary   المفردات الإضافيّة

He is from New York.	هُوِّ مِن نْيويورْك.	هُوَ مِنْ نْيويورْك.
Is he from New York?	هُوِّ مِن نْيويورْك؟	هَل هُوَ مِنْ نْيويورْك؟
Her name is Sally.	اِسْمْها سالي.	اِسْمُها سالي.
Is her name Sally?	اِسْمْها سالي؟	هَل اِسْمُها سالي؟
I	أَنا	أَنا
you (m.)	اِنْتَ	أَنْتَ
you (f.)	اِنْتِ	أَنْتِ
he	هُوِّ	هُوَ
He is from ____, and of ____ origin also.	هُوِّ مِن ____ ومِن أَصْل ____ كَمان.	هُوَ مِن ____ وَمِن أَصْل ____ أَيْضاً.
She is from ____, and of ____ origin also.	هِيِّ مِن ____ ومِن أَصْل ____ كَمان.	هِيَ مِن ____ وَمِن أَصْل ____ أَيْضاً.
He is from ____, but of ____ origin.	هُوِّ مِن ____ بَس مِن أَصْل ____.	هُوَ مِن ____ وَلْكِن مِن أَصْل ____.
She is from ____, but of ____ origin.	هِيِّ مِن ____ بَس مِن أَصْل ____.	هِيَ مِن ____ وَلْكِن مِن أَصْل ____.
Really?	عَن جَدّ؟	حَقّاً؟
He / she is indigenous.	هُوِّ \ هِيِّ مِن السُّكان الأَصْليين	هُوَ \ هِيَ مِن السُّكان الأَصْليين

LESSON FIVE   الدرس الخامس

Core vocabulary   المفردات الأساسيّة

المعنى	العاميّة الشاميّة	الفصحى
What is your email address? (m.)	شو إيمَيلَك؟	ما عُنْوان بَريدَك الإلِكْترونيّ؟
What is your email address? (f.)	شو إيمَيلِك؟	ما عُنْوان بَريدِك الإلِكْترونيّ؟

المعنى	العاميّة الشاميّة	الفصحى
My email address is ____.	إيميلي ____.	عُنْوان بَريدي الإلِكْترونيّ ____.
What is your phone number? *(m.)*	شو رَقْم تَلِفونَك؟	ما رَقْم هاتِفَك؟
What is your phone number? *(f.)*	شو رَقْم تَلِفونك؟	ما رَقْم هاتِفِك؟
My phone number is ____.	رَقْم تَلِفوني ____.	رَقْم هاتِفي ____.

المفردات الإضافيّة

Extra vocabulary

What is Sarah's email address?	شو إيمَيل سارة؟	ما عُنْوان بَريدِ سارة الإلِكْترونيّ؟
What is Sarah's phone number?	شو رَقْم تَلِفون سارة؟	ما رَقْم هاتِف سارة؟
What is McDonald's phone number?	شو رَقْم تَلِفون ماكْدونالْدْز؟	ما رَقْم هاتِف ماكْدونالْدْز؟
McDonald's phone number is ____.	رَقْم تَلِفون ماكْدونالْدْز ____.	رَقْم هاتِف ماكْدونالْدْز ____.

Invitations

الوحدة الثانية

الدعوات

UNIT TWO GOALS—HOW IS YOUR ARABIC?

أهداف الوحدة الثانية—كيف عربيتك؟

This section lists the unit objectives. While you are working through the lessons in this unit, refer to this list and keep track of your progress toward each objective as you go. By the end of each lesson, you should be able to do the following in Arabic:

Lesson Six

الدرس السادس

- Ask permission to do something in your classroom
- Respond to questions by saying whether you understand them
- Respond to questions by telling whether you know the answer
- Respond to questions by saying whether you remember the answer

Lesson Seven

الدرس السابع

- Find out whether others are free or busy on different days of the week
- Respond to questions about whether you are free or busy on different days of the week
- Identify when the weekend is in different countries and cultures

Lesson Eight

الدرس الثامن

- Make plans to do something with a friend at a certain day and time
- Ask and respond to questions about what time it is
- Begin to understand some cultural differences in time management

Lesson Nine

الدرس التاسع

- Invite someone over to your house or another location
- Accept or defer invitations
- Respond to invitations using the phrase "God willing" appropriately in an Arab cultural context
- Ask and respond to questions about where you want to go

Lesson Ten   الدرس العاشر

- Offer someone tea or coffee when they come over to your house
- Respond politely when someone offers you drinks at their house
- Tell someone some of your likes and dislikes
- Tell how you take your coffee and tea

Classroom Talk: May I . . . ?

كلام الصفّ: هل من الممكن أن...؟

LESSON SIX GOALS

أهداف الدرس السادس

By the end of this lesson, you should be able to do the following:

- Ask permission to do something in your classroom
- Respond to questions by saying whether you understand them
- Respond to questions by telling whether you know the answer
- Respond to questions by saying whether you remember the answer

In this lesson, you will learn how to use Arabic to ask for permission and respond to simple questions from your teacher in class.

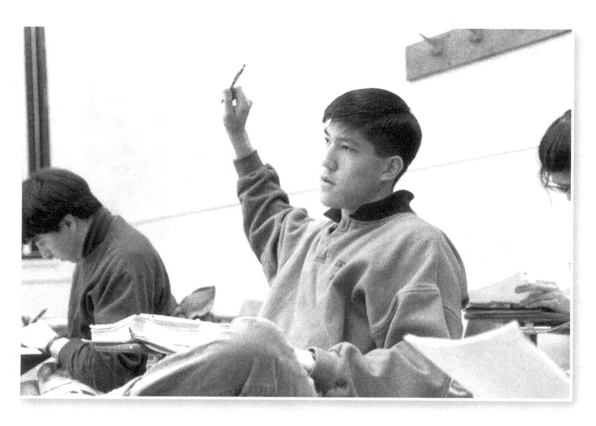

MAY I...?   هل من الممكن أن...؟

Vocabulary 1   مفردات ١

The following phrases can be used to ask permission from your teacher:

المعنى	العاميّة الشاميّة	الفصحى
May I go to the bathroom?	مُمْكِن أروح عَ الحَمّام؟	هَل مِن المُمْكِن أنْ أذهَب إلى الحَمّام؟
May I go drink water?	مُمْكِن أروح أشْرَب مَيّ؟	هَل مِن المُمْكِن أنْ أذهَب لِأشْرَب الماء؟
May I speak in English?	مُمْكِن أحكي إنْكْليزي؟	هَل مِن المُمْكِن أنْ أتَكَلَّم الإنْكْليزيّة؟
May...? Is it possible that...?	مُمْكِن...؟	هَل مِن المُمْكِن أنْ...؟

From now on, you should use only Arabic to ask permission to do these actions. Practice these phrases with your classmates so that you can use them when you need to in class.

Activity 1   Vocabulary practice: نشاط ١   تدريب على المفردات: أفعال
             Classroom verbs   الصف

In this exercise, find a classmate and practice the classroom phrases that correspond with the following pictures:

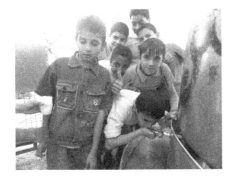 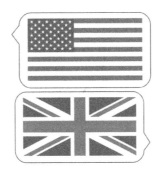 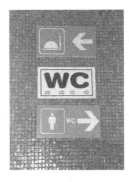

First, practice pointing to the correct picture when your classmate says each phrase. Then switch roles and practice saying the correct phrase when your classmate points to each picture. Finally, continue to practice with these pictures, this time using the full phrase "May I...?"

YES, I KNOW!

نعم، أعرف!

Vocabulary 2

مفردات ٢

These phrases will be useful if your teacher or classmates ask whether you understand something or know something in Arabic:

المعنى	العاميّة الشاميّة	الفصحى
I understand	فْهِمت	فَهِمْتُ
I do not understand	ما فْهِمت	ما فَهِمْتُ
I know	بَعْرَف	أَعْرِف
I do not know	ما بَعْرَف	لا أَعْرِف
I remember	بْتْذَكَّر	أتَذَكَّر
I do not remember	ما بْتْذَكَّر	لا أتَذَكَّر

Activity 2   Reading and conversation: Which of the words do you understand?

نشاط ٢   قراءة ومحادثة: ماذا فهمت من الكلمات؟

In this activity, you will practice reporting what you understand from a list of words. With a classmate, look at the following words and try to identify what you can and cannot understand. Point to each word, read it, and say the appropriate phrase about it: "I understand" or "I don't understand." If there is a word that you understand but your classmate does not, see if you can explain or show the meaning without using English!

These words include words and phrases from Unit One, words and phrases from elsewhere in this book, and names of places that have similar names in Arabic and English. If you see a word that has a letter you do not know, sound out the rest of the letters and see if you can guess the word. (You are not expected to understand every word in this list!)

٥. لَم	٤. اللّيالي	٣. مومْباي	٢. وَ	١. أتلانْتا
١٠. ثَلاث	٩. أب	٨. شو	٧. أَيْنَ	٦. آه
١٥. مَدينة	١٤. ليبيا	١٣. إثْيوبيا	١٢. هُوَ	١١. هُنا
٢٠. أمْريكا	١٩. واو	١٨. مِلْيون	١٧. مُمْتاز	١٦. بَنَما
٢٥. ولاية	٢٤. أهْلاً	٢٣. ثَمانية	٢٢. اِثْنَين	٢١. أنْتِ
٣٠. وَلٰكِن	٢٩. النيل	٢٨. هِيَ	٢٧. واحِد	٢٦. اسْمي
٣٥. مِثْل	٣٤. لُبْنان	٣٣. عِنْدي	٣٢. نيويورْك	٣١. أنا
٤٠. بَيت	٣٩. مِن	٣٨. ميلان	٣٧. لا	٣٦. يَوم

٤٥. لام	٤٤. عُمان	٤٣. مانيلا	٤٢. بَيروت	٤١. مِيامي
٥٠. بَين	٤٩. اليابان	٤٨. ثانَويّ	٤٧. عُمري	٤٦. هَل
٥٥. تونِس	٥٤. اليَمَن	٥٣. أَنْتَ	٥٢. التّالي	٥١. نون
٦٠. ثانِية	٥٩. تَل أَبيب	٥٨. كَيفَ	٥٧. السَّلام	٥٦. ميم

I'm busy today

الدرس السابع

أنا مشغول اليوم

LESSON SEVEN GOALS

أهداف الدرس السابع

By the end of this lesson, you should be able to do the following:

- Find out whether others are free or busy on different days of the week
- Respond to questions about whether you are free or busy on different days of the week
- Identify when the weekend is in different countries and cultures

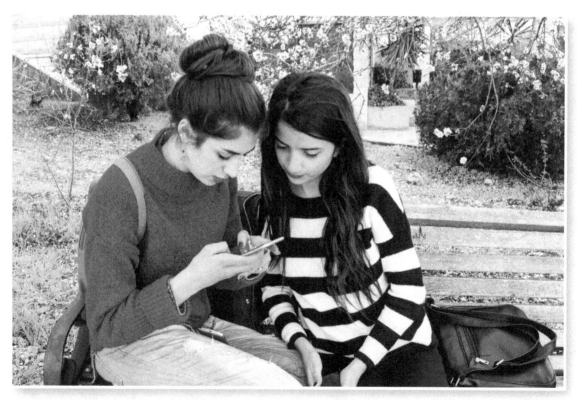

- Which days of the week are you busiest?
- Which days of the week do you do activities outside of school?
- Among your family, friends, or community, is being busy considered a good thing? Why or why not?

I'M BUSY
Vocabulary 1

أنا مشغول

مفردات ١

المعنى	العاميّة الشاميّة	الفصحى
Are you free today? (m.)	فاضي اليوم؟	هَل أَنْتَ فاضي* اليَوْم؟
Are you free today? (f.)	فاضية اليوم؟	هَل أَنْتِ فاضية اليَوْم؟
Yes, I am free. (m.)	آه، أنا فاضي.	نَعَم، أنا فاضي.
Yes, I am free. (f.)	آه، أنا فاضية.	نَعَم، أنا فاضية.
No, I am busy. (m.)	لا، أنا مَشْغول.	لا، أنا مَشْغول.
No, I am busy. (f.)	لا، أنا مَشْغولة.	لا، أنا مَشْغولة.
free available	فاضي / فاضية	فاضي / فاضِية
busy occupied	مَشْغول / مَشْغولة	مَشْغول / مَشْغولة
today	اليوم	اليَوْم
tomorrow	بُكْرا	غَداً

* The word فاضي is given in the vocabulary columns for both الفصحى and العاميّة الشاميّة as a simplification for novice learners. The standard form of this word, in الفصحى, is فاضٍ. Ask your teacher if you would like to know more.

| Activity 1 | Listening: "Are you free today?" | استماع: "فاضية اليوم؟" | نشاط ١ |

In this video, you will see two characters making plans.

Before listening

قبل الاستماع

Watch a few seconds of the video "فاضية اليوم؟" without the sound. Who are the characters in it? Tell a classmate what you remember about these characters from previous videos, using complete sentences in Arabic as much as possible.

Listening

الاستماع

On a separate sheet of paper, write a word or draw a symbol to indicate whether the two characters are free or busy on each day they mention.

غداً Tomorrow	اليوم Today	
		ياسمين Yasmine
		نادين Nadine

Grammar: Questions   القواعد: الأسئلة

In this section, you will review and practice asking yes-or-no questions in Arabic. As you learned in Lesson 4, the patterns for this vary between Levantine dialect and Modern Standard Arabic. Whichever variety of Arabic you are activating in your class, it will be useful for you to be familiar with both varieties. We will begin with Levantine, since this is what we heard in the video in Activity 1 above.

If you are studying Levantine dialect: Listen again to the video and pay attention to how the characters ask questions in Levantine Arabic.

Are you free today?	اِنْتِ فاضْية اليوم؟
Are you free tomorrow?	اِنْتِ فاضْية بُكْرا؟

The character asks these questions with a rising tone of voice. In this way, Arabic is similar to English; we also use rising intonation when asking yes-or-no questions. **In Levantine dialect, the rising tone of voice is the only change between statements and yes-or-no questions.** Compare these statements with their corresponding questions above:

You are free today.	اِنْتِ فاضْية اليوم.
You are free tomorrow.	اِنْتِ فاضْية بُكْرا.

Practice saying the statements and questions aloud with the appropriate change in the tone of your voice.

If you are studying Modern Standard Arabic: As you previously practiced, in Modern Standard Arabic, yes-or-no questions are formed by adding a word to the beginning of a statement. When spoken, yes-or-no questions are pronounced with rising intonation, just as in Levantine dialect and in English. The word that makes a statement into a question is هَل.

This word has no direct equivalent in English. It is a very common word in Arabic, and even if you are focusing on Levantine dialect, you should become familiar with this word since you will encounter it often. Look at the differences between these statements and questions in formal Arabic:

You are busy today.	أَنْتِ مَشْغولة اليَوْم.
You are busy tomorrow.	أَنْتِ مَشْغولة غَداً.

Are you busy today?	هَل أَنْتِ مَشْغولة اليَوْم؟
Are you busy tomorrow?	هَل أَنْتِ مَشْغولة غَداً؟

Practice saying these statements and questions aloud, using the word هَل and changing the tone of your voice as appropriate. With a classmate, think of a number of statements that you know how to say in Arabic and then turn them into yes-or-no questions in both varieties.

Activity 2   Conversation: Are you busy tomorrow?   نشاط ٢   محادثة: هل أنت مشغول غداً؟

In this activity, you will practice finding out when others are free in order to make plans.

Before speaking   قبل المحادثة

Imagine that you want to plan a class outing today or tomorrow, and you want to find out what day is best for the majority of your classmates. On a separate piece of paper, make a chart like this:

غداً **Tomorrow**	اليوم **Today**	الاسم **Name**

Your task is to find out from your classmates whether they are free today or tomorrow. Before starting, practice asking your question in Arabic and prepare to ask classmates of different genders.

Speaking   المحادثة

Find a classmate, write their name on your chart, and ask them whether they are free today and tomorrow. Write a check or an X in the chart based on their answers. Talk to as many classmates as you can in the time you have.

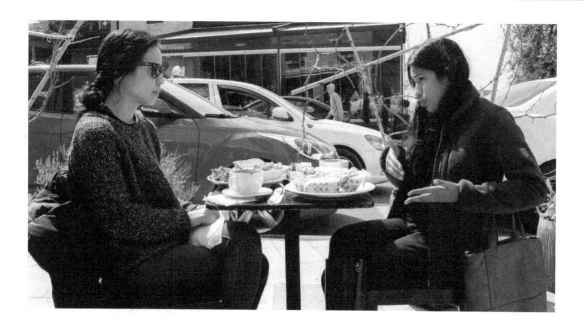

Keep speaking

واصلوا المحادثة

Now, find a classmate you did not talk to earlier and give them a report about the people you have on your list, using their names to say whether they are free or busy today and tomorrow.

After speaking

بعد المحادثة

Now that you have practiced these phrases, create a skit with a classmate based on the video in Activity 1 of this lesson. Watch the video again, then play it with the sound off as you act out your skit. Make sure to include the following elements:

- Greetings
- A question about how the person is doing
- Questions that find out whether they are free or busy for a meeting
- A polite goodbye

Activity 3   Conversation: Two truths and a lie game

نشاط ٣   محادثة: لعبة حقيقتين وكذبة

In order to practice asking yes-or-no questions, play a version of the game two truths and a lie.

Before speaking

قبل المحادثة

Come up with three statements about yourself in Arabic, using your knowledge and vocabulary from this and the previous lessons. You could start your sentences with these phrases:

- أنا فاضي غداً / أنا فاضي بكرا
- أنا مشغول اليوم
- صديقتي ____ من... / صاحبتي ____ من...

- أنا من...
- أنا من أصل...
- عمري...

Two of your statements should be true, and one of your statements should be false. Draw a picture representing your statements or write them in Arabic.

Speaking   المحادثة

Find a classmate and tell them the three statements you have prepared. In response, your classmate should express their skepticism about the statement they find least likely, saying "Really?" and restating the statement they doubt as a question. You can then confirm whether your classmate found your lie. Switch roles, then find a new classmate and repeat the game. To express your skepticism about a fact, use this expression:

Really?	عَن جَدّ؟	حَقّاً؟

			يناير			
الجمعة	الخميس	الأربعاء	الثلاثاء	الاثنين	الأحد	السبت
٦	٥	٤	٣	٢	١	
١٣	١٢	١١	١٠	٩	٨	٧
٢٠	١٩	١٨	١٧	١٦	١٥	١٤
٢٧	٢٦	٢٥	٢٤	٢٣	٢٢	٢١
			٣١	٣٠	٢٩	٢٨

I'M FREE ON FRIDAY

Vocabulary 2

أنا فاضي يوم الجمعة

مفردات ٢

المعنى	العاميّة الشاميّة	الفصحى
(a) day	يوم	يَوْم
today	اليوم	اليَوْم
tomorrow	بُكْرا	غَداً
the day after tomorrow	بَعْد بُكْرا	بَعْدَ غَد
days of the week	أيّام الأُسْبوع	أيّام الأُسْبوع
Sunday	يوم الأَحَد	يَوْم الأَحَد
Monday	يوم الاِثْنين	يَوْم الاِثْنَيْن
Tuesday	يوم الثَّلاثا	يَوْم الثَّلاثاء
Wednesday	يوم الأَرْبعا	يَوْم الأَرْبعاء
Thursday	يوم الخَميس	يَوْم الخَميس
Friday	يوم الجُمْعة	يَوْم الجُمْعة
Saturday	يوم السَّبْت	يَوْم السَّبْت

In both الفصحى and العاميّة الشاميّة, it is acceptable to say any day of the week with or without the word يوم at the beginning. For example, when referring to Sunday, you could say either يوم الأحد or الأحد.

Activity 4	Listening and reading: Days of the week and numbers	نشاط ٤ استماع وقراءة: أيام الأسبوع والأرقام

This activity will help you draw connections among words you already know in Arabic and practice your observational skills.

Before listening

قبل الاستماع

Before listening, count from one to ten in Arabic with your classmates. Do you hear any numbers that sound similar to the days of the week?

Listening

الاستماع

In this chart are the numbers one through seven and the days of the week lined up. Read or listen to each row in the chart and pay attention to what is similar and different between these words. Then, write down what you notice. Be specific, saying more than "they are similar." Write down which letters or sounds are similar and different between them.

ملاحظات Notes	أيام الأسبوع Days of the week	الأرقام Numbers
	يوم الأَحَد	واحِد
	يوم الاِثْنَيْن	اِثْنان / اِثْنَيْن
	يوم الثُّلاثاء	ثَلاثة
	يوم الأَرْبِعاء	أَرْبَعة
	يوم الخَميس	خَمْسة
	يوم الجُمْعة	سِتّة
	يوم السَبْت	سَبْعة

Work with your classmates to be as specific as possible about similarities and differences. Why do you think these sets of words sound similar? Why do you think certain days sound different from the numbers? Discuss with your teacher. You will use your observations in the next activity.

Activity 5   Reading: Three-consonant word roots

نشاط ٥   قراءة: الجذر الثلاثي

In the previous activity, you observed how words containing the same or similar letters have related meanings. You will learn more about that phenomenon in this activity.

Before reading

قبل القراءة

Think about the English words "grandiose," "aggrandize," and "grandeur." All three contain the word "grand," meaning magnificent or large, and have related meanings. Now think about the words "eject," "inject," and "reject": what letters do they share, and how are their meanings related? All come from the Latin word for "to throw." What about the words "sing," "sang," "song," and "sung"? What letters and meanings do these words have in common? What other groups of words can you think of that sound similar and have related meanings? What do these words share, and what makes them different?

In Arabic, words that have similar sounds and related meanings share a *root*—this is a linguistic term for the basic core of a word. Recognizing roots of words and understanding how words with the same root relate to each other can help you learn Arabic vocabulary and guess the meaning of unfamiliar words.

Roots in Arabic are made up of three consonants in a fixed order. Letters and short vowels can be added before, after, or in between these root letters to form words whose meanings are related to the root.

The following three tables each contain a set of words that share the same root. Examine the words and discuss with a partner which letters and short vowels have been added to the root in each case.

shared three-consonant root: ك ب ر	
large (adj.)	كَبير
larger (adj.)	أكْبَر
enlarged (adj.)	مُكَبَّر
enlargement (n.)	تَكْبير
grandeur (adj.)	كِبْرِياء

shared three-consonant root: ث ل ث	
three	ثَلاثة
Tuesday (n.)	الثُّلاثاء
a third (n.)	ثُلْث
third (adj.)	ثالِث
triangle (n.)	مُثَلَّث

shared three-consonant root: ع ب ر	
four	أرْبَعة
Wednesday (n.)	الأرْبَعاء
a quarter (n.)	رُبْع
fourth (adj.)	رابِع
square (n.)	مُرَبَّع

At this early stage in your Arabic studies, you do not have to learn how roots work in detail. For now, you will learn how to recognize the three consonants of a root when looking at two words that have a common root. You should try to hear how the words sound similar and observe the relationship between the meanings of the two words.

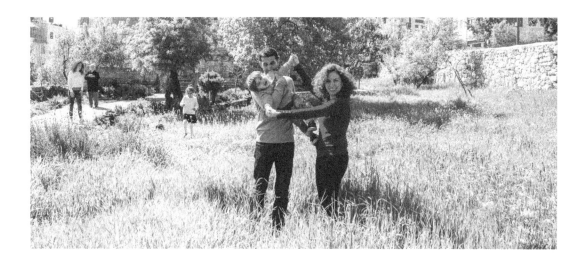

Reading القراءة

Read the following collection of words aloud:

vegetarian	نَباتيّ	colors	ألْوان	nocturnal	لَيْلي
night	لَيْل	wealth	أمْوال	she sleeps	تَنام
similar to	مِثْلَ	representation	تَمْثيل	a second	ثانية
he plants (a seed)	يُنْبِت	color	لَوْن	a dream	مَنام
trio	ثُلاثي	funding	تَمْويل	two	اِثْنَيْن
a third	ثُلْث				

Now, work together with a classmate to find the eight pairs of words that have the same root. Using a chart like the one below, write each of the eight pairs in their won space. Next to each pair, record the three letters you think constitute the shared root of the paired words. Keep the following pointers in mind:

- Not every word starts with its first root letter.
- Root letters must be in the same order.
- There will be a relationship between the meanings of words that share a root.

الجذر Root	المفردان Two Words	
		.١
		.٢
		.٣
		.٤
		.٥

	المفردان Two Words	الجذر Root
.٦		
.٧		
.٨		

After reading بعد القراءة

Discuss your answers with your classmates. Remember that you do not need to learn or remember these particular words! From now on, use your new skills at identifying roots when you learn new vocabulary. It will help you memorize and sometimes even guess the meaning of new words.

Activity 6   Listening and conversation: استماع ومحادثة: متى العطلة؟   نشاط ٦
When is the weekend?

The days that make up the workweek and weekend vary from country to country. In this listening activity, you will learn about different weekends around the world.

Before listening قبل الاستماع

Look at the following cartoons and discuss with your classmates and teachers: Which days of the week make you feel like this? Can you figure out which days of the week these cartoons are describing? Read aloud the sound that the woman in the cartoon is making and ask your teacher about when people use this sound.

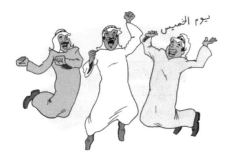
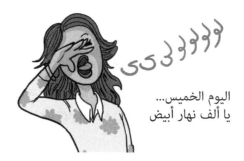

Before starting the listening passage, familiarize yourself this word:

weekend day(s) off holiday	عُطْلة	عُطْلة

Work with a classmate to create an Arabic sentence to describe when the weekend is in your country or other countries you are familiar with: "In [country name], the weekend is [days' names]."

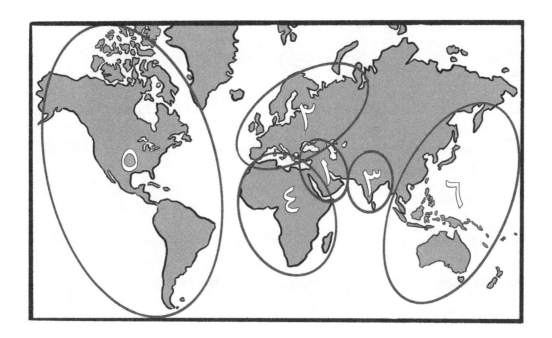

Listening   الاستماع

This activity includes six different audio recordings, each describing the weekends in countries
in different regions of the world. Listen to the audio recording(s) about the region(s) assigned
to you and take note of the weekend for each country. (Use the table provided by your teacher
or create your own.) The countries included have seven different possible weekends:

يوم الأحد Sunday	يوم السبت ويوم الأحد Saturday and Sunday	يوم السبت Saturday	يوم الجمعة ويوم الأحد Friday and Sunday	يوم الجمعة ويوم السبت Friday and Saturday	يوم الجمعة Friday	يوم الخميس ويوم الجمعة Thursday and Friday

Below are the country names you will listen for:

٣	٢	١
إثيوبيا / Ethiopia تنزانيا / Tanzania تونس / Tunisia الجزائر / Algeria جيبوتي / Djibouti السودان / Sudan ليبيا / Libya مصر (miSr) / Egypt المغرب / Morocco نيجيريا / Nigeria	ألمانيا / Germany (almaaniyaa) روسيا / Russia فرنسا / France	أفغانستان / Afghanistan إسرائيل / Israel إيران / Iran تركيا / Turkey السعودية / Saudi Arabia سوريا / Syria العراق / Iraq لبنان / Lebanon اليمن / Yemen فلسطين / Palestine

٦	٥	٤
أستراليا / Australia إندونيسيا / Indonesia Brunei / بروناي China / الصين Philippines / الفلبين Japan / اليابان	الأرجنتين / Argentina برازيل / Brazil Colombia / كولومبيا Mexico / المكسيك الولايات المتحدة الأمريكية / USA	إثيوبيا / Ethiopia تنزانيا / Tanzania Tunisia / تونس Algeria / الجزائر Djibouti / جيبوتي Sudan / السودان Libya / ليبيا Egypt (*miSr*) / مصر Morocco / المغرب Nigeria / نيجيريا

Speaking   المحادثة

After you have determined the weekends for the countries from your assigned region(s), find a classmate who listened to different audio recording(s). Ask and answer questions in Arabic to find out about the weekends in countries that you did not hear about in the previous phase. Use the following question and take note of the response:

When is the weekend in ____?	إيمتى العُطْلة في ____؟	مَتى العُطْلة في ____؟

Talk with as many people as necessary until you have noted the weekend for every country listed.

After listening and speaking   بعد الاستماع والمحادثة

Now that you have organized the countries by weekend days, complete the following tasks to explore the reasons that might explain the differences in weekends around the world (it is acceptable to use English):

- Identify as many Arab countries from the audio recordings as you can. What is the pattern of weekends and where are there exceptions?
- Identify as many majority-Muslim countries from the audios as you can. Which of these countries fit with the pattern in Arab countries and which are different?
- Use the internet to research some of the reasons behind the diversity in weekends around the world.

Challenge yourself: On the following page is a cartoon from Qatar about a proposed change in the weekend. It shows the "latest public opinion poll" about the change. Identify all of the days of the week mentioned in the cartoon, comparing the shapes of the letters. Then talk with your classmates and teacher about what the cartoon is trying to say.

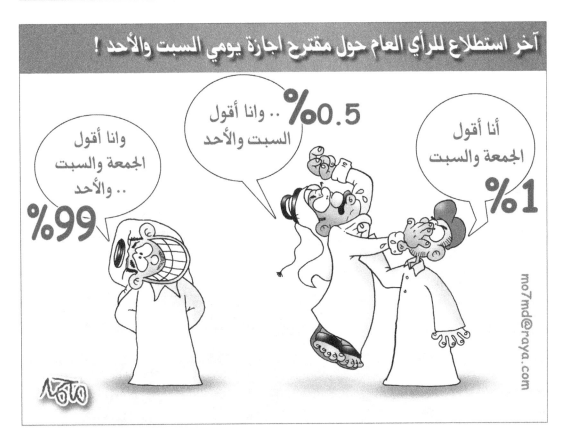

Activity 7   Listening: Films on TV   استماع: أفلام على التلفزيون   نشاط ٧

In Arab countries, there are a number of popular TV channels that play Hollywood movies with Arabic subtitles. In this activity, you will practice understanding schedules for when some of those movies appear on TV.

Before Listening   قبل الاستماع

Talk about some of the movies you think are great with your classmates. Take turns mentioning names of movies, and then let your classmates respond with some of the following phrases.

The movie is excellent.	الفيلْم مُمتاز.	الفيلْم مُمتاز.
The movie is good.	الفيلْم مْنيح.	الفيلْم جَيِّد.
I don't know the movie.	ما بَعرَف الفيلْم.	لا أعرِف الفيلْم.

Listening   الاستماع

Imagine that you have some American friends living in an Arab country who want to watch American movies on an Arab TV channel, but they are having trouble understanding the commercials and deciding what they should watch on which day.

You will listen to two different commercials for two different TV channels. Write down the names of the movies showing on each day on each channel, using the chart that follows. Add any other information that you can hear about the film in the commercials.

MBC2	Fox Movies		
		Sunday	الأحد
		Monday	الاثنين
		Tuesday	الثلاثاء
		Wednesday	الأربعاء
		Thursday	الخميس
		Friday	الجمعة

After listening   بعد الاستماع

Prepare your recommendations about the movies that are playing each day. Prepare a short presentation in Arabic, saying what you think of the movies on each day. Follow the model below for your sentences, making each one your own.

On Thursday, the movie *Shrek* is excellent, but I don't know the movie *Star Wars*.	يوم الخَميس، فيلْم "شْرِك" مُمْتاز بَس ما بَعْرَف فيلْم "سْتار ووْرْز".	يَوْم الخَميس، فيلْم "شْرِك" مُمْتاز وَلْكِن لا أَعْرِف فيلْم "سْتار ووْرْز".

When you have practiced this independently, record it as an audio recording and submit it to your teacher. For further practice with the days of the week, create a commercial for your own movie channel that plays your favorite movies. Record this and submit to your teacher.

Activity 8   Listening: A voice message   استماع: رسالة صوتية   نشاط ٨

Imagine that you have been assigned a group project with four other classmates, and you need to find a lunch period when you can all meet. You have asked each member of your group to tell you when they are free during the week so that you can schedule a meeting, and they each respond to you by leaving a voice message on a messaging app.

Listening for general understanding

Create a chart like the one below on a separate piece of paper. Listen quickly to each of the four voice messages (audio) to find out who they are from. Write the name of each person in the right-hand column of the chart below.

الخميس Thursday	الأربعاء Wednesday	الثلاثاء Tuesday	الاثنين Monday	الأحد Sunday	الاسم Name

Close listening

Listen to each of the voice messages again and mark in the chart whether the person is free or busy on each day. You could draw a picture, a symbol, or write an Arabic word. Then decide which will be the best day for the group to meet.

After listening

Use the chart below, based on the Monday through Friday schedule, to indicate your own (real or invented) availability during a lunch or other break. Chat with as many classmates as possible to find out when they are available to hold a group study session.

When you talk with each classmate, keep these things in mind to make sure that you are interacting in a culturally appropriate way:

- Greet each other appropriately.
- Ask the other person how they are doing.
- Use the appropriate words according to your classmate's gender.
- Say goodbye before moving on to your next classmate.

الجمعة Friday	الخميس Thursday	الأربعاء Wednesday	الثلاثاء Tuesday	الاثنين Monday	الاسم Name

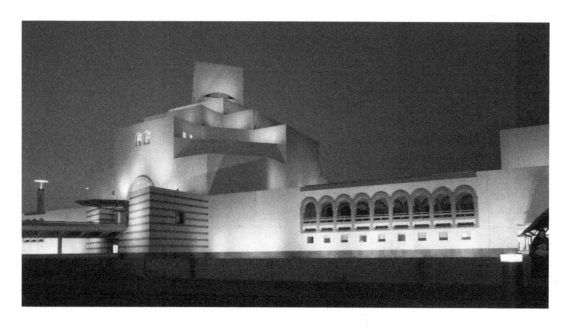

Activity 9   Reading: A museum schedule   نشاط ٩   قراءة: جدول المتحف

The following is from a flyer about the Arab Museum of Modern Art in Qatar.

تاريخ المكتبة

كانت المكتبة في البدء مستودعاً لحفظ مراجع الفن المأخوذة من مكتبة الشيخ حسن بن محمد بن علي آل ثاني الخاصة. وعلى مر السنين نمت وازدادت هذه المجموعة وقفاً لاحتياجات القيّمين ثم تم مراجعتها وازدادت المجموعة توسعاً لتلبي احتياجات المتحف.

ساعات العمل والدخول

الأحد	١١:٠٠ – ١٨:٠٠
الاثنين	مغلق
الثلاثاء – الخميس	١١:٠٠ – ١٨:٠٠
الجمعة	١٥:٠٠ – ٢١:٠٠
السبت	١١:٠٠ – ١٨:٠٠

مغلق في اليوم الأول من العيد.

To help plan an upcoming student trip to Qatar, you have been asked to create a visual representation of the museum's hours. Create a chart such as the following and shade in the hours when the museum is open.

	Sunday	Monday	Tuesday	Wednesday	Thursday	Friday	Saturday
6:00–8:00 a.m.							
8:00–10:00 a.m.							
10:00 a.m.–12:00 p.m.							
12:00–2:00 p.m.							
2:00–4:00 pm							
4:00–6:00 p.m.							
6:00–8:00 p.m.							
8:00–10:00 p.m.							

Challenge yourself: In the flyer, what do you think the word مُغْلَق means, from the context? What other words can you recognize or guess from this advertisement?

At what time?

في أيّ ساعة؟

LESSON EIGHT GOALS

أهداف الدرس الثامن

By the end of this lesson, you should be able to do the following:

- Make plans to do something with a friend at a certain day and time
- Ask and respond to questions about what time it is
- Begin to understand some cultural differences in time management

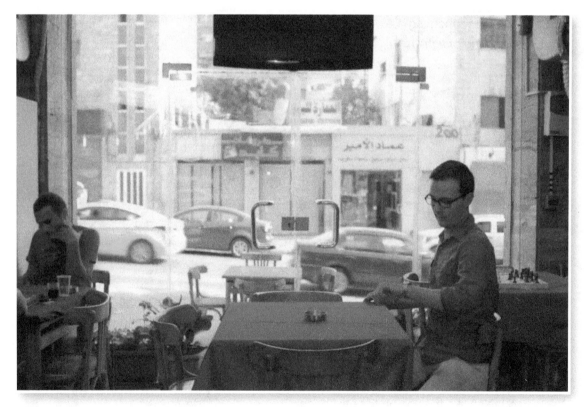

- How do you manage your time?
- How do people from different cultures view time differently?

WHEN?   مَتى؟

Vocabulary 1   مفردات ١

Practice these new greetings in games and conversation practice, as instructed by your teacher:

المعنى	العاميّة الشاميّة	الفصحى
When?	إيمْتى؟	مَتى؟
in the morning	الصُّبْح	في الصَّباح
noon noontime	الظُّهُر	الظُّهْر
in the afternoon	بَعْد الظُّهُر	بَعْدَ الظُّهْر
in the evening	المَسا	في المَساء
at night	باللَّيل	في اللَّيْل
good morning (literally: "morning of prosperity")	صَباح الخَير	صَباح الخَيْر
response to "good morning" (literally: "morning of light")	صَباح النّور	صَباح النّور
good evening (literally: "evening of prosperity") (said after noon or later)	مَسا الخَير	مَساء الخَيْر
response to "good evening" (literally "evening of light")	مَسا النّور	مَساء النّور

Activity 1   Listening: What happened today?   نشاط ١   استماع: ماذا حدث اليوم؟

Samir's parents are out of town unexpectedly. He has been left in charge of the house and taking their phone calls. At the end of each day, he relays the most important messages back to them via voicemail because they cannot text or email easily.

Listening   الاستماع

Create two tables like the one on the next page:

الأحد	الإثنين	الثلاثاء	الأربعاء	الخميس	الجمعة	السبت

Listen to Samir's messages to his parents. For each message, write the time of day (morning, noon, afternoon, evening, or night) in the cell below the day of the week mentioned. It is okay if you do not understand the content of the messages, but you may be able to pick up on some other familiar words and cognates with English, meaning words that sound similar and have a similar meaning in both languages.

Keep listening   واصلوا الاستماع

Samir's parents responded to Samir's messages with voice messages of their own. Listen to the messages they left him using the second table you created to mark the time of day under the corresponding day of the week. Jot down words that you understood or recognize.

Activity 2   Conversation: When do you do   محادثة: متى تفعلون هذا؟   نشاط ٢
this?

In this activity, you will find out about some of your classmates' daily routines.

Before speaking   قبل المحادثة

When do you do the following? Point to each picture and tell a classmate whether you do the depicted action in the morning, afternoon, evening, or night. You do not need to know how to say the action in Arabic.

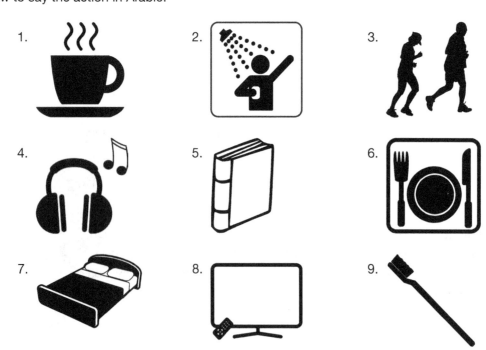

Speaking   المحادثة

Your teacher will give you a card with either an image or a word. You are responsible for polling as many classmates as you can to find out when they usually do the activity on your card. Keep a tally by making a chart like the one below. To conduct your poll and respond to others', use the following sentence structures as you point to a card with an activity on it:

When do you do this? *(m.)*	إيمْتى بْتِعْمَل هٰذا؟	مَتى تَفْعَل هٰذا؟
When do you do this? *(f.)*	إيمْتى بْتِعْمَلي هٰذا؟	مَتى تَفْعَلين هٰذا؟
I do this in the morning.	أَنا بَعْمَل هاذا الصُّبْح.	أَنا أَفْعَل هٰذا في الصَّباح.
I do not do this.	أَنا ما بَعْمَل هاذا.	أَنا لا أَفْعَل هٰذا.

Keep a tally of the responses that you receive on a table like this:

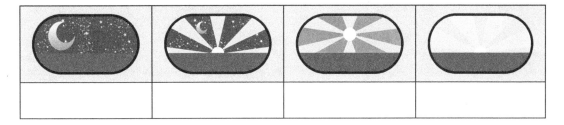

After speaking   بعد المحادثة

Tell your classmates how many people do your activity at each of the four times, using the times of day and the numbers you know in Arabic. You do not need to know how to say the activity in Arabic; just show your card.

Activity 3   Conversation: Assistant   محادثة: مساعد   نشاط ٣

You are the CEO of a large, successful company. Because you are so busy, your assistant takes care of all of your appointments for you. In this activity, your assistant will first learn about your availability for meetings and then use that information to schedule some interviews with the media.

Before speaking   قبْل المحادثة

First, create two Monday to Thursday schedules like the ones on the following page, labeling one of them ا and one of them ب (or use the handout your teacher gives you). Then, indicate your availability for the four days by circling the part of day that you are free in schedule ا. You can create a fake schedule for yourself as CEO of a huge company; you do not have to follow your real-life schedule.

الخميس Thursday	الأربعاء Wednesday	الثلاثاء Tuesday	الاثنين Monday

Speaking   المحادثة

Find a classmate and take turns being the CEO and being the assistant. Communicate your availability (from schedule أ above) over the next four days to your assistant. Make sure you exchange greetings and other pleasantries before discussing business. Follow your teacher's example and the following instructions:

- When it is your turn to act as the assistant, ask the CEO when they are available and keep track by circling or crossing out the times as appropriate on schedule ب.
- When it is your turn to the act as the CEO, tell your assistant when you are available based on the schedule you already completed for yourself (schedule أ).

Keep talking   واصلوا المحادثة

You will now work with a new classmate. This time, take turns being the assistant and being a journalist. The goal of the journalist is to get an interview with the CEO. The goal of the secretary is to safeguard the CEO's time and only schedule an interview when the CEO is free.

In order to complete this task, first review what you already know and figure out how you could say "she is free" or "he is busy." As in the prior part of the activity, both parties should make sure that they greet each other and exchange pleasantries before discussing business. Follow the appropriate instructions below, given your role:

- As the assistant, you will need to give the name of your boss when talking to the journalist. You will use the CEO's schedule (from schedule ب) that you asked about in the previous part to answer the journalist's questions.

- As journalist, you must state your name and identify the newspaper or news outlet where you work. (Use the phrase "I am from . . ." with the name of the newspaper or TV channel.) You must ask the secretary questions about when the CEO is free. You will use your schedule from schedule I above to try to find a time in common. You may not end up with an interview if you and the CEO do not have any openings at the same time.

WHAT TIME IS IT?

Vocabulary 2

كم الساعة؟

مفردات ٢

المعنى	العاميّة الشاميّة	الفصحى
What time is it?	كَم الساعة؟	كَم الساعة؟
At what time . . . ?	أيّ ساعة...؟	في أيّ ساعة...؟
(clock showing 1:00)	الساعة واحْدة	الساعة الواحِدة
(clock showing 2:00)	الساعة ثِنْتَين	الساعة الثانِية
(clock showing 3:00)	الساعة ثَلاثة	الساعة الثالِثة
(clock showing 4:00)	الساعة أَرْبَعة	الساعة الرابِعة
(clock showing 5:00)	الساعة خَمْسة	الساعة الخامِسة

المعنى	العاميّة الشاميّة	الفصحى
	الساعة سِتّة	الساعة السادسة
	الساعة سَبْعة	الساعة السابِعة
	الساعة ثَمانية	الساعة الثامِنة
	الساعة تِسْعة	الساعة التاسِعة
	الساعة عَشَرة	الساعة العاشِرة
	الساعة اِحْدَعْش	الساعة الحادِية عَشَرة
	الساعة اِثْنَعْش	الساعة الثانِية عَشَرة
a.m.		صَباحاً
p.m.		مَساءً

Practice saying the times you have learned:

1. With a classmate, take turns saying aloud the time represented by each clock below.
2. When you are done, take turns asking each other "What time is it?" in Arabic. The other person must answer with a time depicted by one of the clocks below. Then, the classmate who asked for the time must demonstrate their understanding by pointing to the clock that represents that time.

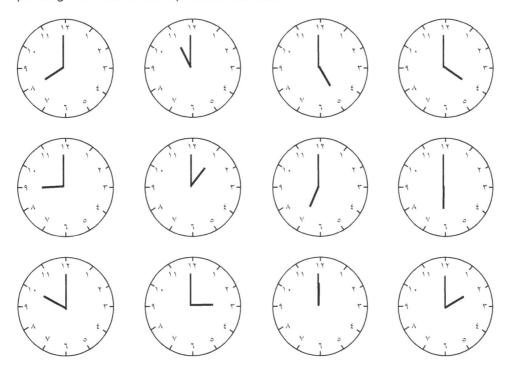

Vocabulary 3

مفردات ٣

In this lesson, we will only be looking at fractions of the hour rather than minutes (quarter, third, half). To say "a quarter" (15 minutes), "a third" (20 minutes), and "a half" (30 minutes) past the hour, use و in your construction:

المعنى	العاميّة الشاميّة	الفصحى
(clock showing 5:15)	الساعة خَمْسة ورُبُع	الساعة الخامِسة والرُبع
(clock showing 6:20)	الساعة سِتّة وثُلْث	الساعة السادِسة والثُلْث

المعنى	العاميّة الشاميّة	الفصحى
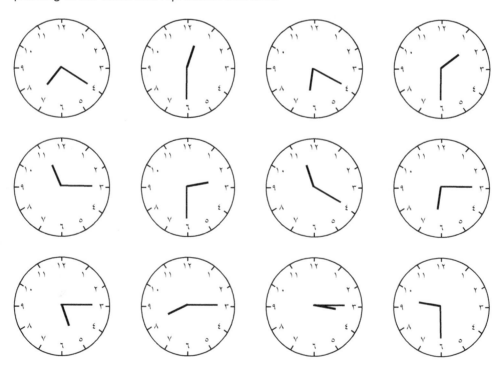	الساعة تِسْعة ونُص	الساعة التاسِعة وَالنِصْف
and	و	وَ
a quarter	رُبُع	رُبْع
a third	ثُلْث	ثُلْث
a half	نُص	نِصْف

Activity 5 Vocabulary practice: One thirty	نشاط ٥ تدريب على المفردات: الساعة الواحدة والنصف

Practice saying the times you have learned:

1. With a classmate, take turns saying aloud the time represented by each clock below.

2. When you are done, take turns asking each other "What time is it?" in Arabic. The other person must respond with a time depicted by one of the clocks below. Then, the classmate who asked for the time must demonstrate their understanding by pointing to the clock that represents that time.

Vocabulary 4   مفردات ٤

To express that the time is a quarter or a third *to* the (next) hour, you will use إِلّا.

المعنى	العاميّة الشاميّة	الفصحى
	الساعة ثِنتَين إلّا رُبُع	الساعة الثانِية إلّا رُبْعاً
	الساعة ثَلاثة إلّا ثُلْث	الساعة الثالِثة إلّا ثُلْثاً
except for minus *(use this for expressing "till" or "to" the hour)*	إلّا	إلّا

Activity 6	Vocabulary practice: A quarter to two	نشاط ٦ تدريب على المفردات: الساعة الثانية إلّا ربعاً

Practice saying the times you have learned:

1. With a classmate, take turns saying aloud the time represented by each clock below.
2. When you are done, take turns asking each other "What time is it?" in Arabic. The other person must answer with a time depicted by one of the clocks below. Then, the classmate who asked for the time must demonstrate their understanding by pointing to the clock that represents that time.

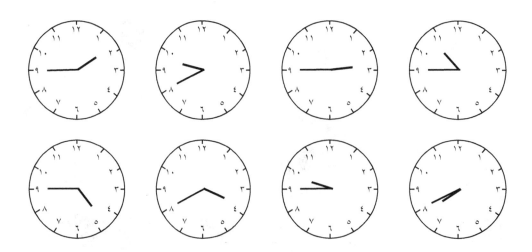

| Activity 7   Listening: "What time is it?" | استماع: "كم الساعة؟"   نشاط ٧ |

In this video, you will hear some people asking each other for the time.

| Listening for general understanding | الاستماع للفهم العام |

Write down the times of day that you hear in each scene (morning, etc.).

الساعة	رقم المشهد Scene number
	١
	٢
	٣
	٤

| Close listening | الاستماع الدقيق |

In Scene 2, David uses a different phrase to ask what time it is. This phrasing is used in many varieties of Levantine dialect. What does he say?

| After listening | بعد الاستماع |

Practice asking several classmates what the time is, modeling your exchange on what you saw in the video.

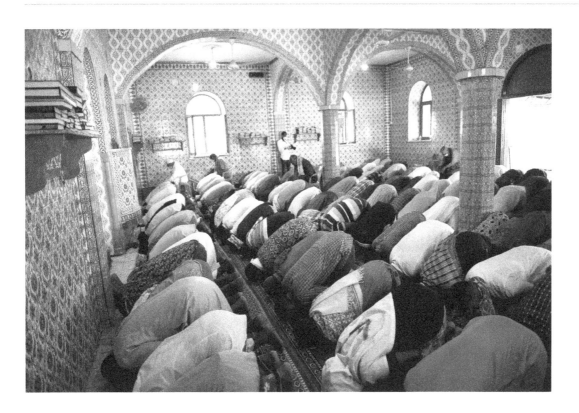

| Activity 8 | Vocabulary practice: Prayer time | | نشاط ٨ | تدريب على المفردات: وقت الصلاة |

Many observant Muslims around the world pray five times a day. In pairs, practice reading the following Muslim prayer times for August 19, 2022, in different cities around the world. The five prayer times are different every day, even in the same city, because they are based on the movement of the sun and the earth. Times have been rounded to the nearest quarter-hour.

صَلاة العِشاء Nightfall Prayer	صَلاة المَغْرِب Sunset Prayer	صَلاة العَصْر Afternoon Prayer	صَلاة الظُّهْر Noon Prayer	صَلاة الفَجْر Dawn Prayer	المدينة
٩:٠٠ مساءً	٧:٤٥ مساءً	٤:٤٥ مساءً	١:٠٠ مساءً	٤:٣٠ صباحاً	Boston, MA
٨:٠٠ مساءً	٦:١٥ مساءً	٣:٣٠ مساءً	١٢:٠٠ ظهراً	٤:٠٠ صباحاً	Riyadh, Saudi Arabia
٧:٠٠ مساءً	٦:٠٠ مساءً	٢:١٥ مساءً	١٢:٠٠ ظهراً	٤:٤٥ صباحاً	Jakarta, Indonesia

Challenge yourself: Look up the Muslim prayer times for today in your city and tell a classmate what they are in Arabic (you may round to the nearest quarter-hour).

| Activity 9 | Writing and conversation: The time is now … o'clock | نشاط ٩   كتابة ومحادثة: الساعة الآن... |

If you need to contact someone in another part of the world, it helps to be able to figure out the time difference between two cities.

Before writing   قبل الكتابة

Look at the following times around the world and practice saying them aloud. Can you figure out the time difference between each city? Write the time difference on a separate sheet of paper and indicate the difference using +/- hours, with London time as the base.

بغداد Baghdad	نيويورك New York	طوكيو Tokyo	مومباي Mumbai	ريو دي جانيرو Rio de Janeiro	القاهرة Cairo	لندن London
٤:٠٠ مساءً	٨:٠٠ مساءً	١٠:٠٠ مساءً	٦:٣٠ مساءً	١١:٠٠ صباحاً	٣:٠٠ مساءً	١:٠٠مساءً

Writing   الكتابة

Create a blank table based on the chart above, with three rows and seven columns. Above your table, label the columns in Arabic with same seven city names used above. Then, number the rows from one to three.

   To fill out your chart, read the first statement below and record the information it reports in the first row of your chart. Then, using the time differences you deduced from above, fill in the remaining cells of the first row with the times in the other six cities. Be sure to write using Eastern Arabic numerals and include the day of the week in each cell. Repeat this process in the second and third rows of your chart, using the second and third statements below.

١. الساعة في بغداد (Baghdad) ٣:٣٠ صباحاً يوم الأحد.
٢. الساعة في القاهرة (Cairo) ٦:١٥ مساءً يوم الاثنين.
٣. الساعة في نيويورك (New York) ١٢:٢٠ مساءً يوم الخميس.

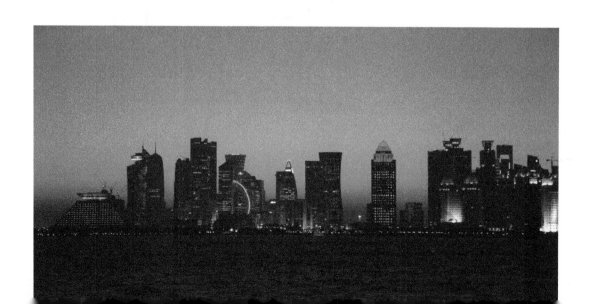

After writing   بعد الكتابة

Point to a time and city and have your classmate tell you the time indicated. Make sure to correct any errors you may hear.

Activity 10 Listening: When do you want to...?   استماع: متى تريد أن...؟   نشاط ١٠

In this activity, you'll practice recognizing whether a message is addressed directly to a person, talking about someone else, or talking about the speaker.

Before listening   قبل الاستماع

As a review, write down on a separate piece of paper (and in Arabic as much as you can) what clues to listen for to find out whether an Arabic speaker is talking about themselves, talking about someone else, or addressing someone directly.

Listening for general understanding   الاستماع للفهم العام

The first time you listen to the voice messages, listen for the clues you noted, and mark down whether the speaker is addressing someone, talking about someone else, or speaking about themselves. You may hear someone being addressed and someone talking about themselves in the same message; if so, mark more than one box.

Talking about themselves	Talking or asking about someone else	Addressing someone directly	
			.١
			.٢
			.٣
			.٤
			.٥

Close listening   الاستماع الدقيق

What time is specified in each voicemail?

_____ .١

_____ .٢

_____ ٣.
_____ ٤.
_____ ٥.

Challenge yourself: Listen again and identify the gender of the person speaking, being spoken about, or being addressed.

Activity 11 Conversation: When do CEOs wake up?

نشاط ١١   محادثة: متى يستيقظ المديرون الكبار؟

In this activity, you will share the wake-up times of current and former CEOs of major corporations.

Before speaking   قبل المحادثة

Tell a classmate what time you wake up each day of the week. Use the verb:

I wake up	بَصْحى	أَصْحو

Speaking   المحادثة

Create a table on a separate sheet of paper with headings like the one below. Your teacher will give you an identity of a CEO along with the time they wake up each morning. This will be your identity. Exchange your waking time information with the other "CEOs" in your class and note the responses in the chart below.

في الساعة	من (الشركة) From (the company)	الاسم Name

Activity 12 Listening: What time is the match?

نشاط ١٢   استماع: في أيّ ساعة المباراة؟

European soccer is very popular in the Arab world. You will hear an announcement of the times that a variety of soccer matches will be played.

Before listening   قبل الاستماع

Television and radio announcements often use Modern Standard Arabic to tell time, as you will hear in the one in this audio. Review the list of vocabulary words for telling time in Modern Standard Arabic or listen to the vocabulary list and write down some of the similarities and differences you notice between the Modern Standard and the Levantine dialect ways of expressing time.

Listening   الاستماع

Write down the time each match will begin.

في الساعة	المباراة The match	
	Marseille—Lyon	١. مارسيليا—ليون
	Liverpool FC—Chelsea FC	٢. ليفربول—تشيلسي
	Arsenal FC—Watford FC	٣. آرسنال—واتفورد
	Burnley FC—Leicester City FC	٤. بيرنلي—ليستر سيتي
	Sunderland AFC—Tottenham Hotspur FC	٥. سندرلاند—توتنهام
	Inter Milan—Lazio	٦. إنتر ميلان—لاتسيو

After listening   بعد الاستماع

In Arabic, compare your answers with a classmate.

Challenge yourself: Create a similar announcement of sporting events taking place in your school, community, or state during a particular week or month. Share your announcement with classmates to practice stating the time of each event in Modern Standard Arabic. Which game might you want to watch in person or on television?

Culture: Time   الثقافة: الوقت

One of the most common reasons for intercultural misunderstanding is differing cultural concepts of time. In Arab cultural contexts, people are often flexible about the start and end times of events, especially in informal social situations. This flexibility may take new-comers to Arab cultural contexts by surprise, as in the following experiences shared by students studying abroad in the Arab world: arriving an hour late to an Arab wedding yet being among the first guests in attendance, with plenty of time until the celebrations began; being invited to a dinner at 7:00 p.m. but not eating until well past 9:00 p.m.; going on an outing with friends that ends up lasting eight hours. In your family or community, what might the

outcome be if you encountered the above situations? In your journal or on a separate piece of paper, respond to the following prompts in order to prepare for a class discussion:

- How do members of your family or community view the concept of time and punctuality?
- In what situations are you expected to adhere to a particular schedule, and in what situations is it typical to go about your activities at a pace you decide?
- Have you ever witnessed or been involved in a situation where peoples' expectations about time came into conflict? What factors do you think contributed to the conflict or misunderstanding?
- If you are familiar with multiple communities or cultures, how does the concept of time differ between them? Have you had an interaction with someone from another culture that has a different concept of time? What about regional or personal differences—do you think there are varying concepts of time within your country or your community?

Taking what you learned from your class discussion, with a classmate, make a list of situations in which people have different expectations about time. You will refer to your notes and this discussion in a later activity.

Activity 13   Listening: "A meeting time"   نشاط ١٣   استماع: "موعد"

In this video, "موعد," you will see characters encounter some differences in the concept of time between American and Arab cultures.

Before listening   قبل الاستماع

Answer the following questions on a separate piece of paper to share in class:

1. Imagine you have agreed to meet a friend at a coffee shop at 11:30 a.m. What time would you try to arrive? When would you actually get there?
2. Now imagine that your friend has not yet arrived. How long would you wait for them?

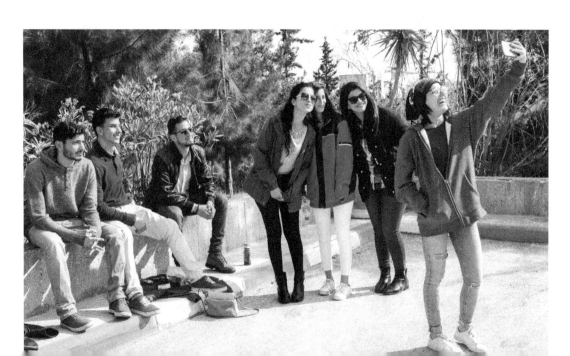

Listening   الاستماع

Listen and watch the video enough times to get a sense of what is happening. Then decide
if the following sentences are true or false. If false, tell a classmate the correct information.

1. عصام is busy on Saturday.
2. توماس and عصام agree to meet at 5:00 p.m.
3. توماس arrives at the café at 5:15 p.m.
4. عصام arrives at the coffee shop at 5:15 p.m.

After listening   بعد الاستماع

There are a few instances in these clips where Thomas acted in a way that some would
say is not culturally appropriate in the Arab world. With a classmate, identify at least two
instances. Then, create a skit that shows how Thomas might behave in a more culturally
appropriate manner at these times. You do not need to stick to the video script. Practice
the new version with your classmate and be prepared to present the scene in front of the
class.

Activity 14 Conversation: It's about time   نشاط ١٤   محادثة: مسألة وقت

Working with a classmate and drawing from your class discussion and list about concepts
of time across regions and cultures, come up with a skit that reflects these differences. It is
important to choose a situation that enables you to showcase the Arabic you have learned
so far, such as making a plan with someone for a particular time and place. Remember to
include the following elements:

- At least one of the new greetings
- Questions asking how someone is
- Days of the week
- Time of day
- Ways of telling time
- Appropriate phrases for excusing yourself

Here are some useful phrases that you can incorporate:

What's this?!	شو هٰذا؟!	ما هٰذا؟!
You're late! *(m.)*	اِنْتَ مِتْأَخِّر!	أَنتَ مُتَأَخِّر!
You're late! *(f.)*	اِنْتِ مِتْأَخِّرة!	أَنتِ مُتَأَخِّرة!

After speaking   بعد المحادثة

In English, list the situations and misunderstandings related to time your classmates came
up with. Add it to your journal entry about the differing cultural conceptions of time.

Activity 15   Reading: Text message from a friend   نشاط ١٥   قراءة: رسالة قصيرة من صديق

A friend wants you to come over to his house and is trying to find a time you are both free. Read the text message you received. What can you understand?

Reading   القراءة

> مرحبا، انت فاضي يوم الجمعة الساعة خمسة ونص، أو ممكن الأحد الساعة عشرة ونص الصبح؟ أنا ممكن رح أكون فاضي يوم الخميس الساعة أربعة ونص بس ما بعرف، ممكن أكون مشغول.

> أهلاً، هل أنت فاضي يوم الجمعة في الساعة الخامسة والنصف، أو الأحد في الساعة العاشرة والنصف في الصباح؟ أنا ربما سأكون فاضياً يوم الخميس في الساعة الرابعة والنصف ولكن لا أعرف ربما سأكون مشغولاً.

Create a table like the one below and keep track of the times mentioned in the message and whether you are free or busy then:

فاضي أم مشغول؟	الساعة	اليوم

After reading   بعد القراءة

Write a response to this text message on a separate sheet of paper telling your friend the time(s) that might work for you based on their schedule. If none of the proposed times work, offer two additional days and times that work for you.

You have to come over!

الدرس التاسع

من اللازم أن تجيء عندي!

LESSON NINE GOALS

أهداف الدرس التاسع

By the end of this lesson, you should be able to do the following:

- Invite someone over to your house or another location
- Accept or defer invitations
- Respond to invitations using the phrase "God willing" appropriately in an Arab cultural context
- Ask and respond to questions about where you want to go

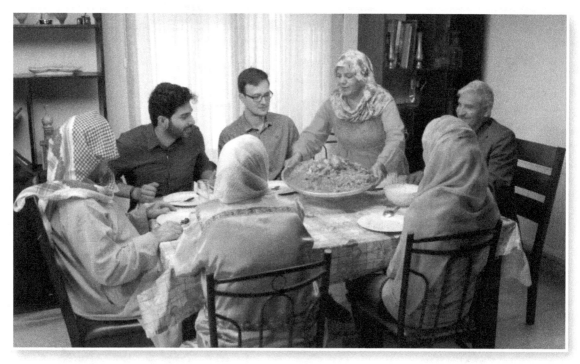

In the Arab world, inviting someone to have coffee, tea, or a meal at one's home is an important custom and a sign of hospitality, friendship, and generosity.

- What does your family usually do when you have guests over?

PLEASE COME OVER

Vocabulary 1

تفضّل عندي

مفردات ١

المعنى	العاميّة الشاميّة	الفصحى
Please come over. (m.)	تْفَضَّل عِنْدي.	تَفَضَّل عِنْدي.
Please come over. (f.)	تْفَضَّلي عِنْدي.	تَفَضَّلي عِنْدي.
You have to come over! (m.)	لازِم تِجي عِنْدي!	مِن اللازِم أَنْ تَجيءَ عِنْدي!
You have to come over! (f.)	لازِم تِجي عِنْدي!	مِن اللازِم أَنْ تَجيئي عِنْدي!
must have to	لازِم	مِن اللازِم أَنْ
possibly might	مُمْكِن	مِن المُمْكِنِ أَنْ
I am sorry (m.)	مَعْلَيش‡	(أَنا) آسِف*
I am sorry (f.)	مَعْلَيش	(أَنا) آسِفة
God willing hopefully	إنْ شاءَ الله	إنْ شاءَ الله
I will see you around! (m.)	بَشوفَك، إنْ شاءَ الله!	أَراكَ، إنْ شاءَ الله!
I will see you around! (f.)	بَشوفِك، إنْ شاءَ الله!	أَراكِ، إنْ شاءَ الله!
I want to go to …	بِدّي أروح عَلى…§	أُريد أَنْ أَذْهَب إلى…
my house my home	بَيْتي	بَيْتي

*The word آسِف in Arabic is less versatile than the word "sorry" in English; whereas "sorry" in English can be used in a variety of situations, آسِف is generally used only to apologize and acknowledge responsibility for doing something objectionable.

‡The word معليش is presented here as a way to excuse oneself for not being able to attend. It has multiple other uses in Levantine dialect beyond this meaning.

§In Levantine Arabic, the word على is sometimes abbreviated as ع. You will hear both, but focus on being able to use one or the other.

Activity 1   Listening: "You have to come over!"

استماع: "لازِم تِجي عِندنا!"   نشاط ١

In this video, you will watch or a scene in which one person receives an invitation from another. You may find it a lot to process at once; focus on getting the overall meaning.

Before listening   قبل الاستماع

Think back to the last time you invited someone over to your house or were invited over to someone else's house. How did you let them know that you really wanted them to come over? Have you ever invited someone over just to be polite? Has someone in your family ever told you to invite someone over just to be polite?

Listening for general understanding   الاستماع للفهم العام

Jot down your answers to these questions here or on a separate piece of paper:

1. Do ياسمين and أم راية know each other already?
2. Which person invited the other to their house?
3. When will the visit take place?

Close listening   الاستماع الدقيق

Try to answer these questions, listening as many times as you need to:

4. How many times did the person inviting the other reiterate her invitation?
5. How did the other person respond to the invitation? Note as many ways as you hear.

Activity 2   Listening: Busy today   استماع: مشغول اليوم   نشاط ٢

You will listen to a recording of several statements in which people respond to various invitations (you will not hear the invitations, just the responses). You will have to judge whether the person has accepted the invitation, declined it, or given an ambiguous answer.

Before listening   قبل الاستماع

Brainstorm some different Arabic words someone might use to: accept an invitation, decline an invitation, and respond ambiguously to an invitation. Then, create a table like the one on the next page, with ten rows.

Listening for general understanding   الاستماع للفهم العام

Listen for the times of day mentioned in each audio. Next to the number of each statement, write the time mentioned in the statement (you do not need to write the day).

Close listening   الاستماع الدقيق

Using the table you created at the start of this activity, listen to the series of replies to an invitation and record the following information:

- If the person has declined the invitation or is not able to make it at that time, put an ✗.
- If the person accepted the invitation, put a check mark ✔.
- If the person gave an ambiguous answer and you wouldn't be able to know for sure if they are free or not, put a question mark (?).

✔ X ?	الساعة	رقم **Number**
		١
		٢

بعد الاستماع

You will listen to a series of voice messages. Imagine that these messages were left on your phone while you were studying abroad in the Middle East. Practice responding to each one, either in a few words or a complete sentence if you can. Model your responses on what you heard in Activity 2.

Culture: *In shaa' allaah*

Even before starting to study Arabic, you might have known that إن شاء الله *in shaa' allaah* is widely used in Arab culture. The phrase literally means "God willing" and is used by both religious and secular Arabic speakers. Understanding exactly what it means will take some practice and depend on the specific context.

Discussing future events

When discussing a future event or an anticipated outcome, many Arabic speakers say إن شاء الله as a way to indicate that outcomes are ultimately in God's hands. The expression reflects a shared understanding that upcoming events are never certain to humans, whether they are in the near or distant future. You will hear it used in various contexts: an engaged couple may utter the phrase when informing others of plans for their wedding next year, a teacher may say it when detailing the itinerary for a field trip the following week, and a taxi driver may use the expression to confirm that they have heard the passenger's destination and will take them there safely, إن شاء الله.

"I hope"

إن شاء الله can also more specifically convey that you are hoping something will happen in the future—for example, "إن شاء الله our basketball team will win the game tonight."

Noncommittal response

Across different cultural contexts, speakers use different communicative strategies to decline invitations and requests politely. What expressions do your family members and friends use when you invite them to do something that they do not want to do? For Arabic

speakers, إن شاء الله can play this role by acting as a noncommittal response. If a speaker does not want to commit to something or does not wish to make another person feel obliged to do something, they may use إن شاء الله.

Look over the following situations in which you might use إن شاء الله while speaking Arabic. How would you respond to these situations in English?

The situation	Your response	What it means here
Someone calls you to confirm that you are coming over for dinner the next day.	See you then, *in shaa' allaah.*	You are planning to be there, but you acknowledge that there could always be circumstances outside your control that prevent you from going.
You see someone you have not seen in a long time.	How are you? *In shaa' allaah you're well.*	You hope the person is doing well.
Someone invites you to a movie you want to see, but you are busy.	Some other time, *in shaa' allaah.*	Here the meaning of إن شاء الله is more like "hopefully." You could suggest an alternate time to show you really want to see the movie.
Someone invites you to a movie you do not really want to see.	*in shaa' allaah*	You show that you like and respect the person enough to not refuse them out-right, but you still do not commit.
Someone you know slightly invites you to coffee, but you are not sure if the invitation is sincere.	*in shaa' allaah*	You give the person an out by not agree-ing right away. If they are sincere, they will make more of an effort to get you to go.
Someone asks why you do not have a husband, wife, or children yet.	In the future, *in shaa' allaah.*	You do not want to discuss your personal decisions about children and marriage. You evade the discussion by expressing a vague commitment to having those things in the future.
Someone asks why you do not want to be a doc-tor or pursue another high-status career.	We will see, *in shaa' allaah.*	You do not want to discuss your career goals with others. You avoid the conver-sation by implying that you might change your mind in the future.

Activity 3   Listening: In shaa' allaah   استماع: إن شاء الله   نشاط ٣

Watch the video "لازم تِجي عندنا!" from Activity 1 again. This time, pay close attention to how the speakers use the expression إن شاء الله.

Listening for general understanding   الاستماع للفهم العام

Keep track of the expression إن شاء الله. Write down how many times do you hear it during the video.

Close listening   الاستماع الدقيق

In how many different contexts do you hear the phrase used? What do the speakers mean when they say it in each context?

After listening   بعد الاستماع

In class, divide into groups. In your group, create a skit based on **one** of the following scenarios, using the phrase إن شاء الله in a culturally appropriate way as many times as you can:

1. You are greeting someone and tell them that *hopefully* they are well.
2. You are making plans with someone—*hopefully* they are free at a certain time.

Perform your skit in front of the class. When your classmates perform, count how many times each group uses إن شاء الله in a *culturally appropriate* way. Which group was most successful at using إن شاء الله appropriately the greatest number of times?

DO YOU WANT TO . . . ?   هل تريد أن...؟

Grammar 1: I want, you want   قواعد ١: أريد، تريد

You have seen in previous lessons that many words in Arabic change according to grammatical gender; to address or describe a person, Arabic speakers use linguistic forms that correspond with that person's gender. Verbs are one of the groups of words that carry

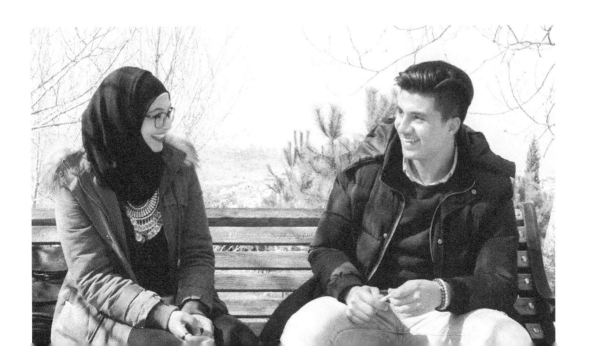

grammatical gender markings in Arabic. Moreover, as you will now learn, Arabic verbs change form depending on whether they are used by a speaker to talk about themselves, to address another person, or to speak about another person. The linguistic term for changing the form of a verb is "verb conjugation." You already conjugate verbs unconsciously in the language(s) you learned from infancy. For example, without even thinking about it, native speakers of many varieties of English say "I want" when talking about themselves but "she want<u>s</u>" when talking about a woman. For now, you will only learn the "I" and "you" forms of verbs in Arabic. You will learn more verb conjugation patterns later.

Look over the vocabulary words or listen to the audio. What patterns do you notice? Jot down some notes on a separate piece of paper or discuss with your classmates.

Vocabulary 2   مفردات ٢

المعنى	العاميّة الشاميّة	الفصحى
I want to go to …	بدّي أروح عَلى...	أُريد أَنْ أذهَب إلى...
Do you want to come? (m.)	بِدَّك تجي؟	هَل تُريد أَنْ تَجيء؟
Do you want to go? (f.)	بدّك تْروحي؟	هَل تُريدين أَنْ تَذهَبي؟
I want (to)	بِدّي	أُريد (أَنْ)
you want (to) (m.)	بِدَّك	تُريد (أَنْ)
you want (to) (f.)	بدِّك	تُريدين (أَنْ)
I go (to)	أروح (عَلى)	أَذهَب (إلى)
you go (to) (m.)	تْروح (عَلى)	تَذهَب (إلى)
you go (to) (f.)	تْروحي (عَلى)	تَذهَبين / تَذهبي (إلى)
I come	أجي	أجيء
you come (m.)	تِجي	تَجيء
you come (f.)	تِجي	تَجيئين / تَجيئي

If you are studying Modern Standard Arabic: You will notice that there are two slightly different forms of the verb when speaking to a woman. The meaning is exactly the same for both, and the difference is grammatical. You will learn more about this difference in Unit 3.

If you are studying Levantine dialect: You will notice that "to want" in Levantine dialect looks different from the other verbs you have seen in this lesson and in the vocabulary section. The reason for this is that "to want" is technically not a verb in Levantine Arabic. Instead, this word changes the way that nouns do. Compare the different forms of "to want" with the words for "my name," "your name," "my age," and "your age."

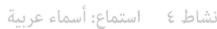

Activity 4   Listening: Arabic names   استماع: أسماء عربية   نشاط ٤

You will listen to a series of Arab names and decide whether they refer to a man or woman, given how the speaker in the audio addresses a person with each name.

Before listening   قبل الاستماع

Read over the list of names to see if you recognize any. If you do, jot down a note about which gender you have heard this name used for.

Listening   الاستماع

Listen carefully to how each person is addressed. Based on your knowledge of verb conjugations, mark whether each Arab name is used for a man or a woman in the recording. Listen a second time if you need to.

Name in Latin script	الاسم بالحروف العربية	M. or F.?
tawfiiq	تَوْفيق	
Hasan	حَسَن	
daliyaa	داليا	
ᶜabiir	عَبير	
riyaaD	رِياض	
Haniin	حَنين	
Husaam	حُسام	
riim	ريم	

After listening   بعد الاستماع

Stop the audio after each sentence and pretend you are the person being addressed. Try to respond to each sentence, even if just with a single word like "yes," "no," or a time.

Activity 5   Practicing grammar: I, you   التدريب على القواعد: أنا، أنتَ،   نشاط ٥
أنتِ

In this game, you will practice conjugating the new verbs you have learned.

Before practicing your grammar   قبل التدريب على القواعد

In pairs, construct two large dice by making cubes out of paper, following the instructions from your teacher.

On the first cube, write each of the following words **twice**, such that one word appears on each side of the cube: أنا, أنتَ, أنتِ. On the second cube, write each of the following words **twice** as well, such that one word appears on each side of the cube: "want," "come," and "go."

Pick a partner. Roll both of your dice at once. You should see one personal pronoun (أنا, أنتَ, or أنتِ) and one verb ("want," "come," or "go") face up on each die. When you see the combination, call out the verb that is showing, conjugated for the personal pronoun that is showing. For example: The first die shows أنتَ; the second die shows "go." Therefore, you must call out تَذْهَب or تْروح in Arabic.

Start by working cooperatively with your classmate to get the right conjugation. You can look at your notes if you need to. When you feel comfortable, switch to competition mode:

- Give yourself one point if you say the verb, conjugated correctly in Arabic, before your classmate does. No looking at your notes or at the textbook!
- Give yourself one extra point if you use the verb in a complete sentence of three or more words.
- Both partners can earn a point by saying a complete sentence as long as the sentences are different from each other; if they are the same, neither person receives a point.
- If you get it wrong, your partner gets a chance to say the right conjugation and earn the point.
- If neither of you can get the right answer, neither of you gets a point.

When your teacher tells you that the time is up for your game, get up and look for a new partner and start a new game.

Culture: Insisting   الثقافة: الإصرار

Think back to the video you watched in Activities 1 and 3. How many times did one person ask the other to come over to their house? How did the person being invited respond?

In Arab culture, hospitality is considered extremely important. When you interact with someone you are not close to, certain "rules" govern hospitality for both hosts and guests. It is part of basic politeness to offer drinks to visitors or to invite acquaintances over to your house, whether or not it is convenient for you. For those who receive offers of tea or coffee or invitations to another person's home, it is also polite not to accept right away. This shows that you are not trying to take advantage of someone else's generosity or do not want to inconvenience your host. As a rule of thumb, wait for the person to offer *at least three times* before you accept. Think back to the video, or watch it again if you cannot remember: how did one person insist that the other come over?

When you are close to someone—like a good friend or close family member—you can skip the formalities. You might refuse only once, or you might accept immediately if you are already sure the person is sincere. These "rules" are flexible. Depending on the community, the ages of the people involved, and how close their relationship is, invitations and responses may play out very differently. The principles behind the actions, however, will be the same: a host seeks to welcome someone generously, while a guest tries not to take advantage of their host or cause them to go to unnecessary trouble. When you interact with people of an Arab background, let these ideas guide your actions when it comes to invitations or visits to someone's home.

Activity 6   Conversation: You have to!   نشاط ٦   محادثة: لازم!

Imagine that you are studying abroad in the Arab world. Since you are away from your family, you want to invite as many classmates and friends over as possible this weekend.

Before speaking   قبل المحادثة

Look at the blank schedule on the next page. Your goal is to try to schedule each friend at a different time, so you can see as many friends as possible. Here are some sample phrases you can use to discuss invitations:

Can you come over? (f.)	مُمْكِن تِجي عِنْدي؟	هَل مِن المُمْكِن أَنْ تَجيئي عِنْدي؟
I want to come but . . .	بِدّي أَجي بَس...	أُريد أَنْ أَجيء وَلكن...
You have to come over! (m.)	لازِم تِجي عِنْدي!	مِن اللازِم أَنْ تَجيء عِنْدي!

Before you start, review with a classmate the following:

* The times and days of the week you will need
* Some phrases you could use to defer an invitation if you are not sure whether to accept or not
* Some phrases you could use to accept an invitation
* Some phrases you could use if you are not available at a certain time

Speaking   المحادثة

Talk to as many classmates as you can and invite them over to your house—or be invited over to their houses. Mark down your plans on your schedule. If someone invites you over at a time you have already scheduled something, you must say that you are busy and find another time. Be sure *not* to agree right away when some invites you over! Likewise, remember to insist several times that your classmates come over to show that your invitation is sincere.

الساعة	يوم الجمعة Friday	يوم السبت Saturday
١٠:٠٠		
١٢:٠٠		
٢:٠٠		
٤:٠٠		
٦:٠٠		
٨:٠٠		
١٠:٠٠		

After speaking   بعد المحادثة

1. Reflect on the interactions you just had. Who successfully insisted?
2. Tell a classmate what plans you have made—in Arabic, of course.

Activity 7   Conversation: When and where?   محادثة: أين ومتى؟   نشاط ٧

In the next activity, you will practice extending and negotiating invitations. Your teacher will assign you a specific role to play. You can choose a new Arab name to help yourself get into the role of your secret identity.

Before speaking   قبل المحادثة

When you receive your role, do not reveal it to your classmates! Just jot down some of the words and phrases you think you will need to use. You will do the role-play twice—once as someone who invites others and once as someone who receives invitations. Be sure to stick to your role both times.

Speaking   المحادثة

Keep track of the invitations you extend or receive during the **first** role play. Create a table on a separate sheet of paper with headings like those on the next page. Whom did you successfully invite or accept an invitation from? When will you meet them? Where will you go?

مَتى؟ When?	أَيْنَ؟ Where?	مَعَ مَن؟ With whom?

Keep speaking   واصلوا المحادثة

Keep track of the invitations you extend or receive during the **second** role play. Whom did you successfully invite and from whom did you accept an invitation? When will you meet them? Where will you go? Continue adding more details in the table you created.

After speaking   بعد المحادثة

1. Who in your class did a good job of remaining in character? What did they do that made them believable?
2. Share some of your plans with a classmate you did not talk to, using Arabic.

Activity 8   Conversation: You have to   محادثة: من اللازم أن تجيء   نشاط ٨
come over   عندي

In this activity, you will create a skit demonstrating some of the polite behaviors you have learned.

Before speaking   قبل المحادثة

Divide into small groups in your class. With your group, create a skit in which at least one person invites another to his or her home. Be sure to include the following components:

- Polite greetings
- An invitation to someone's home
- Polite refusal
- Agreement on a time and day
- Taking leave politely

Remember to change the form of the verb you are using depending on whether you are talking about yourself or addressing a classmate. Likewise, be sure to change the form of any adjectives you use depending on the gender of the person you are speaking about.

Do not write a script for your skit. Instead, speak the words of your interaction spontaneously!

Speaking   المحادثة

Present your skit to your classmates and watch their skits. Does each group include all the elements needed to make a convincing conversation? Does it seem culturally authentic?

Grammar 2: Negation—I want, I don't want

قواعد ٢: النفي- أريد، لا أريد

You have learned how to say what you want. How do you say what you do not want?

المعنى	العاميّة الشاميّة	الفصحى
I do not want	ما بِدّي	لا أُريد
you do not want (m.)	ما بِدَّك	لا تُريد
you do not want (f.)	ما بِدِّك	لا تُريدين

نشاط ٩	Activity 9	Practicing grammar: I do not want a hamburger	التدريب على القواعد: لا أريد هامبرغراً

In this activity, you will practice saying what you want and do not want.

Before speaking   قبل المحادثة

Look over the pictures below of things that have similar names in Arabic and English.
Which ones do you want? Write a list or silently make a list in your head of the items that
you want and do not want.

Speaking   المحادثة

Tell a classmate which items you want and which you do not want.

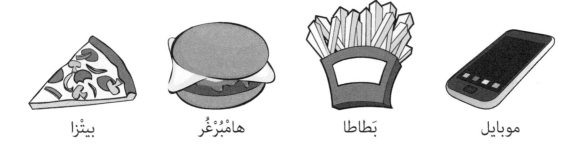

بيتْزا   هامْبُرْغُر   بَطاطا   موبايل

نشاط١٠	Activity 10	Conversation: Which name do you want?	محادثة: أي اسم تريد؟

What Arabic name would you choose for yourself if you could choose one now? In this
activity, you will talk about names you would want for yourself.

Before speaking   قبل المحادثة

Look over the names you have seen in your book or class so far and choose one that you
would want to have for yourself. If you already have an Arabic name, choose another name
you like. Practice telling a classmate "I want the name ____."

I want the name ____.	بدّي اِسم ____ .	أُريد اسم ____ .

How would you ask another classmate, "Do you want the name ___?" Remember these tips about asking questions in Arabic:

If you are studying Modern Standard Arabic: Create yes-or-no questions by adding the word هَل at the beginning of the statement and speaking with rising intonation.

If you are studying Levantine Arabic: Create yes-or-no questions by speaking the sentence with rising intonation.

Speaking   المحادثة

On a separate piece of paper, draw a T-chart with columns for "yes" and "no," as below:

نعم Yes	لا No

Poll your classmates by asking them whether they would want the name you have chosen. Record their answers in your T-chart. How many other people in your class would want this name?

After speaking   بعد المحادثة

Use the numbers you know to say how many students want and do not want the name you chose. What is the most popular name in the room?

Grammar 3: Two verbs in one sentence   قواعد ٣: فعلان في جملة واحدة

Sometimes we need to use two verbs consecutively to express something. When you combine two or more verbs in Arabic, it is important to note that you must always conjugate (change the forms of) both verbs in the sentence. This principle is equally true in Modern Standard Arabic and Arabic dialects, even though conjugation patterns differ across varieties. Read the following examples that you have encountered previously:

I want to go to . . .	بدّي أروح على...	أُريد أَنْ أَذهَب إلى...
You want to go to . . . *(m.)*	بِدَّك تْروح على...	تُريد أَنْ تَذهَب إلى...
You want to go to . . . *(f.)*	بِدِّك تْروحي عَلى...	تُريدين أَنْ تَذهَبي...

If you are studying Modern Standard Arabic: To include a second verb after "I want," use the word أَنْ to link the two verbs.

Activity 11 Conversation: Do you want to go to the city?	نشاط ١١ محادثة: هل تريد أن تذهب إلى المدينة؟

Where in your city or state would you like to go? In this activity, imagine that you have some relatives coming to visit you from out of town. You want to show them the best destinations around your city or state, but you are not sure where to take them. To figure out what the best destinations are before your relatives arrive, you decide to invite your classmates to visit different places with you to see how they react.

Before speaking   قبل المحادثة

Pick a destination you would like to go to and write it down on a separate piece of paper. Prepare to invite your classmates to go to this destination. How will you ask them? Make sure you know how to address each gender correctly.

Speaking   المحادثة

On a separate piece of paper, draw a T-chart with three columns:

لازم! Definitely, it's a must!	ممكن Possibly	لا No

Invite your classmates by asking each one, "Do you want to go to . . . ?" Record the answers in your chart.

After talking   بعد المحادثة

Share your poll results with your classmates, using the numbers you know in Arabic to tell how many people said لازم and ممكن, لا, to your destination. What was the most popular destination in the class? Where will you be taking your relatives when they come visit?

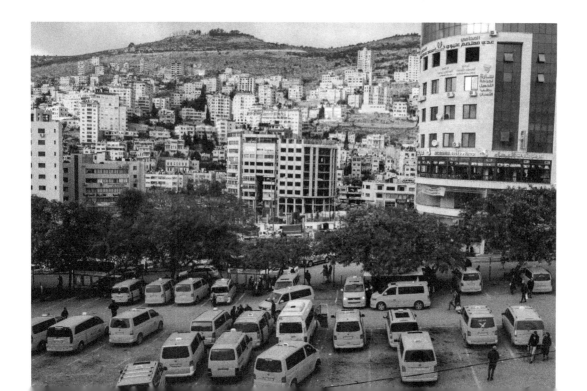

Would you like some coffee?

LESSON TEN GOALS

أهداف الدرس العاشر

By the end of this lesson, you should be able to do the following:

- Offer someone tea or coffee when they come over to your house
- Respond politely when someone offers you drinks at their house
- Tell someone some of your likes and dislikes
- Tell how you take your coffee and tea

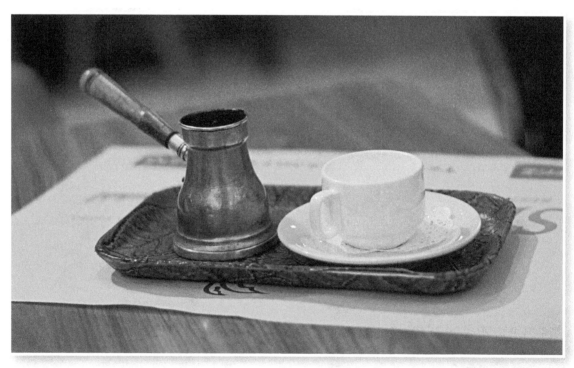

Look at the Arabic coffee pot and mug above:

- How does the way Arabic coffee is served look different from, or similar to, the way coffee is served in your culture?
- What do you usually offer people to eat or drink when they come to your home?

WHAT WOULD YOU LIKE TO DRINK?   ماذا تريد أن تشرب؟

Vocabulary 1   مفردات ١

المعنى	العاميّة الشاميّة	الفصحى
Would you like some coffee? *(m.)*	تِشْرَب قَهْوة؟	هل تُريد أن تَشْرَب القَهْوة؟
Would you like some coffee? *(f.)*	تِشْرَبي قَهْوة؟	هل تُريدين أنْ تَشْرَبي القَهْوة؟
Would you like coffee or tea? *(m.)*	تِشْرَب قَهْوة ولّا شاي؟	هل تُريد أنْ تَشْرَب القَهْوة أم الشاي؟
Would you like coffee or tea? *(f.)*	تِشْرَبي قَهْوة ولّا شاي؟	هل تُريدين أنْ تَشْرَبي القَهْوة أم الشاي؟
coffee	القَهْوة	القَهْوة
tea	الشاي	الشاي
here you go go ahead *(m.)*	تْفَضَّل	تَفَضَّل
here you go go ahead *(f.)*	تْفَضَّلي	تَفَضَّلي
thank you *(in the context of receiving coffee or tea)*	شُكْراً يِسْلَموا	شُكْراً
you're welcome	أَهْلا وسَهْلا	عَفْواً

Activity 1   Listening: "Would you like   استماع: "تشربي قهوة؟"   نشاط ١
                  some coffee?"

In this activity, you will observe a home hospitality interaction.

Before listening   قبل الاستماع

Discuss or journal about these questions in English: What does hospitality mean in your family or community? What do you do when someone comes over to your house to make them feel welcome?

Listening for general understanding   الاستماع للفهم العام

Watch the video "تشربي قهوة؟" to learn more about hospitality in Arab culture.

1. How does the host show the guest they are welcome in this video? On a separate sheet, jot down any observations you can make, words or phrases you hear, or things you see, using English or Arabic.

2. What do you notice about the way Arabic coffee is prepared? How is it different from or similar to American coffee or types of coffee from other cultures? Write one to two sentences in English.

Close listening   الاستماع الدقيق

3. How many times do you hear the word تفضّل؟ Who says it? When does this person say it?

4. What drinks does the host offer?

Challenge yourself: Listen for the phrase ما بيصير. What do you think it means?

Activity 2   Culture and conversation: ثقافة ومحادثة: تفضّل   نشاط ٢
             tafaDDal

One word you heard in the video "شو تشربي؟" was تفضّل. In what context did the speaker use it? You have probably heard this word in your classroom. When does your teacher use it? The word تفضّل is an extremely common word in Arabic that can mean a variety of things based on the context. In this activity, you will learn more about the different contexts in which you can say this word.

Before speaking   قبل المحادثة

Find a partner. Your teacher will give you a short scenario of a situation in which you would use the word تفضّل. Prepare a skit based on your scenario. Your skit does not need to have much dialogue. It is more important is that you demonstrate a situation in which you would say تفضّل. Remember that the word تفضّل changes depending on the gender of the person you are talking to.

Speaking   المحادثة

Present your skit to your classmates. If your class is large, you may want to present to another pair rather than to the whole class.

After speaking   بعد المحادثة

When can you use the word تفضّل؟ Watch your classmates' skits and take notes on the different situations you see.

Activity 3   Listening: Where is this coffee from?

نشاط ٣   استماع: من أين هذه القهوة؟

Tea or coffee look very different depending on the country or culture of origin.

Before listening

قبل الاستماع

Look over the following images of tea and coffee. Where do you think each one is from? It is okay if you're not sure—make your best guess. Share a few of your guesses with a classmate. Remember that you know how to say where a person or thing is from using Arabic.

Listening

الاستماع

Number a separate piece of paper from one to nine. When you hear each statement, write the letter of the picture it describes next to the number.

a.
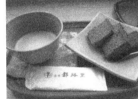

b.
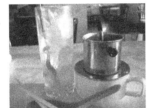

c.
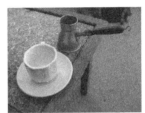

d.
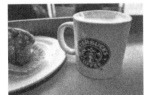

e.
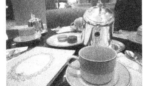

f.
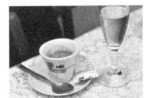

g.
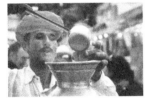

h.
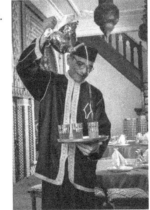

i.
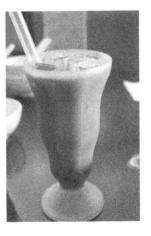

Vocabulary 2

مفردات ٢

How do you express in Arabic whether or not you like something? In the previous lesson, you learned how to conjugate, or change, verbs depending on whether you are talking about yourself or addressing someone else. Look over the vocabulary on the next page and listen to the audio. How are the patterns here similar to or different from the other verbs you have learned?

المعنى	العاميّة الشاميّة	الفصحى
I like	بَحِبّ	أُحِبّ
you like (m.)	بِتْحِبّ	تُحِبّ
you like (f.)	بِتْحِبّي	تُحِبّين
I do not like	ما بَحِبّ	لا أُحِبّ
you do not like (m.)	ما بِتْحِبّ	لا تُحِبّ
you do not like (f.)	ما بِتْحِبّي	لا تُحِبّين

Activity 4   Listening: I like …

نشاط ٤   استماع: أحبّ...

In the next activity, you will hear someone talking about what they like and do not like. You will then have an opportunity to tell your classmates whether you like or dislike the same items.

Before listening

قبل الاستماع

You will hear someone mention a series of likes and dislikes, represented by the pictures below and on the next page. Look over the images. With a classmate, point to each item and try to say what is in the picture in Arabic. If there is anything that you do not know how to say in Arabic, ask your teacher or a classmate using the Arabic question phrases you have learned.

Listening

الاستماع

Number a separate piece of paper from one to twelve. Mark whether the person in the recording likes or dislikes each item as you hear it mentioned:

- Write نعم or a check mark if the speaker likes the item in the picture.
- Write لا or an X if the speaker does not like it.

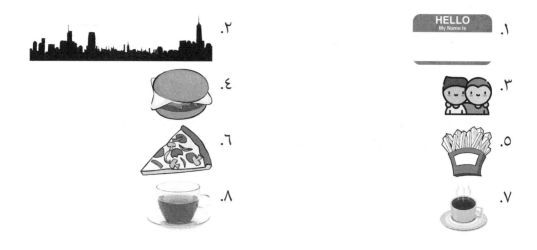

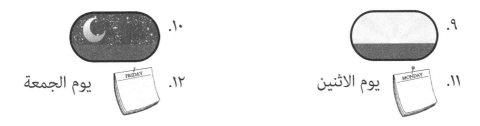

٩.

١١. يوم الاثنين

١٠.

١٢. يوم الجمعة

After listening
بعد الاستماع

1. Tell a classmate the things you like and dislike in the pictures, using what you heard in the audio as a model. Mention as many of the things in the pictures as you can and use complete sentences.

2. The speaker mentions some things, like coffee, that are a "must" for him. Is coffee or tea a must for you? Are there any fast-food restaurants that you have to go to? Tell your classmate.

| Activity 5   Conversation: Do you like the singer . . . ? | محادثة: هل تحب المغني...؟   نشاط ٥ |

In this activity, you will poll your classmates to find out what they think of a movie, singer, TV show, or band.

Before speaking
قبل المحادثة

Think of a movie, singer, TV show, or band you would like to ask your classmates about. It does not have to be something that you, yourself, like. Write it down on a separate piece of paper. Then, draw a T-chart like the one below on your piece of paper:

لا No	نعم Yes

Speaking
المحادثة

Ask your classmates one at a time whether they like the movie, singer, TV show, or musical group you chose, and record their answers on your chart. Make sure you think about the gender of the person you are speaking to when you ask them.

After speaking
بعد المحادثة

Using the numbers you have learned, share how people like and dislike the thing you asked about. What is the most popular movie, TV show, singer, or band in the class?

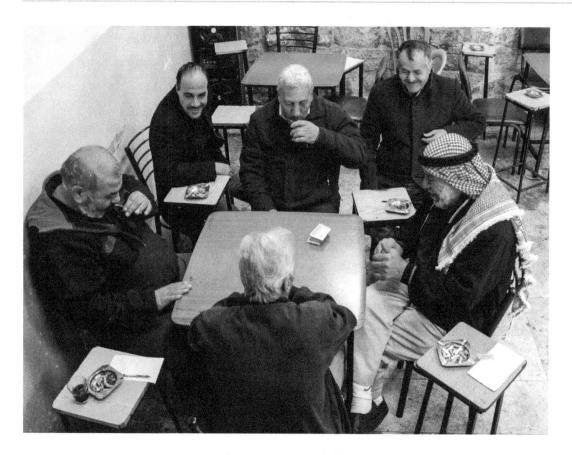

Activity 6 Listening: Tea or coffee?

نشاط ٦ استماع: شاي أو قهوة؟

In some countries, coffee is the most popular drink, while in others, most people drink tea. You will listen to some audio explaining the most popular caffeinated drink in different countries around the world. Remember that both tea and coffee are consumed widely in all of these countries; the passage just focuses on which one people in that country drink more of.

Before listening

قبل الاستماع

Look over the list of country names below and on the next page and try to guess what each one is in English. If you aren't sure, ask your teacher "Where is ____?" in Arabic, and they will point to the country on a map.

Number a separate sheet of paper from one to twenty-four, as in the list below. Then, make a prediction for each country: Do you think people drink more coffee or tea there? Write down what you think will people in that country drink more often.

Listening

الاستماع

Listen to the passage two or three times and check your predictions. You will hear the countries mentioned in the same order that they are listed.

٢. أمريكا / amriikaa   ١. كندا / kanada

٤. البرازيل / al-baraaziil   ٣. المكسيك / al-maksiik

٦. كولومبيا / kuuluumbiyaa   ٥. فنزويلا / fanizwiilaa

٨. إسبانيا / isbaaniyaa	٧. تشيلي / tshiilii
١٠. ألمانيا / almaaniyaa	٩. فرنسا / faransaa
١٢. بريطانيا / briiTaaniyaa	١١. إيطاليا / iiTaaliyaa
١٤. إيران / iiraan	١٣. الجزائر / al-jazaa'ir
١٦. مصر / miSr	١٥. تُركيا / turkiyaa
١٨. السعودية / as-saᶜuudiya	١٧. المغرب / al-maghrib
٢٠. جنوب أفريقيا / januub afriiqiyaa	١٩. كينيا / kiiniyaa
٢٢. روسيا / ruusiyaa	٢١. اليابان / al-yaabaan
٣٤. الهند / al-hind	٢٣. الصين / aS-Siin

نشاط ٧   محادثة: هل تحب أن تشرب   Activity 7   Conversation: Do you like to
القهوة أو الشاي؟   drink coffee or tea?

You just learned about countries where coffee is more popular and countries where tea is more popular. Is your class representative of the country you live in? Poll your classmates to find out what they like to drink.

Before speaking   قبل المحادثة

Practice how to ask your classmates what they like to drink. To do this, you will have to combine familiar words into new combinations. Use these sentences as models:

Do you like to drink tea? (m.)	بِتْحِبّ تِشْرَب شاي؟	هَل تُحِبّ أَنْ تَشْرَب الشاي؟
Yes, I like to drink tea.	آه، بَحِبّ أَشْرَب شاي.	نَعَم، أُحِبّ أَنْ أَشْرَب الشاي.
Do you like to drink coffee? (f.)	بِتْحِبّي تِشْرَبي قَهْوة؟	هَل تُحِبّين أَنْ تَشْرَبي القَهْوة؟
No, I don't like to drink coffee.	لا، ما بَحِبّ أَشْرَب قَهْوة.	لا، لا أُحِبّ أَنْ أَشْرَب القَهْوة.

Draw a table on a separate piece of paper to keep track of your classmates' preferences using the one below as a model:

القهوة Coffee	الشاي Tea	القهوة والشاي Coffee and tea	لا شيء Nothing

Speaking   المحادثة

Poll your classmates to find out what they drink and keep track of the results on your chart.

After speaking   بعد المحادثة

Compare your results with those of a classmate, using the Arabic numbers you know. What is the most popular drink in your class?

Activity 8   Conversation: When do you   محادثة: متى تشرب القهوة؟   نشاط ٨
               drink coffee?

In this activity, you will ask your classmates more detailed questions about their coffee and tea drinking habits.

Before speaking   قبل المحادثة

You will need to poll your classmates about their coffee and tea drinking habits. Plan ahead how you will phrase your questions to gather the following information:

- *When* each classmate likes to drink coffee or tea
- Whether they *like* coffee or tea

Challenge yourself: Plan ahead how you will find out these details:

- Whether they *have to* drink coffee or tea
- Whether they *want to* drink coffee or tea

Speaking   المحادثة

Circulate among your classmates and find one person in your class who fits each of the descriptions on the handout that your teacher gives you. On the handout, write the person's name who matches that description. Try to get a "blackout bingo," finding someone who fits each description. Try to talk to as many classmates as possible!

Culture: Insisting on coffee   الثقافة: الإصرار على القهوة

Think back to the video "تشربي قهوة؟" from Activity 1. How did the host insist that the guest drink coffee? How many times did they offer the guest coffee before the guest agreed? Watch the video again if you need to.

    As you learned in the previous lesson, insisting that someone come over to your house—and refusing if someone invites you over—can both be important aspects of polite behavior. These actions demonstrate generosity as a host and a reluctance to burden someone as a guest. The same principle can apply to offering someone coffee or tea:

- If someone offers you coffee or tea during a meeting, at a shop, or at their home after you happened to stop by unannounced, it is polite to refuse the offer several times. Your refusal helps show that you do not wish to inconvenience them or take advantage of their hospitality. Accept after the person insists that you drink something.

- If someone invites you over to their house specifically for coffee, or is a close friend or family member, you do not need to refuse as many times—once is usually enough. If you are close enough to the person, you do not need to refuse at all.

Activity 9   Conversation: At the market   نشاط ٩   محادثة: في السوق

American visitors shopping in an Arab market may find that shop owners offer them tea or coffee to drink at the shop if they stay a long time and show a particular interest in the shop. This is a good occasion to practice saying no to coffee or tea the first time it is offered, since it is offered by someone you do not know well.

Before speaking   قبل المحادثة

Brainstorm some vocabulary you know that you can use in each situation below on a separate piece of paper:

1. You are a shop owner who wants to insist that a customer drink something.
2. You are a customer who wants to *politely* refuse coffee or tea the first time it is offered.

Speaking   المحادثة

Create a short skit with a classmate showing what happens when a customer comes to shop in an Arab *suuq*, and a shop owner offers them coffee. Be sure to include these components:

- Polite greetings
- An offer of coffee or tea
- The customer refusing initially
- The shop owner insisting
- The customer eventually accepting

Remember to change the verbs you are using depending on the gender of the person to whom you are speaking.

After speaking   بعد المحادثة

Talk with your classmates about which skit you thought best represented polite behavior.

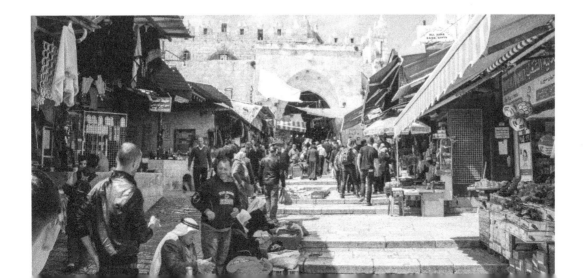

WITH SUGAR OR WITH MILK?

Vocabulary 3

بالسكر أو بالحليب؟

مفردات ٣

المعنى	العاميّة الشاميّة	الفصحى
with sugar	بِالسُّكَّر	بِالسُّكَّر
without sugar	بَلا سُكَّر	بِلا سُكَّر
with milk	بالحَليب	بالحَليب
without milk	بَلا حَليب	بِلا حَليب
sugar	السُكَّر	السُّكَّر
milk	الحَليب	الحَليب

Activity 10 Listening: Where do they drink coffee with milk?

نشاط ١٠   استماع: أين يشربون القهوة بالحليب؟

Whether or not a person drinks milk and sugar with their tea and coffee is a habit strongly influenced by culture. Many cultures consider it inappropriate to add sugar to certain types of tea or milk to certain types of coffee. Other cultures, meanwhile, consider it a must to mellow the taste of tea or coffee with these additions.

Before listening   قبل الاستماع

Look back at the pictures of coffee and tea around the world in Activity 3. Tell a classmate: Which drinks do you think have sugar in them? Which drinks do you think have milk in them?

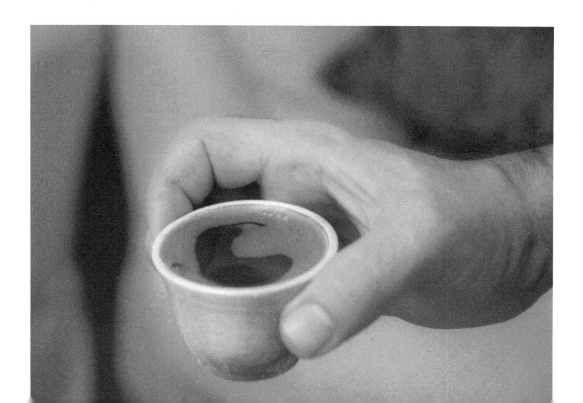

Listening   الاستماع

Number a separate sheet of paper from one to nine. You will hear a series of statements about coffees and teas from different parts of the world, as represented in the earlier pictures in Activity 3. Note on your paper whether people in each place tend to take their tea or coffee with sugar or milk, according to the listening passage. Note that the observations in the audio reflect broad generalizations. In any society, you may find people who drink coffee and tea in different ways. For example, although it is common for Americans to drink coffee with milk and sugar, you can also find many Americans who take their coffee black.

بالحليب؟	بالسكر؟	Place
		al-yaabaan / اليابان .١
		almaghrib / المغرب .٢
		al-hind / الهند .٣
		briiTaaniyaa / بريطانيا .٤
		taaywaan / تايوان .٥
		amriika / أمريكا .٦
		iiTaaliyaa / إيطاليا .٧
		fiiyatnaam / فيتنام .٨
		al-urdunn / الأردن .٩

After listening   بعد الاستماع

In English, journal or discuss with a classmate the following questions in regard to your own community or another community or culture you are familiar with. If you know more about one of the places mentioned in the listening, share your knowledge with your classmates.

- How do people in this community or culture take their coffee and tea?
- What norms does this community or culture have around when and where people drink coffee or tea?
- How and to what extent do these norms vary within this community or culture?

Culture: What is Arabic coffee?   الثقافة: ما هي القهوة العربية؟

"Arabic coffee" as used in this lesson is also called "Turkish coffee" in many parts of the Arab world and even sometimes in the United States. Although coffee originally came from Yemen, it was popularized by the Ottoman Turks who ruled large swathes of the Middle East for centuries. In fact, the word "coffee" in English comes from the Arabic word *qahwa* via Turkish, after the drink was spread into Europe by the Ottoman Turks.

This kind of coffee is made very differently from American coffee. Unlike American coffee, which can be made automatically in a coffeemaker, Arabic coffee is brewed in a special metal pot over a burner or open flame, requiring constant attention. Moreover, whereas American coffee can be left to sit before serving, Arabic coffee is served immediately in a small, espresso-like cup called a فِنْجان *finjaan*. In Egypt and in Jordan, "Turkish coffee" must have a layer of foam when served, while in Lebanon it must be served without it. Coffee blends in the Arab world range from lightly to darkly roasted and, especially in the Gulf countries, are often infused with spices such as cardamom, cinnamon, cloves, saffron, ginger, and nutmeg.

While Americans add sugar to each mug of coffee individually, Arabs add sugar to the coffee pot itself when preparing "Turkish coffee." They do so before the coffee comes to a boil, and it would be considered an error in etiquette to add more sugar afterwards. Accordingly, when you order Arabic coffee at a café or drink it at a friend's house, you must specify beforehand how sweet you want your coffee to be as it will be made fresh and customized to your preference. Ask your teacher if you would like to learn the vocabulary for telling someone how much sugar you want.

In the Arab world, coffee is not traditionally seen as an energy drink that you grab at a coffee shop and leave. Rather, it is an essential part of daily social interactions, life events, and special occasions. In many Arab countries, a special, usually sweet, coffee is served after the birth of a new child or during the ceremonial signing of a marriage contract, while a bitter coffee is served at funerals. An everyday invitation for coffee symbolizes the cultural expectation to sit and share news with friends.

There are other types of coffee that are common in different parts of the Arab world. In North Africa, coffee drinking patterns were influenced more by the French than by the Ottomans. In Jordan and the Arabian Peninsula, what is sometimes called "Bedouin coffee" involves roasting coffee beans over a fire then grinding them with cardamom for a rich, flavorful brew. Ask your teacher and others you know: What kinds of coffee and tea are popular in the various parts of the Arab world? If you have lived in the Arab world or visited an Arab home in any country, what kinds of tea and coffee did you drink or see?

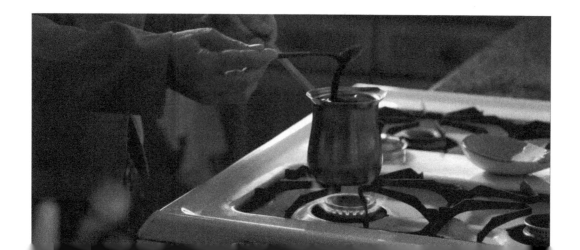

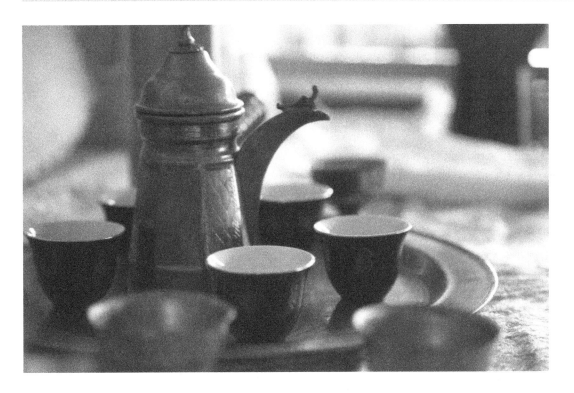

نشاط ١١   محادثة: كيف تحب قهوتك؟   Activity 11   Conversation: How do you like your coffee?

How do you like to drink your coffee? Be ready to tell your classmates your preferences and ask them about theirs.

قبل المحادثة   Before speaking

You can ask your classmates whether they like milk or sugar in their drinks using structures you already know:

How do you like your coffee? *(m.)*	كَيْف قَهْوَتَك؟	كَيْف تُحِبّ قَهْوَتَك؟
How do you like your coffee? *(f.)*	كَيْف قَهْوَتك؟	كَيْف تُحِبّين قَهْوَتك؟
How do you like your tea? *(m.)*	كيف بِتحِبّ الشاي؟	كَيْف تُحِبّ الشاي؟
How do you like your tea? *(f.)*	كيف بِتْحِبّي الشاي؟	كَيْف تُحِبّين الشاي؟
I like tea with milk and sugar.	بحِبّ الشاي بِالسُّكَّر وبِالحَليب.	أُحِبّ الشاي بِالسُّكَّر وَبِالحَليب.

Speaking

المحادثة

Ask your classmates how they like their coffee and tea. Record their responses as tally marks on a separate sheet of paper or on the handout from your teacher. Below are some possible beverage choices that people may have:

الشاي

القهوة

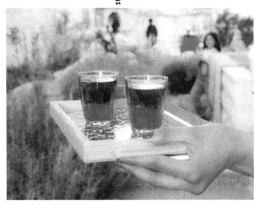

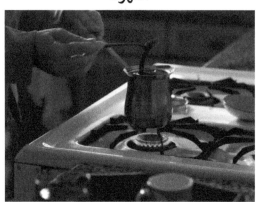

القَهْوة بالسُّكَّر

الشاي بالسُّكَّر

القَهْوة بالحَليب

الشاي بالحَليب

القَهْوة بالسُّكَّر وبالحَليب

الشاي بالسُّكَّر وبالحَليب

القَهْوة بلا سُكَّر وبلا حَليب

الشاي بلا سُكَّر وبلا حَليب

After speaking

بعد المحادثة

What is the most common preference in your class? Use the numbers you know to compare the number of people who like their tea and coffee each way.

Activity 12 Listening: American coffee

نشاط ١٢   استماع: قهوة أمريكية

What might happen when an American who is not very culturally aware travels to the Arab world and wants to order Arabic coffee? In the next video, you will see one misunderstanding that might happen.

Before listening

قبل الاستماع

What are some differences and similarities you have learned between American and Arabic coffee? State as many as you can in Arabic.

Listening

الاستماع

Watch the video "قهوة أمريكية؟" and answer the questions below:

1. What did the customer order?
2. What cultural misunderstanding occurred?

After listening

بعد الاستماع

Write or discuss the following questions with a classmate in English:

3. Based on your knowledge of Arab culture, what are some other cultural misunderstandings you imagine might happen if you were to order coffee or tea at a café in the Arab world before having studied Arabic?
4. What cultural misunderstandings have you observed when you encountered hospitality from another culture for the first time or saw someone else offered hospitality from a culture new to them?
5. Create a skit showing a cultural misunderstanding *other* than the one pictured in the video, in any culture you know about. Here are some questions to think about in your planning:
    *   What misunderstanding might occur if an Arab visited an American-style café for the first time?
    *   What misunderstanding might occur if someone not from your community visited you at home for the first time?
    *   What misunderstanding might happen if someone visited a café or home in another country or culture you are familiar with for the first time? For example, if you are very familiar with Mexican traditions, what do you think would happen if someone new to Mexican culture visited a Mexican home or café for the first time?
6. Present the skit to your classmates and see if they can identify the misunderstanding that occurred.

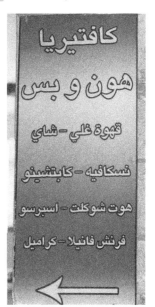

Activity 13 Reading: At the café

نشاط ١٣   قراءة: في المقهى

Although traditional cafés in the Arab world serve only Arabic coffee and tea (and do not have written menus), most large cities in the region have Western-style cafés that offer a wide range of American and European coffee drinks.

Look over the café menu. It is okay to feel overwhelmed by the amount of text. Do not worry—you are not expected to understand everything! Instead, focus on identifying familiar organizing elements: Where are the prices? Where are the category headings?

Reading   القراءة

مشروبات آخرى		مشروبات غازية		قهوة	
شاي	8	كوكاكولا	7	قهوة عربية	8
زهورات	8	سبرايت	7	قهوة أمريكية	12
الشاي الوردي	8	سبرايت دايت	7	قهوة فرنسية	12
شاي أخضر	10	فانتا	7	قهوة اليوم	15
شاي بالليمون	10	سفن أب	7	قهوة اليوم بلا كافيين	15
شاي بالنعناع	10	كوكاكولا دايت	7	قهوة فرنسية بالحليب	15
شاي بالحليب	15	بيبسي	7	قهوة فرنسية بالتوفي	15
شوكولاتة ساخنة	15	ماء معدني	7	قهوة فرنسية بالفانيلا	15
عصير ليمون	12	صودا	10	نسكافيه	15
عصير برتقال	15	كرز مع صودا وكريمة	15	إسبرسو	10
عصير كيوي	17			إسبرسو دبل	15
عصير مانجا	15	مأكولات		كافيه لاتيه	15
عصير برتقال	15	توست جبن	8	كافيه موكا	15
عصير بندورة	15	سندوتش دجاج	12	كابتشينو	15
عصير جزر	15	سندوتش لحم	12	قهوة بطعم البندق	15
عصير جريب فروت	15	سندوتش تونا	12	قهوة بطعم الجوز	15
عصير مانجا مع فراولة	15	كروسان	6	قهوة بطعم العسل	15
عصير جزر مع برتقال	15	دونات	6	قهوة بطعم الشوكولاتة	15

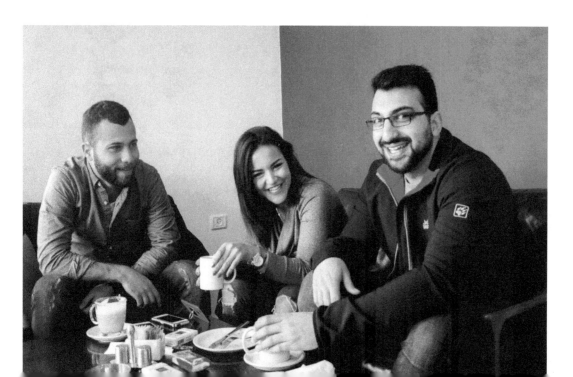

Imagine visiting the café whose menu you see. As at many American or European cafés, you are overwhelmed with options!

Scan the menu for words you *can* understand. You may not have seen them before in Arabic, but there are many words in common with English. Which drinks would you want to order? Create a table like the one below on a separate sheet. Then, writing in Arabic script, list the name of every drink you understand in the appropriate column, given whether you would want to order it or not.

Write down as many items as you can. If you read Arabic letters slowly, you may only write down a few items. If you read quickly, you may write down a lot. Either way is fine as long as you are putting in your best effort to read and understand as many words as you can. If you encounter a word you cannot understand at all, just move on to the next one.

لا أريد... 👎	أريد.... 👍

After reading 1   بعد القراءة ١

This menu is based on a menu from Stars & Bucks Café (*not* Starbucks!) in Ramallah, a city in the Palestinian Territories. The Palestinian Territories use shekels, the currency of Israel. Look up the exchange rate. How expensive or cheap are these items compared to a café in your city?

After reading 2   بعد القراءة ٢

Use the Arabic you know to ask your classmates what they want from the menu and to share what you want and do not want.

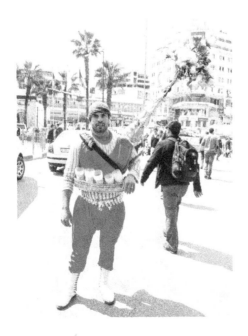

Unit Two
Vocabulary

مفردات الوحدة الثانية

المعنى	العاميّة الشاميّة	الفصحى
May I go to the bathroom?	مُمْكِن أروح عَ الحَمّام؟	هَل مِن المُمْكِن أَنْ أَذْهَب إلى الحَمّام؟
May I go drink water?	مُمْكِن أروح أَشْرَب مَيّ؟	هَل مِن المُمْكِن أَنْ أَذْهَب لِأَشْرَب الماء؟
May I speak in English?	مُمْكِن أحكي إنْكْليزي؟	هَل مِن المُمْكِن أَنْ أَتَكَلَّم الإنْكْليزيّة؟
May . . . ? Is it possible that . . . ?	مُمْكِن...؟	هَل مِن المُمْكِن أَنْ...؟
I understand	فْهِمِت	فَهِمْتُ
I do not understand	ما فْهِمِت	ما فَهِمْتُ
I know	بَعْرِف	أَعْرِف
I do not know	ما بَعْرَف	لا أَعْرِف
I remember	بَتْذَكَّر	أتَذَكَّر
I do not remember	ما بَتْذَكَّر	لا أتَذَكَّر

157

LESSON SEVEN
Core vocabulary

الدرس السابع
المفردات الأساسيّة

المعنى	العاميّة الشاميّة	الفصحى
Are you free today? (m.)	فاضي اليوم؟	هَل أَنْتَ فاضي اليَوْم؟
Are you free today? (f.)	فاضْية اليوم؟	هَل أَنْتِ فاضية اليَوْم؟
Yes, I am free. (m.)	آه، أنا فاضي.	نَعَم، أَنا فاضي.
Yes, I am free. (f.)	آه، أنا فاضْية.	نَعَم، أَنا فاضية.
No, I am busy. (m.)	لا، أنا مَشْغول.	لا، أَنا مَشْغول.
No, I am busy. (f.)	لا، أنا مَشْغولة.	لا، أَنا مَشْغولة.
free available	فاضي / فاضْية	فاضِي / فاضِية
busy occupied	مَشْغول / مَشْغولة	مَشْغول / مَشْغولة
today	اليوم	اليَوْم
tomorrow	بُكْرا	غَداً
(a) day	يوم	يَوْم
the day after tomorrow	بَعْد بُكْرا	بَعْدَ غَد
days of the week	أَيّام الأُسْبوع	أَيّام الأُسْبوع
Sunday	يوم الأَحَد	يَوْم الأَحَد
Monday	يوم الاِثْنين	يَوْم الاِثْنَين
Tuesday	يوم الثَّلاثا	يَوْم الثُّلاثاء
Wednesday	يوم الأَرْبعا	يَوْم الأَرْبِعاء
Thursday	يوم الخَميس	يَوْم الخَميس
Friday	يوم الجُمْعة	يَوْم الجُمْعة
Saturday	يوم السَّبْت	يَوْم السَّبْت

Extra vocabulary   المفردات الإضافيّة

المعنى	العاميّة الشاميّة	الفصحى
Really?	عَن جَدّ؟	حَقّاً؟
weekend day(s) off holiday	عُطْلة	عُطْلة
When is the weekend in ____?	إيمتى العُطْلة في ____؟	مَتى العُطْلة في ____؟
The movie is excellent.	الفيلْم مُمتاز.	الفيلْم مُمتاز.
The movie is good.	الفيلْم مْنيح.	الفيلْم جَيِّد.
I don't know the movie.	ما بَعرَف الفيلْم.	لا أعرِف الفيلْم.

LESSON EIGHT   الدرس الثامن

Core vocabulary   المفردات الأساسيّة

المعنى	العاميّة الشاميّة	الفصحى
When?	إيمتى؟	مَتى؟
in the morning	الصُّبُح	في الصَّباح
noon noontime	الظُّهُر	الظُّهْر
in the afternoon	بَعْد الظُّهُر	بَعْدَ الظُّهْر
in the evening	المَسا	في المَساء
at night	باللَيل	في اللَيْل
good morning (literally: "morning of prosperity")	صَباح الخَير	صَباح الخَير
response to "good morning" (literally: "morning of light")	صَباح النّور	صَباح النّور

المعنى	العامّيّة الشاميّة	الفصحى
good evening *(literally: "evening of prosperity")* *(said after noon or later)*	مَسا الخَير	مَساء الخَيْر
response to "good evening" *(literally "evening of light")*	مَسا النّور	مَساء النّور
What time is it?	كَم الساعة؟	كَم الساعة؟
At what time...?	أَيّ ساعة...؟	في أَيّ ساعة...؟
	الساعة واحْدة	الساعة الواحِدة
	الساعة ثْنْتَين	الساعة الثانِية
	الساعة ثَلاثة	الساعة الثالِثة
	الساعة أَرْبَعة	الساعة الرابِعة
	الساعة خَمْسة	الساعة الخامِسة

المعنى	العامّيّة الشاميّة	الفصحى
	الساعة سِتّة	الساعة السادِسة
	الساعة سَبْعة	الساعة السابِعة
	الساعة ثَمانية	الساعة الثامِنة
	الساعة تِسْعة	الساعة التاسِعة
	الساعة عَشَرة	الساعة العاشِرة
	الساعة إحْدَعْش	الساعة الحادِية عَشَرة
	الساعة اتْنَعْش	الساعة الثانِية عَشَرة
a.m.		صَباحاً
p.m.		مَساءً

المعنى	العاميّة الشاميّة	الفصحى
	الساعة خَمْسة ورُبُع	الساعة الخامِسة والرُبع
	الساعة سِتّة وثُلْث	الساعة السادِسة وَالثُلث
	الساعة تِسْعة ونُص	الساعة التاسِعة وَالنِصْف
and	و	وَ
a quarter	رُبُع	رُبْع
a third	ثُلْث	ثُلْث
a half	نُص	نِصْف
	الساعة ثِنتَين إِلّا رُبُع	الساعة الثانِية إِلّا رُبْعاً
	الساعة ثَلاثة إِلّا ثُلْث	الساعة الثالِثة إِلّا ثُلْثاً
except for minus *(use this for expressing "till"* *or "to" the hour)*	إِلّا	إِلّا

Extra vocabulary   المفردات الإضافيّة

المعنى	العاميّة الشاميّة	الفصحى
When do you do this? (m.)	إيمتى بْتِعْمَل هاذا؟	مَتى تَفْعَل هٰذا؟
When do you do this? (f.)	إيمتى بْتِعْمَلي هاذا؟	مَتى تَفْعَلين هٰذا؟
I do this in the morning.	أنا بَعْمَل هاذا الصُّبْح.	أَنا أَفْعَل هٰذا في الصَّباح.
I do not do this.	أنا ما بَعْمَل هاذا.	أَنا لا أَفْعَل هٰذا.
I wake up	بَصْحى	أَصْحو
What's this?!	شو هاذا؟!	ما هٰذا؟!
You're late! (m.)	إنْتَ مِتْأَخِّر!	أَنْتَ مُتَأَخِّر!
You're late! (f.)	إنْتِ مِتْأَخِّرة!	أَنْتِ مُتَأَخِّرة!

LESSON NINE

الدرس التاسع

Core vocabulary   المفردات الأساسيّة

المعنى	العاميّة الشاميّة	الفصحى
Please come over. (m.)	تْفَضَّل عِنْدي.	تَفَضَّل عِنْدي.
Please come over. (f.)	تْفَضَّلي عِنْدي.	تَفَضَّلي عِنْدي.
You have to come over! (m.)	لازِم تِجي عِنْدي!	مِن اللازم أَنْ تَجيء عِنْدي!
You have to come over! (f.)	لازِم تِجي عِنْدي!	مِن اللازم أَنْ تَجيئي عِنْدي!
must . . . have to . . .	لازِم...	مِن اللازم أَنْ...
possibly . . . might . . .	مُمْكِن...	مِن المُمْكِن أَنْ...
I am sorry. (m.)	مَعْلَيش	(أَنا) آسِف
I am sorry. (f.)	مَعْلَيش	(أَنا) آسِفة
God willing hopefully	إنْ شاء الله	إنْ شاءَ الله
I will see you around! (m.)	بَشوفَك، إنْ شاء الله!	أَراكَ، إنْ شاءَ الله!

المعنى	العاميّة الشاميّة	الفصحى
I will see you around! (f.)	بَشوفِك، إنْ شاء الله!	أراكِ، إنْ شاءَ الله!
I want to go to . . .	بِدّي أروح عَلى...	أُريد أَنْ أَذْهَب إلى...
my house my home	بَيْتي	بَيْتي
Do you want to come? (m.)	بِدّك تِجي؟	هَل تُريد أَنْ تَجيءَ؟
Do you want to go? (f.)	بِدّك تْروحي؟	هَل تُريدين أَنْ تَذْهَبي؟
I want (to)	بِدّي	أُريد (أَنْ)
you want (to) (m.)	بِدّك	تُريد (أَنْ)
you want (to) (f.)	بِدّك	تُريدين (أَنْ)
I go (to)	أروح (عَلى)	أَذْهَب (إلى)
you go (to) (m.)	تْروح (عَلى)	تَذْهَب (إلى)
you go (to) (f.)	تْروحي (عَلى)	تَذهَبين / تَذهبي (إلى)
I come	أجي	أَجيء
you come (m.)	تِجي	تَجيء
you come (f.)	تِجي	تَجيئين / تَجيئي
I do not want	ما بِدّي	لا أُريد
you do not want (m.)	ما بِدّك	لا تُريد
you do not want (f.)	ما بِدّك	لا تُريدين

المفردات الإضافيّة

Extra vocabulary

المعنى	العاميّة الشاميّة	الفصحى
Can you come over? (f.)	مُمْكِن تِجي عِنْدي؟	هَل مِن المُمْكِن أَنْ تَجيئي عِنْدي؟
I want to come but . . .	بِدّي أجي بَس...	أُريد أَنْ أَجيء وَلْكِن...
You have to come over! (m.)	لازِم تِجي عِنْدي!	مِن اللازِم أن تَجيء عِنْدي!
I want the name ___.	بِدّي اِسم ___.	أُريد اسم ___.

المعنى	العاميّة الشاميّة	الفصحى
I want to go to . . .	بِدّي أروح على...	أُريد أَنْ أَذْهَب إلى...
You want to go to . . . (m.)	بِدَّك تْروح على...	تُريد أَنْ تَذْهَب إلى...
You want to go to . . . (f.)	بِدَّك تْروحي عَلى...	تُريدين أَنْ تَذْهَبي...

LESSON TEN
Core vocabulary

الدرس العاشر
المفردات الأساسيّة

المعنى	العاميّة الشاميّة	الفصحى
Would you like some coffee? (m.)	تِشْرَب قَهْوة؟	هل تُريد أَنْ تَشْرَب القَهْوة؟
Would you like some coffee? (f.)	تِشْرَبي قَهْوة؟	هل تُريدين أَنْ تَشْرَبي القَهْوة؟
Would you like coffee or tea? (m.)	تِشْرَب قَهْوة وِلّا شاي؟	هل تُريد أَنْ تَشْرَب القَهْوة أم الشاي؟
Would you like coffee or tea? (f.)	تِشْرَبي قَهْوة وِلّا شاي؟	هل تُريدين أَنْ تَشْرَبي القَهْوة أم الشاي؟
coffee	القَهْوة	القَهْوة
tea	الشاي	الشاي
here you go go ahead (m.)	تْفَضّل	تَفَضّل
here you go go ahead (f.)	تْفَضّلي	تَفَضّلي
thank you (in the context of receiving coffee or tea)	شُكْراً يِسْلَموا	شُكْراً
you're welcome	أَهْلا وسَهْلا	عَفْواً
I like	بَحِبّ	أُحِبّ
you like (m.)	بِتْحِبّ	تُحِبّ
you like (f.)	بِتْحِبّي	تُحِبّين

المعنى	العاميّة الشاميّة	الفصحى
I do not like	ما بَحِبّ	لا أُحِبّ
you do not like *(m.)*	ما بِتْحِبّ	لا تُحِبّ
you do not like *(f.)*	ما بِتْحِبّي	لا تُحِبّين
with sugar	بِالسُّكَّر	بِالسُّكَّر
without sugar	بَلا سُكَّر	بِلا سُكَّر
with milk	بِالحَليب	بِالحَليب
without milk	بَلا حَليب	بِلا حَليب
sugar	السُّكَّر	السُّكَّر
milk	الحَليب	الحَليب

Extra vocabulary

المفردات الإضافيّة

المعنى	العاميّة الشاميّة	الفصحى
Do you like to drink tea? *(m.)*	بِتْحِبّ تِشْرَب الشاي؟	هَل تُحِبّ أَنْ تَشْرَب الشاي؟
Yes, I like to drink tea.	آه، بَحِبّ أَشْرَب الشاي.	نَعَم، أُحِبّ أَنْ أَشْرَب الشاي.
Do you like to drink coffee? *(f.)*	بِتْحِبّي تِشْرَبي القَهْوة؟	هَل تُحِبّين أَنْ تَشْرَبي القَهْوة؟
No, I don't like to drink coffee.	لا، ما بَحِبّ أَشْرَب القَهْوة.	لا، لا أُحِبّ أَنْ أَشْرَب القَهْوة.
How do you like your coffee? *(m.)*	كَيف قَهْوَتَك؟	كَيْف تُحِبّ قَهْوَتَك؟
How do you like your coffee? *(f.)*	كَيف قَهْوَتِك؟	كَيْف تُحِبّين قَهْوَتَك؟
How do you like your tea? *(m.)*	كيف بِتحِبّ الشاي؟	كَيْف تُحِبّ الشاي؟
How do you like your tea? *(f.)*	كيف بِتْحِبّي الشاي؟	كَيْف تُحِبّين الشاي؟
I like tea with milk and sugar.	بحِبّ الشاي بِالسُّكَّر وَبِالحَليب.	أُحِبّ الشاي بِالسُّكَّر وَبِالحَليب.

Free Time

وقت الفراغ

UNIT THREE GOALS—HOW IS YOUR ARABIC?

أهداف الوحدة الثالثة—كيف عربيتك؟

This section lists the unit objectives. While you are working through the lessons in this unit, refer to this list and keep track of your progress toward each objective as you go. By the end of each lesson, you should be able to do the following in Arabic:

Lesson Eleven

الدرس الحادي عشر

- Ask and respond to questions about what your homework is
- Find out when your test is

Lesson Twelve

الدرس الثاني عشر

- Ask and respond to questions about what hobbies you like
- Tell others what you do in your free time
- Invite others to participate in some of your hobbies or favorite activities with you

Lesson Thirteen

الدرس الثالث عشر

- Ask and respond to questions about how much you like particular activities
- Tell how often you do particular activities
- Tell how you feel about doing activities in the future
- Report about what activities other people like to do

Lesson Fourteen

الدرس الرابع عشر

- Ask and respond to questions about the places that you go to during a typical week
- Explain why you go places in a typical day or week
- Tell what order you do different activities in
- Report information about others' daily schedules

Classroom Talk: What is the homework?

الدرس الحادي عشر

كلام الصفّ: ما هو الواجب؟

LESSON ELEVEN GOALS

أهداف الدرس الحادي عشر

By the end of this lesson, you should be able to do the following:

- Ask and respond to questions about what your homework is
- Find out when your test is

In this lesson, you will learn how to use Arabic to ask and answer questions about homework and tests.

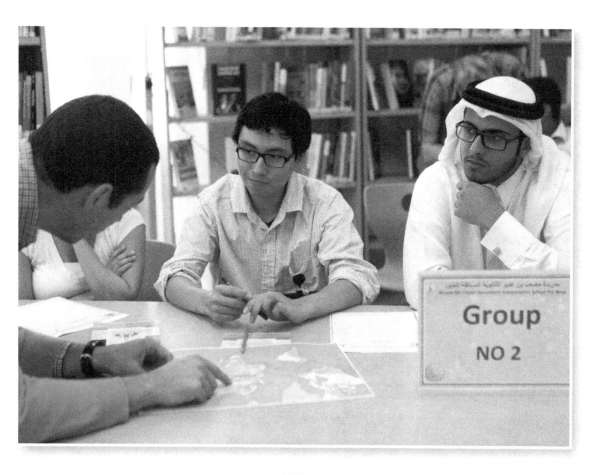

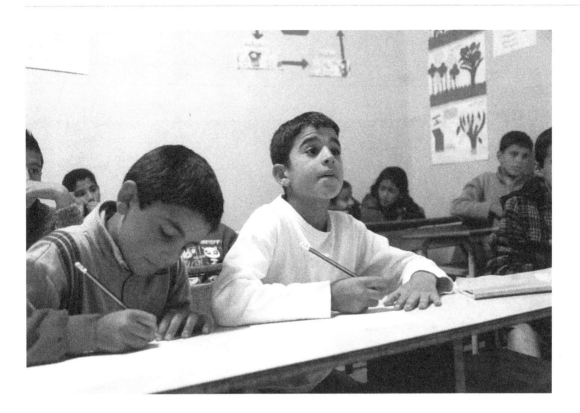

WHEN IS THE TEST?

متى الامتحان؟

Vocabulary

المفردات

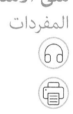

المعنى	العاميّة الشاميّة	الفصحى
What is the homework today?	شو الواجِب اليوم؟	ما هُوَ الواجِب اليَوْم؟
What is the homework for tomorrow?	شو الواجِب لِبُكرا؟	ما هُوَ الواجِب لِيَوْم الغَد؟
What is the homework for ____ [day of the week]?	شو الواجِب لِيوم الـ ____؟	ما هُوَ الواجِب لِيَوْم الـ ____؟
The homework is . . .	الواجِب هُوِّ...	الواجِب هُوَ...
The homework is activity number ____.	الواجِب هُوِّ النَّشاط رَقْم ____.	الواجِب هُوَ النَّشاط رَقْم ____.
The homework is activities number ____ to number ____.	الواجِب هُوِّ النَّشاطات رَقْم ____ إلى رَقْم ____.	الواجِب هُوَ النَّشاطات رَقْم ____ إلى رقم ____.
When is the test?	إيمْتى الاِمْتِحان؟	مَتى الاِمْتِحان؟

Activity 1   Listening: Homework schedule   استماع: جدول الواجبات   نشاط ١

What is the homework schedule for the week? On the audio, you will hear a teacher give a schedule for the week's homework.

Before listening   قبل الاستماع

Look over the schedule below. What country might this schedule be from, based on your knowledge of school schedules and weekends in different countries?

Listening   الاستماع

Listen to the teacher giving the weekly homework schedule. Keep track of the following on the schedule:

- What activities are assigned each day?
- When is there a test?

يوم الخميس	يوم الأربعاء	يوم الثلاثاء	يوم الاثنين	يوم الأحد

Activity 2   Conversation: What is the schedule?   محادثة: ما هو الجدول؟   نشاط ٢

For the next activity, you will get to make up homework assignments for your class on a weekly schedule.

Before speaking   قبل المحادثة

Create two blank weekly schedules like the one below. On the first one, write down which activities you might assign for each day of next week (you can assign as many as you want, assigning at least one each day). Include at least one test in your schedule too.

يوم الجمعة	يوم الخميس	يوم الأربعاء	يوم الثلاثاء	يوم الاثنين

Speaking   المحادثة

1. Imagine that you were out of class when your teacher announced the homework for next week. Turn to a classmate and ask them what the homework is for each day and when the test is. Record the information that they provide on your second weekly schedule.

2. When you have finished asking your classmates questions, trade roles. This time your classmate will pretend to have been absent and ask you about the homework and test next week. Tell them the information that you wrote down on the schedule you created in before listening section.

Activity 3   Reading and writing:
                 The homework this month

نشاط ٣   قراءة وكتابة: الواجب لهذا الشهر

Create a calendar in Arabic for your class this month, based on the example below, which first appeared in Lesson 7. After creating the calendar, write down as much information as you can in Arabic about the homework and tests you had or will have.

الجمعة	الخميس	الأربعاء	الثلاثاء	الاثنين	الأحد	السبت
						يناير
٦	٥	٤	٣	٢	١	
١٣	١٢	١١	١٠	٩	٨	٧
٢٠	١٩	١٨	١٧	١٦	١٥	١٤
٢٧	٢٦	٢٥	٢٤	٢٣	٢٢	٢١
			٣١	٣٠	٢٩	٢٨

In my free time,
I like to . . .

الدرس الثاني عشر

في وقت الفراغ، أحبّ
أن...

UNIT TWELVE GOALS

أهداف الدرس الثاني عشر

By the end of this lesson, you should be able to do the following:

- Ask and respond to questions about what hobbies you like
- Tell others what you do in your free time
- Invite others to participate in some of your hobbies or favorite activities with you

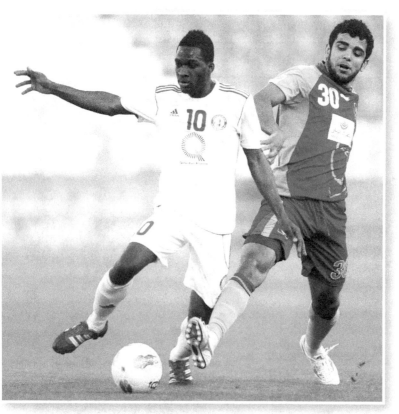

Some sports, such as soccer, are much more popular in the Arab world (and other regions) than in the United States. Other sports, such as baseball and American football, are more popular in the United States than elsewhere.

- How do cultural norms influence the hobbies that are important to you?

MY HOBBIES ARE . . .
Vocabulary 1

هواياتي هي...

مفردات ١ 🎧

المعنى	العاميّة الشاميّة	الفصحى
my hobbies	هِواياتي	هِواياتي
in (my) free time	بْوَقْت الفَراغ	في وَقْت الفَراغ
I like to read.	بَحِبّ أَقْرَأ.	أُحِبّ أَنْ أَقْرَأ.
I do not like to read.	ما بَحِبّ أَقْرَأ.	لا أُحِبّ أَنْ أَقْرَأ.
also and also	كَمان وكَمان	أَيْضاً وأَيْضاً
I like to draw/paint.	بَحِبّ أَرْسُم.	أُحِبّ أَنْ أَرْسُم.
I like to study.	بَحِبّ أَدْرُس.	أُحِبّ أَنْ أَدْرُس.
I like to listen to music.	بَحِبّ أَسْمَع موسيقى.	أُحِبّ أَنْ أَسْتَمِع إلى الموسيقى.
I like to watch TV.	بَحِبّ أَتْفَرَّج عَلى التِّلِفْزْيون.	أُحِبّ أَنْ أُشاهِد التِّلِفِزْيون.
I like to watch movies.	بَحِبّ أَتْفَرَّج عَلى الأَفْلام.	أُحِبّ أَنْ أُشاهِد الأَفْلام.
I like to play video games.	بَحِبّ أَلْعَب أَلْعاب الفيديو	أُحِبّ أَنْ أَلْعَب أَلْعاب الفيديو
I like to go on the Internet.	بَحِبّ أَفوت عَلى الإِنْتَرْنِت.	أُحِبّ أَنْ أَدْخُل في الإِنْتَرْنِت.
I like to shop.	بَحِبّ أَتْسَوَّق.	أُحِبّ أَنْ أَتَسَوَّق.

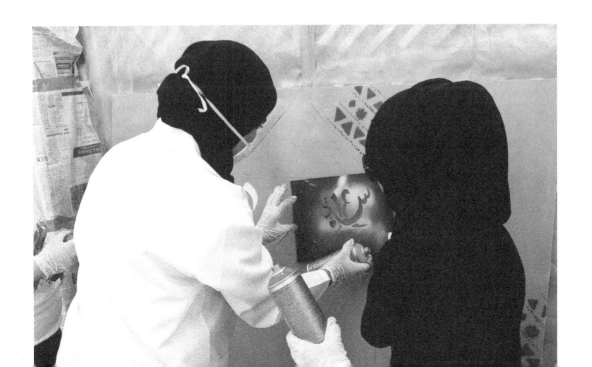

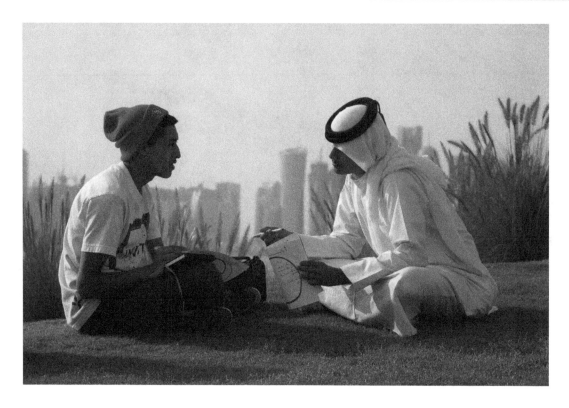

Culture: Borrowed words   الثقافة: كلمات من لغات أخرى

One of the ways that the Arabic dialects differ from one another relates to the borrowing of words from other languages. Each dialect tends to borrow the most heavily from the languages of the colonial powers who occupied the lands where the dialect has historically been spoken. For instance, North African varieties are liberally sprinkled with French loanwords, whereas Iraqi dialect has many words borrowed from English and Turkish. The global dominance of English in such fields as science and technology has meant that Arabic speakers, even in countries not formerly colonized by the British, have borrowed various technological terms from English. These include إنترنت and موبايل, which you have heard used in earlier chapters. Note that scholars of the Arabic language have created words using Arabic roots and patterns to express the same ideas as these two borrowings and others; however, the words borrowed from English are often more commonly used in dialect. For example, a computer is called a حاسوب in Modern Standard Arabic, but in speaking, virtually everyone will say كمبيوتر. The same is true for "shopping" (التسوق) and شوبنغ) and "mall" (مول and مركز تسوق), though the balance between the use of foreign words and Arabic words in such cases varies from community to community.

One subcategory of borrowed words is those where a dominant brand name is used to describe any product of the same type, even if it is not made by the same company. What do you usually call a soft drink? If you are from the southern United States, chances are you call a soft drink a "coke," even if it is Sprite, Fanta, or Pepsi. You will hear an example of this later on in a video: any home game console is usually called a بلايستايشن, even if it really is an Xbox.

What are some borrowed words that you use? What brand names have become synomous with certain products?

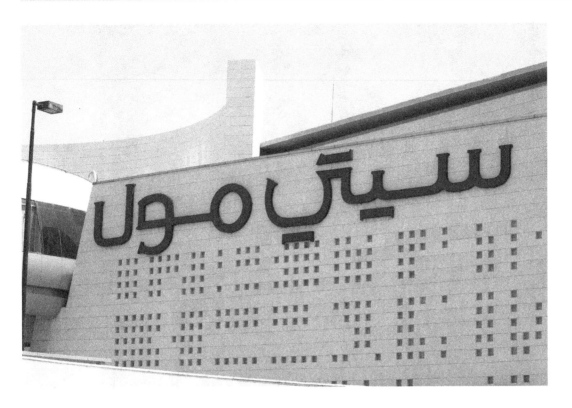

Activity 1   Listening: My hobbies

نشاط ١   استماع: هواياتي

In this activity, you will practice listening to questions. You do not need to respond verbally, so focus on understanding the questions and pay attention to how they are phrased.

Before listening

قبل الاستماع

On a separate sheet of paper, draw a line down the middle. Label one side with a heart or the word أُحِبّ; on the other side draw a wastebasket or the phrase لا أُحِبّ.

Listening

الاستماع

Your teacher will ask your class a series of questions. Each question will ask if you like certain hobbies. If you say نعم to the question, draw a picture of that activity on the side of your paper with the heart. If you say لا to the question, draw a picture representing that hobby on the side with the wastebasket.

After listening

بعد الاستماع

Compare your drawing with that of someone else in your class. If you see an interest that you have in common, point to their drawing and tell them that you enjoy this interest, too. Use this sentence as a model:

| I like to shop, too! | أَنا كَمان بحِبّ أَتْسَوَّق! | أَنا أَيضاً أُحِبّ أَنْ أَتَسَوَّق! |

Challenge yourself: Ask your classmate whether they like an activity and respond enthusiastically, using the question forms you heard your teacher use. Use these sentences as models:

Do you like to shop? *(m.)*	بِتحِبّ تِتْسَوَّق؟	هَل تُحِبّ أَنْ تَتَسَوَّق؟
Do you like to shop? *(f.)*	بِتحِبّي تِتْسَوَّقي؟	هَل تُحِبّين أَنْ تَتَسَوَّقي؟
Me too!	أنا كَمان!	أنا أيضاً!

Activity 2   American teens   استماع: الشباب الأمريكيون   نشاط ٢

In the next listening activity, you will learn how much time American teens spend on different activities each day.[1]

Before listening   قبل الاستماع

To express how long someone spends on something, use a word you know from Unit 2 that has a separate but related meaning: ساعة.

(for) an hour every day	ساعة كُلّ يوم	ساعة كُلّ يَوْم
(for) three hours every day	ثَلاث ساعات كُلّ يوم	ثَلاث ساعات كُلّ يَوْم
an hour	ساعة	ساعة
hours	ساعات	ساعات

   How much time do you think the average teen spends on each of the activities below? Create a numbered list on a separate sheet of paper based on the activities in the table below and on the next page. Write down a guess for how long the average teenager spends on each per day. (Time for studying or homework is separate from time spent on the Internet; the survey only counted the length of time teens did things for fun.)

النشاط	كم ساعة في اليوم؟	
١.	Guess:	Actual:
٢.	Guess:	Actual:
٣.	Guess:	Actual:
٤.	Guess:	Actual:

النشاط	كم ساعة في اليوم؟	
٥.	Guess:	Actual:
٦.	Guess:	Actual:
٧.	Guess:	Actual:

Listening   الاستماع

Listen to the passage about the pastimes of American teens. For each item, write down how long the average teen does these things daily (times have been rounded to the nearest fifteen minutes).

After listening   بعد الاستماع

On another piece of paper, create a table that looks like the one below. Rearrange the activities in order from longest to shortest, drawing a picture to represent the activity. In the next row, order your own activities from those you spend the most time on to those you spend the least time on. What do you spend the most time on? What do you spend the least time on? Jot down how much time you think you spend on each thing on average. Focus on the activities in this lesson—do not include things like eating and sleeping.

Challenge yourself: Complete the table in Arabic letters.

Shortest time ← → Longest time						
						Average American teen's activities
						My activities

    When you are ready, present your list to a classmate or to the whole class by saying the activities you do and how long you do them in order.

Grammar: More about verb conjugations   القواعد: المزيد عن تصريف الأفعال

You have already been exposed to multiple verbs in context and learned how to conjugate them for the pronouns أنا, أنتَ, and أنتِ. Now you will learn more about the two different verb conjugation patterns that you have been exposed to. These patterns vary between العاميّة الشاميّة and الفصحى. Focus on the variety of Arabic that you are learning; if you are curious about the similarities and differences, look at the other variety.

If you are studying Modern Standard Arabic: review these familiar sentences that contain verbal phrases with more than one verb, looking for similarities and differences between the verbs:

I like to drink tea.	أُحِبّ أَنْ أَشْرَب الشاي.
Do you like to drink tea? *(m.)*	هَل تُحِبّ أَنْ تَشْرَب الشاي؟
Do you like to drink tea? *(f.)*	هَل تُحِبّين أَنْ تَشْرَبي الشاي؟

If you look at the prefixes of the two verbs in each row, you will notice similarities: the verbs about أنا start with أ, and the verbs about أنتَ and أنتِ all start with ت. In other respects, you will notice some differences: the verbs about أنتِ have two different suffixes, ـي and ـين. The two verbs in each row (e.g., أَشْرب and أحِبّ) follow two distinct conjugation patterns. The most significant difference between them is that one includes a final ن in the suffix of the أنتِ form, and one does not.

Below are tables presenting the two conjugation patterns with the same verb. They are labeled with the grammatical terms for these patterns.*

Pattern for Indicative Verbs (i.e., Independent Verbs) المُضارِع المَرْفوع	
I draw	أَرْسُم
you draw *(m.)*	تَرْسُم
you draw *(f.)*	تَرْسُمـين

Pattern for Subjunctive Verbs (i.e., Dependent Verbs) المُضارِع المَنْصوب	
I like to draw.	أُحِبّ أَنْ أَرْسُم.
You like to draw. *(m.)*	تُحِبّ أَنْ تَرْسُم.
You like to draw. *(f.)*	تُحِبّين أَنْ تَرْسُمـي.

*There are other differences between these conjugation patterns in Modern Standard Arabic that have to do with the short vowels—a, u, or i—used at the end of verbs. However, these grammatical differences are not presented in the table, and we will not focus on them here, because they do not change the fundamental meaning of the word.

When do we use each of these different patterns? The pattern for indicative verbs is used to express states of being that are generally or always true (e.g., "I like") or habitual

actions that are done repeatedly or regularly (e.g., "I draw"). The pattern for subjunctive verbs, by contrast, appears after another verbal phrase (e.g., أُحِبّ أَنْ), which takes the pattern for indicative verbs. In general, the pattern for subjunctive verbs is used to refer to actions that are dependent on something else in the sentence.‡ There are certain other verbs and phrases that "activate" this pattern. The ones you know are easy to recognize, because they all include the word أَنْ:

مِن اللازِم أَنْ	مِن المُمْكِن أَنْ	أُريد أَنْ	أُحِبّ أَنْ
		تُريد أَنْ	تُحِبّ أَنْ
		تُريدين أَنْ	تُحِبّين أَنْ

It will take time for you to master the difference between these two patterns for conjugating verbs. Remember that if you have a verb following the word أَنْ, then the أَنتِ form must drop the ن at the end of the verb.

If you are studying Levantine dialect: review these familiar examples of sentences that contain verbal phrases with more than one verb, looking for the similarities and differences between the verbs:

I like to drink tea.	بَحِبّ أَشْرَب شاي.
Do you like to drink tea? *(m.)*	بِتْحِبّ تِشْرَب شاي؟
Do you like to drink tea? *(f.)*	بِتْحِبّي تِشْرَبي شاي؟

You may notice the differences first: The first verb in each row (meaning "like") starts with بـ, while the second verb in each row (meaning "drink") does not. You can also see similarities: the prefixes and suffixes of the verbs about أَنتَ have the prefix تـ in common, and the verbs about أَنتِ have the prefix تـ and the suffix ـي. The two verbs in each row (e.g., بحِب and أشرب) follow two different conjugation patterns. The most significant difference between them is the presence and absence of بـ at the beginning of each verb. So far, you have seen these different patterns applied only to certain verbs, but they can both be used with any verb.

Below and on the next page are tables presenting the two conjugation patterns with the same verb. They are labeled with the grammatical terms for these patterns.

Pattern for Indicative Verbs (i.e., Independent Verbs)	
I draw	بَـرْسُم
You draw. *(m.)*	بْتِـرْسُم
You draw. *(f.)*	بْتِـرْسُمـي

Pattern for Subjunctive Verbs (i.e., Dependent Verbs)	
I like to draw.	بَحِبّ أَرْسُم.
You like to draw. *(m.)*	بِتْحِبّ تِرْسُم.
You like to draw. *(f.)*	بِتْحِبّي تِرْسمِي.

When do we use each of these different patterns? The pattern for indicative verbs (with بـ at the beginning) is used to express states of being that are generally or always true (e.g., "I like") or habitual actions that are done repeatedly or regularly (e.g., "I draw"). The pattern for subjunctive verbs, by contrast, appears after another verb (e.g., بحبّ), which takes the pattern for indicative verbs. In general, the pattern for subjunctive verbs (those without بـ at the beginning) is used to refer to actions that are dependent on something else in the sentence.[‡] There are certain other verbs and phrases that "activate" this pattern, and the ones you know so far include the following:

لازِم	مُمْكِن	بِدّي	بحِبّ
		بِدّك	بتْحِبّ
		بِدّك	بتْحِبّي

It will take time for you to master the difference between these two patterns for conjugating verbs. When expressing a state of being or habitual action, use بـ at the beginning of the verb. When using a verb after one of the words noted above, do not use بـ.

[‡]This description and the terms "independent" and "dependent" to describe these grammatical phenomena come from El-Said Badawi, Adrian Gully, and Michael G. Carter, *Modern Written Arabic: A Comprehensive Grammar* (London: Routledge, 2010), 598.

Activity 3   Practicing grammar: Verbs   التدريب على القواعد: الأفعال   نشاط ٣

In this activity, you will practice activating the different verb conjugations you just learned.

Before practicing   قبل التدريب

Construct two large dice by making cubes out of paper following your teacher's instructions. On the first cube, draw pictures on each side representing six different activities

(of your choice) from the list in Vocabulary 1. On the second cube, write the following words, phrases, or images on each side of the cube:

في وَقْت الفَراغ	كُلّ يَوْم	♥
"want to"	لازِم	مُمْكِن

Practice   التدريب

Pair up with another student. Roll both of your dice at once. One die will show an activity and one will show an additional phrase. When you see the combination, ask your classmate a question that incorporates the hobby and the phrase, using the correct conjugation. For example:

The first die shows 🎧; the second die shows كُلّ يوم. You then ask your classmate the following question:

Do you listen to music every day? *(m.)*	بْتِسْمَع موسيقى كُلّ يوم؟	هَل تَسْتَمِع إلى الموسيقى كُلّ يَوْم؟
Do you listen to music every day? *(f.)*	بْتِسْمَع موسيقى كُلّ يوم؟	هَل تَسْتَمِعين إلى الموسيقى كُلّ يَوْم؟

Start by working cooperatively with your classmate to get the right conjugation. See how long you can extend a conversation based on each dice roll. When your teacher tells you that the time is up for your conversation, get up and look for a new classmate to start a new practice session with.

Activity 4   Conversation and reading: نشاط ٤   محادثة وقراءة: التسوّق عبر
Shopping online   الإنترنت

In this activity you and your classmates will ask and answer questions about shopping habits. As an interviewer, you will play the role of a researcher learning about people's shopping habits. As an interviewee, you will either be assigned the role of a person living in the Arab world or you will talk about your own personal shopping habits.

Before speaking   قبل المحادثة

Your teacher will give you a role to play. On your slip of paper, you will find out whether you are playing yourself or a person living in the Arab world. If you are playing yourself, fill out the slip of paper with information about your own shopping habits, writing in Arabic as much as you can. If you are playing the role of someone residing in the Arab world, read your slip to find out who you are and what you like.

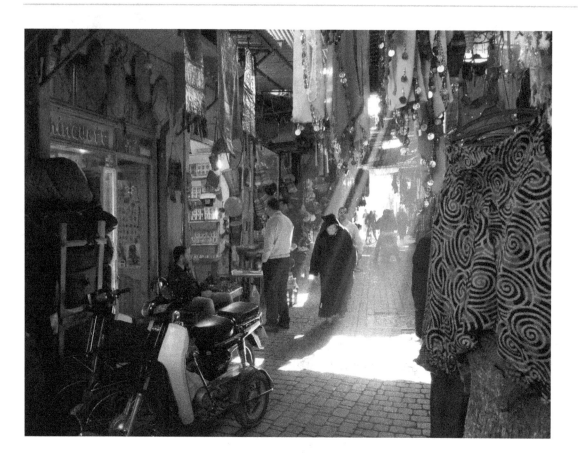

Speaking   المحادثة

Interview your classmates to find out who likes shopping online and who does not. Some of your classmates will be acting as people living the Arab world, based on real statistics about internet shopping in the Arab world.[2] Be sure to ask your classmates what their names are and where they are from in order to know if you are talking with someone residing in your country or the Arab world. As you talk to your classmates, record who likes to shop online and who does not in a table like the one below.

من بلَدي		من البلاد العَرَبية	
لا يتسوّقون في الإنترنت 👎	يتسوّقون في الإنترنت 👍	لا يتسوّقون في الإنترنت 👎	يتسوّقون في الإنترنت 👍
Total: _____	Total: _____	Total: _____	Total: _____

After speaking   بعد المحادثة

Summarize your findings and share them with the class, using the numbers you know to
report how many residents of your country versus those of the Arab world said yes or no to
your question.

| Activity 5 | Conversation: Do you like to…? | محادثة: هل تحب أن...؟ | نشاط ٥ |

In this activity, you'll review how to ask whether your classmates like to do certain
activities.

Before speaking   قبل المحادثة

Look over the hobbies pictured below. Practice the verb forms you will use to ask your
classmates whether they like to do each hobby, remembering to pay attention to gender
agreement. Share with a classmate the questions you came up with. Then, on a separate
sheet of paper, create a table like the one below and on the next page, with a picture for
each of the activities (or use the sheet from your teacher).

Speaking   المحادثة

Ask your classmates whether they like or dislike the following activities, and write down the
name of the person who answers your question. Circle either the thumbs-up or thumbs-
down sign to show how your classmate answered.

👎 👍	الاسم	النشاط
👎 👍	الاسم: _____	⬜ ١.
👎 👍	الاسم: _____	🎧 ♪ ٢.
👎 👍	الاسم: _____	🎞 ٣.
👎 👍	الاسم: _____	🎨 ٤.
👎 👍	الاسم: _____	🛍 ٥.
👎 👍	الاسم: _____	📕 ٦.

👎 👍	الاسم	النشاط
👎 👍	الاسم: _____	.٧ 🎮
👎 👍	الاسم: _____	.٨ 💻
👎 👍	الاسم: _____	.٩ 👨‍🎓

Activity 6   Listening and conversation: Do you want to watch TV at my house?

نشاط ٦   استماع ومحادثة: هل تريد أن تشاهد التلفزيون في بيتي؟

In Unit 2, you learned how to invite others to your house for coffee or tea. In this activity, you will practice inviting others to do some of these activities with you at your house.

Before listening

قبل الاستماع

On a separate sheet of paper, create a chart like the one on the next page.

Listening

الاستماع

You will hear a series of voice messages someone has left inviting people to do different activities. For each activity, do the following:

1. Mark the day and time when the person is being invited over.
2. Note the activity the person is being invited to do, either by drawing a picture or writing in Arabic letters.

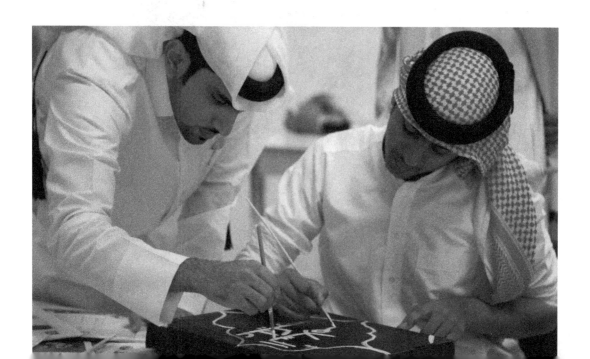

	يوم الأحد	يوم الاثنين	يوم الثلاثاء	يوم الأربعاء	يوم الخميس	يوم الجمعة	يوم السبت
١:٠٠							
٢:٠٠							
٣:٠٠							
٤:٠٠							
٥:٠٠							
٦:٠٠							
٧:٠٠							
٨:٠٠							
٩:٠٠							

After listening   بعد الاستماع

Listen to the voice messages again as a class, pausing after each one. Pretend that this voice message was left on your phone. Turn to a classmate and give a short response to the invitation, using two or more words to respond.

Challenge yourself: Respond in a complete sentence or two!

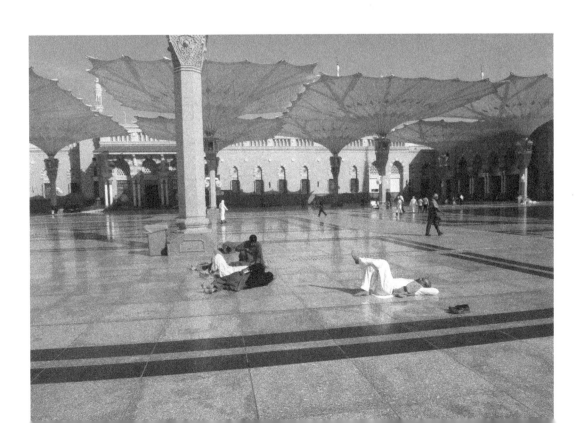

Before speaking　قبل المحادثة

1. Choose three activities to invite someone else to do. Write them down in Arabic letters or draw pictures on your table.
2. Decide what day and time you want to do each activity and pencil them in the table.
3. Speak aloud to yourself to practice saying your invitations, paying attention to gender agreement. You can use many of the same phrases that you learned in previous lessons.

Speaking　المحادثة

Talking with one classmate at a time, take turns inviting each other over to your house to do the activities you have chosen. Decide whether you are free or busy based on whether you already have something else to do at that time. In a table like the one below, write down the names of those who are free to come over and those who are busy. Recall the following pointers:

- Be polite and insist that someone come over!
- When you are invited over, don't agree right away.

النشاط:		النشاط:		النشاط:	
الساعة:	اليوم:	الساعة:	اليوم:	الساعة:	اليوم:
لا، مشغول/ مشغولة	نعم، فاضي/ فاضية	لا، مشغول/ مشغولة	نعم، فاضي/ فاضية	لا، مشغول/ مشغولة	نعم، فاضي/ فاضية

Activity 7　Reading: Free time in Saudi Arabia　نشاط ٧　قراءة: وقت الفراغ في السعودية

What does free time look like in the Arab world? The following table gives some information about free time in Saudi Arabia for people between 15 and 29.[3]

Before reading　قبل القراءة

Skim the two tables, focusing on the format and the headings in the top row. What information is each table giving?

النسبة – الذكور 👳	النسبة – الإناث 🧕	ساعات من وقت الفراغ في اليوم
٧٪	١٣٪	من ٠ إلى ساعتين (٢) في اليوم
١٨٪	٢٨٪	من ٢ إلى ٣ ساعات في اليوم
٤٣٪	٣٧٪	من ٤ إلى ٦ ساعات في اليوم
٢٤٪	١٥٪	من ٧ إلى ١٢ ساعة في اليوم
٨٪	٦٪	من ١٢ إلى ١٨ ساعة في اليوم

النسبة		هل تفعل هذا في وقت الفراغ؟
لا	نعم	
٤٥٪	٥٥٪	أشاهد التلفزيون
٦٧٪	٣٣٪	أتكلّم على الهاتف
٩٠٪	١٠٪	أشرب القهوة في المقهى
٤٤٪	٥٦٪	أرى أصدقائي
٦١٪	٣٩٪	أدخل في الإنترنت
٧١٪	٢٩٪	أقرأ

Reading for general understanding
القراءة للفهم العام

Search for the answers to the following questions. Write your answers on a separate sheet of paper, including at least one thing from the chart that supports each of your responses. Use quotation marks if you copy directly from the chart.

1. Who has more free time in Saudi Arabia, young men or young women?
2. What are the two most common activities for young people in Saudi Arabia to do during their free time?
3. What is the least common activity for young people in Saudi Arabia to do during their free time?

Close reading
القراءة الدقيقة

The two charts above are presented in a dry format. An editor for an online magazine has asked you to create an engaging infographic to represent the information instead. Choose one of the above charts and create an infographic using pictures and charts to quickly communicate the information to readers.

Here are some sample formats that you can build on for your infographic. You can also be creative and use any other format you want.

- To show how much time young people have, create a pie chart for men and a different pie chart for women to compare the two.

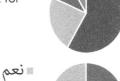

- To show how many people participate in one certain activity, use a pie chart with just two slices.

نعم ▪
لا ▪

- You can also put your data into a bar graph:

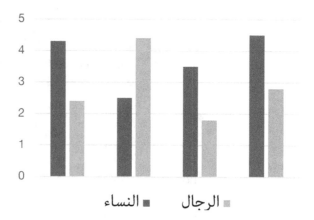

النساء ■   الرجال ■

Challenge yourself: Survey ten classmates to find out how much free time they have or whether they do a certain activity in their free time. Add this information to your infographic in order to show a comparison between youth in Saudi Arabia and youth in the United States.

I LIKE SPORTS
Vocabulary 2

أحبّ الرياضة
مفردات ٢

المعنى	العاميّة الشاميّة	الفصحى
I like to play . . .	بَحِبّ أَلْعَب...	أُحِبّ أَنْ أَلْعَب...
I like to watch . . .	بَحِبّ أَتْفَرَّج على...	أُحِبّ أَنْ أُشاهِد....
sports	الرِّياضة	الرِّياضة
soccer (football)	كُرة القَدَم	كُرة القَدَم
basketball	كُرة السَّلّة	كُرة السَّلّة
American football	كُرة القَدَم الأَمْريكِيّة	كُرة القَدَم الأَمْريكِيّة
I like to swim.	بَحِبّ أَسْبَح.	أُحِبّ أَنْ أَسْبَح.
the sport of swimming	السِّباحة	السِّباحة
I like to dance.	بَحِبّ أَرْقُص.	أُحِبّ أَنْ أَرْقُص.

Activity 8   Listening: Where is this team from?

نشاط ٨   استماع: من أين هذا الفريق؟

How well do you know American and European sports teams? In this activity, you will hear a series of clues about teams in different cities. Can you figure out which team each sentence is describing?

Before listening

قبل الاستماع

Number a separate sheet of paper from one to twelve. In the listening, you will hear the word فَريق ("team") used. You do not need to memorize this word, but you can choose to learn it if you want to.

team	فَريق	فَريق

Look over the team names below. Which ones do you recognize? Use the Arabic you know to tell a classmate what sport is associated with each team.

Listening

الاستماع

You will hear twelve clues. For each clue, write the name of the team you think the sentence is referring to on your numbered sheet of paper.

Packers

Real Madrid

Seahawks

Lakers

Bulls

Patriots

Thunder

Bayern Munich

Juventus

Cowboys

Manchester United

Heat

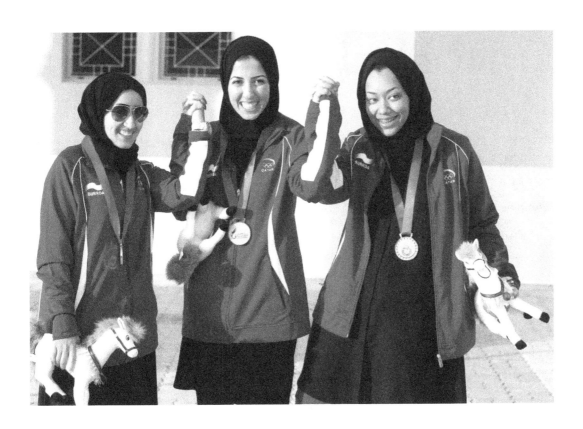

After listening 1   بعد الاستماع ١

Go through the list with a classmate. For each team mentioned, tell your classmate whether you like to watch that team. If you don't know, you can also say ما بعرف or لا أعرف.

After listening 2   بعد الاستماع ٢

Create your own list of sports teams. Try to stump a classmate by telling them the type of sport and where the team plays, such as "basketball in the city of Boston." See if they can guess the sports team you are thinking of. You can use soccer, basketball, and American football teams in any city and country.

Activity 9	Listening: "Yasmine's Hobbies"	نشاط ٩ استماع: "هوايات ياسمين"

In the video "هوايات ياسمين," ياسمين is practicing her Arabic at home by making videos of herself talking about her interests and her life in the United States. She made videos of herself in both Levantine dialect and Modern Standard Arabic.

Listening for general understanding   الاستماع للفهم العام

Watch and listen to ياسمين as she discusses her hobbies. Using the sheet of these activities from your teacher, circle the symbols that represent hobbies she likes, and write an *x* by symbols that represent hobbies that she does not like. Keep in mind that if you are listening to the video in Levantine dialect, you will hear ياسمين use verb forms that use the بـ prefix.

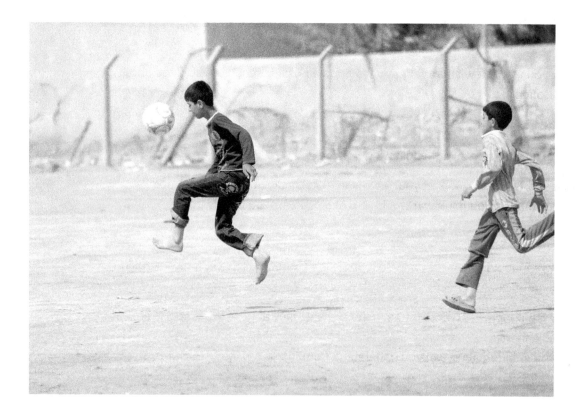

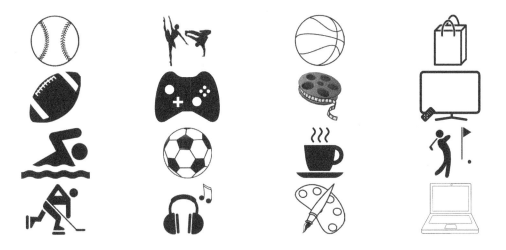

Close listening   الاستماع الدقيق

Listen again and focus on the sports: which sports does ياسمين like (or not like)
to watch, and which does she like to play? Draw symbols near the pictures to show your
understanding.

After listening   بعد الاستماع

Using what ياسمين says as a model, tell a classmate about your own hobbies and interests using the vocabulary you know in Arabic. If you have the technology available, make
a video of yourself talking about your hobbies. Play the video back: what could you do to
improve your speaking?

| Activity 10 Reading: What sports are | قراءة: ما الرياضات المتوفّرة في | نشاط ١٠ |
| available at this school? | هذه المدرسة؟ | |

In this activity, you will review information from a Middle Eastern school's web page about
the sports they offer.

Before reading   قبل القراءة

Tell a classmate in Arabic each of the following:

1. What sports are available at your school that you know how to say in Arabic?
2. What sports do you think you would find at a school in the Middle East?

Reading   القراءة

Look over the webpage on the next page describing the sports available at Imtiyaaz Academy, a private international school:

3. Circle the sports you recognize as many times as they appear. What sports are
   available there?
4. What other information can you understand from the web page?

5. How many cognate words can you find in the webpage? What hints do they give you about the text?

يشارك الطلاب الرياضيون في أكاديمية الامتياز في منافسات محلية وعلى مستوى الشرق الأوسط ضمن رياضات تنافسية فردية وجماعية. وتشتمل الرياضات التي يتنافس فيها الطلاب ما يلي:

- الكرة الطائرة / كرة القدم / كرة السلة
  - للبنين والبنات دون ١٤ سنة
  - للبنين والبنات - المنتخبات المدرسية للناشئين
  - للبنين والبنات - المنتخبات المدرسية
- تنس الريشة / السباحة
  - لفرق البنين والبنات
- ألعاب القوى
  - سباقات السرعة
  - سباقات المسافات الطويلة
  - الرمي
  - القفز
- تنس الطاولة / الكريكيت / كرة الشبكة
  - لفرق البنين والبنات

- بطولات رابطة أنشطة مدارس الشرق الأدنى (NESAC) التي ستشارك فيها أكاديمية الامتياز العام القادم: كرة الطائرة فئة المتمرسين ٢٦-٣٠ أكتوبر (المدرسة الأمريكية الدولية، الكويت)
- السباحة ١٦-١٩ نوفمبر (المدرسة الأمريكية الدولية في مصر، القاهرة)
- كرة الطائرة فئة المبتدئين ١٩-٢٣ أكتوبر (المدرسة الأمريكية الدولية، الكويت)
- كرة القدم فئة المبتدئين ١٨-٢٢ يناير (المدرسة الأمريكية الدولية في أبو ظبي، الإمارات)
- كرة القدم فئة المتمرسين ٧-١١ ديسمبر (أكاديمية قطر، الدوحة)
- كرة السلة فئة المبتدئين ٢٩ فبراير - ٨ مارس (المدرسة الأمريكية الدولية، الكويت)
- كرة السلة فئة المبتدئين ٢٩ فبراير - ٨ مارس (المدرسة الأمريكية الدولية في مصر، القاهرة)
- ألعاب القوى ١٤-١٧ أبريل (الكلية الأمريكية في القاهرة، مصر)
- الفرقة الموسيقية والغناء الجماعي (الكورال) ٨-١٢ فبراير (المدرسة الأمريكية الدولية، الكويت)

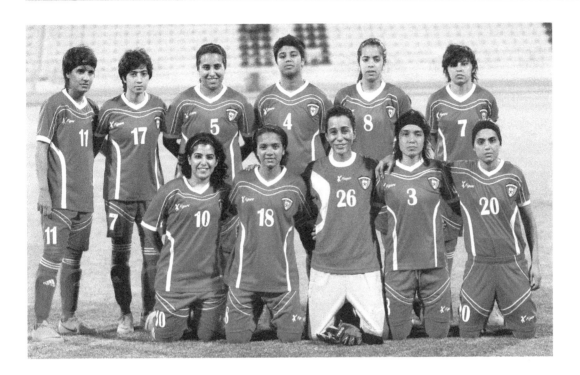

After reading   بعد القراءة

Your school has asked you to create a list of school sports and activities for your school, to be displayed in Arabic on the school webpage. Write a list and think about any other information you can give, such as practice times and coaches.

Activity 11 Listening and conversation: استماع ومحادثة: ماذا تشاهد؟   نشاط ١١
What do you watch?

In this activity, you'll find out what the most popular sports in the US are, as judged by the number of people who watch major sporting events on TV.

Before listening   قبل الاستماع

What are the most-watched sports on TV in the United States? Write your guesses of the four most-watched sports on a separate sheet of paper. Write each sport's name in Arabic letters or draw a picture for it.

   Share your guesses with a classmate, using the sport and the numbers you know. For example, you could say: كرة السلة رقم واحد.

Listening for general understanding   الاستماع للفهم العام

You will hear a short "radio segment" on the most popular sports to watch on television in the United States.[4] Listen for the sports in the pictures. For each sport, write down any information you hear about it. You will hear some sports mentioned whose names you have not previously learned in Arabic, but these words are borrowed from English.

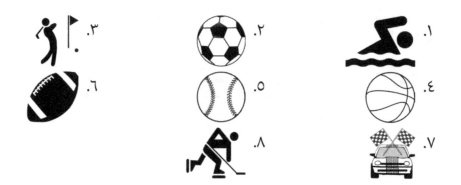

Close listening   الاستماع الدقيق

Listen for the phrase كأس العالم. What sport is it related to? What do you think it might mean, in the context?

Speaking   المحادثة

Do you think the most-watched sport among students in your class is the same as that in the United States overall? Ask your classmates whether they watch each of these sports, and record your answers on a separate sheet. You can use the phrase "Do you like to watch . . . ?"

Do you like to watch . . . ? (m.)	بِتْحِبّ تِتْفَرَّج عَلى...؟	هَل تُحِبّ أَنْ تُشاهِد...؟
Do you like to watch . . . ? (f.)	بِتْحِبّي تِتْفَرَّجي عَلى...؟	هَل تُحِبّين أَنْ تُشاهِدي...؟

After talking   بعد المحادثة

Based on the information you have gathered about your classmates' sports-watching preferences, which four sports are the most watched in your class? Which sport is number one in your class? How does the list compare to preferences in the United States generally?

Activity 12 Listening: "Taghreed and Issam's Hobbies"   نشاط ١٢   استماع: "هوايات تغريد وعصام"

In this video, you will see عصام and تغريد discussing their hobbies and interests.

Before listening   قبل الاستماع

Play a few seconds of the video, then pause it when you can see the characters. What do you remember about تغريد or عصام? Tell a classmate the information you remember

in Arabic. On a separate sheet of paper, create a table with each character's name in the headings like the one below.

عصام	تغريد

Listening for general understanding   الاستماع للفهم العام

Watch the video and listen to تغريد and عصام discuss their hobbies together. Draw symbols (or write words) in your table to record their likes and dislikes. Keep in mind that if you listen to the video in Levantine dialect, you will hear them use verbs with the بـ prefix.

Close listening   الاستماع الدقيق

Answer the following questions:

1. What kind of music does تغريد like?
2. What does each person like to watch on TV?
3. What does each person like to do on the internet or on their phone?

After listening   بعد الاستماع

Think of a sibling or a friend you are close to. Do you share the same interests? With a classmate, create a dialogue between two siblings or two close friends talking about their interests. Model your speech on تغريد and عصام. Practice several times, then present to another pair or to the rest of your class.

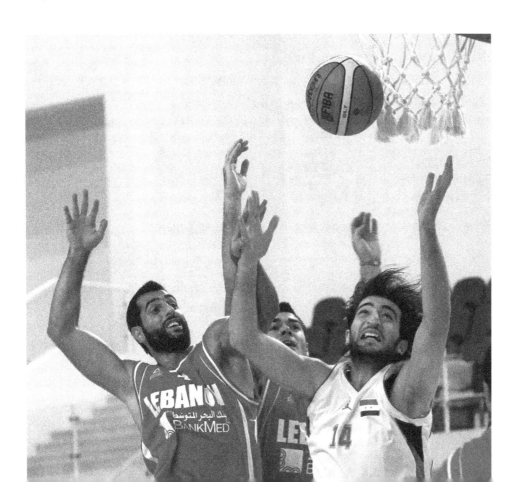

Activity 13 Listening and conversation:
What time is the match?

نشاط ١٣ استماع ومحادثة: في أي ساعة
المباراة؟

To promote exercise and good health, the Qatari government hosts a yearly sports event for students called "Schools Olympic." Students from schools all over the country compete in national championships in a variety of sports at the Aspire Sports Complex.

Listening

الاستماع

While visiting Qatar, you decide to attend the championship Schools Olympic competition. When you arrive, you hear an announcement for the times and places different sports will take place. Listen to the announcement and jot down the times for each sport. Listen carefully; they may not be in the same order as listed on the table, and you may hear other sports listed that you do not need to note down.

Because this announcement is in Modern Standard Arabic, times are listed in Modern Standard Arabic as well. You may find these times challenging to understand, so focus on identifying familiar words and sounds.

في الساعة...	الرياضة
	⚽ ١.
	🏊 ٢.
	🏀 ٣.
	🥋 ٤.

Challenge yourself: After writing down all the times, listen for the words مَلْعَب and مَسْبَح. Can you guess what they might mean? Practice identifying the root of both words, as you learned to do in Unit 2. (Hint: a good rule of thumb to follow is that م is often not part of the root of a word.) Then look for a word in your sports vocabulary list that shares the same root.

Guess about meaning	Word from vocabulary list with a shared root	Root	
			١. مَلْعَب
			٢. مَسْبَح

Speaking

المحادثة

Pick one sporting event that you want to attend at the Schools Olympic competition. Invite your classmates to go with you to watch and see how many you can get to agree. Create a table like the one below and use it to record the results of your conversations.

1. Which sport would you like to watch? Write it down in Arabic or draw a picture.
2. Invite your classmates to go watch with you. How many are going to go?

إن شاء الله	لا	نعم

Activity 14 Reading: Sports in the newspaper

نشاط ١٤   قراءة: الرياضة في الجريدة

In the following activity, you will skim newspaper headlines and try to decide which category each headline belongs to.

Before reading

قبل القراءة

Part of the purpose of this activity is to practice skimming words written in different fonts, so don't worry if you find some fonts harder to read than others—that is normal. With a classmate, brainstorm some of the words you might see in headlines about the following topics:

- Event announcements
- الرياضة
- التكنولوجيا

Create a table that looks like the example on the next page, with 11 rows.

Reading

القراءة

Skim the headlines on the next page, using the following strategies:

1. Look for the word or words in each headline that help you to recognize the topic of the headline. Write each topic in the second column of the table, labeled الكلمات المهمة.
2. For each headline, write a check in the column that shows the category that best fits the topic of the headline based on the words you understood.

Example: In headline 1, you recognize the word السباحة. You write it in the table and then check the column labeled الرياضة because you know that this headline has something to do with sports.

التكنولوجيا	الرياضة	Event announcement	الكلمات المهمة	الرقم
	✔		السباحة	١.
				٢.

١. الأطفال في حاجة إلى تدريبات مكثفة للوصول إلى مستوى آمن في السباحة

٢. الكمبيوتر "يحدد شخصيتك أفضل من الأصدقاء"[5]

٣. **رونالدو: ضمنت صفحة في كتاب عظماء كرة القدم[6]**

٤. قطر تنضم للاتحاد الآسيوي لكرة القدم الأمريكية[7]

٥. **أرخص هاتف إنترنت من مايكروسوفت[8]**

٦. **«ثقافة الوادي الجديد» ينظم إنشطة فنية وثقافية حتى ١٥ يناير[9]**

٧. فلسطيني يسبح بجليد "هدى" تضامنا مع غزة وسوريا[10]

٨. **«الحب والحرب» في مكتبة الإسكندرية الثلاثاء ٢٥ يناير[11]**

٩. مايكروسوفت تطلق "موبايل" يستمر شحنه شهرًا كاملاً[12]

١٠. الشباب مع الحكمة في افتتاح دولية دبي لكرة السلة[13]

١١. **«تطوير الكادر الحكومي».. ندوة بمكتبة القاهرة السبت[14]**

After reading   بعد القراءة

Ask your teacher to help you find an Arabic news source, whether on paper or online, and skim several headlines to sound out words. How many proper nouns or words can you recognize in each headline?

Activity 15 Conversation: Where will you go?   نشاط ١٥ محادثة: أين ستذهب؟

Imagine that you are a travel agent for wealthy clients. Sometimes they aren't sure where they want to travel, so you take an inventory of their interests beforehand and ask them about which activities they want to do while on vacation. Then, you advise them on a good location to travel to based on their interests. For example, if someone really likes swimming and reading, then a trip to a Hawaiian beach may be the best place for them. If they love to shop, then Paris or Dubai might be a better vacation.

Before speaking   قبل المحادثة

Make sure you know how to talk about all of the hobbies in the pictures. When you play the role of travel agent, how will you phrase your question? When you play the role of client, which activities will you say you want to do the most on your trip?

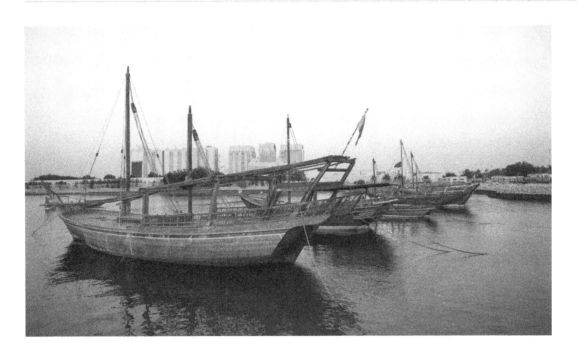

Speaking
المحادثة

Choose a role to start with and start speaking. The "travel agent" will ask the client whether they want to do each of the activities depicted in the icons below. The client will respond with something that indicates their level interest, such as ممكن, لازم, لا, نعم, or أعرف لا.
The travel agent will write down all of the client's responses. Then switch roles conduct the interview again.

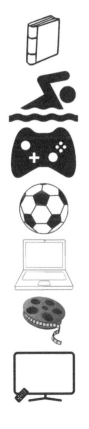

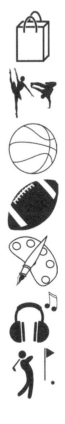

After speaking   بعد المحادثة

Where would you recommend your "client" go on vacation? Write it down and tell them
using the phrase لازم or من اللازم أن, which can also mean "should" in addition to meaning
"must" or "have to."

Activity 16 Listening and conversation: نشاط ١٦   استماع ومحادثة: "لجين
"Lujain, the Jordanian girl"   الأردنّية"

Watch the video of Lujain, a Jordanian girl, talking about some of the things she likes. You
may find some words difficult to understand; this video segment was not scripted for Arabic learners, so Lujain talks at a pace natural to her, uses a wide variety of vocabulary, and
doesn't try to enunciate. It's good practice to listen to native speakers who are not slowing
their speech down too much.

Listening   الاستماع

Create a table like the one below and write any interests you understand in the box on the
left. You may be able to guess some new words from the video as well.

لُجَين	أنا

Speaking   المحادثة

Write down your own interests in the table above. Then share them with your classmates.
Think about letting yourself speak as naturally as Lujain speaks; try to say everything several times until you can do it smoothly.

Activity 17 Conversation: Celebrity   نشاط ١٧   محادثة: هوايات المشاهير
hobbies

In this activity, you will pretend to be famous people and share information about your
hobbies.

Before speaking   قبل المحادثة

What do you know about the hobbies of celebrities? Write down the names of two famous
people you are interested in and learn about hobbies or activities they like to do.

Speaking   المحادثة

You will take on the identity of a celebrity, either a celebrity you researched, or one
assigned to you by your teacher. Assume this identity and speak in the first person about
your hobbies and what you like.

Speaking in Arabic with your classmates one by one, introduce yourselves to each other and talk about what you like to do. When you find another celebrity with at least one hobby in common, write down his or her name and what hobby or hobbies you both like to do in a table like this.

هوايات مشتركة Hobbies in common	الاسم

After speaking   بعد المحادثة

Look at your list of celebrity matches. What activities do you want to do with different celebrities? Tell a classmate in Arabic.

Activity 18 Listening: "Joya, a Lebanese girl"   نشاط ١٨   استماع: "جويا اللبنانيّة"

Watch Joya, a Lebanese teenager, talk about the things she likes to do in her free time. Like Lujain, whom you saw earlier in this lesson, Joya is not trying to slow her speech down for language students to understand. If you feel frustrated, don't worry; it's natural to struggle to understand native speakers when they are speaking quickly. The more you practice listening and recognizing this type of speech, the easier it will become. You will not be able to understand everything; just focus on listening for words you do understand.

Before listening   قبل الاستماع

In this video, Joya is speaking in the Lebanese variety of Arabic. Even if you are not studying informal Arabic in your class, it is helpful to recognize words that are similar in informal and Modern Standard Arabic but pronounced slightly differently.

If you are studying Modern Standard Arabic, review the pronunciation of vocabulary words from this chapter that have a ق in them. How is ق pronounced in Levantine dialect? How will these words sound in Levantine dialect in the video?

Listening   الاستماع

On a separate piece of paper, write down any activities you recognize that Joya mentions she likes to do. Check your answers with a classmate and with your entire class.

After listening   بعد المحادثة

Reflection: You probably noticed that Joya used the word فوتبول rather than كرة القدم. Why do you think she chose to use a foreign word? What do you think this says about how people in Lebanon see English?

Do you read a lot every day?

الدرس الثالث عشر

هل تقرأ كثيراً كلّ يوم؟

LESSON THIRTEEN GOALS

أهداف الدرس الثالث عشر

By the end of this lesson, you should be able to do the following:

- Ask and respond to questions about how much you like particular activities
- Tell how often you do particular activities
- Tell how you feel about doing activities in the future
- Report about what activities other people like to do

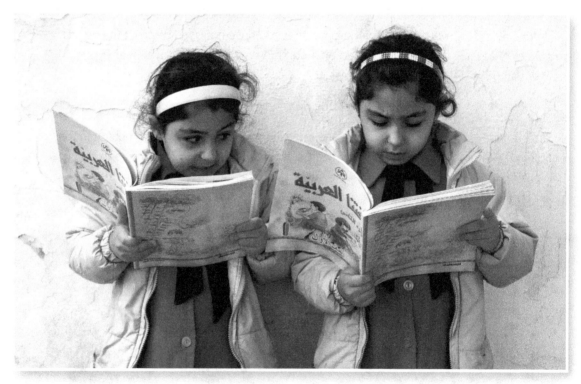

- On which activities do you spend the most time? On which do you spend the least?
- What is the latest fad in hobbies among people you know?
- Are there many hobbies that you hope to try in the future?
- Are there any that you never would try?

HOW MUCH DO YOU LIKE TO DO THIS?

كم تحب أن تفعل هذا؟

Activity 1   Listening: What does Nisreen do in her free time?

نشاط ١   استماع: ماذا تفعل نسرين في وقت الفراغ؟

In this listening activity, you'll practice understanding profiles of some young Jordanians and what they like to do in their free time.

Before listening

قبل الاستماع

Before listening, turn to the Vocabulary 1 list in Lesson Twelve and work with your class-mates to identify the three-letter roots of each of the verbs. Create a table for yourself that looks like this:

الجذر Root	الفعل Verb
د ر س	أدرس

    In this recording, you will hear verb forms that you have not used before, but you will be able to recognize the meaning based on a common root. You may have heard your teacher using these forms already in class.

Listening for general understanding

الاستماع للفهم العام

Number a separate piece of paper from one to seven, with a space for each person in the recording. Listen to the recording to identify the activities that each person likes to do in their free time. Next to each number, write either the letter for the activities that they do based on the images on the next page or the activities each person likes to do in Arabic.

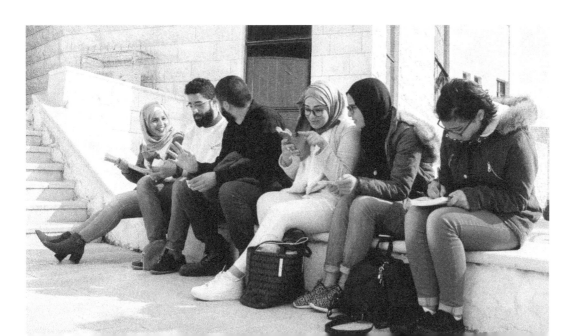

الاسم			
٤. عَلي	٣. نِسْرين	٢. عِماد	١. حُسَيْن
	٧. رَزان	٦. أَحْمَد	٥. نائلة

الهوايات في وقت الفراغ		
a.	b.	c. أصدقاء \ أصحاب
d.	e.	f.
g.	h.	i.
j.	k.	l.
m.	n.	o.
p.		

Close listening   الاستماع الدقيق

How are the verbs in this recording different from what you are familiar with? Write down any ideas you have before continuing to the next section to learn about this with your teacher.[1]

Grammar 1: Verb conjugation: "he" and "she"   القواعد ١: تصريف الأفعال :"هو" و"هي"

In the previous recording, you heard the forms of verbs that describe what "he" and "she" do. Now you will learn to use these conjugations yourself.

Read the below examples aloud. Notice how these forms are both similar to and different from forms that you have already learned.

المعنى	العاميّة الشاميّة	الفصحى
He likes to play . . .	بيحِبّ يِلْعَب...	يُحِبّ أَنْ يَلْعَب...
She likes to play . . .	بِتْحِبّ تِلْعَب...	تُحِبّ أَنْ تَلْعَب...

Now return to the listening in Activity 1 of this lesson and listen to the recording again, paying attention to how the letters ي or تـ are added as a prefix to each of the verbs.

For reference and comparison, here are the forms of these verbs you are familiar with already:

I like to play . . .	بَحِبّ أَلْعَب...	أُحِبّ أَنْ أَلْعَب...
You like to play . . . *(m.)*	بِتْحِبّ تِلْعَب...	تُحِبّ أَنْ تَلْعَب...
You like to play . . . *(f.)*	بِتْحِبّي تِلْعَبي...	تُحِبّين أَنْ تَلْعَبي...

There are more pronouns and verb forms in Arabic; ask your teacher if you would like to know more. Making the different forms of these basic conjugations part of your working knowledge is an essential step toward effective communication in Arabic.

Activity 2 Grammar: "He plays," "she plays"	نشاط ٢ تدريب على القواعد: "يلعب،" "تلعب"

As you have done for the conjugations you have learned already, you will identify in this activity the **stem** of a verb and the **prefixes** and **suffixes** that are added to it. One way to think about the forms of the verb "play" that you see above is as a tree: the **stem** is on the trunk or root of the tree, and the forms with added **prefixes** and **suffixes** are on the branches.

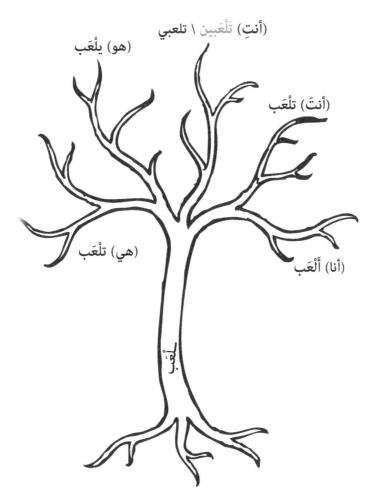

By itself, the stem of this verb is not a word; it needs to be combined with a prefix and/or suffix to a create complete word. Using the following chart or on a separate sheet of paper, write the prefixes and suffixes that are attached to the verb stem for each of these pronouns, as in the example with أنا:

___ هي   ___ هو   ___ أنتِ   ___ أنتَ   أ ___ أنا

Which two forms are the same? Pay attention to these closely, as they can be confusing for learners.

You will continue to practice these forms throughout this chapter and beyond. At first, you will have to think carefully to use these forms correctly, but soon it will become easy. Complete the practice exercises that your teacher assigns to you.

Vocabulary 1   مفردات ١

المعنى	العاميّة الشاميّة	الفصحى
a lot	كْثير	كَثْيراً
a little	شْوَيْ	قَليلاً
but	بَس	وَلْكِن
I prefer (to)	بَفَضِّل	أُفَضِّل (أنْ)

Challenge yourself: Look at this slogan written in dialect on a billboard in Jordan. Can you find the words that have the same roots as كثير and قليل؟

Activity 3   Listening and conversation: استماع ومحادثة: كثيراً أم قليلاً؟   نشاط ٣
A lot or a little?

In this activity, you will listen to the same recording as in Activity 1 ("What does Nisreen do in her free time?"). This time, you'll gather additional information.

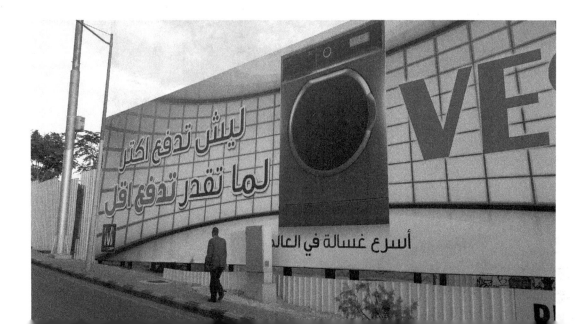

Before listening   قبل الاستماع

Find the chart you filled out while listening to the recording in Activity 1. With a classmate, take turns pointing to each activity in the pictures and saying كثيراً \ كثير if you like it a lot or قليلاً \ شوي if you like it a little.

Listening   الاستماع

Listen to the recording and add any extra information you are able to understand that you didn't understand when you completed Activity 1. How much do the people in the recording like each activity?

Speaking   المحادثة

1. Interview a classmate to find out about how much he or she likes the activities mentioned in the recording. Create a new chart for your classmate. For each activity, ask a follow-up question about whether they like (or dislike) those activities *a lot* or *a little*.

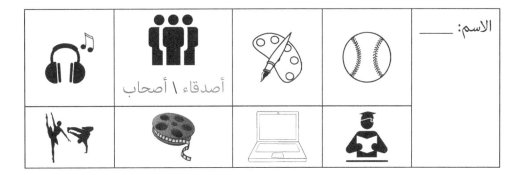

2. Record yourself reporting on your classmate's preferences, trying to imitate the language and tone of the recording.

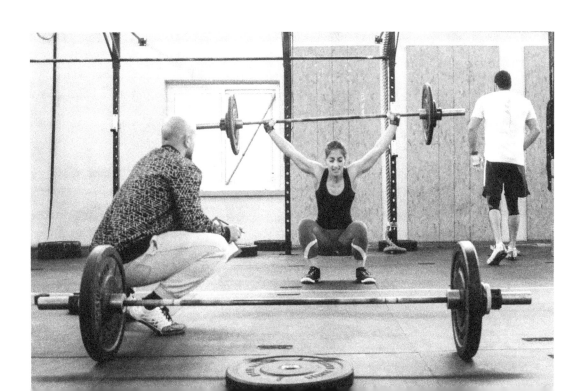

Activity 4   Listening: "Nadine and   نشاط ٤   استماع: "هوايات نادين
            Ashraf's hobbies"   وأشرف"

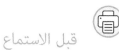

In this activity, you'll learn more about نادين and أشرف.

Before listening   قبل الاستماع

Review what you know about the hobbies of characters featured in videos so far: ياسمين,
تغريد, and عصام. With a classmate, say as many sentences as you can about the characters using the هو and هي forms of the verbs.

Listening for general understanding   الاستماع للفهم العام

Watch the video "هوايات نادين وأشرف" to hear أشرف and نادين discuss their hobbies.
Pay attention to when each person is talking about themselves and when they are talking
about their sibling. Record your notes about the hobbies, likes and activities of each person in a table like this.

أشرف	نادين

Listen as many times as you need to include as many details as possible about each
person's preferences. Check with your classmates to confirm that you understood each
person's preferences, using Arabic.

Close listening   الاستماع الدقيق

Fill in the blanks for the variety you are studying.

الفصحى:

١. [٠:٢٢] نادين: ولكن أشرف من المستحيل أن ____ كرة القدم الأمريكية أو كرة
       السلة. هو لا ____ـهما ابداً!

٢. [٠:٤٥]أشرف: ولكن نادين لا ____ أن ____ الأفلام ولا ____ ومن المستحيل أن ____
       ألعاب الفيديو.

٣. [٠:٥٣]نادين: نعم، ____ أن ألعب الألعاب بالموبايل أحياناً.

العاميّة الشاميّة:

١. [٠:٢٤] نادين: بس أشرف مستحيل ____ ع كرة القدم الأمريكية أو ع كرة السلة.
       هو ما ____ـهم ابداً!

٢. [٠:٤٦]بس نادين ما ____ ع أفلام ولا ____ ومستحيل ____ بلايستايشن.

٣. [٠:٥٣]نادين: آه ____ ألعب ألعاب بالموبايل أحياناً.

After listening   بعد الاستماع

Based on the information you have about the different character's hobbies, write or say six sentences comparing or contrasting different characters' likes and dislikes in different areas.

Culture: Traditional games   الثقافة: الألعاب الشعبية التقليدية

If you walk by a typical local coffeehouse in the Arab world, you are likely to see men (and sometimes women) chatting with friends, reading the newspaper, or playing one of three games. الطاولة (backgammon—literally, "table") is a very popular game. There are several variations, but all involve two players rolling dice to move their pieces to the other side of the board. Historians believe الطاولة is the oldest board game in the world, and early versions of it have been found at different archaeological sites in modern-day Iran and Iraq dating back to 3,000 BC.

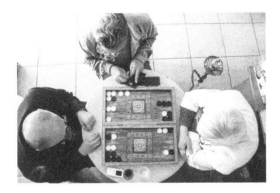
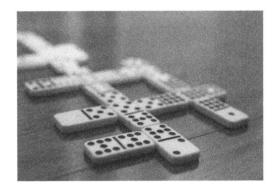

Another game you may see is الدومينو (dominoes), a popular game that originated in China, before the modern version was developed by Italian missionaries in the 18th century. Each player is dealt a hand of seven rectangular tiles, each half of which has between zero and six dots or "pips." The winner is the first person to successfully play all of their tiles.

You're probably already familiar with الشَّطْرَنْج (chess), but you might not know its Middle Eastern origins. الشَّطْرَنْج was invented in Persia (modern-day Iran) and introduced to Western Europe in the 8th century by the Muslims ruling Spain. The phrase "checkmate" to announce one player's victory is a combination of Arabic and Persian: الشاه مات (the shah/king died). الشَّطْرَنْج involves only skill, not a combination of skill and luck like the other two games.

Activity 5   Conversation: Which stars do   نشاط ٥   محادثة: من تحبّ من النجوم؟
              you like?

In this activity, you will practice expressing your preferences and how much you like something.

Before speaking   قبل المحادثة

Before beginning, practice forming the questions and answers that you will use: Start by reviewing the different forms of the verbs أفضّل \ بفضّل and أحب \ بحب that you will use when talking with classmates. Similar to أحبّ \ بحب, the verb أفضّل \ بفضّل often appears

as an indicative (independent) verb in Arabic. In الفصحى, the verb أفضّل can can be followed by أن and a subjunctive (dependent) verb. In العاميّة الشاميّة, the verb بفضّل can take the prefix بـ and be followed by a subjunctive (dependent) verb without the prefix بـ.

For practice, use the items القهوة and الشاي to discuss preferences. Review with a neighbor how you can ask about the following:

1. Whether someone likes coffee a lot
2. Whether someone likes tea a little
3. Whether someone prefers coffee or tea

Speaking   المحادثة

In this exercise, poll each of your classmates to learn their thoughts about two different celebrities. Create a table like the one at the bottom of the page. Write the names of the two celebrities in the two columns, under the numbers 1 and 2. When you interview a classmate, write their name in the right-hand column before asking them whether they like each celebrity. Follow up to learn how much they like each celebrity, and which celebrity they prefer, using the following as a model for your follow-up questions:

Do you like ____ a lot or a little? (m.)	بِتْحِبّ ____ كْثير ولّا شْوَي؟	هَل تُحِبّ ____ كَثيراً أَم قَليلاً؟
Do you like ____ a lot or a little? (f.)	بِتْحِبّي ____ كْثير ولّا شْوَي؟	هَل تُحِبّين ____ كَثيراً أَم قَليلاً؟
Do you prefer ____ or ____? (m.)	بِتْفَضّل ____ ولّا ____؟	هَل تُفَضّل ____ أَم ____؟
Do you prefer ____ or ____? (f.)	بِتْفَضّلي ____ ولّا ____؟	هَل تُفَضّلين ____ أَم ____؟

Make sure that you ask and respond to questions using full sentences. Record each person's answer in the table. When you have talked with enough people, calculate the total numbers of each of the different opinions.

	2			1		
	:الاسم _____			:الاسم _____		
هل يفضّل / تفضّل...؟	هل يحب \ تحب...؟		هل يفضّل / تفضّل...؟	هل يحب \ تحب...؟		الاسم ↓
	كثيراً	قليلاً		كثيراً	قليلاً	

After speaking   بعد المحادثة

Once you have spoken with enough people and recorded their responses in your chart,
review the information you collected. Calculate how many classmates like each celebrity
a lot and how many like each celebrity a little. Then, calculate how many classmates prefer each celebrity. You will prepare to give a short report on what you learned: describe
the opinion of at least three different classmates and of the class as a whole. Use these
phrases to make general statements about the class's opinion:

| The class likes . . . | الصَّفّ بيحِبّ... | الصَّفّ يُحِبّ... |
| The class prefers . . . | الصَّفّ بيفَضِّل... | الصَّفّ يُفَضِّل... |

In your spoken report, compare your classmate's opinions with your own opinion, using the
words you know for "also" and "but." When you are ready, record your report as an audio
file and send it to your teacher.

Activity 6   Conversation: I like soccer, but   محادثة: أحب كرة القدم ولكنّي   نشاط ٦
             I prefer basketball   أفضّل كرة السلة

In this activity, you will practice telling which hobbies you like more than others.

Before speaking   قبل المحادثة

On a separate piece of paper, draw a large circle and write your name in the middle. Select
five different hobbies or activities that you have **different** opinions about (positive, negative,
or in between) and sketch a symbol for each one around your name. Here is an example
diagram drawn by a student named Nancy:

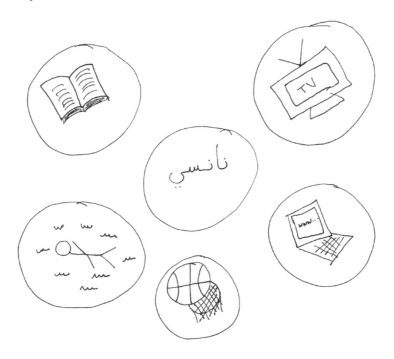

Before speaking with your classmates, independently practice speaking in full sentences to tell how much you like or dislike the hobbies on your drawing.

Speaking   المحادثة

In this activity, you will work with a classmate. Don't forget to exchange greetings and ask how your classmate is doing before you start the conversation about hobbies! Ask your classmate about the hobbies on their diagram. Make sure that you ask follow-up questions to gather information about which activities they prefer and how much they like (or dislike) each activity. Try to extend the conversation as long as possible. What other follow-up questions about the hobbies or activities in the person's diagram could you ask?

Find two more classmates and repeat this conversation. For each person, write or draw the activities they tell you about in a table, ordered from most to least liked.

Challenge yourself: If you are confused about which of two activities a person likes, ask clarifying questions in Arabic.

طالب ٣	طالب ٢	طالب ١	
			Most liked ↑ ↓ Least liked

After speaking   بعد المحادثة

Prepare a short oral presentation about the preferences of one of the people you spoke with in the previous conversation. Talk about their likes and dislikes and indicate their preferences. Record your statement and send the recording to your teacher for evaluation.

Challenge yourself: Compare and contrast that person's opinions with your own, using word such as بس / لكن and كمان / أيضاً.

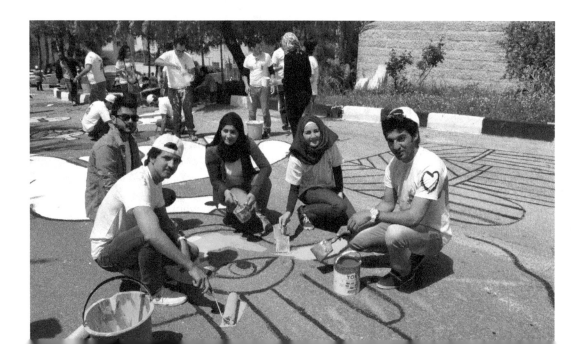

DO YOU DO THAT EVERY DAY?

Vocabulary 2

هل تفعل هذا كلّ يوم؟

مفردات ٢

المعنى	العاميّة الشاميّة	الفصحى
sometimes	أَحْياناً	أَحْياناً
always	دائماً	دائماً
every day	كُلّ يوم	كُلّ يَوْم
every week	كُلّ أُسْبوع	كُلّ أُسْبوع

Activity 7   Conversation: Honestly? You really do that?

نشاط ٧   محادثة: هل حقّاً تفعل هذا؟

In this activity, you'll practice asking your classmates more questions about their hobbies and interests.

Before speaking

قبل المحادثة

Review the names of the days of the week that you learned in Unit 2. Share with a class-mate the following information:

- An activity you want to do today
- An activity you want to do tomorrow
- An activity you want to do the day after tomorrow

Speaking

المحادثة

Think back to what you have already learned about your classmates when asking them about their hobbies in earlier conversations. Now you will learn about how much (and how often) they actually do those activities. For example, if someone likes to read, you can ask one of these two questions:

Do you always read? (m.)	إِنْتَ دائماً بْتِقْرا؟	هَل أَنْتَ دائماً تَقْرا؟
Do you always read? (f.)	إِنْتِ دائماً بْتِقْرَأي؟	هَل أَنْتِ دائماً تَقْرَأين؟
Do you actually read? (m.)	عَن جَدّ إِنْتَ بْتِقْرا؟	هَل أَنْتَ حَقّاً تَقْرا؟
Do you actually read? (f.)	عَن جَدّ إِنْتِ بْتِقْرَأي؟	هَل أَنْتِ حَقّاً تَقْرَأين؟

If you hear someone saying something that seems impressive, unlikely, or hard to believe, you can express your skepticism with the following question. If you want to affirm that what you are saying is true, you can respond with the same word.

| Really?
(literally: swear to God?) | وَاللّٰه؟ | وَاللّٰه؟ |
| Yes, really! | آه، وَاللّٰه! | نَعَم، وَاللّٰه! |

Ask follow-up questions to the classmates who have already told you about their hobbies to find out exactly when they do these activities. Be specific in your questions and find out how often each week and which days of the week the person does each activity. Record the information you learn on a separate piece of paper. Speak with at least two people.

Challenge yourself: Find out how many hours the person spends each day on each activity.

After speaking   بعد المحادثة

Choose one of the people you spoke with and create a weekly schedule for them, labeled with the days of the week. On each day, draw a picture or write a word in Arabic to indicate the activity they do and how much time they spend on it.

Activity 8   Reading and conversation: نشاط ٨   قراءة ومحادثة: أين في العالم
              Where in the world do people   يقرأ الناس كثيراً؟
              read a lot?

Different cultures emphasize different types of media consumption. In this activity, you'll learn about the media habits of some people from around the world.

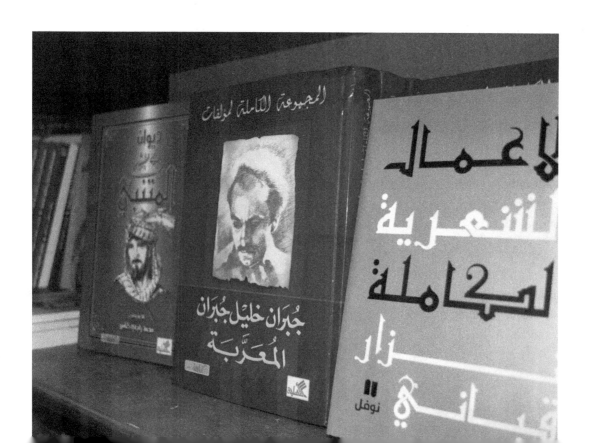

Before reading, tell a classmate how much time you spend with the following types of media:

For each kind of media activity, do you do it always? Never? Every day? How many hours do you spend on each activity every week?

In the following pages, there are several charts that shows the amount of time that four people from around the world spend with different kinds of media each week. (Each person's usage is close to the average usage in his or her country in 2005.)[2]

Your teacher will assign you one table (و, ا, or ي) to read. First, read about the four people on your table. Be ready to write or say a few statements about the people on your table:

1. Who uses a particular kind of media *a lot* or *a little* each week, compared with the others?
2. For each person, which kind of media besides television do they *prefer*?

When you are done, use Arabic to check your answers with a classmate who has the same table.

Find a classmate who has a different table than you and do the following steps:

3. Ask your classmate questions about the people on their table, including where they are from and how many hours they consume each type of media each week.
4. Write the information on the second page of your chart.

Repeat these steps with a classmate who has the third chart. At this point, all eight rows on the second page of your chart should be complete.

Now that the information on your chart is complete, work independently to answer the following questions about the whole group of people. For each person, write their name and their country of origin.

5. Who goes on the internet a lot?
6. Who goes on the internet a little?
7. Who listens to the radio a lot?
8. Who listens to the radio a little?
9. Who reads a lot?

10. Who reads a little?
11. Who watches TV a lot?
12. Who watches TV a little?

After reading   بعد القراءة

Prepare a short presentation about some of the information in the table. Choose one of the people whose information you gathered from a classmate. Describe that person's media usage in detail, addressing each of the questions below. Record this presentation as an audio file and send it to your teacher to check.

13. How many hours does the person spend on each type of media each week?
14. Which type(s) of media do they prefer?
15. Do you think that they consume each media type a lot or a little?

| جدول ١ | | | | |
| كم ساعة في الأسبوع...؟ | | | | |
أستخدم الكمبيوتر أو أدخل في الإنترنت	أقرأ	أستمع إلى الراديو	أُشاهد التلفزيون	
١٠ ساعات	٨ ساعات	٩ ساعات	٢١ ساعة	اسمه: عُمَر من مصر
١٣ ساعة	٥ ساعات	٥ ساعات	١٩ ساعة	اسمه: شيا هاو من تايوان
١٢ ساعة	٦ ساعات	١٠ ساعات	١٦ ساعة	اسمها: مارتا من إسبانيا
٩ ساعات	٦ ساعات	٢١ ساعة	١٤ ساعة	اسمه: بَنيسيو من الأرجنتين

جدول و كم ساعة في الأسبوع...؟				
أستخدم الكمبيوتر أو أدخل في الإنترنت	أقرأ	أستمع إلى الراديو	أُشاهد التلفزيون	
٩ ساعات	٧ ساعات	٤ ساعات	١٨ ساعة	اسمه: محمد من السعودية
١٠ ساعات	٣ ساعات	٣ ساعات	١٥ ساعة	اسمها: سيو هيون من كوريا
٩ ساعات	٦ ساعات	١٠ ساعات	١٩ ساعة	اسمه: إيثان من أمريكا
١١ ساعة	٨ ساعات	ساعتين ٢	١٦ ساعة	اسمها: ماي من الصين

جدول ي كم ساعة في الأسبوع...؟				
أستخدم الكمبيوتر أو أدخل في الإنترنت	أقرأ	أستمع إلى الراديو	أُشاهد التلفزيون	
٦ ساعات	٦ ساعات	١١ ساعة	١٢ ساعة	اسمه: فرانسيسكو من المكسيك
١٢ ساعة	٩ ساعات	١٣ ساعة	٢٢ ساعة	اسمها: نان من تايلاند
٨ ساعات	١١ ساعة	٤ ساعات	١٣ ساعة	اسمها: تانفي من الهند
٦ ساعات	٦ ساعات	٧ ساعات	١٥ ساعة	اسمه: ماركو من إيطاليا

Activity 9   Listening: "What do you like to read?"   نشاط ٩   استماع: "شو بتحبي تقرأي؟"

In the video "شو بتحبي تقرأي؟" you'll see رابة and تغريد talk about some of their interests.

Before listening   قبل الاستماع

Watch the video "شو بتحبي تقرأي؟" for a few seconds to see who is in the video. Pause the video and tell a classmate as much as you remember about any of the characters onscreen in Arabic.

Listening   الاستماع

Listen and write down what رابة and تغريد like to do in their free time. When you have written down as many hobbies as you can understand, create a Venn diagram like the one below to show the overlap in their hobbies.

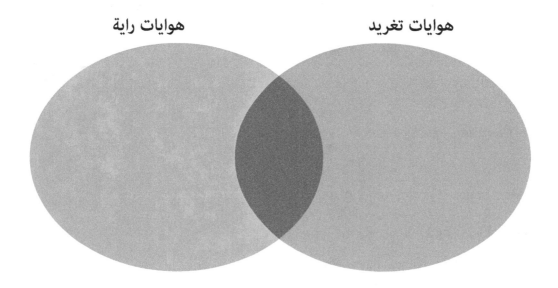

هوايات رابة   هوايات تغريد

After listening   بعد الاستماع

Check the information in your Venn diagram by comparing with a classmate. Use the words ولكن / بس if رابة and تغريد like different activities, and the words أيضاً / كمان if they like the same activities:

رابة بتْحِبّ ___، بَس تغْريد ما بِتْحِبّ ___.	رابة تُحِبّ ___، وَلٰكِن تَغْريد لا تُحِبّ ___.
تَغْريد بتْحِبّ ___، ورابة كَمان بِتْحِبّ ___.	تَغْريد تُحِبّ ___، ورابة أيْضاً تُحِبّ ___.

Challenge yourself: تغريد mentioned several Arab authors she enjoys. Who are they? Research one of them online.

Vocabulary 3   مفردات ٣

المعنى	العامِيّة الشامِيّة	الفصحى
It is possible that . . . Might . . . Maybe . . .	مُمْكِن...	مِن المُمْكِن أَنْ...
Must . . . Have to . . . Should . . .	لازِم...	مِن اللازِم أَنْ...
It is impossible that . . . Definitely won't . . .	مُسْتَحيل...	مِن المُسْتَحيل أَنْ...

After each of these phrases, you should use a subjunctive (dependent) verb. Remember
that this means that in الفصحى, verbs conjugated for أنتِ will take the suffix ـي, while in
العامِيّة الشامِيّة, verbs will not take the prefix بـ.

Activity 10 Conversation: I definitely won't   نشاط ١٠   محادثة: مِن المستحيل أن
see that movie!   أشاهد هذا الفيلم!

In this activity, you'll exchange opinions about movies with your classmates.

Before speaking   قبل المحادثة

On a separate sheet of paper, brainstorm a list of movie titles that you have seen recently
and some favorite movies that you have seen in the past. Make sure your list of movies
includes some movies you like a lot and some that you do not like.

Challenge yourself: Sort the list that you make into genres. Here is a list of some film
genres; you will notice that most of these words are similar to English:

- أَفْلام دْراما
- أَفْلام رومانْسِيّة

- أَفْلام أَكْشَن
- أَفْلام كوميدِيا
- أَفْلام تَشْويق (thriller / suspense)

Speaking   المحادثة

Talk with a classmate and exchange advice and recommendations about what movies to
see from your lists. Write what you hear from them on a separate sheet of paper. You can
use the following phrases:

لازِم تِتْفَرَّج / تِتْفَرَّجي عَلى...	مِن اللازِم أَنْ تُشاهِد / تُشاهِدي...
مُمْكِن تِتْفَرَّج / تِتْفَرَّجي عَلى...	مِن المُمْكِن أَنْ تُشاهِد / تُشاهِدي...

Challenge yourself: Extend your conversation.

- Give your opinion of the movie using words like "good" or "excellent."
- Ask who is in the movie, if you haven't seen it already.
- Tell what genres you like and dislike.

After speaking　　بعد المحادثة

After your conversation, review the movies you wrote down. Write or say your reactions to six of the movies, including the following information:

- Two movies you must watch
- Two movies you might watch
- Two movies you definitely won't watch

Grammar 2: He wants to, she wants to　　القواعد ٢: يريد أن، تريد أن

You have learned how to say "I want to" and "you want to" when addressing others. How do you say "he wants to" and "she wants to"? Extend your knowledge from the other forms that you have learned: on a separate sheet of paper, create conjugation charts or conjugation trees with your classmates and check them with your teacher. Here are some reminders about grammar:

If you are learning Modern Standard Arabic: You can use the phrase أُريد أنْ and combine it with other verbs, in the same way that is possible with أُحِبّ أنْ. When used in this way, أُريد will follow the indicative (independent) verb pattern, while the verb that comes after أن will follow the subjunctive (dependent) verb pattern.

If you are learning Levantine dialect: Remember that بدّي and its other forms (بدَّك, etc.) are not technically verbs. Instead of taking verb prefixes and suffixes, it takes the possessive pronoun endings. Verbs that come directly after بدّي and its other forms should follow the subjunctive (dependent) pattern and not take the prefix بـ.

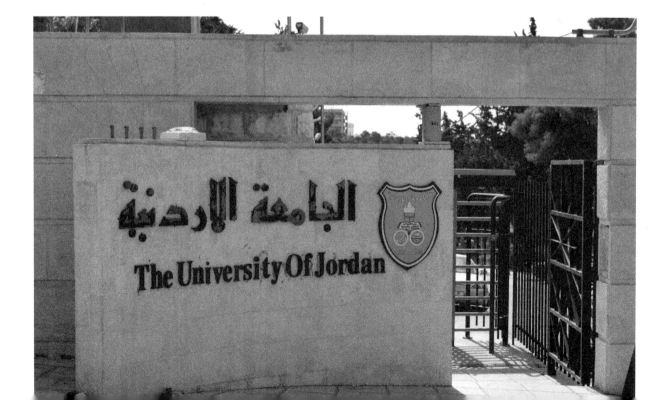

Activity 11 Conversation: In college   نشاط ١١   محادثة: في الجامعة

In this exercise, you will converse with a college advisor about the activities you might do when you go to college.

Before speaking   قبل المحادثة

On a separate sheet of paper, record some ideas about:

- Three to five activities you want to do in college
- Two to three activities you do not want to do in college

Speaking   المحادثة

You will work with a classmate, with one person playing the role of a college advisor and one person playing the role of a high school student who is their advisee.

College advisor: Ask your advisee what they want to do in college. You can use the phrases:

in college	بالجامْعة	في الجامِعة
What do you want to do in college? *(m.)*	شو بِدَّك تِعْمَل بِالجامْعة؟	ماذا تُريد أَنْ تَفْعَل في الجامِعة؟
What do you want to do in college? *(f.)*	شو بِدِّك تِعْمَلي بِالجامْعة؟	ماذا تُريدين أَنْ تَفْعَلي في الجامِعة؟

Client: Tell your college advisor what you want or do not want to do in college. You can use the phrases:

in college	بالجامْعة	في الجامِعة
In college, I want to . . .	بِالجامْعة، بدّي...	في الجامِعة، أُريد أَنْ...

Find a new classmate and repeat. Switch roles, such that you play the role of college advisor at least twice and gather the preferences of at least two students.

Continue speaking   واصلوا المحادثة

Playing the role of a college advisor, meet with another classmate also playing the role of a college advisor. Report what you learned about your advisees, using the following structures:

	بِالجامْعة، بِدُّه...	في الجامِعة، يُريد أَنْ...
	بِالجامْعة، بِدّها...	في الجامِعة، تُريد أَنْ...

With your classmate, give recommendations for where each advisee should study in college. Use the word لازم to mean "should" if you are confident in your recommendation and ممكن to mean "might" or "could" if you are less certain.

After speaking   بعد المحادثة

After practicing, record your recommendations about the two people you talked with during part as a voice message and send it to your teacher for evaluation.

Activity 12   Reading and conversation: نشاط ١٢   قراءة ومحادثة: النوادي!
            Clubs!

In this activity, you will talk with your classmates to find people to join a club نادي based on your shared interests. For this activity, instead of using your own interests, you will take on an identity that your teacher gives you.

Reading   القراءة

When you receive the sheet of paper describing your interests, do the following:

1. Choose a new name for yourself.
2. Read each of the statements to understand "your" opinions about different hobbies.
3. Take special note of the hobbies that you strongly like or dislike, as these will be important to finding people with corresponding interests.

Challenge yourself: Add details to your assumed identity. For example, if your sheet says you like watching TV, add some details about what kind of TV you like.

Speaking   المحادثة

Talk with your classmates one by one to learn about what activities they like and dislike. Your goal is to identify people who have similar or compatible interests and to form a نادي with them. Talk with many different people. If you have common interests with any of them, record their name and your common interests in a table like this one:

الاهتمامات المشتركة Shared interests	الاسم

After speaking   بعد المحادثة

After speaking with many people, join together in a group with three to five people who share at least one interest. Your task is to form a club with these people; talk with them in Arabic to decide what kind of club you will form. Working together with the other members of ناديكُم (your club), create a poster advertising your club. Use images and text to show the activities of the club. Add other details, such as when and where you will meet.

Sometimes I go to . . .

الدرس الرابع عشر

أحياناً أذهب إلى...

LESSON FOURTEEN GOALS

أهداف الدرس الرابع عشر

By the end of this lesson, you should be able to do the following:

- Ask and respond to questions about the places that you go to during a typical week
- Explain why you go places in a typical day or week
- Tell what order you do different activities in
- Report information about others' daily schedules

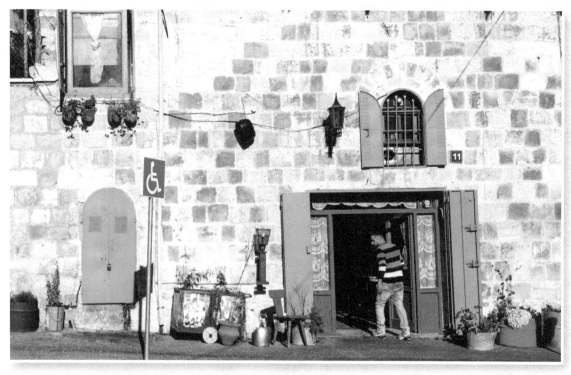

- Where do you spend most of your time?
- What are your favorite places in your city?
- Are there places to which you like to go alone or prefer to invite company?

225

WHERE DO YOU GO EVERY DAY?

Vocabulary 1

أين تذهب كلّ يوم؟

مفردات ١

المعنى	العاميّة الشاميّة	الفصحى
the house (the) home*	البَيْت	البَيْت
(the) school	المَدْرَسة	المَدْرَسة
the library the bookstore	المَكْتَبة	المَكْتَبة
(the) work	الشُّغُل	العَمَل
the restaurant	المَطْعَم	المَطْعَم
the field the stadium	المَلْعَب	المَلْعَب
the café	القَهْوة‡ الكافيه§	المَقْهى

*The nouns in this list with "(the)" before them are usually definite in Arabic when used to say where an activity is taking place. For example, "I study at home" is usually expressed as أدرس في البيت and "I go to school" as أذهب إلى المدرسة. You will learn more about this in نشاط 1.

‡This refers to a traditional café.

§This refers to a European-style café.

Activity 1   Conversation: Hello, is Sawsan home?

نشاط ١   محادثة: ألو، هل سوسن في البيت؟

In this activity, you will be making calls and answering the telephone to find out the where-abouts of your friends.

Before speaking

قبل المحادثة

Quiz a classmate on the names of places from the vocabulary. Say the word in Arabic and have your classmate point to the corresponding image below.

Speaking

المحادثة

d. أُسامة	c. رَمزي	b. رامي	a. سَوْسَن
h. رَزان	g. حَنا	f. إلياس	e. رَشيد

Your teacher will give you a slip of paper with the whereabouts of half of the people above. With a partner, act out phone conversations in which you imagine that you are calling the home phone number of the other four friends to find out where they are. Write their responses in the spaces on the slip of paper given to you. Do not forget to greet the person answering the phone and thank them before hanging up. In Arabic, a person picking up the phone will generally start the conversation by saying أَلو.

After speaking   بعد المحادثة

Look at the places you wrote down and at the vocabulary list. You will notice that most of these words begin with الـ in Arabic, even though "the" might not typically be used with equivalent expressions in English. For example, "at school" in English is usually expressed as في المدرسة in Arabic. Usage of the definite article varies between English and Arabic, and mastering the underlying grammatical patterns is often challenging for non-native speakers of either language. With a classmate, practice saying where each person is again, being sure to use الـ correctly in Arabic.

نشاط ٢   محادثة: أين أنت في الساعة...؟   Activity 2   Conversation: Where are you at . . . o'clock?

In this activity, you will tell your classmates your whereabouts at certain times of the day.

Before speaking   قبل المحادثة

On a separate sheet of paper, create a table like the one below. In the middle column, write down (in Arabic) your whereabouts on a typical Tuesday at each given time.

يوم الثلاثاء		
أين صديقي \ صديقتي؟	أين أنا؟	الساعة
		٦:٠٠ صباحاً
		٩:١٥ صباحاً
		١٢:٠٠ ظهراً
		٣:٣٠ بعد الظهر
		٦:٠٠ مساءً
		٨:٤٥ مساءً

Speaking   المحادثة

Ask questions of a classmate to find out where they are at certain times and record their whereabouts in the left-hand column of your table. Don't forget to say أنا أيضاً or أنا كمان when you find yourselves at the same place at the same time.

After speaking
بعد المحادثة

Your classmate from the previous exercise forgot their cell phone. Since you were with them last, their parents contact you to ask their whereabouts. Respond to text messages from their parents and remember to pay attention to the time!

الفصحى:

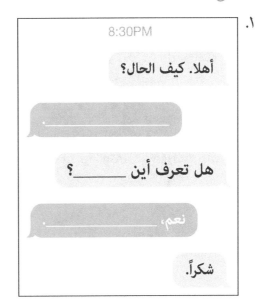

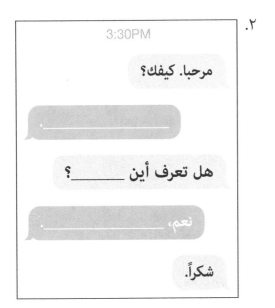

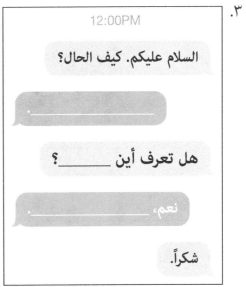

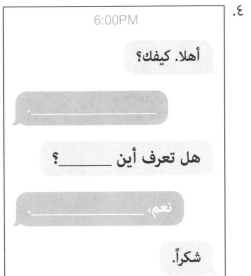

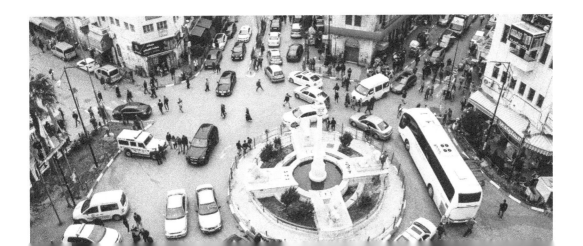

العاميّة الشاميّة:

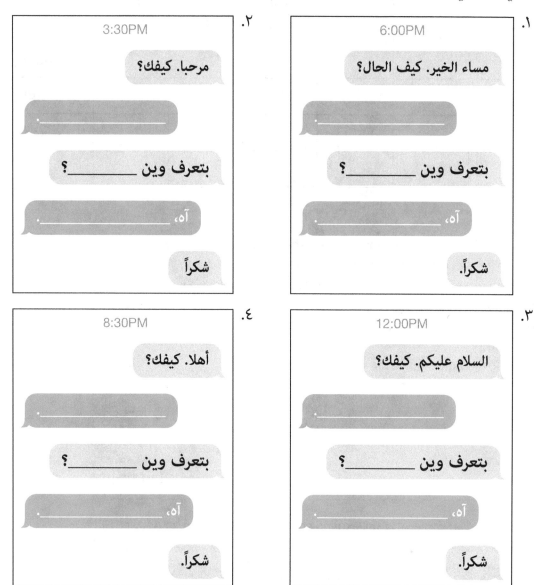

Imagine that an Arab exchange student is coming to live with you and your family. The exchange organization has asked you to draw up a simple weekly schedule in Arabic.

Before writing   قبل القراءة

On a separate sheet of paper, create a schedule like the one on the next page. In each box of the schedule, record the following information:

1. Where you are likely to be at that time
2. What you are likely to be doing if it is something you know how to say in Arabic

	يوم الأحد	يوم الاثنين	يوم الثلاثاء	يوم الأربعاء	يوم الخميس	يوم الجمعة	يوم السبت
الصباح							
بعد الظهر							
المساء							
الليل							

Writing   الكتابة

Some study abroad organizations like to know the schedule of potential host families so they can match them with an exchange student who shares similar interests. Write a draft note to a study abroad organization that summarizes your weekly schedule in several sentences. (If you are studying العاميّة الشاميّة, remember that you should use the indicative (independent) verb pattern, beginning with the prefix بـ, when you talk about regular, habitual activities.)

You can use the following sentence starters to help you:

في الصباح، أنا...
من يوم الاثنين إلى يوم الجمعة، أنا...
في الليل، أحياناً أنا... وأحياناً أنا...

Be sure to save what you wrote. You will expand on it later in this lesson, in Activity 19.

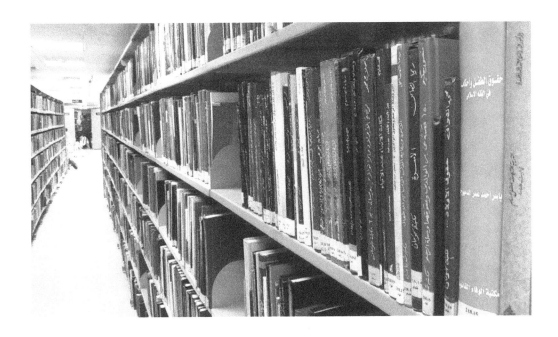

Grammar 1: Place name pattern

القواعد ١: اسم المكان

In the previous lessons, you have gained some exposure to roots. You have learned that words that share the same root are often related in core meaning. For example, أَسبَح and السِباحة are both related to swimming. They both share the same three letter root, س-ب-ح. What other words have you noticed that sound alike?

In Arabic there are also *patterns*. These are specific combinations of letters and short vowels that are added to roots to create particular meanings. In English, when you add the suffix *–er* to many verbs, as in "swim*er*," "read*er*," and "think*er*," you create a word meaning someone or something that performs the action expressed by the verb. Likewise, if you attach the prefix *inter-* to certain words, it adds the meaning of "between," as in "*inter*national," "*inter*change," and "*inter*action." In Arabic, it is common for patterns to add letters to the beginning, end, and/or middle of roots—not just the beginning or end, as in English. The three root letters will remain in the word.

Look back at the vocabulary list. What do مَطعَم and مَلعَب have in common? The shared consonants and vowels that are not part of the root of these words make up the pattern. Your teacher may want to discuss this more with you in class; it is something you will learn much more about if you keep studying Arabic. The concept is extremely important in Arabic, and once you crack this code of patterns, you will be able to make more informed guesses as to the meaning of unfamiliar words and learn vocabulary more easily.

Vocabulary 2

مفردات ٢

المعنى	العاميّة الشاميّة	الفصحى
my friend's house (m.)	بَيت صاحْبي	بَيت صَديقي
my friend's house (f.)	بَيت صاحِبْتي	بَيت صَديقَتي
the shopping mall	المول	مَركَز التَّسَوُّق
downtown	وَسْط البَلَد	وَسَط البَلَد
the club (sports or social club)	النّادي	النّادي
the movie theater the cinema	السّينَما	السّينَما
the market (traditional open-air market or shopping district)	السّوق	السّوق
with me	مَعي	مَعي

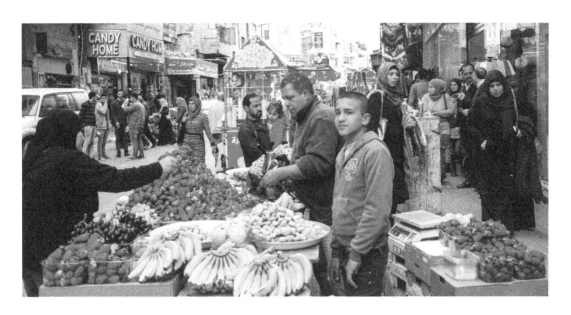

نشاط ٤	استماع: هل تريد أن تجيء معي؟	Activity 4 Listening: Do you want to come with me?

In this activity, you'll listen to a series of voice messages about making plans.

Before listening   قبل الاستماع

Before listening, look over the images of different places. With a classmate, say at least one phrase or sentence about each image.

a.   b.   c.

d.   e.   f.

g.   h.   i.

On a separate sheet of paper, create a table like the one below with nine rows.

معلومات آخرى	اليوم والساعة	الصورة (.a، .b، .c...)
		١.
		٢.

Listening   الاستماع

You will hear a series of nine voice messages. Listen as many times as you need to in order to fill out your table, following the instructions below.

1. Write down the day of the week and time mentioned in the message.
2. Jot down any other details you understand, such as the name of the individual calling and other things mentioned.

After listening   بعد الاستماع

Using your notes, pretend you are relaying each message to the person for whom it was intended. Recreate a new voice message talking *about* the person. For example, "Mohammed wants to go to the club today at 12:00pm." Remember to conjugate verbs for هو and هي.

Grammar 2: Possessive construction   القواعد ٢: الإضافة

As you have noticed in expressions like بيت صديقي / بيت صاحبي from the new vocabulary, Arabic neither uses apostrophes (as in "my friend's house") nor requires an additional word (as in "the house *of* my friend") to express possession. How do we tell when something belongs to someone in Arabic? Look at the examples below that show possession, and go over how to pronounce them with your teacher:

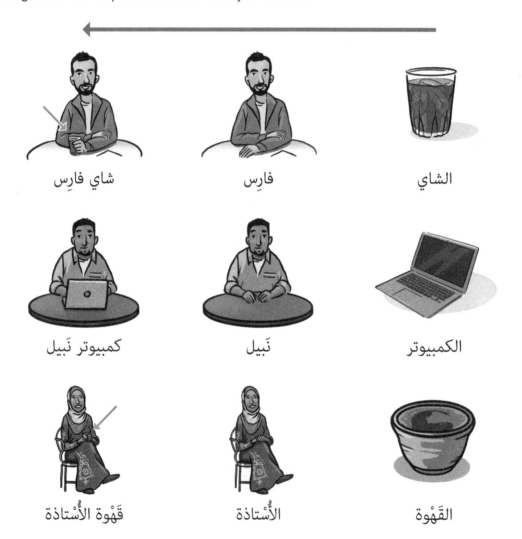

شاي فارِس	فارِس	الشاي
كمبيوتر نَبيل	نَبيل	الكمبيوتر
قَهْوة الأُسْتاذة	الأُسْتاذة	القَهْوة

The combinations of words in the left column that show possession are all examples of the grammatical construction called الإضافة. You have seen this construction before,

in phrases such as ولاية ألاباما and مَدينة سان فرانْسيسْكو. This is the way to express possession or belonging in Arabic. What do you notice about the pronunciation of the ة in the first word of an إضافة phrase?

Finally, notice that the first word of this construction never has the definite article in Arabic, الـ. Remember to drop the الـ on the first word when you form الإضافة.

Activity 5   Practicing grammar: نشاط ٥   تدريب على القواعد: الإضافة
           Possessive construction

Now practice this new structure by figuring out how to say the following concepts. Use the examples from your class discussion as models.

1. Pizza restaurant
2. Sam's house
3. Sports club
4. The Shawnee School
5. The tea market
6. Starbucks Café
7. Susan's (female) friend
8. Barnes and Noble Bookstore

Challenge yourself: Try to create these phrases:

9. Soccer stadium
10. Maria's teacher's house

Activity 6   Conversation: The biggest US   نشاط ٦   محادثة: أكبر المطاعم الأمريكية
           fast-food chains in the world   للوجبات السريعة في العالم

In this activity, you will find out which US fast food restaurants or cafés have the most stores worldwide.

Before speaking   قبل المحادثة

1. Tell a classmate what you think the top three US fast food chains are, using the إضافة construction. For example, you could say: مطعم تشيبوتليه رقم واحد.
2. Practice reading the list of chains that are in the top twelve. Do not forget to add "restaurant" or "café" before the name and to pay attention to pronunciation.
3. Guess their world popularity by ranking them from one to twelve on a separate piece of paper.

Ranking (Actual)	Ranking (Guess)	اسم المَطْعَم
		دَنْكِن دونَتْس
		آرْبيز

Ranking (Actual)	Ranking (Guess)	اسم المَطْعَم
		ماكْدونالْدز
		بَرْجَر كينْج
		تاكو بَل
		ستارْبَكْس
		بيتْزا هَت
		دومينوز
		ديري كْوين
		كَي أف سي (دجاج كنتاكي)
		صَبواي
		بابا جونْز

Speaking   المحادثة

4. Your teacher will distribute the numerical order for these restaurants. Exchange the ranking you received with a classmate, remembering to use this structure for your statements:

مطعم ـــــ رقم ـــــ.

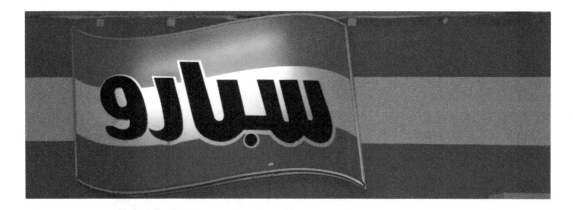

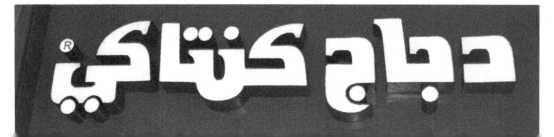

Continue speaking   واصلوا المحادثة

5. Choose two of your favorite restaurants and cafes from this list. Ask your classmates if they like them and which one they prefer. Write down their answers in a
table like the one below:

2				1				
اسم المطعم: ـــــــــــــــــ				اسم المطعم: ـــــــــــــــــ				اسم الطالب ↓
	يحبّ/تحبّ؟				يحبّ/تحبّ؟			
يفضّل / تفضّل؟	كثيراً	قليلاً	لا	يفضّل / تفضّل؟	كثيراً	قليلاً	لا	

After speaking   بعد المحادثة

6. Talk with someone you didn't interview already. Report on your classmates' preferences. Remember to use the proper form of the verb for هو and هي.

7. Tell your classmate: what restaurant does the class prefer? Remember that you
can use the phrases:

The class likes . . .	الصَّفّ بيحِبّ...	الصَّفّ يُحِبّ...
The class prefers . . .	الصَّفّ بيفَضِّل...	الصَّفّ يُفَضِّل...

Activity 7   Reading: What's in this hotel?   قراءة: ماذا يوجد في هذا الفندق؟   نشاط ٧

The following reading includes information about a hotel's amenities.

Before reading   قبل القراءة

With a classmate, take turns answering the following questions:

1. Where would you like to travel and stay in a hotel?

2. What amenities do you want to have there? For example, a pool, a club . . .

You can use the following word and phrase:

hotel	فُنْدُق	فُنْدُق
In the hotel, I want . . .	بِالفُنْدُق، بِدّي...	في الفُنْدُق، أُريد...

Reading

القراءة

As you read, answer the following:

3. What words for places and amenities do you recognize? Circle them all.

4. What other information can you figure out? Look for loan words from English.

5. What words do you see that may share roots with words that you have learned before?

6. In the last category of this list are some numbers followed by كم; can you guess what this might be? (Hint: it is *not* the word for "how much.")

7. Look over the names of places you were able to find. Are any of them in the إضافة structure? If so, underline them. Practice reading them aloud, paying attention to the proper pronunciation.

Challenge yourself: If you studied the patterns for places more in depth, circle the words that follow the placename pattern (مَفعلة or مَفعل).

الفندق[1]

العمل عن بعد	الطعام والشراب
• مركز لرجال الأعمال	• ٧ مطاعم (مطعم إفطار فيه مخبز خاص) بوفيه للغداء يوميًا
• مكتب في الغرف	• بار/استراحة
• مركز المؤتمرات	• كافيتيريا
• محطة كمبيوتر	• بار على المسبح
	• خدمة الغرف على مدار ٢٤ ساعة
الخدمات	• مقهى في مدخل الفندق
• مكتب استقبال مفتوح ٢٤ ساعة	• متجر للطعام
• خدمات الكونسيرج	• مصرف مفتوح ٢٤ ساعة
ماذا يوجد في الجوار؟	**أنشطة يمكن ممارستها**
• سوق مدينة جميرا (١.١ كم)	• مسبح مكشوف
• ملعب دبي لكرة القدم (١ كم)	• بار على حمام السباحة
• مركز تسوق لجميرا (٤.١ كم)	• نادي صحي
• شاطئ (٥.٠ كم)	• ملعب الجولف في الموقع
• موقف للحافلات والمواصلات العامة (٢.٠ كم)	• ملعب التنس في الموقع
• متحف دبي (٣.٠ كم)	• نادي صحي متكامل الخدمات
	• ساونا
	• نادي ليلي
	• دروس البيلاتيس
	• طاولة بلياردو
	• مركز يوغا

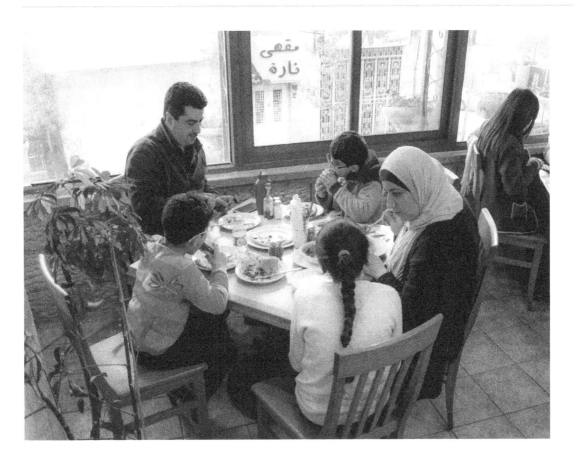

Activity 8   Speaking: A place I really like   محادثة: مكان أحبّه كثيراً   نشاط ٨

In this activity, you will share some of your favorite places in your town or city.

Before speaking   قبل المحادثة

Create a table like the one below. For each category on the far right, write the name of one
such place you like a lot in the column labeled اسم المكان. Write the full name using Arabic
letters as much as you can.

2	1	اسم المكان	المكان
			سينما
			مطعم
			مقهى / كافيه
			مركز تسوّق / مول
			مكتبة
			سوق

Speaking   المحادثة

Talk with two classmates separately about their favorite places and record their answers in the columns labeled 1 and 2. Pay attention to the favorite places that you have in common (if any).

After speaking   بعد المحادثة

With a classmate you haven't talked with yet, take turns answering the following questions:

1. Which places mentioned would you never go to?
2. Which places would you possibly go to?
3. Which places do you definitely want to go to?

Activity 9   Reading: The club   نشاط ٩   قراءة: النادي

You will read a map of a social club in Cairo, Egypt.

Before reading   قبل القراءة

Look at the image on the next page. In Arabic, name as many activities and sports as you can that you can do at this club.

Reading   القراءة

Read the legend for the map on the next page. As you read, complete the following:

1. Circle all the names for fields/courts/stadiums and sports that you see.
2. Circle all the other places that you recognize.
3. Circle all the words that might share a root with a word that you have learned. Try to guess what the new words might mean.
4. Guess the meaning of the following phrases:

    حمام سباحة = ____   الألعاب اليابانية = ____

5. Return to the names of places that you were able to find. Underline the places that are in the إضافة structure such as بيت صاحبي, مركز تسوّق, and مدينة نيويورك.

Challenge yourself: Look for the grammatical pattern for places (مَـ ____ ____ ____/مَفعل أو مَـ ____ ____ ____ ة/مَفعلة) that we learned about previously. Your teacher will share with you the meaning of the roots and you can guess the meaning of the placename words.

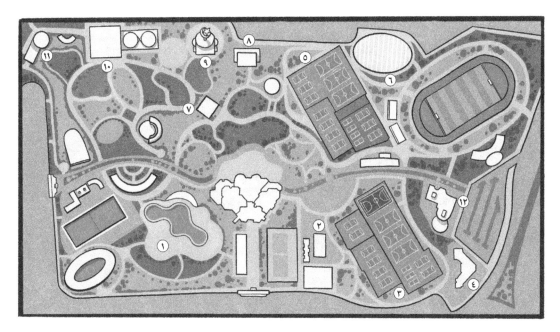

<table>
<tr><td>

٦. محلات وأسواق

• مبنى محلات ومطاعم وكافتيريا

٧. قاعة احتفالات

٨. مبنى ثقافيّ

٩. مسجد

١٠. مقهى ومطعم "القاهرة الجديدة"

١١. نادي صحيّ

١٢. مبنى الألعاب اليابانيّة

</td><td>

٣. منطقة الملاعب ١

• ملاعب كروكيه

• ملاعب التنس

• كرة السرعة

• ملاعب السلة

• ملعب خماسي

• ملاعب اليد

• ملاعب طائرة

• منطقة استراحة لاعبين

٤. المبنى الإداريّ

٥. منطقة الملاعب ٢

• ملعب كرة القدم

• ملعب اليد

• ملعب الفولي

• ملعب الجولف

• مطعم وقاعة الاجتماعات

• مبنى تغيير الملابس

• كافاتيريا

</td><td>

١. مبنى خدمات حمامات السباحة

• حمام السباحة

• حمام سباحة الأطفال

• مبنى الخدمات

• كافتيريا

٢. منطقة حمامات السباحة

• الصالة المغطاة لحمام السباحة

• حمام السباحة الأولمبيّ

• حمام سباحة غطس

• حمام سباحة ترفيهي

• مبنى تغير ملابس

</td></tr>
</table>

Take turns sharing the following information with a classmate:

6. Where in the club you want to go

7. Where in the club you definitely wouldn't go

8. Where in the club you might go

Culture: The club   الثقافة: النادي

Think back to the club you read about in the previous activity. If you were a member of this club, which facilities might you use the most? Do you have a similar club in your area or a place that offers these facilties? Is it popular? Who usually frequents it and has access to it? Are clubs of this type common in the region or country where you live?

In much of the Arab world, the نادي (club) is a popular institution. A نادي is loosely similar to a country club in the United States: both usually require a membership or guess past for entry, but a نادي tends to be more accessible to middle-class residents in the surrounding community. Some clubs are exclusive to those who work in certain professions and their family members, such as clubs for police officers or engineers. Typically, a نادي includes a swimming pool, a gym, restaurants and cafes, tennis courts, and other facilities, like party halls, where cultural and holiday programming frequently takes place. Many families will go to their نادي after school or on the weekend to socialize or play sports.

Professional sports teams are also always based at a نادي instead of in a city or state, as in the United States. Instead of rooting for the Chicago Bears or Atlanta Dream, an Egyptian might cheer on نادي الأهلي or نادي الزمالك, and a Jordanian would cheer on نادي الوحدات or نادي الفيصلي—pairs of rival clubs in Cairo and Amman respectively. Most public schools do not offer their own sports teams, so students who want to participate in competitive sports often do so by joining a league connected to a club.

Activity 10 Conversation: Receptionist   نشاط ١٠ محادثة: مكتب الاستقبال في
                     desk at the club   النادي

In this activity, imagine that you are working at the reception desk at a club in Egypt called نادي القاهرة الجديدة.

Before speaking   قبل المحادثة

Based on what you learned about clubs in the Arab world, make a list of the facilities and activities you can expect clubs to have there. Then make note of your answers to the following questions:

1. If you were able to obtain a job at such a club, in which facility would you like to work?
2. Where would you dislike working?

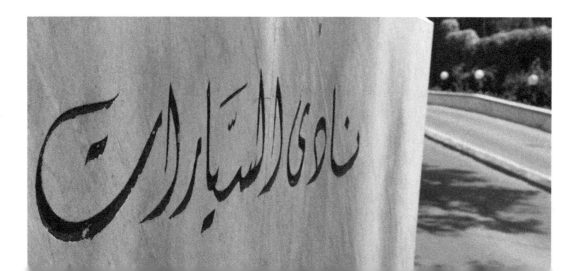

You can use the phrase:

I want to work at . . .	بِدّي أَشْتَغِل في...	أُريد أَنْ أَعْمَل في...

3. Your teacher will give you a slip of paper with places and activities this club features. Mark their location on the map in English or Arabic.

Speaking   المحادثة

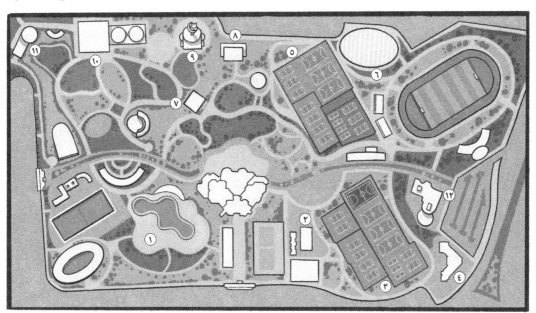

You will take turns being a receptionist at the club or a member at the club:

- If you are a receptionist, use the map you have marked for guidance. If you do not know the location of a facility or activity that a member asks you about, tell them that you do not know.
- If you are a member, use the slip of paper given to you by your teacher to ask where you must go. If the receptionist does not know, you can move to speak to another receptionist in the classroom.

Activity 11 Listening: "You have to come with me!"   نشاط ١١   استماع: "لازم تجي معيّ!"

You will listen to a discussion between ياسمين and نادين when they meet by chance.

Before listening   قبل الاستماع

In Lesson 9, you learned how to insist when inviting someone over and offering a drink to guests. Review with a classmate the following:

1. What are some polite phrases for insisting?
2. What are some polite phrases for refusing or deferring an invitation?

Listening   الاستماع

Watch the video titled "اللازم تجي معي!" as many times as you need to answer the following questions:

3. Where is نادين going?
4. What are some of the activities she mentions they can do there?
5. How many times did نادين ask ياسمين to join her?
6. When are they planning to go?

After listening   بعد الاستماع

As you saw in the video, it is generally considered polite to refuse invitations, like offerings of tea and coffee, before accepting them in Arab culture.

Using this video as a guide, create a skit with a classmate about one of the places that you love or prefer from Activity 8 in this lesson. In the skit, you should try to convince your classmate to come with you to this place. Follow the model provided by your teacher. Your skit must include these elements:

- Greetings
- Exchanging pleasantries
- At least one place and what you can/will do there
- Insisting and refusing in a culturally appropriate manner

WHY DO YOU WANT TO GO TO . . . ?   لماذا تريد أن تذهب إلى...؟

Vocabulary 3   مفردات ٣

المعنى	العاميّة الشاميّة	الفصحى
Why . . . ?	لَيش...؟	لماذا...؟
in order to . . .	عَشان...	لِـ...

Activity 12 Reading and writing: Why?   نشاط ١٢   قراءة وكتابة: لماذا؟

In this activity, you will read and create text message exchanges between two individuals.

Before reading   قبل القراءة

With a classmate, review the verbs depicted below and on the next page for the pronouns "I" and "you."

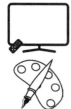
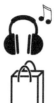

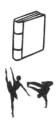
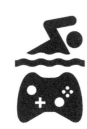

القراءة

Reading

Read the text message exchanges in which friends Majid (a man) and Iman (a woman) discuss where they are and why. Talk with a friend in Arabic to answer these questions:

- Where is each character?
- Why are they there?

العاميّة

الفصحى

١.

كيفك؟

الحمد لله. وانت كيفك؟

الحمد لله. وينك؟

أنا بمطعم.

ليش؟

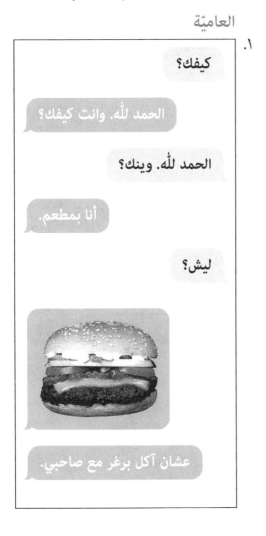

عشان آكل برغر مع صاحبي.

١.

كيف الحال؟

بخير الحمد لله. وأنت كيف حالك؟

بخير. أين أنت؟

أنا في مطعم.

لماذا؟

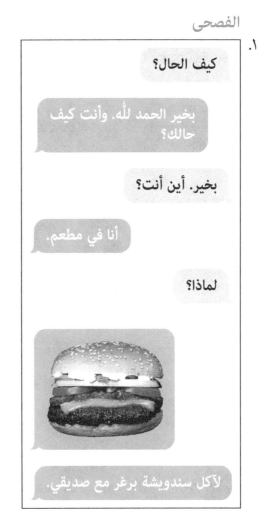

لآكل سندويشة برغر مع صديقي.

العاميّة   الفصحى

٢.   ٢.

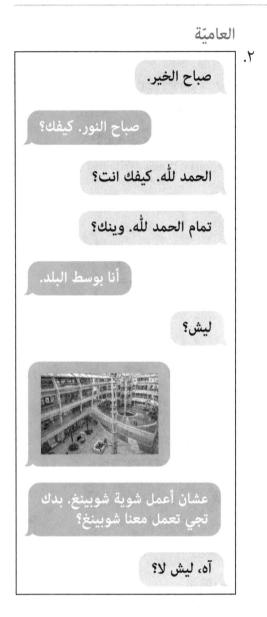

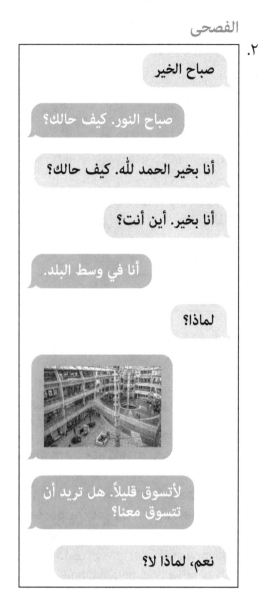

Writing
الكتابة

Create your own text message exchange with a partner in which you discuss where you are and why. Take turns writing and use complete sentences. Make sure to include the following elements:

- An exchange of greetings and "how are you?"
- Asking where the other person is and responding
- Asking why the other person is in that place
- Using عشان or لـ to explain why you are in each place

Add pictures if possible and share your written exchange with your classmates.

After reading and writing
بعد القراءة والكتابة

Text or email a classmate in Arabic in the evening or on the weekend to find out where he or she is and why. Take a screenshot of your conversation and submit it to your teacher.

Activity 13 Conversation: May I go to ...

نشاط ١٣   محادثة: من الممكن أن أذهب إلى...

Your teacher will divide your class in half. One half will play the role of teenagers and the other the role of parents in a conversation about going different places.

Before speaking

قبل المحادثة

Write down where you want to go this week on different days and at different times in a table like the one below.

لماذا؟	في الليل	في المساء	بعد الظهر	في الصباح	
					يوم الأحد
					يوم الثلاثاء
					يوم السبت

Speaking

المحادثة

Your teacher will assign you to play a teenager or a parent:

- If you are playing a teenager, tell your "parent" all the places you want to go and why. If they tell you no, you should ask them why and protest, offering more reasons to make them accept.

- If you are playing a parent, tell your "teenager" yes or no to each place and time that they mention (be sure to vary your responses). Press them by asking why they want to go to each place if they forget to offer a reason. If you are saying no, you can rebut by offering your own reason as to why you are refusing. For example, they might have school or work during that time! You can use this phrase:

It's not possible!	ما بيصير!	لا يُمْكِن!

After you are done, switch roles.

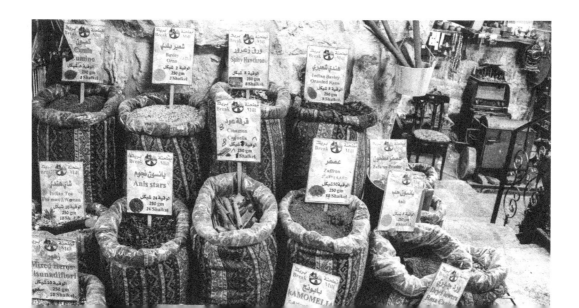

| Vocabulary 4 | | مفردات ٤ |

المعنى	العاميّة الشاميّة	الفصحى
before school	قَبِل المَدْرَسة	قَبْلَ المَدْرَسة
after school	بَعْد المَدْرَسة	بَعْد المَدْرَسة
and then . . .	وبَعْدَين...	ثُمَّ...

Activity 14   Listening: My routine on Monday

نشاط ١٤   استماع: برنامجي يوم الاثنين

You will be listening to three recordings of people talking about a typical Monday.

Before listening

قبل الاستماع

Where do you go and what do you do on Mondays? Using a separate sheet of paper or the diagram provided by your teacher, list four places where you do different activities on Mondays in the order that you do them.

Listening

الاستماع

You will listen to three people talk about their activities on a Monday. Complete a similar diagram for each of them.

After listening

بعد الاستماع

What are the similarities and differences between you and the three other individuals? Talk with a classmate. Make sure to use the habitual form of the verbs and also use كمان or ولكن or بس and أيضاً.

Activity 15   Reading: A visit to Kuwait City

نشاط ١٥   قراءة: زيارة إلى مدينة الكويت

You will be reading a one-day itinerary for Kuwait City created on an internet travel message board.[2]

Before reading

قبل القراءة

Look at the pictures. Pretend you are a travel guide who wants to encourage tourists to visit the places pictured. Decide on an order in which the tourists should visit these places, then tell them why they must go there and what they can do there. Use the connector "then" to tell what order tourists might do these activities in.

a.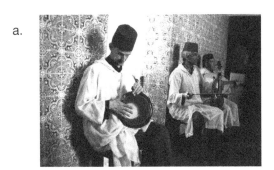

b.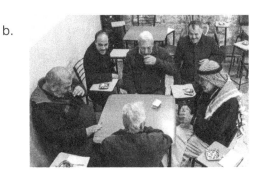

c.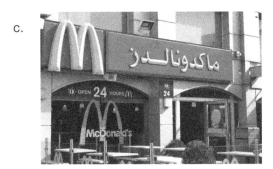

d.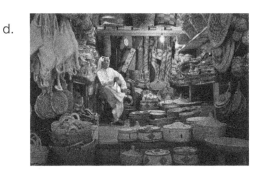

e.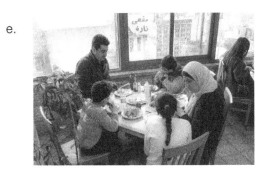

f.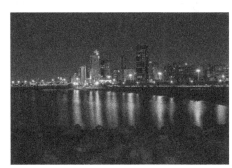

Reading   القراءة

Read the sentences below and on the next page. Then do the following:

1. Match each sentence with the image that it goes with.
2. Place them in order by looking for clues such as the new connectors you have learned or time of day (morning, afternoon, etc. or the exact time).

الفصحى:

	Photo	Order
أ. ثم يمكنك أن تذهب إلى مقهى للشاي أو للقهوة في الساعة العاشرة في الصباح.		
ب. في الليل يمكنك الذهاب إلى مركز تسوق حيث تتسوق أو تشاهد فيلماً في السينما.		

	Photo	Order
ج. وثم يمكنك أن تذهب إلى الأسواق القديمة في المدينة القديمة كسوق الصفافير أو سوق السلال في حوالي الساعة الثالثة.		
د. يمكنك أن تبدأ الصباح في الساعة التاسعة والنصف بأكل بوفيه الفطور في مطعم البلد (مطعم لبنانيّ) في برج الخدمة.		
هـ. قبل أن تذهب إلى مركز التسوق في المساء من اللازم أن تذهب إلى حفلة الرقص والموسيقى في نادي الكويت الثقافي لتشاهد الرقص العربي وتستمع إلى الموسيقى العربية وإلى الآلات العربية كالعود والطبل.		
و. ثم بعد المقهى، في حوالي الساعة الثانية والربع من اللازم أن تأكل الغداء في مطعم أمريكي كماكدونالدز.		

العاميّة الشاميّة:

	Photo	Order
أ. بعدين بتقدر تروح على كافيه للشاي أو للقهوة الساعة عشرة الصبح.		
ب. بالليل بتقدر تروح على مول اسمه مارينا مول وتتسوق أو تتفرج على فيلم في السينما.		
ج. وبعدين ممكن تروح على الأسواق القديمة في المدينة القديمة زي سوق الصفافير أو سوق السلال تقريبا الساعة ثلاثة.		
د. الساعة تسعة ونص الصبح ممكن تأكل ببوفيه الفطور في مطعم البلد (مطعم لبنانيّ) ببرج الخدمة.		
هـ. قبل ما تروح على المول المسا لازم تروح على حفلة الرقص والموسيقى في نادي الكويت الثقافي عشان تتفرج على الرقص العربي وتسمع الموسيقى العربية والآلات العربية زي العود والطبل.		
و. وبعدين بعد الكافيه، الساعة اثنين وربع تقريبا لازم تأكل الغدا في مطعم أمريكي زي ماكدونالدز.		

After reading   بعد القراءة

Which places in Kuwait City would you like to visit? Write a short schedule for yourself for a visit that includes three to four places depicted in the pictures using complete sentences.

Activity 16 Listening and conversation:
           A daily schedule

نشاط ١٦   استماع ومحادثة: برنامج يومي

In this activity, you'll learn more about some familiar characters through videos.

Before listening

قبل الاستماع

Chat for at least two minutes with a classmate about some places you go and things you do on a typical day.

Listening

الاستماع

Watch and listen to the video that your teacher assigns you. You will hear either ياسمين, محمود, نادين or أشرف talking about their daily schedules. Listen to your video enough times to understand specific details about when and how often the person or people do certain things or go certain places. Record this information in a table like the following. Make sure to write the information in the chart under the correct name or names. Pay attention to the differences between days of the weekend and workdays or school days.

أشرف		نادين		محمود		ياسمين	
متى؟	أين يذهب؟	متى؟	أين تذهب؟	متى؟	أين يذهب؟	متى؟	أين تذهب؟

Speaking

المحادثة

After listening, talk in Arabic with your classmates who listened to the same video to confirm that you got the same information. Next, talk with classmates who watched the other videos, and ask and answer questions to fill in the information on the chart. Make sure to ask about weekend days and school days or work days for each person.

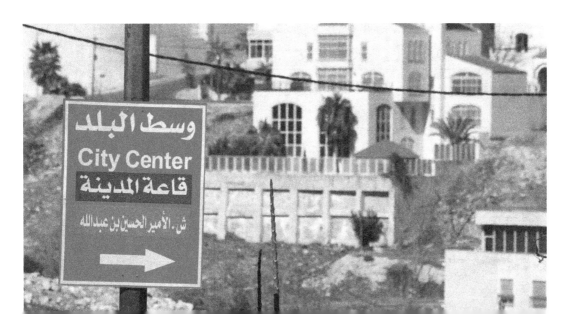

After speaking

بعد المحادثة

Make a recording about yourself and your daily schedule, modeled on the video you watched. Submit it to your teacher.

Activity 17 Conversation: Tour guide

نشاط ١٧ محادثة: مرشد سياحيّ

In this activity, imagine that you got a summer job at a travel agency creating one-day itineraries for people visiting your hometown.

Before speaking

قبل المحادثة

Using the lists you've created before about your favorite places as a starting point, brainstorm an itinerary for a first-time visitor to your city or town. For at least two or three places, think of a reason why someone should go there and the best time of day to go. Afterward, decide on an order for the itinerary and think of how you will use the connectors such as ثم or بعدين to give the order.

لماذا؟	متى؟	اسم المكان

Speaking

المحادثة

Your teacher will assign you to the role of either the boss or an employee at the travel agency.

If you are playing the role of the employee: Tell your boss your vision for a day visit, remembering to use the connectors and to indicate the time of day at which each portion of the visit will occur (e.g., morning, afternoon, or the exact time). You must offer a reason for your choice for at least two places.

If you are playing the role of the boss: Draw another chart similar to the one in قبل المحادثة and use it to take notes of the order, times, and reasons.

When you have finished, repeat the role-play with another classmate, this time playing the role you did not originally play.

Activity 18 Conversation: Arab brother or sister

نشاط ١٨ محادثة: أخ عربيّ أو أخت عربيّة

Imagine that you received a prestigious scholarship to study abroad for one month in the Arab world. You will be meeting virtually with a potential host brother or host sister to determine who will be the best roommate for you.

1. Complete the questionnaire handout like the one below with information about yourself. You will use this when talking with your potential host brother or sister.
2. With a classmate, brainstorm as many questions as you can that you'd like to ask your potential host sibling.

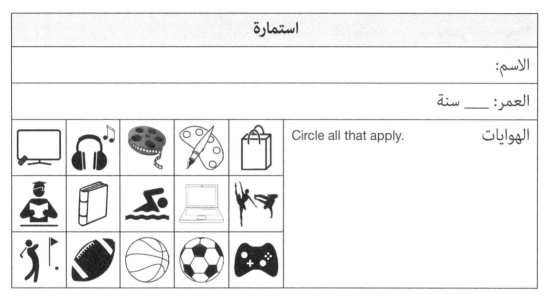

	استمارة
	الاسم:
	العمر: ___ سنة
Circle all that apply.	الهوايات

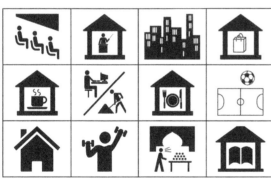

Circle the places you go to on a typical school day and write numbers for the order in which you go to them.

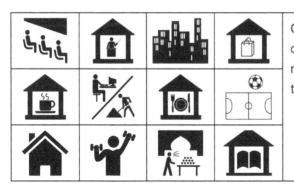

Circle the places you go to on a typical day you do not have school and write numbers for the order in which you go to them.

You will either play the role of an Arab host sibling or yourself. Your teacher will tell you which role you will play first. When you are the Arab host sibling, you will use the "identity card" that your teacher gives you to know what you like and what you do.

When you are yourself, use your own form. Talk with your classmates who are playing Arab host siblings. Take notes on each person's information using the blank form given to you.

After speaking   بعد المحادثة

With whom are you most compatible? To inform your decision, review the notes you have taken to look for similarities. With a new classmate, share some of the similarities using كمان or أيضاً and differences using بس or ولكن.

نشاط ١٩   كتابة: جدول أسبوعي، الجزء الثاني

Activity 19 Writing: A weekly schedule, part two

In this activity, you'll add detail to a previous writing assignment you created in Activity 3 of this lesson.

Before writing   قبل الكتابة

Go back to the weekly schedule you made for yourself in Activity 3 and review the sentences you wrote about your daily activities:

1. Look over the weekly schedule you made. What can you add to it, using the words you have learned since the last time you worked on it?
2. Read over your draft of your note to the study-abroad organization summarizing your schedule. Consider the following:
   - Where can you add words that tell **when** or **in what order** you do different activities? Draw an arrow to show where you could add these words.
   - Where can you add words that tell **why** you do different activities? Write the word عشان or ل to show where you could expand a sentence to tell why you go a certain place or do a certain activity.

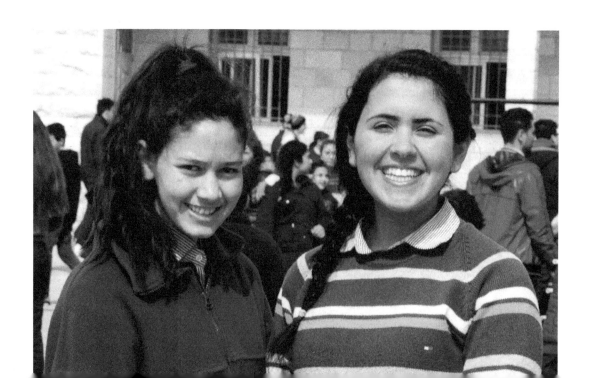

Start writing

الكتابة

Rewrite your note to the study abroad organization to include a more detailed picture of your week. Be sure to include these elements:

- As many activities and places as you can
- The order in which you do these activities
- Why you do certain activities or go certain places

After writing

بعد الكتابة

Trade notes with a classmate after you are done writing. Imagine that you are an employee at an exchange organization reading this note. Using a sticky note, write a short reaction to your classmate and place it on the bottom of his or her note. Here are some sample comments you could make:

انتَ مشغول كثير!	أنتَ مشغول جدّاً!
انتِ مشغولة كثير!	أنتِ مشغولة جدّاً!
بتلعبي الرياضة كثير!	تلعبين الرياضة كثيراً!
بتروح على المسبح كثير!	تذهب إلى المسبح كثيراً!

Unit Three
Vocabulary

مفردات الوحدة الثالثة

LESSON ELEVEN

Core vocabulary

الدرس الحادي عشر

المفردات الأساسيّة

المعنى	العاميّة الشاميّة	الفصحى
What is the homework today?	شو الواجِب اليوم؟	ما هُوَ الواجِب اليَوْم؟
What is the homework for tomorrow?	شو الواجِب لِبُكرا؟	ما هُوَ الواجِب لِيَوْم الغَد؟
What is the homework for ____ [day of the week]?	شو الواجِب لِيوم الـ ____؟	ما هُوَ الواجِب لِيَوْم الـ ____؟
The homework is . . .	الواجِب هُوّ...	الواجِب هُوَ...
The homework is activity number ____.	الواجِب هُوّ النَّشاطِ رَقْم ____.	الواجِب هُوَ النَّشاط رَقْم ____.
The homework is activities number ____ to number ____.	الواجِب هُوّ النَّشاطات رَقْم ____ إلى رَقْم ____.	الواجِب هُوَ النَّشاطات رَقْم ____ إلى رقم ____.
When is the test?	إيمتى الإمْتِحان؟	مَتى الإمْتِحان؟

LESSON TWELVE

Core vocabulary

الدرس الثاني عشر

المفردات الأساسيّة

المعنى	العاميّة الشاميّة	الفصحى
my hobbies	هِواياتي	هِواياتي

المعنى	العاميّة الشاميّة	الفصحى
in (my) free time	بْوَقْت الفَراغ	في وَقْت الفَراغ
I like to read.	بْحِبّ أَقْرَأ.	أُحِبّ أَنْ أَقْرَأ.
I do not like to read.	ما بْحِبّ أَقْرَأ.	لا أُحِبّ أَنْ أَقْرَأ.
also and also	كَمان وكَمان	أَيْضاً وأَيْضاً
I like to draw/paint.	بْحِبّ أَرْسُم.	أُحِبّ أَنْ أَرْسُم.
I like to study.	بْحِبّ أَدْرُس.	أُحِبّ أَنْ أَدْرُس.
I like to listen to music.	بْحِبّ أَسْمَع موسيقى.	أُحِبّ أَنْ أَسْتَمِع إلى الموسيقى.
I like to watch TV.	بْحِبّ أَتْفَرّج عَلى التِّلِفِزْيون.	أُحِبّ أَنْ أُشاهِد التِّلِفِزْيون.
I like to watch movies.	بْحِبّ أَتْفَرّج عَلى الأَفْلام.	أُحِبّ أَنْ أُشاهِد الأَفْلام.
I like to play video games.	بْحِبّ أَلْعَب أَلْعاب الفِيديو	أُحِبّ أَنْ أَلْعَب أَلْعاب الفِيديو
I like to go on the Internet.	بْحِبّ أَفوت عَلى الإِنْتَرْنِت.	أُحِبّ أَنْ أَدْخُل في الإِنْتَرْنِت.
I like to shop.	بْحِبّ أَتْسَوَّق.	أُحِبّ أَنْ أَتَسَوَّق.
I like to play . . .	بْحِبّ أَلْعَب...	أُحِبّ أَنْ أَلْعَب...
I like to watch . . .	بْحِبّ أَتْفَرّج عَلى...	أُحِبّ أَنْ أُشاهِد...
sports	الرِّياضة	الرِّياضة
soccer (football)	كُرة القَدَم	كُرة القَدَم
basketball	كُرة السَّلّة	كُرة السَّلّة
American football	كُرة القَدَم الأَمْريكِيّة	كُرة القَدَم الأَمْريكِيّة
I like to swim.	بْحِبّ أَسْبَح.	أُحِبّ أَنْ أَسْبَح.
the sport of swimming	السِّباحة	السِّباحة
I like to dance.	بْحِبّ أَرْقُص.	أُحِبّ أَنْ أَرْقُص.

Extra vocabulary   المفردات الإضافية

(for) an hour every day	ساعة كُلّ يوم	ساعة كُلّ يَوْم
(for) three hours every day	ثَلاث ساعات كُلّ يوم	ثَلاث ساعات كُلّ يَوْم
an hour	ساعة	ساعة
hours	ساعات	ساعات
team	فَريق	فَريق

LESSON THIRTEEN   الدرس الثالث عشر

Core vocabulary   المفردات الأساسيّة

المعنى	العاميّة الشاميّة	الفصحى
He likes to play . . .	بيحِبّ يِلْعَب...	يُحِبّ أَنْ يَلْعَب...
She likes to play . . .	بِتْحِبّ تِلْعَب...	تُحِبّ أَنْ تَلْعَب...
I like to play . . .	بَحِبّ أَلْعَب...	أُحِبّ أَنْ أَلْعَب...
You like to play . . . (m.)	بِتْحِبّ تِلْعَب...	تُحِبّ أَنْ تَلْعَب...
You like to play . . . (f.)	بِتْحِبّي تِلْعَبي...	تُحِبّينَ أَنْ تَلْعَبي...
a lot	كْثير	كَثْيراً
a little	شْوَيْ	قَليلاً
but	بَس	وَلكِن
I prefer (to)	بَفَضِّل	أَفَضِّل (أَنْ)
sometimes	أَحْياناً	أَحْياناً
always	دائماً	دائماً
every day	كُلّ يوم	كُلّ يَوْم
every week	كُلّ أُسْبوع	كُلّ أُسْبوع
It is possible that . . . Might . . . Maybe . . .	مُمْكِن...	مِن المُمْكِن أَنْ...

المعنى	العاميّة الشاميّة	الفصحى
Must . . . Have to . . . Should . . .	لازِم...	مِن اللازِم أنْ...
It is impossible that . . . Definitely won't . . .	مُسْتَحيل...	مِن المُسْتَحيل أنْ...

Extra vocabulary المفردات الإضافية

المعنى	العاميّة الشاميّة	الفصحى
Really? (literally: swear to God?)	وَاللّه؟	وَاللّهِ؟
Yes, really!	آه، وَاللّه!	نَعَم، وَاللّه!
in college	بِالجامْعة	في الجامِعة
What do you want to do in college? (m.)	شو بِدَّك تِعْمَل بِالجامْعة؟	ماذا تُريد أنْ تَفْعَل في الجامِعة؟
What do you want to do in college? (f.)	شو بِدِّك تِعْمَلي بِالجامْعة؟	ماذا تُريدين أنْ تَفْعَلي في الجامِعة؟
In college, I want to . . .	بِالجامْعة، بِدّي...	في الجامِعة، أُريد أنْ...

LESSON FOURTEEN الدرس الرابع عشر
Core vocabulary المفردات الأساسيّة

المعنى	العاميّة الشاميّة	الفصحى
the house (the) home	البَيْت	البَيْت
(the) school	المَدْرَسة	المَدْرَسة
the library the bookstore	المَكْتَبة	المَكْتَبة
(the) work	الشُّغُل	العَمَل
the restaurant	المَطْعَم	المَطْعَم
the field the stadium	المَلْعَب	المَلْعَب

المعنى	العاميّة الشاميّة	الفصحى
the café	القَهْوة الكافيه	المَقْهى
my friend's house (m.)	بَيت صاحْبي	بَيْت صَديقي
my friend's house (f.)	بَيت صاحِبْتي	بَيْت صَديقَتي
the shopping mall	المول	مَرْكَز التَّسَوُّق
the downtown	وَسْط البَلَد	وَسَط البَلَد
the club *(sports or social club)*	النّادي	النّادي
the movie theater the cinema	السّينَما	السّينَما
the market *(traditional open-air market or urban shopping district)*	السّوق	السّوق
with me	مَعي	مَعي
Why . . . ?	لَيش...؟	لِماذا...؟
in order to . . .	عَشان...	لِ...
before school	قَبِل المَدْرَسة	قَبْلَ المَدْرَسة
after school	بَعْد المَدْرَسة	بَعْد المَدرَسة
and then . . .	وبَعْدَين...	ثُمَّ...

Extra vocabulary   المفردات الإضافية

المعنى	العاميّة الشاميّة	الفصحى
The class likes . . .	الصَّفّ بيحِبّ...	الصَّفّ يُحِبّ...
The class prefers . . .	الصَّفّ بيفَضِّل...	الصَّفّ يُفَضِّل...
hotel	فُنْدُق	فُنْدُق
In the hotel, I want . . .	بالفُنْدُق، بِدّي...	في الفُنْدُق، أُريد...
I want to work at . . .	بِدّي أَشْتَغِل في...	أُريد أَنْ أَعْمَل في...
It's not possible!	ما بيصير!	لا يُمْكِن!

Family

الوحدة الرابعة

العائلة

UNIT FOUR GOALS—HOW IS YOUR ARABIC?

أهداف الوحدة الرابعة—كيف عربيتك؟

This section lists the unit objectives. While you are working through the lessons in this unit, refer to this list and keep track of your progress toward each objective as you go. By the end of each lesson, you should be able to do the following in Arabic:

Lesson Fifteen

الدرس الخامس عشر

- Find out what exercises in your textbook you should work on
- Understand directions about which activity to turn to
- Tell who is present in your class

Lesson Sixteen

الدرس السادس عشر

- Share who is in your immediate family
- Give some information about your immediate family
- Talk about some of the other people you are close to, such as friends and significant others
- Specify family relationships using the إضافة construction (e.g., "Ahmed's brother")
- Ask and respond to questions about your siblings
- Tell when you have two of something, such as brothers or sisters

Lesson Seventeen

الدرس السابع عشر

- Describe your friends and family with some adjectives
- Tell what your friends and family are *not* like
- Compare your friends and family by saying who is ____-er than others
- Talk about others' friends and family

Lesson Eighteen

الدرس الثامن عشر

- Say how old members of your family are
- Exchange information using numbers up to one hundred

- Talk about what you and your friends or family like to do as a group using verb conjugations for "we"
- Ask and talk about what others' families or friends like to do as a group using verb conjugations for "they" and "you" (plural)
- Ask questions about others' families using a variety of question words

Lesson Nineteen ‏الدرس التاسع عشر‎

- Tell how often you do different activities
- Tell whether you do activities with friends, family, or by yourself
- Write a letter to someone explaining how often you do things with your friends and how often you do them with your family

Classroom Talk:
On which page?

الدرس الخامس عشر

كلام الصفّ: في أيّ صفحة؟

LESSON FIFTEEN GOALS

أهداف الدرس الخامس عشر

By the end of this lesson, you should be able to do the following:

- Find out what exercises in your textbook you should work on
- Understand directions about which activity to turn to
- Tell who is present in your class

In this lesson, you will learn how to use Arabic to ask and answer questions about navigating different activities in your book.

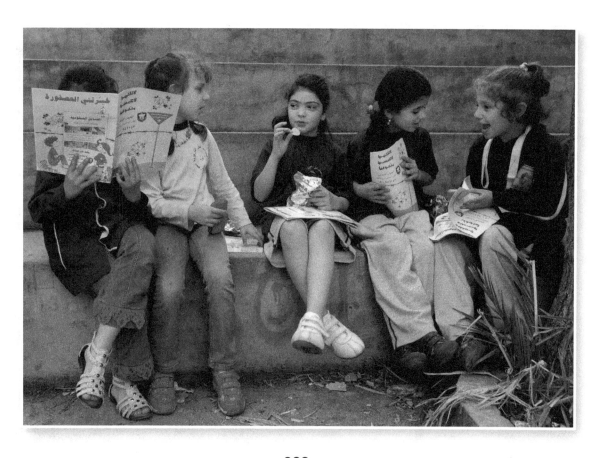

WHERE IN THE BOOK?   أين في الكتاب؟

Vocabulary 1   مفردات ١

المعنى	العاميّة الشاميّة	الفصحى
Where . . . ?	وَين...؟	أَيْنَ...؟
book	كْتاب	كِتاب
notebook	دَفْتَر	دَفْتَر
Which ____ ?	أَيّ ____ ؟	أَيّ ____ ؟
On/In which ____ ?	بِأَيّ ____ ؟	في أَيّ ____ ؟
page	صَفْحة	صَفْحة
activity	نَشاط	نَشاط
number	رَقْم	رَقْم
lesson	دَرْس	دَرْس

Activity 1   Reading: What's the homework?   نشاط ١   قراءة: ما الواجب؟

You have been given a series of homework assignments and the directions for which activities to complete are all in Arabic. Read the list of assignments below and look up each assigned activity in your textbook. Write down the name of each activity and the page number on a separate piece of paper and check with a friend to make sure you recorded the same information.

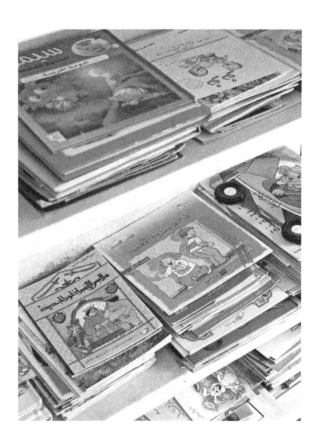

- الواجب: الدرس ١٢—نشاط ٧
- الواجب: الدرس ١٤—نشاط ١٧
- الواجب: كل نشاط في الدرس ١١
- الواجب: الدرس ١٣ من نشاط ٩ حَتّى نشاط ١١

Activity 2   Conversation: Where in the book?   نشاط ٢   محادثة: أين في الكتاب؟

Do you ever find that everyone else in the class has already flipped to the same page in their textbook, but you weren't paying attention and aren't sure where to look? Practice finding out where you should be.

Before speaking   قبل المحادثة

If you aren't sure what activity you're supposed to be working on, how could you use Arabic to find out? By yourself or with a classmate, figure out how to ask the following questions in Arabic:

- On which page?
- Which number?
- Where in the book?
- Which activity?
- Which lesson?

Speaking   المحادثة

Find a classmate and take turns playing two different roles:

- Partner A: Pick an activity in the textbook. You are a student who is paying attention and knows what is going on in class.
- Partner B: You are a student who was daydreaming in class. You want to find out what activity you are supposed to be on. In Arabic, ask your classmate what activity he or she is working on, without looking. Then, flip to that activity and check to make sure you are on the right one.

Switch roles in order to practice asking and answering questions about what page you should be on.

After speaking   بعد المحادثة

A friend has been absent from Arabic class. Write out the homework for them for at least two weeks, giving as much information as you can. You can use your real homework schedule provided by your teacher or make up the assignments using the activities you looked at with your partner.

WHO IS IN CLASS?   من موجود في الصفّ؟

Vocabulary 2   مفردات ٢

المعنى	العاميّة الشاميّة	الفصحى
professor teacher	أُسْتاذ / أُسْتاذة	أُسْتاذ / أُسْتاذة
teacher *(usually in a school setting)*	مُعَلِّم / مُعَلِّمة	مُعَلِّم / مُعَلِّمة

المعنى	العاميّة الشاميّة	الفصحى
student	طالِب / طالْبة	طالِب / طالِبة
students *(all-male or mixed group)*	طُلّاب	طُلّاب
students *(all-female group)*	طالْبات	طالِبات
present *(in class)*	موجود / موجودة	مَوْجود / مَوْجودة
absent	غايِب / غايْبة	غائِب / غائِبة
class	صَفّ	صَفّ

Culture: Seek knowledge   الثقافة: اطلب العلم

The word طالب comes from the verb طَلَبَ, which means "to seek" or "to ask for." Just as a teacher is someone who teaches, a student in Arabic is defined as someone who seeks knowledge. The Prophet Mohammed is said to have exhorted Muslims to "اُطْلُبوا العِلْم"—"Seek knowledge even in China." Read the saying in Arabic—how many words or roots do you recognize? One of the amazing things about the Arabic language is the fact that Arabic speakers can read and understand texts and sayings from more than a thousand years ago. For a comparison, search for an Anglo-Saxon text online, and see how many words you can recognize in the earliest form of English.

Activity 3   Listening: Attendance report   نشاط ٣   استماع: تقرير حضور

The computerized attendance system is broken today, so teachers are having to phone in their attendance. Listen to a voicemail from one of the teachers and create a written record of the attendance by marking down whether each person is present.

Before listening   قبل الاستماع

Read the names on the attendance list and write هو or هي to show whether you think each name is for a male student or a female student.

Listening for general understanding   الاستماع للفهم العام

Complete the attendance report according to what you hear on the recording.

موجود أم غائب	هو / هي	الاسم
تقرير الحضور		
الصفّ: _____		
		١. زكي
		٢. سامية
		٣. سوسن
		٤. سميحة
		٥. شيرين
		٦. عزّ الدين
		٧. طارق
		٨. فاتن
		٩. ماجد
		١٠. نصر

Close listening   الاستماع الدقيق

Listen again, paying attention to whether each name is a male or female name, correcting your initial guesses when necessary.

Challenge yourself: Listen for the following two words. What do you think they mean, from context?

- غايبين
- موجودين

After listening   بعد الاستماع

Create a voicemail with the attendance for one of your classes today. Share it with your teacher or a classmate.

Activity 4   Conversation: Is Ahmed there?   محادثة: هل أحمد موجود؟   نشاط ٤

Your boss has asked you to call and find out the availability of some people he wants to speak with today. You must call their office and find out if they're around.

1. Your teacher will give you a list of names of people to inquire about. Go over the names and make sure you know whether each is a name for a man or woman. If you aren't sure, use Arabic to ask your teacher or a classmate.

2. The word موجود is useful not only for telling whether someone is present in class, but also for asking for someone on the phone. If you call and want to know if someone is there, use the following phrases:

| Is Ahmed there? | أَحْمَد موجود؟ | هَل أَحْمَد مَوْجود؟ |
| Is Samira there? | سَميرة موجودة؟ | هَل سَميرة مَوْجودة؟ |

Practice using these phrases with the names you received.

If you have received نسخة أ, find a classmate who has نسخة ب, or vice versa. Pretend to call your classmate on the phone and try to find out whether the top four names on your sheet are available. Mark down your classmate's response. When you have asked about all of the people on your sheet, switch roles.

Write your boss a note summarizing the availability of the people you called.

Activity 5   Conversation: Who is absent today?   نشاط ٥   محادثة: من غائب اليوم؟

In this activity, you will practice talking about who is present and absent in your class.

Answer the following two questions with a classmate:

١. كم طالباً في صف العربية؟*
٢. من غائب عن صف العربية اليوم؟

*In Modern Standard Arabic, we add تنوين الفتح to a word if it comes after the word كَم. This does not change the meaning of the word. Ask your teacher if you would like to know more.

Your teacher will give you one question to ask the rest of your classmates; write that question in a chart similar to the one on the next page, on a separate piece of paper. Walk around the room and talk with your classmates. Ask each classmate you encounter your

question and write down the names of those you have spoken to and their response. When a classmate asks you a question, try to answer in a complete sentence.

	السؤال
	أسماء الطلاب

I like my family and friends

الدرس السادس عشر

أحبّ عائلتي
وأصدقائي

LESSON SIXTEEN GOALS

أهداف الدرس السادس عشر

By the end of this lesson, you should be able to do the following:

- Share who is in your immediate family
- Give some information about your immediate family
- Talk about some of the other people you are close to, such as friends and significant others
- Specify family relationships using the إضافة construction (e.g., "Ahmed's brother")
- Ask and respond to questions about your siblings
- Tell when you have two of something, such as brothers or sisters

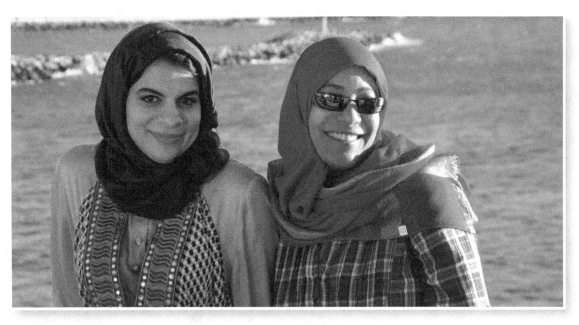

- How many generations of your family do you see regularly?
- Who are the most important people in your social circle of family and friends?
- What does family mean in different cultures you are familiar with?

WHO IS IN YOUR FAMILY?

Vocabulary 1

من في عائلتك؟

مفردات ١

المعنى	العاميّة الشاميّة	الفصحى
family	عَيلة	عائِلة
mother	أُمّ إمّ	أُمّ
father	أَب	أَب
husband	جوز	زَوْج
wife	مَرة	زَوْجة
partner (m.)	شَريك	شَريك
partner (f.)	شَريكة	شَريكة
brother	أخ	أخ
brothers	إخْوان	إخْوة
sister	أُخْت إخْت	أُخْت
sisters	إخْوات	أخَوات

Activity 1   Practicing vocabulary:
Stepparents

نشاط ١   التدريب على المفردات: زوج
الأم وزوجة الأب

The family tree below has a family with stepparents in it. Where are they?

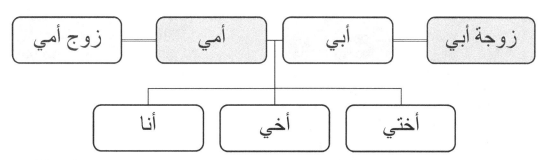

What do you notice about the words for stepparents? Find and write down the
word for:

    1. My stepmother (my father's wife): _____

    2. My stepfather (my mother's husband): _____

Cultural norms around family structure vary across the world and are shaped by many different factors, such as political and economic interests and religious beliefs. Even within a community, people may have different kinds of families and use different words to refer to their family members. Ask your teacher if wish to refer to members of your family but need additional vocabulary. Using the words you have already learned, figure out how to say the following:

3. My stepfather (my father's husband): _____
4. My stepmother (my mother's wife): _____

Challenge yourself:

5. My mother's partner (f.): _____
6. My mother's partner (m.): _____
7. My father's partner (f.): _____
8. My father's partner (m.): _____

Activity 2   Listening: A picture of my family   استماع: صورة عائلتي   نشاط ٢

In this activity, you will listen to a recording of someone naming the members of their family.

Before listening   قبل الاستماع

Look at the pictures of the families below. Say what role you think each person plays in relation to the person who is named—the mother? The brother?

Listening   الاستماع

With a classmate, listen to the recording. Imagine that you are the person who is speaking—but you don't have to say anything. Instead, just point to the person in the photo as you hear each person mentioned, pretending that you are showing them your family.

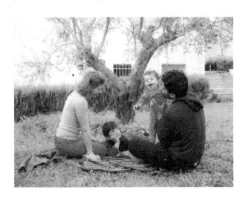 .b

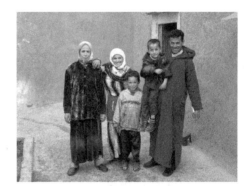 .a

After listening 1   بعد الاستماع ١

On a separate sheet of paper, draw a picture of the people in your family (or use a photo). You could use your real family or make up an imaginary family. Describe the people in the picture to your classmate, imitating the video. Tell your classmate who all the people in the

picture are, including their relationship to you and their names. Remember to think about how to change verbs when you are talking about yourself and about others.

Challenge yourself: Say at least one fact about each family member, besides their name. For example, what is something each person likes?

After listening 2 بعد الاستماع ٢

Write a caption for your image, listing everyone who appears in it.

Activity 3   Listening: She's Ahmed's mother   نشاط ٣   استماع: هي أم أحمد

In this activity, practice identifying the members of others' families.

Before listening   قبل الاستماع

In previous lessons, you learned about using the إضافة construction to show ownership, as in the following phrases:

شاي أحمد مطعم ماكدونالدز كمبيوتر نبيلة

Look at the pictures below. One person in each picture has been indicated by name. With a classmate, practice using the إضافة to say who the other people in the photo are in relation to this person.

Listening   الاستماع

A friend has sent you some pictures of family friends over Skype and is telling you who is in each picture.

   1. Listen to the recording and point to the person you think your friend is talking about when they mention each one.

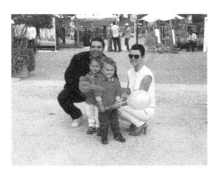   .b   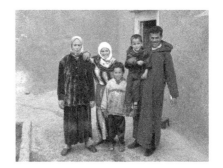   .a

   2. Listen to the recording again. Show a classmate which family members you pointed to by pointing to them again as you listen.

After listening   بعد الاستماع

Using the same picture of your family—real or fake—that you drew for Activity 2, complete the following:

3. Show the picture to a different partner and explain who the family members are in Arabic.

4. Swap pictures with your partner and describe your partner's family to a third partner. Use Arabic to explain who they are in relationship to this person.

| Activity 4   Reading: Who are they? | قراءة: مَن هؤلاء؟   نشاط ٤ |

In this activity, you'll learn about a culturally appropriate way of referring to certain family members.

Reading for general understanding   القراءة للفهم العام

Who are the people in the pictures? What information does the caption give?

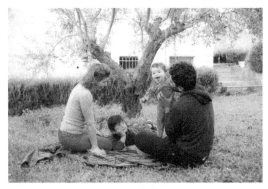
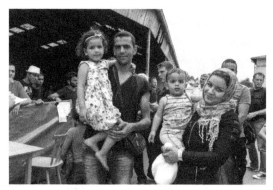

من اليمين إلى اليسار: أبو زياد ونور وزياد وأم زياد يقضون يوم عطلة في الحديقة.

من اليمين إلى اليسار: أم فادي وفادي وأبو فادي ونبيلة في مدينة الدوحة.

Close reading   القراءة الدقيقة

Journal or discuss with a partner in English: What do you notice about the parents' names? How are they different from the way you would list your parents' names in a caption?

Notice the variation on the spelling of أب, too. It becomes أبو when part of an إضافة. You will learn more about this later in the chapter.

After reading   بعد القراءة

Find two to three celebrity family photos online. Print them out and write complete captions using the same style as the photos above.

Culture: Abuu Ahmed   الثقافة: أبو أحمد

In your community, is there any special way of addressing people who are parents? How would your parents be referred to in an Arabic-speaking society? In a previous activity, you looked at some captions of photographs where the parents were referred to as "so-and-so's father" and "so-and-so's mother." Referring to parents as "mother of ____" ("*Umm* ____") and "father of ____" ("*Abuu* ____") is common across the Arab world; friends, neighbors, family members, and co-workers may all use these titles rather than a person's first name. Parents are referred to using the name of their oldest son or oldest daughter

if they don't have any sons. A man whose oldest son is named أحمد would be called أبو أحمد by many of the people who know him, and Ahmed's mother would be known as أم أحمد. Watch for this in the videos that accompany this unit. While "*Abuu*" is sometimes used as a stereotypical Arabic name, it is in fact not used as a name on its own in Arabic-speaking societies.

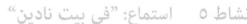

Activity 5   Listening: "At Nadine's house"   نشاط ٥   استماع: "في بيت نادين"

In the video titled "في بيت نادين," the character ياسمين visits the home of her friend نادين for the first time and meets her family.

Before listening   قبل الاستماع

What are some phrases or words you already know that you are likely to hear in the context of an introduction? Brainstorm with a classmate.

Listening for general understanding   الاستماع للفهم العام

Who is in the family? Note all of the family members and any information you hear about them, such as their name or age.

Close listening   الاستماع الدقيق

1. At 0:51, how does نادين say "my brother"? Write this down as you hear it. This variation is commonly used in Levantine dialect. If you are learning primarily العاميّة الشاميّة, you should memorize it and use it.

2. **Challenge yourself:** At 1:24, ياسمين responds to أشرف using a polite phrase said after hearing someone else's age. What does she say?

After listening   بعد الاستماع

3. ياسمين wants to write an entry in her diary summarizing her day. Fill in some information about عائلة نادين on a separate sheet of paper.

التاريخ: _____
اليوم زرت بيت ياسمين وتعرفت على عائلتها لأول مرة. أحب عائلتها كثيراً.
في عائلة نادين:
_____
_____
_____
_____
_____
كان اليوم يوماً طويلاً وممتعاً! إلى اللقاء!

| Activity 6   Listening: Yasmine asks about Nadine's family | استماع: ياسمين تسأل عن عائلة نادين   نشاط ٦ |

If you see someone you haven't seen in a month or so, do you ask them how their family members are? If so, about whom do you ask? In this video, you'll see a polite style of inquiry common in Arab culture.

Before listening   قبل الاستماع

Look over the words for family members below in Arabic. Which are phrased so that they refer to a member of one's own family (using "my"), and which are phrased so that you could use them when asking about someone else's family (using "your")? Create two headings—"my family members" and "your family members"—on a separate sheet of paper and rewrite each word under the appropriate one.

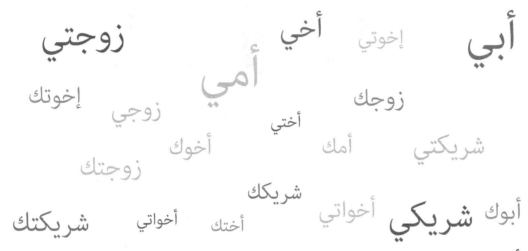

You may notice that two terms for family members are spelled a little differently: أخوك and أبوك both include the letter و. These terms are two of a group of five nouns that behave a little differently when used in an إضافة or with an attached pronoun. With the exception of أبي and أخي, for now, as a rule of thumb, remember that أب and أخ often include a و when you add a pronoun to them.

In العاميّة الشاميّة, the words أخوي "my brother" and أبوي "my father" also have this و in them.

Listening   الاستماع

In Arab culture, it is considered polite to ask how someone's family members are doing, especially if you know those family members personally.

Watch the video of ياسمين running into أشرف. What family members are mentioned in this segment? Point to them in the picture, and check what you heard with a classmate.

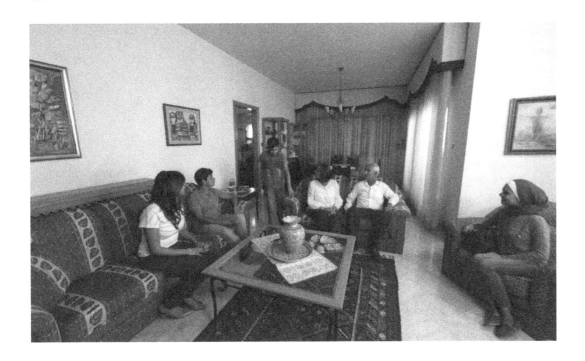

Challenge yourself: At 0:20, ياسمين uses a phrase that means "say hi to them for me." What does she say? How does أشرف respond?

After listening   بعد الاستماع

Imagine that you are living in the Middle East and attend a wedding where you encounter many people you haven't seen in months. With your classmates, practice the extended greetings you would use with them, modeled on the style of the video. Try to respond in complete sentences as much as possible.

Activity 7   Reading and writing: Writing   قراءة وكتابة: كتابة بريد   نشاط ٧
              an email   إلكتروني

In this activity, you'll start to learn how to write emails in Arabic. Respond to the following questions on a separate sheet of paper.

Before reading   قبل القراءة

1. What are some Arabic phrases you know that you could use to write an email to a friend?
2. What phrases might you use when writing to a teacher?

Reading   القراءة

3. What kind of email do you think this is—personal or formal? What in the text gives you clues?

4. Circle all the familiar words you see in the email. Don't worry; you are not expected to understand everything! Look in particular for greetings and for mentions of family members.

5. Underline any stylistic elements, such as greetings, common questions, and sign-offs. (Take note of these to use or adapt for your own writing in the next stage.)

6. This email uses a version of the phrase ياسمين used to mean "say 'hi' to them for me." Where is it? Whom does Rula tell Ruqayya to say hi to?

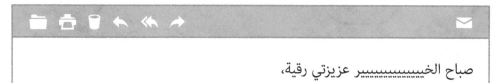

صباح الخيــــــــــير عزيزتي رقية،

مرحبا كيفك؟ شو اخبارك؟ شو أخبار عيلتك؟ كيف أخوك وأختك؟ إن شاء الله كل شي ممتاز، انا كثير منيحة بس زعلانة شوي لاني ما بدي اخذ الامتحانات النهائية بكرا، بس شو منساوي. ماما وبابا بيسلموا عليك كثير. حبيت أقولك اني انبسطت كثير بتلفونك وسماع اخبارك آخر مرة حكينا. يلا سلمي على أخوك وأختك وكل العيلة وان شاء الله منشوفكم قريبا، وخلينا على اتصال.

رولة

Writing   الكتابة

You have been missing an Arab friend of yours whom you met on a study abroad trip. Write them a short email that includes the stylistic elements you identified above.

نشاط ٨   استماع: ماريا أم مقابل أم ماريا   Activity 8   Listening: Maria is a mother vs. Maria's mother

The إضافة construct is often difficult for native speakers of English, and mistakes made because of this difficulty can cause confusion. Practice identifying the meaning of different phrases that may sound similar to English speakers but have very different meanings.

Before listening   قبل الاستماع

Read the phrases below. What do you think is the difference in meaning between them? Discuss with a classmate.

١. أم خديجة ـــــ خديجة أم
٢. أحمد أب ـــــ أبو أحمد

Listening   الاستماع

Number a separate sheet of paper from one to six. You will hear a series of phrases and sentences. Next to the number of each statement on your paper, write the letter of the picture it best describes.

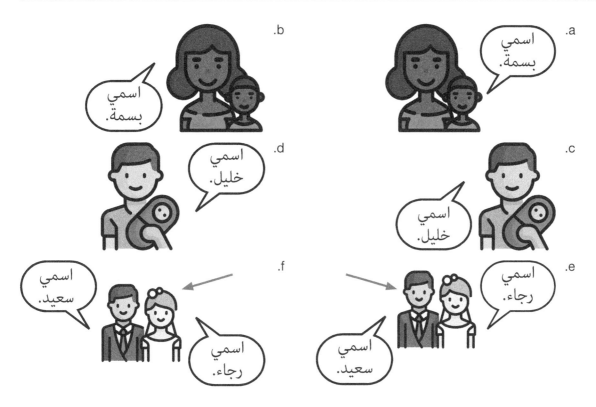

After listening   بعد الاستماع

Find a photo of the family of a celebrity you know about—you can use the same photo you used in Activity 4. In a small group, speak in Arabic about who is in the photo and how they are related to the celebrity.

Activity 9   Conversation: A present for   محادثة: هدية لأخي   ٩ نشاط
my brother

You are trying to think of gifts to buy your family and decide to talk with a friend about it. Your friend will suggest items from a flyer they received in the mail.

Before speaking   قبل المحادثة

Write at least three to five sentences about what your family members like and dislike, using what you already know in Arabic. You can base your writing on a fake family or a real family, such as your own or a celebrity's. Write about three to five family members, giving at least one complete sentence per family member. Be sure to conjugate verbs for هو and هي where appropriate, as in the following example:

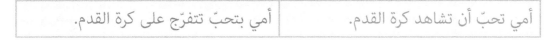

| أمي بتحبّ تتفرّج على كرة القدم. | أمي تحبّ أن تشاهد كرة القدم. |

Challenge yourself: Write about three to five family members, giving at least one compound sentence per family member and using أيضاً or كمان and ولكن or بس to link ideas as follows:

أمي بتحبّ تتفرّج على كرة القدم وكمان بتحبّ تتفرّج على كرة السلّة، بس ما بتحبّ تلعب كرة القدم ولا كرة السلّة.	أمي تحبّ أن تشاهد كرة القدم وأيضاً تحبّ أن تشاهد كرة السلّة، ولكنّها لا تحبّ أن تلعب كرة القدم أو كرة السلّة.

Speaking   المحادثة

In this part of the activity, you will talk with a classmate about what your family members like or dislike. You will take turns talking about your family and recommending gifts from a flyer you received in the mail.

When talking about your family: Tell your classmate about what your family members like or dislike, based on what you wrote. After you settle on a recommendation, write down what you plan to buy for each family member.

When recommending items from the flyer: Based on what you hear from your classmate about their family, suggest a gift from the catalogue below, which you received in the mail. Ask follow-up questions if you need to get more details about what someone would prefer.

أغراض وهدايا لكل أفراد العائلة!			
كرة (كرة القدم)	كرة (كرة السّلة)	كتاب	راديو
كرة (بيسبول)	كرة (كرة القدم الأمريكية)	موبايل أندرويد	موبايل آبل
كمبيوتر	تلفزيون	ساعة	عطلة في هاواي
فيلم كوميدي	فيلم أكشن	فيلم دراما	فيلم رومانسي

After speaking   بعد المحادثة

So you don't forget any gift ideas, you decide to make a note in your phone about what each family member would like. Write a note either by hand or in your phone and submit it to your teacher.

DO YOU HAVE BROTHERS?
Vocabulary 2

هل عندك إخوة؟
مفردات ٢

المعنى	العاميّة الشاميّة	الفصحى
I have	عِنْدي	عِنْدي
I don't have	ما عِنْدي	لَيْسَ عِنْدي
you have (m.)	عِنْدَك	عِنْدَكَ
you have (f.)	عِنْدِك	عِنْدَكِ
he has	عِنْدُه	عِنْدَهُ
she has	عِنْدْها	عِنْدَها
Do you have . . . ? (m.)	عِنْدَك...؟	هَل عِنْدَكَ...؟
Do you have . . . ? (f.)	عِنْدِك...؟	هَل عِنْدَكِ...؟

Look over the expressions meaning "have" or "has" above. What are they similar to, among the vocabulary that you have already learned? What are they different from? It is important to remember that عند in Arabic is not a verb—it is a preposition. When you say عندي, you are literally saying "at me."

Activity 10 Conversation: Who doesn't have a TV?

نشاط ١٠   محادثة: من ليس عنده تلفزيون؟

In this activity, find out what your classmates have and do not have.

Before speaking

قبل المحادثة

Many electronics share similar names in Arabic and English. For each of the three items below, decide on two you that will say you have and one that you will say you don't have (it doesn't matter whether you have or don't have these items in real life). Practice saying "I have ____" and "I don't have ____":

• تلفزيون   • كمبيوتر   • موبايل

Speaking

المحادثة

How many bingo squares can you fill in here? Find different people in your class who have or do not have the following things. Make sure that you address your classmates using the correct gender depending on whom you are talking to. Remember that the phrases written in the bingo board are in the third person and are *not* the correct form for asking a question.

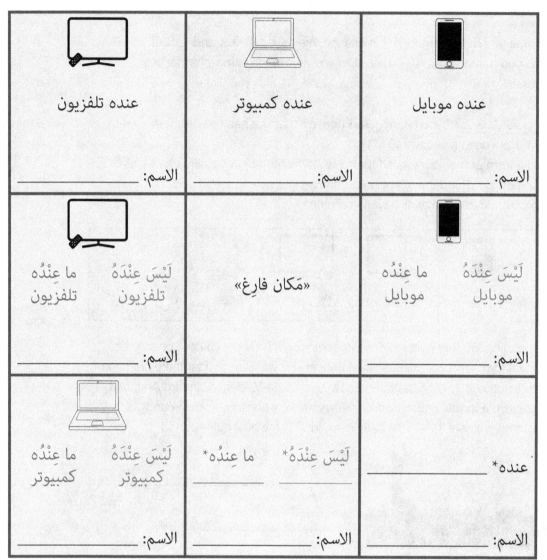

*In this question, insert the name of a social media network you use.

After speaking   بعد المحادثة

Share your results with a classmate in Arabic. Again, be sure to use the correct grammatical form depending on whom you are speaking to.

Activity 11 Listening: Lujain's family   نشاط ١١   استماع: عائلة لجين

Watch the video "لجين 1," which is about a Jordanian girl nicknamed لولو whom you saw previously talking about her hobbies.

Listening   الاستماع

What information did you understand about عائلة لولو? Record as much information as you can after listening two to three times.

After listening

بعد الاستماع

Use the structures you have learned in this chapter like الإضافة and عنده / عندها to tell a classmate what you heard about عائلة لولو. Did you record the same information?

Grammar: The dual

قواعد: المثنّى

In the video "في بيت نادين," you heard نادين confirm that she has two brothers. Watch the video again. How does she say it (0:57)?

نادين used a form of the noun called the "dual," which Arabic speakers use to talk about two of something. Read the following captions of items you asked about earlier to see more examples. What do they all have in common?

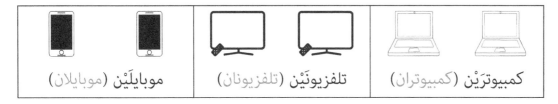

| موبايلَيْن (موبايلان) | تلفزيونَيْن (تلفزيونان) | كمبيوترَيْن (كمبيوتران) |

What **suffix**, or ending, do these words have in common? The suffix you see changes any noun into the **dual** form, and you can use it whenever you want to say that there are two of something. You'll notice that each caption has two words. In Modern Standard Arabic, this suffix has two possible forms. For now, don't worry about when to use each one.*

Below are some words you have already learned with the dual suffix added:

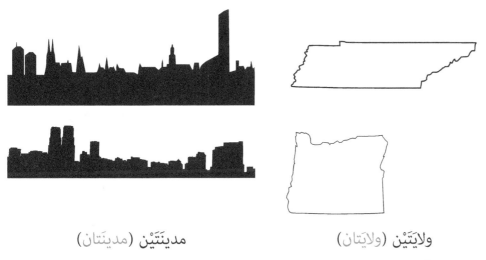

مدينتَيْن (مدينَتان)   ولايتَيْن (ولايَتان)

1. What do you notice about how the dual suffix interacts with the ة at the end of ولاية and مدينة?
2. With a partner, say and write each of the following words with a dual ending:

كِتاب	يوم	اسم	عُطْلة	ساعة

*Which form the dual suffix takes in Modern Standard Arabic depends on factors like whether the word it is attached to is the subject or object of a sentence. Still, both ـَيْن and ـان express the same basic meaning of "two" of whatever noun they are suffixed to. You can ask your teacher if you want to know more.

Activity 12 Practicing grammar: Two
            houses

نشاط ١٢   تدريب على القواعد: بيتان

Following the models presented in the previous activity, write captions on the following pictures:

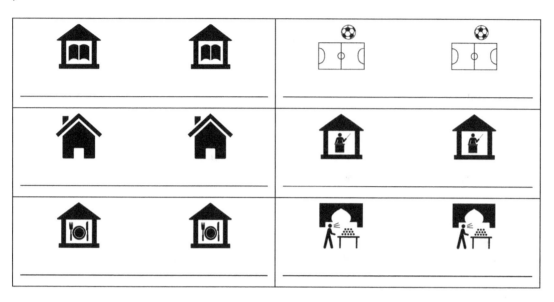

Activity 13 Conversation: Do you
            have...?

نشاط ١٣   محادثة: هل عندك...؟

In this activity, you'll find out which classmates have two of something.

Before speaking

قبل المحادثة

Practicing independently, make sure you know how to say *two* of each of the following images.

Speaking

المحادثة

Can you find anyone in your class who has two of the following? If so, write down that person's name on a separate sheet of paper.

 ٣.   ٢.   ١.

If you cannot find anyone in your class who fits these descriptions, think of a person you know who you think might have two of the other things pictured above. Write down their name.

After speaking   بعد المحادثة

Share your findings with a classmate: Say who in your class has two of the things above. Make sure to use عنده and عندها appropriately, given who you are describing.

Activity 14   Reading: The dual in an advertisement   نشاط ١٤   قراءة: المثنى في إعلان

You'll practice using your knowledge of Arabic grammar to decipher an advertisement and figure out which deal offered is the best.

Before reading   قبل القراءة

Discuss with a classmate: Do you know how much it costs for one year of cellphone or internet service in your area? What about for two years? Does the price change?

Reading   القراءة

Look at the advertisement below for a vehicle-protection service offered by a Jordanian mobile phone company. The service uses a mobile phone app to notify customers when their vehicle has been moved. Look over the chart. Search for the following words and use them to help you understand the ad:

monthly = الشهري   *device* = الجهاز   *commitment* = الالتزام   *Jordanian currency* = دينار.

1. How much does the service cost for one year?
2. For two years?
3. Is "Hasan Track 2" or "Hasan Track 3" a better deal for the customer? Why?

Hasan Track
بتسعدك وبتنسيك الطرق التقليدية لحماية سيارتك من السرقة

رسوم الاشتراك:
الاشتراك بنظام الفاتورة الشهرية

فترة الالتزام	الاشتراك الشهري (دينار)	سعر الجهاز (دينار)	الحزمة
سنة واحدة	100	10	Hasan Track 1
سنتين	100	10	Hasan Track 2
سنتين	0 (مجاناً)	14	Hasan Track 3

Activity 15 Reading: How many children?   نشاط ١٥   قراءة ومحادثة: كم طفلاً؟

The number of children a given family has is influenced by a number of factors, including the family's cultural and religious background and their personal preferences.

Before speaking   قبل المحادثة

Make an estimate: What do you think is the average number of children per family in your class? In the United States?

Speaking   المحادثة

Ask your classmates how many siblings they have, using the following question:

| How many siblings do you have? *(m.)* | كَم أخ وأُخْت عِنْدَك؟ | كَم أخاً وأُختاً عِنْدَكَ؟ |
| How many siblings do you have? *(f.)* | كَم أخ وأُخْت عِنْدِك؟ | كَم أخاً وأُختاً عِنْدَكِ؟ |

Record your answers in a table like this one that you create on a separate sheet. If someone fits into more than one category, write their name down in each category.

ثلاثة إخوة أو أكثر	أختين أختان	أخَّين أخوان*	أخ وأخت	أخت واحدة	أخ واحد

After speaking   بعد المحادثة

Using the information you gathered from your classmates, calculate the average number of children per family in your class.

Reading   القراءة

The following table shows the average number of children per woman in each country. (Note that because this table includes women who don't have any children, the average number of children among women who *do* have children is slightly higher).

*أخ + أخ = أَخَوان—this is an irregular form of the dual that only exists for a few words called الأسماء الخمسة. You can ask your teacher if you'd like to know more.

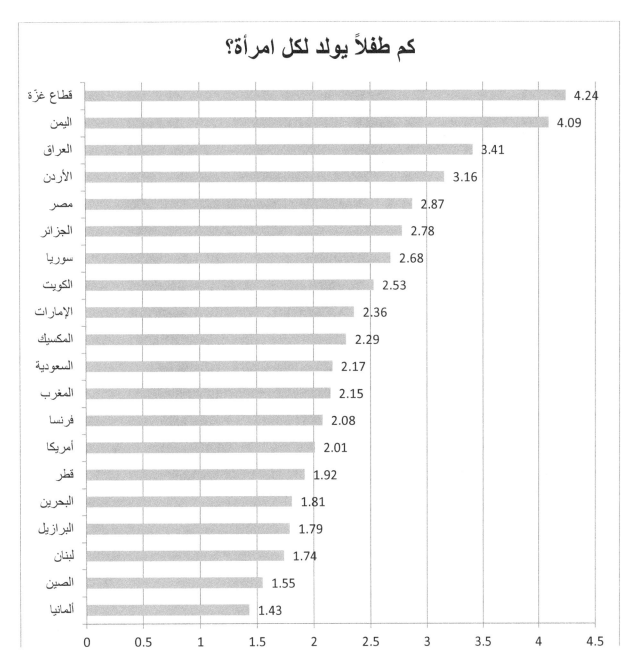

كم طفلاً يولد لكل امرأة؟

1. How does your family compare to the average in your country or a country you know?
2. How does the average family in your class compare?
3. Which Arab countries are on the list?
4. What patterns do you notice?

Activity 16 Conversation: My family's
hobbies   نشاط ١٦   محادثة: هوايات عائلتي

Before exchange organizations select host families for their exchange students, they usually learn about those families to find out what everyone in the family is like—what they like and dislike and what their hobbies are.

Before speaking   قبل المحادثة

Brainstorm:

- Think of as many things as you can to describe four members of your family and social circle, if an exchange organization asked you about them.
- What questions would you ask someone else if you wanted to know more about their family? Write down as many questions as you can think of.

Speaking   المحادثة

Find a classmate and work in pairs, playing two different roles:

Partner A: You are a representative from an exchange organization who has been sent to interview Partner B to find out about their family. You will take notes on what they tell you about their family, ask your questions, and then write a short summary for your exchange organization.

Partner B: You are applying to have your family host an exchange student. The exchange organization has sent its representative, Partner A, to learn about your family. Use your brainstorm ideas above to tell them as much as you can and to answer their questions in Arabic.

When you are done, switch roles.

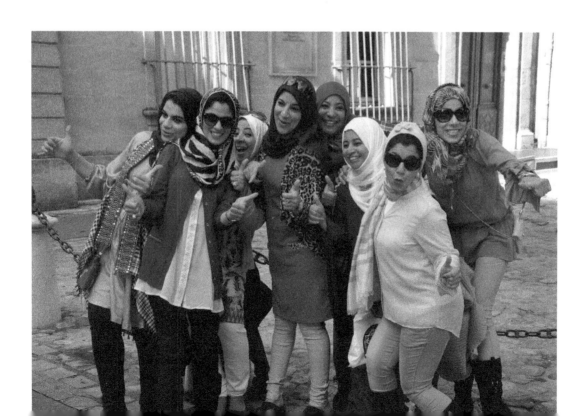

After speaking   بعد المحادثة

Now you're ready to write your report. Write as many sentences as you can about the other person's family, using the إضافة structure to indicate which family member you are talking about.

أُمّ جون بِتحِبّ تْروح عَلى السّينَما.	أُمّ جون تُحِبّ أَنْ تَذهَب إلى السّينَما.

WHO ELSE IS CLOSE TO YOU?   من أيضاً قريب منك؟
Vocabulary 3   مفردات ٣   🎧

المعنى	العاميّة الشاميّة	الفصحى
with	مَعَ	مَعَ
friend (m.)	صاحِب	صَديق
friend (f.)	صاحْبة	صَديقة
friends (all-male or mixed-gender)	أَصْحاب	أَصْدِقاء
friends (all-female)	صاحْبات	صَديقات
beloved dear boyfriend	حَبيب	حَبيب
beloved dear girlfriend	حَبيبة	حَبيبة

Activity 17 Reading and writing: A holiday card	نشاط ١٧ قراءة وكتابة: بطاقة عيد

In Arabic, the words حبيب and حبيبة do not always refer to a romantic partner.

Reading   القراءة

On the next page are cards created for different occasions. To interpret these cards, it will help you to recognize the word:

holiday		عيد

1. What holiday is each card for? Use the text and images as clues.
2. Who does the word حبيب and حبيبة refer to in each?

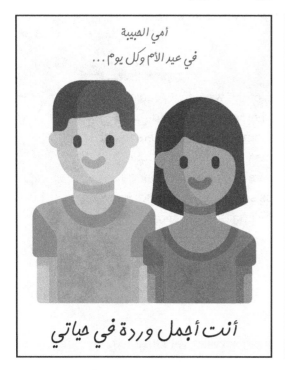

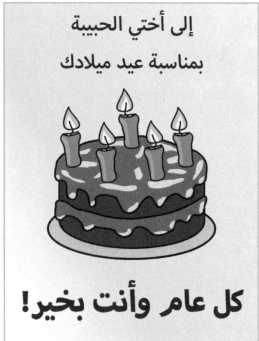

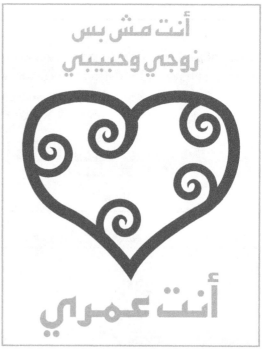

Writing   الكتابة

Create a card to a حبيب or حبيبة, whether romantic or otherwise. The card does not have to be from you to someone in your life—you could choose to write one from the point of view of a celebrity.

Culture: *Habiibii* and *Habiibatii*   الثقافة: حبيبي وحبيبتي

The English translations in your vocabulary list do not show all of the ways that Arabic speakers use حبيبي. In many parts of the Arab world, one of the uses of the word حبيبي is as a term of affection among non-romantic friends the way some English speakers might use a pet name to address their close friends. People sometimes use حبيبي or حبيبتي with strangers as well, the same way that some English speakers (especially in older generations) might use "dear," "sweetheart," or "honey" to address someone they do not know well. When used with family members or romantic partners, the English translations of حبيبي and حبيبتي are closer to "darling" or "beloved."

Activity 18   Conversation: What do you do with your friends?   نشاط ١٨   محادثة: ماذا تفعل مع أصدقائك؟

In this activity, you'll find out whether classmates are busier doing activities with their families or with their friends.

Before speaking   قبل المحادثة

On a separate piece of paper, complete a chart like the following. Your chart should show what you do on different days and at different times on the weekend, as well as with whom you do each activity. You can think about a typical weekend or an ideal weekend you would like to have as you fill out the chart.

مع من	النشاط	
أختي	ألعب ألعاب الفيديو	١. في الصباح يوم السبت
		٢. بعد الظهر يوم السبت

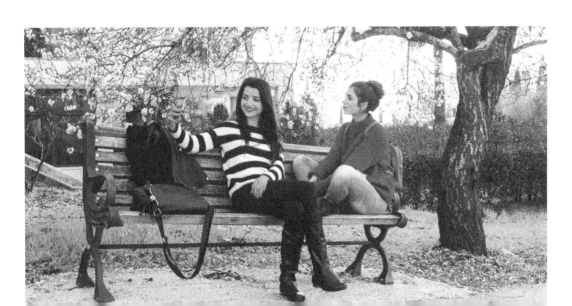

	النشاط	مع من
٣. في المساء يوم السبت		
٤. في الصباح يوم الأحد		
٥. بعد الظهر يوم الأحد		
٦. في المساء يوم الأحد		

Speaking   المحادثة

Count off numbers from ١ to ٦ with your classmates in order to know which of the times from قبل المحادثة you will ask about. For example, if you are assigned ٥, you will ask classmates what they do بعد الظهر يوم الأحد. Use the following questions as models:

ماذا تَفْعَل بَعْدَ الظُّهُر يَوْم الأَحَد؟	شو بْتِعْمَل بَعْد الظُّهُر يوم الأَحَد؟	What do you do Sunday afternoon? (m.)
ماذا تَفْعَل بَعْدَ الظُّهْر يَوْم الأَحَد؟	شو بْتِعْمَلي بَعْد الظُّهُر يوم الأَحَد؟	What do you do Sunday afternoon? (f.)
مَع مَن؟	مَع مين؟	With whom?

Challenge yourself: Ask and answer additional follow-up questions about each activity, such as where or at what time.

    Write down the answers you hear on a chart like the following on a separate piece of paper:

بعد الظهر يوم الأحد		
مع من	النشاط	الاسم
أختها	تلعب ألعاب الفيديو	سميرة

After speaking   بعد المحادثة

Look at the data you collected. How many activities do your classmates do with friends, and how many with family? Create a simple chart and label it in Arabic to summarize what you found.

Activity 19 Conversation: Your family in
              Lebanon

نشاط ١٩ محادثة: عائلتك في لبنان

In this activity, you will imagine that you are a Lebanese American visiting your extended
family in Lebanon for the first time. You have never met most of your extended family there,
but an upcoming family reunion will give you a chance.

Before speaking

قبل المحادثة

With a classmate, review how to say the following:

1. George is my father.
2. I am George's father.
3. Madelina is my mother.
4. I am Madelina's mother.
5. Nabil is my brother.
6. I am Nabil's brother.
7. Tina is my sister.
8. I am Tina's sister.
9. Michele is my wife.
10. I am Michele's wife.
11. Bruno is my husband.
12. I am Bruno's husband.
13. Zaina is my partner.
14. I am Zaina's partner.

Depending on context, the words صاحب / صاحبة and صديق / صديقة may be used
and understood to mean "boyfriend" or "girlfriend," in the sense of a romantic partner.
Review the following examples:

| He is my boyfriend. | هُوَّ صاحْبي. | هُوَ صَديقي. |
| She is Ahmed's girlfriend. | هِيِّ صاحْبة أَحْمَد. | هِيَ صَديقة أَحْمَد. |

Use this information to figure out how to say:

15. Rami is my boyfriend.
16. Amal is my girlfriend.

Speaking

المحادثة

Your teacher will assign you a role in the family to play. Circulate through the family reunion,
meeting your relatives. As is polite in Arab culture, be sure to greet each person, find out
how they are, and let them know that it's nice to meet them. Each person may not reveal all
their relationships to you, so be sure to talk to everyone so that you get a complete picture.

You should meet the following people:

وَديع   أَيْمَن   دانية   مَي   عَلياء   حامِد   فَريد   جاد

لَيلى   نَجاح   رَزان   خَليل   سَميرة   زياد

Be sure to make notes about each person's relationship so you can piece together a family tree later.

After speaking

بعد المحادثة

Create a family tree showing all of the relationships among the relatives you met at the family reunion. Check it with a classmate to make sure that you got all of the family relationships right. When you are done, write an email to your family back in your country telling them everyone you met at the reunion and who those people are. You can use the phrase:

I met . . .	...تْعَرَّفت عَلى	...تَعَرَّفْتُ عَلى

I have a younger brother

الدرس السابع عشر

عندي أخ صغير

LESSON SEVENTEEN GOALS

أهداف الدرس السابع عشر

By the end of this lesson, you should be able to do the following:

- Describe your friends and family with some adjectives
- Tell what your friends and family are *not* like
- Compare your friends and family by saying who is _____-er than others
- Talk about others' friends and family

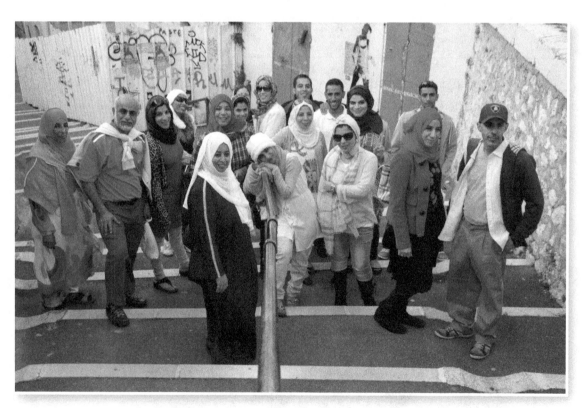

- What are your friends and family like?
- What qualities do you share with your family and friends? What qualities make you different from them?

SHE'S FUN TO BE AROUND

Activity 1   Writing: Reviewing masculine
                          and feminine

هي خفيفة الدم

نشاط ١   كتابة: مراجعة المذكر والمؤنث

In previous chapters, you learned a number of words that change in a predictable way
according to gender by adding ة. Let's review them:

1. Look at this cloud of words and identify pairs of words that are the same except
   for the ة ending.
2. Rewrite the words in the table like the one below, adding a picture, word,
   or phrase to show you know what it means.

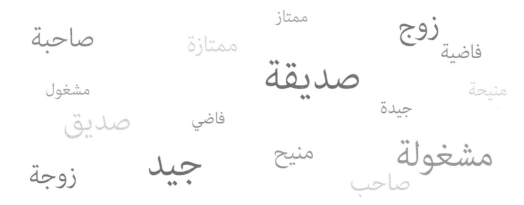

صاحبة   ممتاز   زوج
ممتازة   فاضية
صديقة   منيحة
مشغول   جيدة
صديق   فاضي   مشغولة
زوجة   جيد   منيح   صاحب

What does it mean?	F.	M.

Notice that each of these words is either a **noun (اسم)** or an **adjective (صفة)**. What
is the pattern for differentiating the words for the masculine (مُذَكَّر) and feminine (مُؤَنَّث)

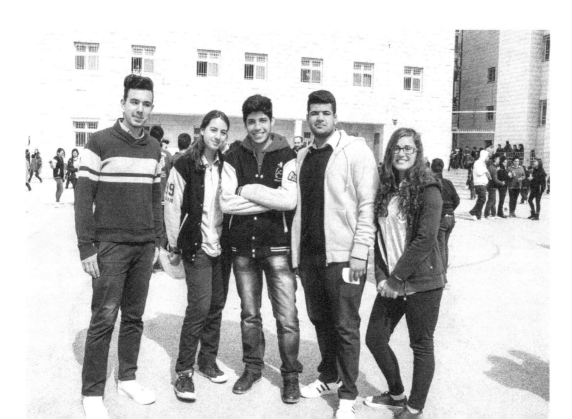

grammatical categories? Most nouns and adjectives in Arabic change with this pattern. Starting with this chapter's lists, most vocabulary words that refer to people (adjectives and nouns) will appear only in the masculine (مُذَكَّر) form. You will have to come up with the feminine (مُؤَنَّث) form on your own.

Vocabulary 1   مفردات ١

المعنى	العاميّة الشاميّة	الفصحى
old a grown-up *(when describing things, this word means "big")*	كْبير (بِالسِّنّ)	كَبير (في السِّنّ)
young a child *(when describing things, this word means "small")*	صْغير (بِالسِّنّ)	صَغير (في السِّنّ)
tall *(when describing things, this word can also mean "long")*	طَويل	طَويل
short	قَصير	قَصير
friendly nice	لَطيف	لَطيف
handsome beautiful	حِلْو	جَميل
smart	ذكي	ذَكِيّ
pleasant fun to be around *(literally: "light of blood")*	خَفيف الدَّمّ	خَفيف الدَّمّ
unpleasant not fun to be around *(literally: "heavy of blood")*	ثْقيل الدَّمّ	ثَقيل الدَّمّ
crazy insane	مَجنون	مَجنون
very tall	طَويل كْثير	طَويل جِدّاً
very	كْثير	جِدّاً

1. Using the vocabulary list, write the مذكر masculine form in the right-hand column
   of a table like the one below. Next, write the مؤنث feminine form of each adjective
   by adding ة / ـة to the end of each word. Remember to pay attention to whether
   the final letter of the مُذَكَّر masculine form is a social or antisocial letter. Then,
   choose either the masculine or the feminine form and draw a doodle that shows
   you know what the word means and label your doodle.

   Note 1: Do not include جِدّاً / كثير (very) because those words modify the adjectives and do not change endings.
   Note 2: When changing the multi-word adjectives (e.g., كبير في السن, ثقيل الدم)
   only the first word changes; that word is the primary adjective.

الصورة	المؤنث	المذكر
طويلة	طويلة	طويل
خفيف الدم	خفيفة الدم	خفيف الدم

2. Draw a picture of yourself and write a sentence describing yourself with as many
   adjectives as possible. Don't forget to use the correct form (مؤنث or مذكر) for
   yourself!

In this activity, practice reading the text of personal ads.

The text on the next page is adapted from a website with personal ads called زواج الأردن.
Talk with a classmate about what you think that might mean. On a separate piece of paper,

create a table with eight numbered spaces, as in the reading below. Use this table to write your notes.

The postings	Titles	
		.١
		.٢

Reading for general understanding

القراءة للفهم العام

On your first reading, focus on the titles, which are to the right of each personal ad in **bold**. On your separate sheet of paper, list all the words you can find next to each number that may refer to a man or a woman, even if you are not sure what the word actually means. Put circles around the masculine words and rectangles around the feminine ones when you write them down.

Close reading

القراءة الدقيقة

Now, look to the postings themselves. These are adapted from an actual website, so you are *not* expected to understand all or even most of what is written here.[1]

♥ زواج الاردن ♥		
انا فتاة عمري ٢٥ سنة مطلقة بدون اولاد جميلة الشكل حنطية البشرة من عائلة محترمة ومحافظة ربة منزل ممتازة طولي ١٦٣ ووزني ٥٢ على خلق ودين ملتزمة والحمد لله رومانسية وحنونة ومخلصة باذن الله تعالى	**ابحث عن زوج رومانسي ولطيف وذكي**	.١
فتاة اردنية من اصل فلسطيني، عمري ٢٧ معي ماجستير وبشتغل في التدريس.. ابحث عن ابن حلال اردني من اصل فلسطيني خلوق ومتعلم	**جادة جداً**	.٢
عمري ٣٧ سنة... جميل الشكل والهيئة.. وضعي المادي جيد.. واريد زوجة تقبل الاقامة في بلد أوروبي معي. لازم تكون طيبة وذكية وتتكلم الانجليزية...	**ابحث عن زوجة عربية**	.٣
انا شاب انيق الشكل اعمل مدقق مالي عمري ٢٧ ابحث عن فتاة للصداقة وان تكون حنونة وجميلة هذا رقمي ٢٢٣٨٢٦٤*** واتس اب	**ابحث عن فتاة جميلة للصداقة**	.٤

♥ زواج الاردن ♥		
شاب يريد الزواج والاستقرار... الحمد لله امتلك شقة للزواج... محترم—ذكي—طموح...	<u>اريد زوجة</u> <u>ممرضة</u>	٥.
شاب عمري ٣٧ سنة اسمي إيهاب أريد امرأة حنونة جميلة وأهم شي عن وجه تحب السهر وانا وضعي المادي جيد جدا للتواصل ٨٣٣٣٤٣***	<u>صداقة</u>	٦.
انا موظف عمري ٢٨ ابحث عن امرأة واقعية العمر ما بين ٣٨—٥٠ فقط من سكان عمان و لا اريد فتاة اصغر مني. بحب ممارسة الرياضة وبحب الطبخ مع شريكتي. واتس او تلفون ٧٦٢٨٩١٣***	<u>امراة واقعية</u> <u>للتعارف</u>	٧.
السلام عليكم انا اسمي حسن عمري ٣٣ سنة انيق المظهر ارغب بالزواج من فتاة محترمة و انيقة انا اسكن في منزل مفروش من جميع الملتزمات لم اتزوج من قبل وضعي المادي متوسط انا طويل وارجو بان لا تكون هي قصيرة ولا طويلة جدا. رقم هاتفي ٥٧٣٥٢٧*** وتس اب او المراسلة على الايميل hasan@*****.com او فيس بوك باسم (حسن ******)	<u>انا شاب جاد</u> <u>جداً وجاهز</u> <u>للزواج ان شاء</u> <u>الله</u>	٨.

1. Search for nouns and adjectives, both masculine and feminine, and write them in your table (draw a circle around masculine words and a rectangle around feminine ones). Keep in mind that some of these may describe the author of the posting while others may describe the person he or she is seeking.

2. Identify adjectives that you have learned and look for other adjectives that you can guess from their spelling and position in the sentences. For example, the appearance of the phrase امرأة واقعية, with two feminine words next to each other, suggests a noun followed by an adjective that modifies it.

3. Can you figure out whether each posting is written by a man or a woman? (Hint: don't rely only on the title!) On your piece of paper, draw a symbol that shows your guess next to each number.

4. There are a few repeated words and phrases in this text. Try to guess the meaning of the phrases below, based on how they appear in the text. Even if you do not guess correctly, it is important to practice the skill of guessing unfamiliar words.

ابحث عن   رومانسية   واتس اب   صداقة

After reading   بعد القراءة

Now that you have read these real-life personal ads, write your own on a separate sheet of paper, pretending that you are a celebrity. Without writing "your" name, use adjectives

to describe both "yourself" (as the celebrity) and the person that "you" are seeking. Write a catchy title for your posting. Include adjectives that you have learned, and make sure to add ة when necessary. When you are finished, trade personal ads with a classmate and see if they can guess which celebrity you impersonated!

Challenge yourself: Incorporate as many new words or phrases that you learned from the reading as possible!

| Activity 4 | Listening: "At Taghreed's house," part one | استماع: "في بيت تغريد،" | نشاط ٤ |

الجزء الأول

In the video titled "في بيت تغريد," observe ياسمين visiting تغريد.

Before listening   قبل الاستماع

Watch through part one of "في بيت تغريد" without the sound (0:00-2:15). In Arabic, tell a classmate some words or phrases you expect to hear, based on the visuals.

Listening for general understanding   الاستماع للفهم العام

On a separate sheet of paper, respond to the questions about the listening:

Who is in عائلة تغريد؟ Listen to confirm the visual cues you noticed earlier. Write each person's name or relationship to تغريد in the right column of a table, like the one below, that you create on a separate sheet of paper.

الوصف	الاسم

Close listening   الاستماع الدقيق

Listen several times to gather more information about the people introduced; write any descriptions or other information about each person in the left column of your table. Finally, below your table, write down as many phrases, familiar and unfamiliar, as you can from the scene. If they are unfamiliar, guess what they mean based on the context.

Challenge yourself: There is one family member mentioned in the video who is not present. Who is this person? What do you learn about him or her?

After listening   بعد الاستماع

With a partner, watch the video with the sound muted and create a "voiceover" for the conversation based on your notes and memory. Decide who will be each character and express the same details about عائلة تغريد.

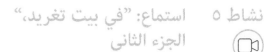

Activity 5   Listening: "At Taghreed's   استماع: "في بيت تغريد،"   نشاط ٥
              house," part two   الجزء الثاني

In part two of the video from Activity 4, you will watch a conversation between ياسمين and
تغريد about عائلة ياسمين in the United States.

Before listening   قبل الاستماع

Watch the video without audio and brainstorm some words or phrases you expect to hear.

Listening for general understanding   في الاستماع للفهم العام

Watch the second part of the video, then respond to the questions about the listening on a
separate sheet of paper:

1. Who is in عائلة ياسمين back home?
2. Write down any extra information you can understand about each of Yasmine's
   family members. What are they like? What hobbies and interests do they have?

Close listening   في الاستماع الدقيق

3. At the beginning of the video, ياسمين and تغريد disagree on the meaning of a big
   family. What does each person say about what a big family means to them? How
   might this reflect a difference between Arab and American cultures?

Challenge yourself: Listen for the following sentences. What do you think they mean?

- اِنْتِ وأَخوكِ أَصْحاب؟
- ما شاء الله عَلَيها كْثير ذَكِيّة!

After listening   بعد الاستماع

Gather pictures of five family members or friends (you can use your own pictures, if possible, or create a fictional family). Then, write a sentence about each person with at least
two adjectives. Follow this example:

أُمّي طَويلة ولَطيفة.

Based on your pictures and your sentences, act out an exchange modeled on the
video with a classmate. Introduce your friends and family members to one another, using
as many phrases and questions as possible from the video. If possible, record a video of
your exchange and share it with your class.

Culture: *Maa shaa' allaah*   الثقافة: ما شاء الله

You have already learned a number of phrases that include the Arabic word for "God" in
them, including إن شاء الله and الحمد لله, which are used in a variety of contexts including
many non-religious situations. Another phrase you will encounter frequently is:

ما شاءَ اللّه

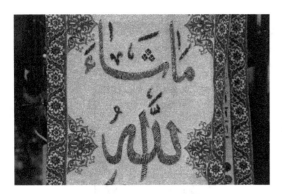 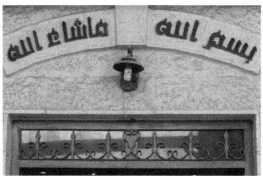

The literal meaning of this phrase is "what God has willed." It expresses praise and thankfulness and is often used when admiring something or someone. The phrase is considered to be a reminder that everything good comes from God. For instance, if you are praising someone's Arabic language skills, you could say:

عربيتك ممتازة، ما شاء الله!!

In some cultures of the Arab world, there is a belief or superstition that directly praising something attracts envy or the evil eye. Some Arabs believe that saying ما شاء الله prevents praise from attracting the evil eye, and some Muslims have the words ما شاء الله written above the door of their home or place of work, or on their car, as a way of bringing blessings. ما شاء الله should always be used when praising people to avoid giving offense. This is especially true when discussing someone's family members with them.

Turn to a classmate and practice complimenting them, using ما شاء الله as part of your praise.

Activity 6   Reading: Negation of adjectives

نشاط ٦   قراءة: نفي الصفات

In Unit 3, you practiced saying that you *do not* do certain activities, using ما or لا. We use different words when saying that you *are not* something. Read the captions next to the diagrams below to discover what these are:

بالعاميّة الشاميّة		بالفصحى
هاي صورة سميرة وأخوها وليد.		هذه صورة فيها سميرة وأخوها وليد.
سميرة طويلة وبتحبّ تلعب كرة السلة كثير.		سميرة طويلة وتحبّ أن تلعب كرة السلة كثيراً.
بس أخوها وليد مِش طويل كثير، فهو ما بحبّ يلعب كرة السلة.		ولكن أخوها وليد لَيْسَ طويلاً جداً، فهو لا يحبّ أن يلعب كرة السلة.

بالعاميّة الشاميّة		بالفصحى
وليد ممتاز بألعاب الفيديو وبحبّ يلعبها كثير.		وليد ممتاز في ألعاب الفيديو ويحبّ أن يلعبها كثيراً.
بس أخته سميرة مِش ممتازة بألعاب الفيديو فما بتحبّ تلعبها.		ولكن أخته سميرة لَيْسَت ممتازة في ألعاب الفيديو، فلا تحبّ أن تلعبها.

Grammar 1: Negating adjectives and nouns
قواعد ١: نفي الصفات والأسماء

Based on what you figured out from the story about وليد and سميرة above, write the words used for negation in the variety of Arabic you are studying in the appropriate chart below. You will need to memorize these words.

If you are studying Modern Standard Arabic:

بالإنكليزية	بالفصحى
(he) is not . . .	
(she) is not . . .	
(I) am not . . .	لَسْتُ

As you noticed in the story above, the word to negate adjectives and nouns changes depending on who you are talking about. In addition to the words in the story, one of the other words is given here for you to learn. You will learn the rest of this set of words in a later chapter.

If you are studying Levantine dialect:

بالإنكليزية	بالعاميّة الشاميّة
(he/she) is not . . . (I) am not . . .	

Here is an Arabic tongue twister to help you remember this word. To understand it, you need to know that the word المِشْمِش means "apricots," and مِشْمِشْنا means "our apricots."

هاذا المِشْمِش مِش مِشْمِشْنا

Figure out the meaning with your classmates and then see who can say it fastest with the right number of syllables.

There are many different ways to say "am not" in different areas of the Arab world. In addition to مِش, you may also hear مُش and مو in the Levant. None of these words changes depending on who you are talking about.

Activity 7 Practicing grammar: Negating sentences	نشاط ٧ التدريب على القواعد: نفي الجمل

Imagine a group of family and friends that is the exact opposite of yours. Practice using words for negation by rewriting the sentences you made up in Activity 4 in a table like the one below, as in the example below. Choose the Arabic variety that your class is focusing on.

الجملة الجديدة		الجملة القديمة
أمي مش طويلة ومش لطيفة	أمي لَيْسَت طويلة ولَيْسَت لَطيفة	أمي طويلة ولطيفة

Activity 8 Practicing grammar: Five questions	نشاط ٨ التدريب على القواعد: خمسة أسئلة

For this activity, divide into groups of three to four and get a set of pictures from your teacher. Take turns being "it." The person who is "it" will choose a picture from the set, without telling the others which person they picked. Other students in the group have five chances to ask yes-or-no questions to identify the chosen person. The person who is "it" must answer the question with "yes" or "no," followed by a complete sentence. After a few turns, switch sets of pictures so that you can practice with the other set. Here is a model of the kind of sentences you can use:

Question:	هُوِّ قَصير؟	هَل هُوَ قَصير؟
Affirmative answer:	آه، هُوِّ قَصير.	نعم، هُوَ قَصير.
Negative answer:	لا، هُوِّ مِش قَصير.	لا، هُوَ لَيْسَ قَصير.

Activity 9 Conversation: Ask your classmates!	نشاط ٩ محادثة: تكلموا مع الزملاء!

In this activity, talk with your classmates one at a time to find out if they have particular kinds of people in their circle of friends and family.

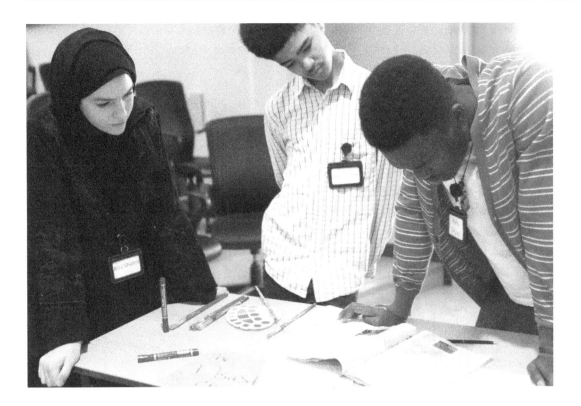

Before speaking قبل المحادثة

Read the list of types of people you are to look for below. With a classmate, figure out how you will phrase the questions that will get you that information, without direct translation. For instance, if the list asks for "a family member who is tall," you could ask, "Do you have a tall brother?" Create a table like the one below to prepare for your conversation.

Speaking المحادثة

With a series of classmates, ask each person questions to find out if they know someone who fits the description. If they do, find out that other person's name by asking ما اسمه؟ or ما اسمها؟ and record it in the table that you created.

Types of people your classmate may know:	Classmate's name:	Who do they know who fits this description?
A teacher who is not nice		
A friend who is crazy but nice		
A family member who is tall		
A parent (mother or father) who is smart		

Types of people your classmate may know:	Classmate's name:	Who do they know who fits this description?
A friend who is short		
A sibling who is older*		
A teacher who is pleasant to be around		
A family member who is beautiful		

After speaking

بعد المحادثة

Report to a classmate or to your whole class about three to five of the people you learned about in your classmates' lives.

*In Arabic, you can say أخ كبير and أخت كبيرة to mean "older brother" and "older sister" respectively.

MY SISTER IS YOUNGER THAN MY BROTHER

أختي أصغر من أخي

Grammar 2: Exploring the comparative form

قواعد ٢: استكشاف وزن "أفعل"

In the previous video, you heard one of the characters say:

$$هِيِّ أَكْبَر مِنّي بِعَشَر سْنين$$

How is the word أكبر similar to كبير? How is it different? Just as with related words that you learned in previous chapters, these words have a **root** in common: they share three letters in the same order and a related meaning. The phrase أكبر من is the **comparative** form of the adjective كبير—instead of "old" it means "older than."

Your teacher will give you a set of cards that include the regular adjectives and the comparative forms. Match them based on root and then fill out the table below with the appropriate forms.

المعنى	Comparative		Adjective
Older than (bigger than)	أَكْبَر مِن	←	كبير
		←	صغير
		←	طويل

المعنى	Comparative		Adjective
		←	قَصير
		←	ذكي
		←	جميل
		←	حلو

Activity 10 Listening: Taghreed's family
and Yasmine's family

نشاط ١٠ استماع: عائلة تغريد وعائلة ياسمين

In this activity, you will rewatch both parts of "في بيت تغريد."

Before listening

قبل الاستماع

First, look back at your notes from the previous times you watched the video. Talking with a classmate, use the comparatives أصغر من and أكبر من to make statements about the different members of عائلة ياسمين and عائلة تغريد.

Listening for general understanding

الاستماع للفهم العام

Watch the videos again. For each pair of names below, write a comparison phrase between them to make a complete sentence. You can use أكبر من and أصغر من to compare people by age.

Challenge yourself: Use other phrases to compare other aspects of the people involved.

عائلة تغريد (الفيديو ١)
١. سناء _____ تغريد
٢. تغريد _____ عصام
٣. شادية _____ قاسم
٤. قاسم _____ سناء
٥. عصام _____ شادية

عائلة ياسمين (الفيديو ٢)
٦. ياسمين _____ يوسف
٧. يوسف _____ ياسمين

Close listening   الاستماع الدقيق

In the video about عائلة ياسمين, listen for the following phrases. Write down what you think they mean and compare your responses with a classmate.

- هو أصغر منك؟
- انتِ أكبر واحدة بالعيلة؟

After listening   بعد الاستماع

In a conversation, share the comparisons you made with your classmates.

Vocabulary 2   مفردات ٢

Review the comparative forms that you already studied in القواعد 2:

المعنى	العاميّة الشاميّة	الفصحى
older than bigger than	أَكْبَر مِن	أَكْبَر مِن
younger than smaller than	أَصْغَر مِن	أَصْغَر مِن
taller than	أَطْوَل مِن	أَطْوَل مِن
shorter than	أَقْصَر مِن	أَقْصَر مِن
nicer than	أَلْطَف مِن	أَلْطَف مِن
more beautiful than	أَحْلى مِن	أَجْمَل مِن
smarter than	أَذْكى مِن	أَذْكى مِن

Activity 11 Vocabulary practice: Guess   نشاط ١١   تدريب على المفردات: إحْزِر
            my number!   رقمي!

Work with a classmate for this game. Take turns playing the role of the chooser and the guesser:

- The chooser picks a number between 1 and 20 and writes it down in a hidden place.
- The guesser says a number, trying to guess the number written down. The chooser responds appropriately, giving a clue using "bigger than" or "smaller than" until the guesser gets the number. Once they find it, switch roles and start again.

Here are some example sentences to use as inspiration:

Question:	رَقْمك عَشَرة؟	هَل رَقْمُك عَشَرة؟
Possible responses:	آه، رَقْمي عَشَرة!	نَعَم، رَقْمي عَشَرة!
	لا، رَقْمي أَكْبَر مِن عَشَرة.	لا، رَقْمي أَكْبَر مِن عَشَرة.
	لا، رَقْمي أَصْغَر مِن عَشَرة.	لا، رَقْمي أَصْغَر مِن عَشَرة.

When the guesser finds your number, use the following phrases to praise them:

That's it!	هاذا هُوِّ!	هٰذا هُوَ!
Bravo! (m.)	يا عَيْني عَلَيْكَ!	يا عَيْني عَلَيْكَ!
Bravo! (f.)	يا عَيْني عَلَيْكِ!	يا عَيْني عَلَيْكِ!

Activity 12 Reading: Tallest buildings in the world   نشاط ١٢   قراءة: أطول بنايات العالم

In this reading, you will learn about some of the tallest buildings in the world.

Before reading   قبْل القراءة

1. On a separate piece of paper, write the numbers ١ through ٩. For each building on the next page, read the name and look at the image, then write down the location

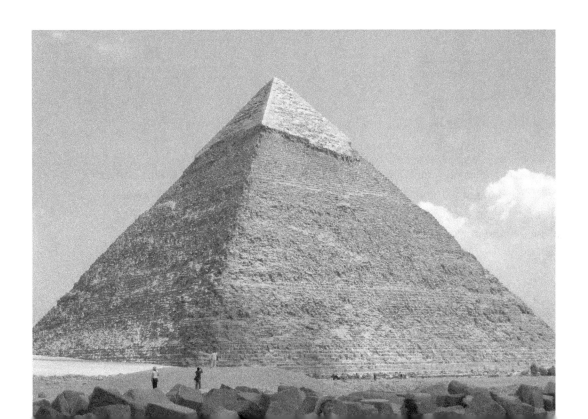

of each building with a location from the answer bank below. If you are not sure, use the Arabic you know to ask a classmate.

 ٢. أبراج البيت

 ١. برج خليفة

 ٤. برج «ويليس»

 ٣. برج الحرية

 ٦. برج توكيو

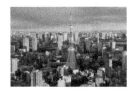 ٥. مبنى "إمباير ستيت"

 ٨. الإبرة الفضائية

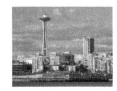 ٧. برج إيفل

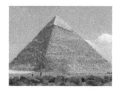 ٩. هَرَم خوفو

ا. مدينة شيكاغو في أمريكا
ب. مدينة مكة في السعودية
ج. مدينة الجيزة في مصر
د. مدينة نيويورك في أمريكا
هـ مدينة سياتل في أمريكا
و. مدينة نيويورك في أمريكا
ز. مدينة باريس في فرنسا
ح. مدينة دبي في الإمارات

2. Which of these buildings would you like to visit? Tell a classmate where you would like to go, using the following sentence as a model:

| I want to visit the Eiffel Tower. | بِدّي أَزور بُرْج إيفل. | أُريد أَنْ أَزور بُرْج إيفل. |

Reading for general understanding   القراءة للفهم العام

With a classmate, look at the table below. What information is it giving? Identify different kinds of information given about each building with your partner.

التكلفة الإجمالية (بالدولار الأمريكي)	مدة البناء (بالسنوات)	سنة البناء	الارتفاع (بالقدم)	الارتفاع (بالمتر)	اسم البناء
١,٥ مليار	٥	٢٠١٠	٢٧١٧	٨٢٨	برج خليفة
٢ مليار	٨	٢٠١٢	١٩٧١	٦٠١	أبراج البيت
٣,٨ مليار	٨	٢٠١٤	١٧٧٦	٥٤١	برج الحرية
١٧٥ مليون	٣	١٩٧٣	١٤٥١	٤٤٢	برج «ويليس»
٢٤ مليون	١	١٩٣١	١٢٥٠	٣٨١	مبنى «إمباير ستيت»
٣٠ مليون	١	١٩٥٨	١٠٩٣	٣٣٣	برج توكيو
١,٥ مليون	٢	١٨٨٩	٩٨٤	٣٠٠	برج إيفل
٤,٥ مليون	١	١٩٦٢	٦٠٥	١٨٤	الإبرة الفضائية
٥ مليار	٢٠	٢٥٥٠ قبل الميلاد	٤٨١	١٤٦	هَرَم خوفو

أطول أبراج العالم

Close reading   القراءة الدقيقة

1. Guess the meaning of the following words: مِلْيار   مِلْيون   بُرْج   أَبْراج
2. Read the following statements about the chart and decide whether they are true (صحيح) or false (خطأ). Write صحيح or خطأ on a separate piece of paper for each one.

١. أبراج البيت أطول من برج ويليس.

٢. البرج في توكيو أقصر من البرج في باريس.

٣. برج الحرية أقصر من مبنى "إمباير ستيت"

٤. البرج من ١٩٣١ أطول من البرج من ١٩٦٢.

٥. هرم خوفو أقصر من برج إيفل.

After reading   بعد القراءة

Now that you have evaluated statements comparing the height of buildings, write four statements on a separate sheet of paper comparing the height of people in your class, some true and some false. Then hand your statements to a classmate to evaluate whether your statements are true or not.

Activity 13 Reading and conversation: Who is the oldest?   نشاط ١٣   قراءة ومحادثة: من الأكبر؟

In this activity, you will learn about some Arab celebrities.

Before reading   قبل القراءة

Below and on the next page is a post from an internet forum. Look at the pictures and discuss with your classmates: who do you think this post is about, based on the pictures and the formatting of the text?

Reading for general understanding   القراءة للفهم العام

What kind of information does the post give about each person? Guess based on words you recognize.

	معلومات عن الفنانين العرب
	حبيت أني أجمع أكبر قدر من المعلومات عن الفنانين العرب أرجو أن يكون موضوع جميل يا ريت الفكرة تعجبكم
١.	**فيروز** الاسم الحقيقي: نهاد رزق وديع حداد تاريخ الميلاد: ١٩٣٥/١١/٢١ مكان الميلاد: مدينة بيروت في لبنان
٢.	**ميريام فارس** الاسم الحقيقي: ميريام فارس تاريخ الميلاد: ١٩٨٣/٥/٣ مكان الميلاد: قرية كفر شلال في لبنان
٣.	**أليسا** الاسم الحقيقي: أليسار زكريا خوري تاريخ الميلاد: ١٩٧٢/١٠/٢٧ مكان الميلاد: بلدة دير الأحمر في لبنان

معلومات عن الفنانين العرب	
٤. **كاظم الساهر** الاسم الحقيقي: كاظم الساهر تاريخ الميلاد: ١٩٥٧/٩/١٢ مكان الميلاد: مدينة الموصل في العراق	
٥. **تامر حسني** الاسم الحقيقي: تامر حسني شريف عباس تاريخ الميلاد: ١٩٧٧/٨/١٦ مكان الميلاد: مدينة القاهرة في مصر	
٦. **وائل كفوري** الاسم الحقيقي: ميشيل إيميل كفوري تاريخ الميلاد: ١٩٧٤/٩/١٥ مكان الميلاد: مدينة زحلة في لبنان	

Close reading   القراءة الدقيقة

1. With a classmate try to guess the meanings of the following words:

ميلاد   تاريخ   حقيقي   مكان

2. Look at how dates are written and write down your own birthdate using Eastern Arabic numerals in the same format.
3. How old is each person in the post? Write their age.

After reading 1   بعد القراءة ١

Get into groups of three classmates. Take turns asking questions about the text to the other members of your group. Pick two people from the post and ask which one of them is older or younger. Follow these models for your question:

مين أكْبَر: ____ ولّا ____؟	مَن أكْبَر: ____ أم ____؟
مين أصْغَر: ____ ولّا ____؟	مَن أصْغَر: ____ أم ____؟

Answer the question as fast as you can, making sure to use a complete sentence that compares who is older or younger. Use these sentences as model responses:

____ أكْبَر مِن ____.	____ أكْبَر مِن ____.

Challenge yourself: Use this structure to express the specific age-difference in years.

___ أَكْبَر مِن ___ بِـ ___ سْنين.	___ أَكْبَر مِن ___ بِـ ___ سَنَوات.

After reading 2   بعد القراءة ٢

After class: choose one of the people listed in the original text and look them up on the internet. What information and videos can you find about them? Who is your favorite?

Activity 14 Writing: Who's older?   نشاط ١٤   كتابة: من أكبر؟

In this activity, you will contrast the ages of some of your classmates.

Before writing   قبل الكتابة

On a separate sheet of paper, create a table like the one below. Record the birth dates of five of your classmates, using the Arabic date formatting that you learned in the previous activity.

تاريخ الميلاد	الاسم
	١.
	٢.

Writing   الكتابة

Now write one sentence about each of the five classmates in your table. In each of these five sentences, compare your classmate's age with that of another classmate or your own. Across your sentences, try to use the following words or phrases at least once:

___ is older than ___ by . . .	___ أَكْبَر مِن ___ بِـ...	___ أَكْبَر مِن ___ بِـ...
___ is younger than___ by . . .	___ أَصْغَر مِن ___ بِـ...	___ أَصْغَر مِن ___ بِـ...
a lot	كْثير	كَثير
a little	شْوَي	قَليل
one year	سَنة	سَنة
two years	سَنْتَيْن	سَنَتَيْن
three years	ثَلاث سْنين	ثَلاث سَنوات

Challenge yourself: Using vocabulary you know from talking about time, figure out how to be more specific with your comparisons: how can you say half a year, a third of a year, or a quarter of a year?

IS THIS YOUR SISTER OR HIS SISTER?

هل هذه أختك أم أخته؟

Grammar 3: Reviewing possessive pronouns

قواعد ٣: مراجعة ضمائر الملكية

In the last lesson, you learned about one way to express possession, الإضافة. You are already familiar with another way to express possession, the possessive pronouns (ضَمائِر المِلْكِيّة). Now you will expand and deepen that knowledge.

Practice   التدريب

المعنى	العاميّة الشاميّة	الفصحى
my name	اِسْمي	اِسْمي
your name (m.)		
your name (f.)		
his name		
her name		

1. First, review how to say your name and others' names by completing the table above on a separate sheet of paper. For now, only fill out the column of the table that has the Arabic variety you are studying.

2. Once you have completed one column, write below your table the part of these words that is the same across all five of them. This word is how you would say "a name" rather than "my name," "his name," etc. The suffixes you see on the end of the words are what give the information about *whose* name it is.

Keep practicing   واصلوا التدريب

3. Now, listen to the recording of the words in the above table, both in الفصحى and العاميّة الشاميّة. Fill in the column that you did not complete earlier, being careful to listen for the short vowels.

4. Check what you wrote with the table on the next page, which contains only the possessive pronoun suffixes, separated from the word they are added to.

5. Look for the similarities and differences between the way the suffixes are written in Modern Standard Arabic and Levantine dialect. Listen again to the recordings of both varieties. Then, write on your separate sheet of paper your observations about both the similarities and differences you observe.

المعنى	العاميّة الشاميّة	الفصحى
my	ـي	ـي
your (m.)	ـَك	ـُكَ
your (f.)	ـِك	ـُكِ
his	ـهْ	ـهُ
her	ـها	ـُها

Even though you are focusing on one variety of Arabic in your learning, you should be familiar with both sets of possessive pronouns because they appear so frequently. Learn one variety to use and be able to recognize the other.

Activity 15 Grammar practice: Possessive pronouns	نشاط ١٥ تدريب على القواعد: ضمائر الملكية

In this activity, you will practice recognizing words with attached pronouns when you see them written.

Before practicing	قبل التدريب

In this activity, you will find words with possessive pronouns attached to them and break them into their component parts.

On a separate sheet of paper, create a table like the one below. For each sentence, fill out your table following these steps:

1. Find at least one word per sentence with a possessive pronoun on it and write it in the table;
    Challenge yourself: Find every example of a possessive pronoun in each sentence.
2. Divide it into its component parts (word and pronoun);
3. Write the meaning in English.

Number 1 has been completed for you as an example; work on number 2 and check your answer with a partner. Don't forget to pay attention to the ة.

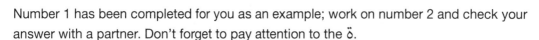

١. وكيف أَهلِك؟   ١. وكيف أَهلك؟
٢. هاي صاحبتي ياسمين.   ٢. هذه صديقتي ياسمين.

Write the meaning	Divide it into its component parts	Find the word from the sentence
Your family	أهل + ك	١. أهلك
		٢.

Start practicing التدريب

Look at the sentences below and complete the chart you started above. Each sentence was spoken in one of the videos that you watched in Lessons 16-17, or will watch in Lesson 18. For those focusing on MSA, the MSA equivalent has also been given.

٣. جدي وستي... كمان بيعيشوا معنا بالبيت.	٣. جدي وجدتي... أيضاً يعيشون معنا في البيت.
٤. تفضلي حبيبتي ياسمين.	٤. تفضّلي حبيبتي ياسمين.
٥. وكيف نادين؟ وأخوك باسم؟*	٥. وكيف نادين؟ وأخوك باسم؟*
٦. عمري ١٢ سنة.	٦. عمري ١٢ سنة.
٧. وكمان بتعرفي أخوي عصام.	٧. وأيضاً تعرفين أخي عصام.
٨. كم عمرها؟	٨. كم عمرها؟
٩. عندي أخ ثاني، اسمه قاسم.	٩. عندي أخ آخر، اسمه قاسم.
١٠. وشو اسمها؟	١٠. وما اسمها؟
١١. هاي أختي شادية وهاي أختي سناء.	١١. هذه أختي شادية وهذه أختي سناء.
١٢. عيلتك كبيرة!	١٢. عائلتك كبيرة!
١٣. عمرها ١٦ سنة.	١٣. عمرها ١٦ سنة.
١٤. هاذا أخوي يوسف.	١٤. هذا أخي يوسف.
١٥. شو بتشتغل أمك؟	١٥. ماذا تعمل أمك؟
١٦. صاحبتي تغريد... هي أكبر منّي.	١٦. صديقتي تغريد... هي أكبر منّي.
١٧. اسمها روزا، هي أمريكية من أصل أرجنتيني.	١٧. اسمها روزا، هي أمريكية من أصل أرجنتيني.
١٨. عن إذنك ماما!	١٨. عن إذنك يا أمي!
١٩. كيف بابا؟ وكيف يوسف؟ شو أخبارهم؟	١٩. كيف أبي؟ وكيف يوسف؟ ما أخبارهم؟

*Recall that أخوك ('your brother') has an additional و. This word, along with the word أب, belongs to a special class of nouns called 'the five nouns'. For now, expect to see and hear these words with the extra و when there is a possessive in العامية الشامية and at times in الفصحى.

Activity 16 Conversation: Where is your grandfather from?   نشاط ١٦   محادثة: مِن أين جدك؟

In this activity you will ask about the origins of the family members of your classmates.

Before speaking قبل المحادثة

First, learn these two family member words in the variety you are learning:

grandfather	جِدّ	جَدّ
grandmother	سِتّ	جَدّة

Prepare for speaking by writing out some family member words with the attached possessive pronouns. On a separate sheet of paper, create a table like the one below and complete the chart, saying each combination aloud as you write. (Remember that أب becomes أبو when a pronoun is added with the exception of أبي.)

	جَدّة \ سِتّ	جَدّ	أم	أب
My . . .			أمّي	
Your (m.) . . .				أَبوكَ
Your (f.) . . .				
His . . .		جدّه		
Her . . .				

Speaking

المحادثة

Your teacher will assign you one of family members to ask about. Rotate around the class-room, asking your classmates where each person's family member is from. Use the following sentences as a model:

Where is your (f.) grandfather from?	مِن وَين جِدِّك؟	مِن أَيْنَ جَدُّكِ؟
My grandfather is from ____.	جِدّي مِن مَدينة ____.	جَدّي مِن مَدينة ____.

If you don't know or don't have a certain family member, you can use a fictional answer. Record what you learn in a table like the one below. When you write the city names, sound out the names and spell them as best you can—do not worry about perfection.

مَن؟	مِن أين؟ أي مدينة؟
أم آلكس	من مدينة نيويورك

واصلوا المحادثة

How would you ask about someone else's family members? Use the following sentences as a model:

Where is Alex's mother from?	مِن وَين أُمّ آلِكْس؟	مِن أَيْنَ أُمّ آلِكْس؟
His mother is from the city of ____.	أُمّه مِن مَدينة ____.	أُمُّهُ مِن مَدينة ____.

Now find out about other families in your classroom by asking your classmates about students you did not directly talk to. Continue to fill in your table from the previous stage.

Finally, check in with some of the students you heard about indirectly, using Arabic to find out whether the information you learned about their family members is correct.

Activity 17   Conversation: Describe your   نشاط ١٧   محادثة: صِف عُائلتك وأصدقائك
family and friends

In this speaking activity, pretend that you are talking to your potential host siblings on a study abroad trip in an Arab country. You will share information with each other about the people who are closest to you, just as the two characters did in "في بيت تغريد," which you watched in Activity 10.

قبل المحادثة

1. In preparation for this conversation, prepare pictures of six of the people who are closest to you. You could print out pictures, draw pictures, create a slide show, or use pictures from your actual social media account, according to what works for your class. You can use real people you are close to or design an imaginary family including celebrities or anyone else.
2. For each person, brainstorm the adjectives you will use to describe him or her, as well as any key phrases you will use. Don't write out full sentences; instead, draw little pictures or write individual words to remind yourself.

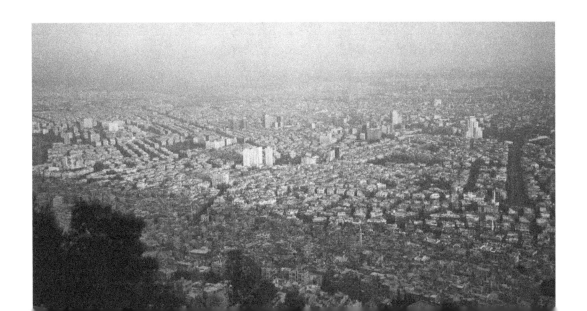

3. Think of three questions you can ask your classmate about their family and friends to get more information. If you're stuck, think about how you can use these question words to make interesting questions:

	شو...؟		ما...؟ ماذا...؟
	وَين...؟		أَيْنَ...؟
	مِن وَين...؟		مِن أَيْنَ...؟
	كَم...؟		كَم...؟

Speaking   المحادثة

4. Find a classmate and show them your pictures, describing each person. Then switch roles and listen while your classmate describes their pictures.

5. When your classmate is speaking, take notes or draw simple pictures so that you can remember the people that they describe to you.

Continue speaking   واصلوا المحادثة

6. Using your diagram, notes and pictures, describe to a third person about the people your classmate has told you about. Use possessive pronouns to say "his brother," "her friend," and so on.

Activity 18 Conversation: At a wedding   محادثة: في حفلة زواج   نشاط ١٨

At weddings in the Arab world—as elsewhere—guests are known to use the party as a chance to get to know who the eligible men and women in the community are and to play "matchmaker." In this role-playing activity, you will play the role of a wedding guest who is looking to find an appropriate match for your children, siblings, or friends.

Before speaking   قبل المحادثة

Your teacher will give you a card with the names and ages of two other people on it. Some of the ages are over twenty. To say the numbers twenty-one through twenty-nine, say the ones digit before the tens digit, connected by و. Use these sentences as models to figure out how to say the ages of your characters.

He is 21 years old.	عُمْرُهُ واحِد وعِشْرين سَنة.	عُمْرُهُ واحِد وَعِشْرين سَنة.
She is 25 years old.	عُمْرُها خَمْسة وعِشْرين سَنة.	عُمْرُها خَمْسة وَعِشْرين سَنة.

Decide how these people are connected to you: Are they your children? Your friends? Your siblings? Write words or images to remind you. If you decide one or both people are your children, you will want to use the following words.

| my son | اِبْني |
| my daughter | بِنْتي |

Use your imagination to make up some information about each of their appearances and personalities:

- What do they like?
- How would you describe them?
- What do they study or work at?
- What do they like to do in their free time?

If you wish, you can also create a name and identity for yourself.

Speaking المحادثة

Pretend that you are at a wedding party and talking with the other guests. You want to introduce yourself and your family (or friends) to others to find out if any of them might be a good match for someone you know. Consider any factors you think are important in finding a match, including age, interests, and personality traits. In Arab countries, it is often considered normal for a man to be a few years older than a woman in a relationship; you can decide whether and how age is an important factor in your matchmaking. After discussing a potential match with another wedding guest, use the following phrases to express your approval or disapproval:

| This is appropriate! | هاذا مُناسِب! | هٰذا مُناسِب! |
| This is not appropriate! | هاذا مِش مُناسِب! | هٰذا لَيْسَ مُناسِباً! |

If you find any possible matches, note the other person's name and reasons for it being a good match.

After speaking بعد المحادثة

As a full class or in a small group, have a debriefing discussion in Arabic about the people you met at the party. Describe any matches that you think might be good and explain why.

Activity 19 Conversation: Humans of Amman نشاط ١٩   محادثة: ناس عمّان

Around the world, including in many Arab countries, people have made social media accounts based on the *Humans of New York* photoblog, showing portraits of people

accompanied by a quote of something they said. In this activity, you and your classmates will talk about the pictures that you find on one of these photoblogs from a city or country in the Arab world.

Before speaking   قبل المحادثة

Search for *Humans of Amman* or *Humans of Beirut* (or a similar photoblog associated with another city) and browse the posts. Collect three or four portraits of people and come up with as many adjectives as possible to describe them.

Challenge yourself: Try to find words that you recognize if there is Arabic text accompanying the pictures!

Speaking   المحادثة

Show your pictures to classmates and discuss what you see. Use the comparative form of the adjectives to compare the people. Who is older or younger than whom? Who is taller, and who is shorter? Who is more beautiful or handsome, in your opinion? If you are speculating about something, use the word ممكن. Make your sentences longer and richer by using بس or ولكن and extend the conversation.

Activity 20 Writing: Humans of My School   نشاط ٢٠   كتابة: ناس مدرستي

In this extension activity, you will create your own series of images about your own school or community.

Before writing   قبل الكتابة

Take pictures (or draw pictures) of six people from your school, some male and some female. If possible, take the pictures while they are doing something they like or in a place that they love. While taking pictures, talk with them about what they are doing, how they are feeling, or something they like and dislike.

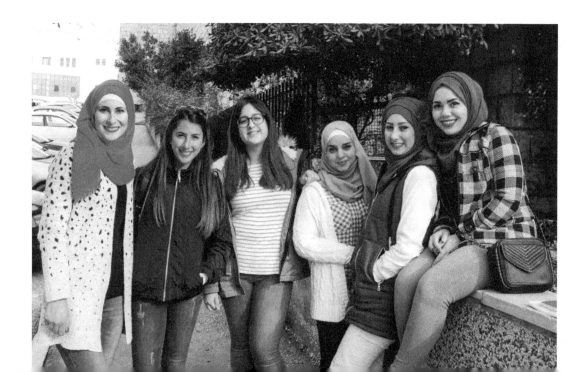

Writing   الكتابة

Write a caption in Arabic to go with each person, based on your conversation. (Do not feel like you need to translate directly!) Use vocabulary from a number of past lessons and include many different adjectives, writing as much as you can.

After writing   بعد الكتابة

Bring your pictures and quotations to class and hang them on the classroom walls. Using sticky notes, write comments in Arabic about what you see and read in other students' pictures, as if you were commenting on a social media post. In your comments, use adjectives to describe the person and the picture. Follow your teacher's instructions about how many comments to write.

My family and I like to …

الدرس الثامن عشر

أنا وعائلتي نحبّ أن...

LESSON EIGHTEEN GOALS

أهداف الدرس الثامن عشر

By the end of this lesson, you should be able to do the following:

- Say how old members of your family are
- Exchange information using numbers up to one hundred
- Talk about what you and your friends or family like to do as a group using verb conjugations for "we"
- Ask and talk about what others' families or friends like to do as a group using verb conjugations for "they" and "you" (plural)
- Ask questions about others' families using a variety of question words

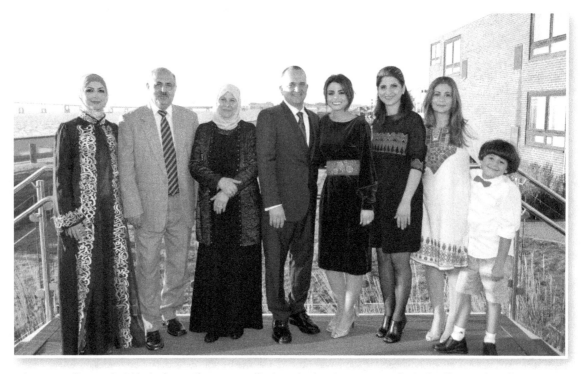

- In your culture, what kind of questions are polite to ask about someone else's family members?
- What kind of questions are considered impolite?

LET'S COUNT TO ONE HUNDRED!

Vocabulary

Learn the numbers between twenty-one and one hundred. In الفصحى, there are two varieties of each number. These represent a grammatical difference but have the same meaning; learn to recognize both.

دعونا نعدّ إلى مئة!

المفردات

المعنى	العاميّة الشاميّة	الفصحى
20	عِشْرين	عِشْرون عِشْرين
21	واحِد وعِشرين	واحِد وَعِشرون واحِد وَعِشرين
22	اِثْنَين وعِشرين	اِثْنان وَعِشرون اِثْنَيْن وَعِشرين
23	ثَلاثة وعِشرين	ثَلاثة وَعِشرون ثَلاثة وَعِشرين
30	ثَلاثين	ثَلاثون ثَلاثين
40	أَرْبَعين	أَرْبَعون أَرْبَعين
50	خَمْسين	خَمْسون خَمْسين
60	سِتّين	سِتّون سِتّين
70	سَبْعين	سَبْعون سَبْعين
80	ثَمانين	ثَمانون ثَمانين
90	تِسْعين	تِسْعون تِسْعين
100	مِيّة	مئة (مائة)*

*These two spellings are pronounced the same way: مِئة. You should be able to recognize both spellings. Ask your teacher which one you should practice writing.

Activity 1   Writing: Numbers twenty to   نشاط ١   كتابة: الأرقام من عشرين إلى
              ninety-nine   تسعة وتسعين

All of the numbers between twenty-one and ninety-nine follow the pattern that is laid out
for twenty-one, twenty-two, and twenty-three above. What is the pattern? On a separate
sheet of paper, write out the full names of the numbers below to practice:

٢. ٣٦	١. ٤٤
٤. ٩٢	٣. ٥٧
٦. ٢٩	٥. ٨٥
٨. ٦١	٧. ٧٣

Activity 2   Listening: The temperature in   نشاط ٢   استماع: درجة الحرارة في
              Arab cities   المدن العربية

In this activity, practice recognizing and using numbers in context.

Before listening   قبل الاستماع

What do you guess is the temperature today in the following American cities? Write down
your guesses next to the name of each city, using Eastern Arabic numerals. If you can,
access a weather website or application to confirm. Use the model sentence below to
share your guesses with your classmates:

The temperature in Boston is 50 degrees Fahrenheit.	الحَرارة في بوسطن ٥٠ دَرَجة فَهْرِنْهايْت.

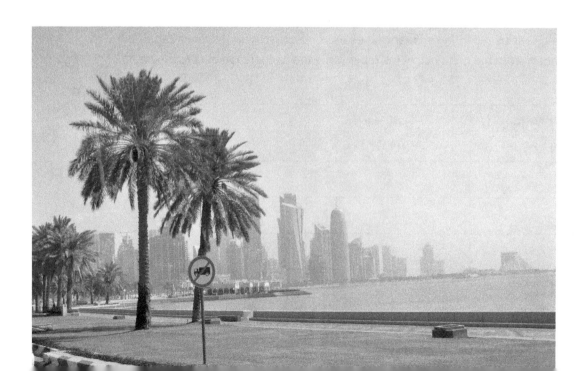

دَرَجة الحَرارة (فَهْرِنْهايْت)	المدينة
	نيويورك
	واشنطن العاصمة
	بوسطن
	سان فرانسسكو
	هيوستن
	شيكاغو

Read the list of Arab cities below aloud, and try to identify each city's name in English and which country it is in.

الاستماع للفهم العام

Listen to this weather report from Lebanese television and write down the names of the cities that the announcer mentions.

المنامة	بغداد	الرياض
صنعاء	أبو ظبي	دمشق
دبيّ	الرباط	عمّان
الكويت	الجزائر	الإسكندريّة

الاستماع الدقيق

Write out the list of cities on a separate sheet of paper in a table like the one below. In this section, you will listen to a recording giving the temperature of each city in Celsius. In most of the world, the Celsius scale is used for measuring temperatures, whereas the Fahrenheit scale is used only in the US, its territories, and a few other places such as the Bahamas.

Listen to the Celsius recording as many times as you need to hear the temperature. Choosing numbers from the bank below the table, write the temperature next to the name of each city.

درجة الحرارة (درجة فهرنهايت)	درجة الحرارة (درجة مئوية)	المدينة
		١. تونس
		٢. الرباط
		٣. القاهرة

درجة الحرارة (درجة فهرنهايت)	درجة الحرارة (درجة مئوية)	المدينة
		٤. بغداد
		٥. دمشق
		٦. عمّان
		٧. الكويت
		٨. الرياض

24   31   23   39   41   35   48   46   29

After listening   بعد الاستماع

Now listen to the Fahrenheit recording, writing down the temperatures that you hear in degrees Fahrenheit for cities 1 through 5 on the list.

Challenge yourself: Write down the temperature mentioned in Fahrenheit for cities 6 through 8.

Activity 3   Listening: Birthday song   الاستماع: سنة حلوة يا جميل   نشاط ٣

Versions of the song "Happy Birthday to You" are common around the world and in many languages. Arabic has a version with different lyrics that follows a similar tune.

Before listening   قبل الاستماع

In which month is your birthday? Use numbers to indicate the month (January = month one, February = month two, etc.). There are other names for months in Arabic, but people often express months this way. Share your birth month with a classmate using the following phrase:

My birthday is in month ____ [number].	عيد ميلادي في شَهْر ____.

Listening   الاستماع

Listen to the birthday song sung for six different people. What are the names and ages of the people in the song?

After listening   بعد الاستماع

Report back to your partner the names and ages you heard.

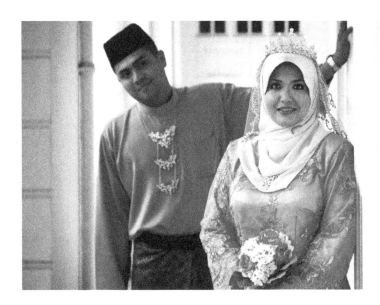
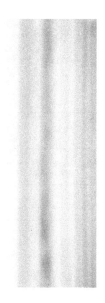

Activity 4   Writing and conversation: قراءة ومحادثة: عمر الزواج   ٤ نشاط
              The age of marriage

In this activity, you will exchange information about average age for marriage in different
countries.

Before reading   قبل القراءة

What word do you know that has the same root as the word الزواج in the phrase
عمر الزواج, the title of this activity? How are their meanings related?

Create a table like the one below, with columns for men's and women's ages for each
country. Read through the country names. Guess the average عمر الزواج for two of the
countries and make a note in pencil.

Speaking with a classmate, share your guesses using the following sentences as a model:

عُمْر الزَّواج لِلرِّجال في فَرَنسا ١٨ سَنة.

عُمْر الزَّواج لِلنِّساء في لُبنان ٢٠ سَنة.

عمر الزواج		
للرجال	للنساء	البلد
		١. أمريكا
		٢. روسيا
		٣. الصين

للرجال	للنساء	البلد
عمر الزواج		
٤. تركيا		
٥. ألمانيا		
٦. السويد		
٧. البرازيل		
٨. لبنان		
٩. المكسيك		
١٠. اليمن		
١١. إندونيسيا		
١٢. الجزائر		
١٣. كينيا		
١٤. مالي		
١٥. الهند		
١٦. السعودية		

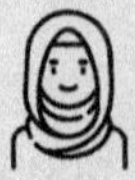

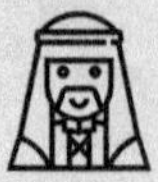

القراءة والمحادثة

Start reading and speaking

Your teacher will hand out strips of paper, each of which shows the average عمر الزواج for women and for men in one of the countries in the chart above. Fill in the data that you got from your teacher. Then, exchange the information you have with your classmates until you complete the entire table. To exchange information with your classmates, you can use this exchange as a model:

كَم عُمْر الزَّواج لِلرِّجال في الصين؟

عُمْر الزَّواج لِلرِّجال في الصّين ٢٥ سَنة.

كَم عُمْر الزَّواج لِلنِّساء في الصّين؟

عُمْر الزَّواج لِلنِّساء في الصين ٢٠ سنة.

When your table is complete, compare your answers with a classmate by making statements in Arabic. If you did not get the same answer as your classmate, find the person who had the information for that country and make sure you communicated correctly.

After reading   بعد القراءة

Answer the following questions, writing out the country names in Arabic.

Challenge yourself: write out the age numbers using full words rather than numerals.

1. Which country has the highest marriage age for men? What is the age? For women? What is the age?
2. Which country has the lowest marriage age for men? What is the age? For women? What is the age?
3. What seems to be the usual gap in marriage age between men and women? In which country is there the smallest marriage gap?
4. Which country has the biggest marriage age gap between men and women? What is the age gap?

Activity 5   Listening: One hundred most powerful Arab women   استماع: أقوى النساء العربيات   نشاط ٥

You will listen to a press release for the ten most powerful Arab women of 2016 according to a site called Arabian Business.[1]

Before listening   قبل الاستماع

In the United States and worldwide, similar lists are compiled each year. Write a short list of powerful women from around the world that you know of or have heard about. Name and describe the individuals on your list in a conversation with a partner, speaking in Arabic. Include each person's name, her country, and her age (an approximate guess is acceptable).

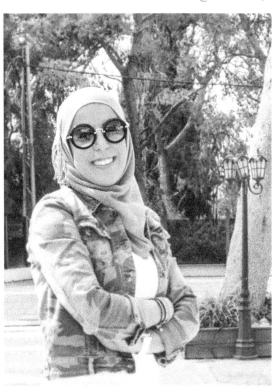

Listening   الاستماع

Create a chart similar to the following on a separate piece of paper. Then, fill out your chart as you listen to the news item about the listed women.

العمر	البلد	الاسم
		١. الشيخة لبنى القاسمي
		٢. زينب السلبي
		٣. ريم الهاشمي
		٤. داليا مجاهد
		٥. نوال المتوكل
		٦. كاتيا بوازا
		٧. نائلة حايك
		٨. لبنى العليان
		٩. زها حديد
		١٠. حنان الكوري

After listening   بعد الاستماع

Research some of the most powerful women in your own country or another country or region of interest. Create a list of five you are interested in, in which you state their names, countries or origins, and ages.

Challenge yourself: Practice writing out their ages in full words rather than using numerals.

نشاط ٦   **Activity 6**   Conversation: How old are these Arab singers?   محادثة: كم أعمار هؤلاء المطربين العرب؟

In this activity, your teacher will give the images, names, and ages of Arab singers. You and a partner will try to guess their correct ages the quickest.

Before speaking   قبل المحادثة

Look over the following structures that will help you complete this activity. Listen to your teacher and classmates as they model the interaction.

Question:	عُمْر نَوال الزُّغْبي ثَلاثة وأَرْبَعين سنة؟	هَل عُمْر نَوال الزُّغْبي ثَلاثة وأَرْبَعون سَنة؟
Possible responses:	آه، عُمْرُها ثَلاثة وأَرْبَعين سنة!	نَعَم، عُمْرُها ثَلاثة وأَرْبَعون سَنة!
	لا، عُمْرُها أَكْبَر مِن ثَلاثة وأَرْبَعين سَنة.	لا، عُمْرُها أَكْبَر مِن ثَلاثة وأَرْبَعين سَنة.
	لا، عُمْرُها أَصْغَر مِن ثَلاثة وأَرْبَعين سنة.	لا، عُمْرُها أَصْغَر مِن ثَلاثة وأَرْبَعين سَنة.

When the guesser finds your number, use the following phrases to praise them:

That's it!	هاذا هُوِّ!	هٰذا هُوَ!
Bravo! *(m.)*	يا عَيني عَلَيْك!	يا عَيني عَلَيْك!
Bravo! *(f.)*	يا عَيني عَلَيْكِ!	يا عَيني عَلَيْكِ!

Speaking   المحادثة

With your partner, decide who will go first. The person going first will show the image to their classmate (make sure to hide the portion that gives the age!). The other partner will guess. Help your classmate by giving them clues using "older than" or "younger than" until the guesser gets the correct age. Immediately switch roles and keep going through all six musical artists.

After speaking   بعد المحادثة

Choose an artist and research online to find out how old they are, where they are from, who their family members are, and what their hobbies are. Then write a magazine blurb in Arabic for the artist with as much information as possible.

Activity 7   Conversation: How old is ...?   نشاط ٧   محادثة: كم عمر...؟

In this activity, practice finding out how old certain people are.

Before speaking   قبل المحادثة

Read the following sentences and try to figure out what they are asking. Then talk with a partner to see if you know the answers.

- كم عمر أوبرا وِنفري؟
- كم عمر أستاذك أو أستاذتك؟

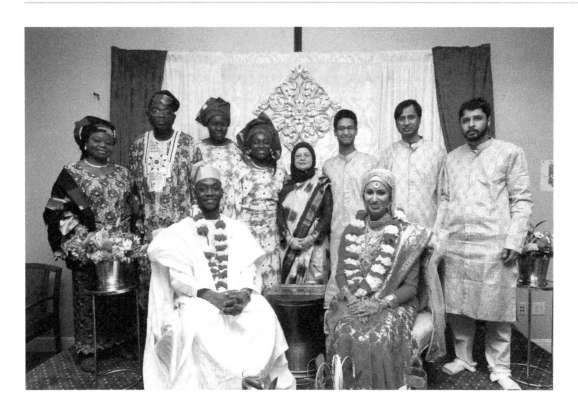

Speaking   المحادثة

Talk with your classmates one at a time and find out the following information, if the
prompts apply to them. Use the questions above as models. Talk with at least four people.

1. Age of a sister
2. Age of a brother
3. Age of a dog (كَلب) or age of a cat (قِطّة، بِسّة)
4. Age of a close friend

After speaking   بعد المحادثة

Write four sentences comparing your answers to those of your classmate's. Use the sentence below as a model:

My sister is 20 years old, and she is older than Chan's sister.	عمر أختي ٢٠ سنة وهي أكبر من أخت تشان.

Activity 8   Reading: *Guinness World Records*   نشاط ٨   قراءة: غينيس للأرقام القياسية

In this drill, you will read about the ages of the oldest and youngest people who earned an
entry in the *Guinness World Records*.

Before reading قبل القراءة

What are some words that you have learned so far that share the same root? Brainstorm together as a class and identify the shared three-letter roots of the words you think of.

Reading القراءة

On a separate sheet of paper, prepare a table to take notes on the following *Guinness World Records* entries. As you read each entry, write down the record holder's name, age, and country, as well as the record they broke. Take notes on the words you were able to guess from context (think about shared roots). Use pictures, flags, or symbols as much as possible instead of translating.

Guinness World Records Entries

١. أكبر لاعب هوكي بريطاني الأصل واسمه روبرت آدمس وهو عمره أربع وثمانون سنة.

٢. أكبر طالب في المدرسة كينيّ الأصل واسمه كيماني نجانجا وعمره أربع وثمانون سنة.

٣. أكبر راقص باليه أمريكي الأصل واسمه فرانك غالي وعمره أربع وسبعون سنة.

٤. أصغر أستاذة أمريكية هي باكستانية الأصل واسمها عالية صابور وعمرها ثماني عشرة سنة.

٥. أصغر لاعب محترف لألعاب الفيديو أمريكي الأصل واسمه فيكتور ديليون وعمره سبع سنوات.

٦. أصغر عازف بيانو يعزف في حفلة رسمية أمريكي الأصل واسمه أيثن بورتنك وعمره تسع سنوات.

٧. أكبر سابحة فازت في الأولمبياد أمريكية الأصل واسمها دارا تورز وعمرها واحدة وأربعون سنة.

٨. أكبر زوجة أسترالية الأصل واسمها مني منرو وعمرها مئة واثنتان سنة وزوجها عمره ثلاث وثمانون سنة.

After reading بعد القراءة

What words were you able to guess from root and context? You probably noticed that a lot of these words are occupations or of people who do a certain action (one who ____). Talk with your classmates and teachers about the pattern that they share. Use this same pattern to guess what the following words would be in Arabic:

Worker = ____   Writer = ____

Writing الكتابة

Write some of your own entries for *Guinness World Records* or search the book online and see which ones you can express using Arabic.

WHAT DO YOU ALL LIKE?

ماذا تحبون؟

Activity 9   Listening: Yasmine talks to her
mother

نشاط ٩   استماع: ياسمين تحكي مع امها

In the video titled "ياسمين تحكّي مع أمها," you will see ياسمين in Jordan video chat with
her mother in the United States.

Before listening

قبل الاستماع

Your teacher will distribute a list of verbs and activities you have learned in previous lessons. Look over the list and be prepared to act them out or draw them in a game of cha-
rades or Pictionary. Working with a partner, decide who will act or draw first while the other
person makes guesses. You will switch roles when your teacher instructs you to. Cross off
the item once your classmate guesses it correctly. You do not need to go through the list in
any particular order.

Then, choose one of the verbs that you acted out. On a separate piece of paper, write
the conjugated forms of this verb that correspond with the pronouns below, and underline
the prefixes and suffixes:

١. أنا
٢. أنتَ
٣. أنتِ
٤. هو
٥. هي

Listening for general understanding

الاستماع للفهم العام

After you listen, name some activities that each of these groups of people like to do:

يوسف وروزا   ياسمين ونادين   ياسمين وتغريد

Close listening

الاستماع الدقيق

Listen again to when راية talks about what she and نادين like to do or to when she discusses what she and تغريد like to do (0:51-1:31). As you listen, complete the following:

1. Write down all the verbs that you hear.
2. What new verb conjugation do you hear? What letters do you think you add to the
   verb stem to create it?

Now, listen to when أم يوسف talks about يوسف and روسا (1:43-2:17) and complete
the following:

3. Write down all the verbs that you hear.
4. What new verb conjugation do you hear? What letters do you add to the verb stem
   to create it?

Culture: "Mom" and "Dad"   الثقافة: "يا ماما" و"يا بابا"

Does your family have a particular way to address children or family members in general? How does أم ياسمين address her at 0:24 and 1:32 in "ياسمين تحكي مع أمها"? In some parts of the Arab world, especially the Levant, you will hear a mother addressing her daughter—or son—as ماما ("Mom"). Likewise, a father often calls his own children بابا ("Dad"), whether speaking with his son or daughter. In fact, any older family member will often address their younger relatives by their own title. For example, a paternal uncle would address his niece or nephew as عَمّو ("Uncle"). This may seem a little confusing at first, but these reversed titles to address children and younger family members are terms of endearment, used the way English speakers might say "baby," "darling," or "sweetie."

Grammar: Conjugating verbs for the pronouns "we," "you" (plural), and "they"   قواعد: تصريف الفعل للضمائر "نحن" و"أنتم" و"هم"

In Lesson 12, you learned the verb conjugation patterns for the singular pronouns in Arabic; now you will learn the patterns for the plural pronouns نحن, أنتم, and هم. Compare the forms of these pronouns between the two varieties and notice how they differ.

we	إِحْنا	نَحْنُ
you (plural)	إِنْتو	أَنْتُم
they	هُمّ	هُم

If you are studying Modern Standard Arabic: Review the familiar verb forms and learn the new ones. The first chart contains the indicative verb pattern, while the second chart contains the subjunctive verb pattern in a phrase following an indicative verb. You will see how, just as with the أنتِ form that drops the final ن in the subjunctive pattern, the أنتم and هم forms also drop the final ن. (The *alif* in those forms is a spelling convention that is not pronounced.)

Pattern for Indicative Verbs (i.e., Independent Verbs) المُضارِع المَرْفوع		
I study	أَدْرُس	أنا
you study (m.)	تَـدْرُس	أنتَ
you study (f.)	تَـدْرُسـين	أنتِ
he studies	يَـدْرُس	هو
she studies	تَـدْرُس	هي
we study	نَـدْرُس	نَحْنُ

Pattern for Indicative Verbs (i.e., Independent Verbs)		
المُضارِع المَرْفوع		
you study (plural)	تَـدرُسون	أنتُم
they study	يَـدْرُسون	هُم

Pattern for Subjunctive Verbs (i.e., Dependent Verbs)		
المُضارِع المَنْصوب		
I like to study.	أُحِبّ أَنْ أَدرُس.	أنا
You like to study. (m.)	تُحِبّ أَنْ تَـدرُس.	أنتَ
You like to study. (f.)	تُحِبّين أَنْ تَـدْرُسي.	أنتِ
He likes to study.	يُحِبّ أَنْ يَـدرُس.	هو
She likes to study.	تُحِبّ أَنْ تَـدرُس.	هي
We like to study.	نُحِبّ أَنْ تَـدرُس.	نَحْنُ
You like to study. (plural)	تُحبّون أَنْ تَـدْرُسوا.	أنتُم
They like to study.	يُحِبّون أَنْ يَـدْرُسوا.	هُم

Remember that the subjunctive form of the verb appears only after certain other verbs or phrases. Here are some of those common phrases (in their plural forms if possible):

مِن اللازِم أَنْ	مِن المُمْكِن أَنْ	نُريد أَنْ	نُحِبّ أَنْ
		تُريدون أَنْ	تُحِبّون أَنْ
		يُريدون أَنْ	يُحِبّون أَنْ

If you are studying Levantine dialect: review these examples of phrases that you heard in the video and take note of the familiar verbs with different suffixes.

We sometimes go to the mall.	أَحْياناً مِنْروح عَلى المول.
We like to go to the University café.	مِنْحِبّ نْروح عَلى كافِتيريا الجامْعة.
We go to the library a lot in order to study.	مِنْروح كْثير عَلى المَكتبة عَشان نِدرُس.

In these examples you can see the prefixes for the احنا forms of the verb include the letter ن. Review the familiar verbs forms below and learn the new ones. The first chart contains the indicative verb pattern, while the second chart contains the subjunctive verb pattern in a phrase following an indicative verb. You will see how all of the indicative forms have a ـب (or ـم) prefix, while the subjunctive forms drop this prefix. (The *alif* in the إنتو and هم forms is a spelling convention that is not pronounced.)

Pattern for Indicative Verbs (i.e., Independent Verbs)		
I study	بَـدْرُس	أنا
you study (m.)	بْتِـدْرُس	أنتَ
you study (f.)	بْتِـدْرُسِـي	أنتِ
he studies	بِيـدْرُس	هو
she studies	بْتِـدْرُس	هي
we study	مْنِـدْرُس	احْنا
you study (plural)	بْتِـدْرُسـوا	إنْتو
they study	بِيـدْرُسـوا	هُمَّ

Pattern for Subjunctive Verbs (i.e., Dependent Verbs)		
I like to study.	بْحِبّ أَدْرُس.	أنا
You like to study. (m.)	بْتِحِبّ تِـدْرُس.	أنتَ
You like to study. (f.)	بْتْحِبّي تِـدْرُسِـي.	أنتِ
He likes to study.	بِيحِبّ يِـدْرُس.	هو
She likes to study.	بْتِحِبّ تِـدْرُس.	هي
We like to study.	مْنِحِبّ نِـدْرُس.	احْنا
You like to study. (plural)	بْتْحِبّوا تِـدْرُسـوا.	إنْتو
They like to study.	بِيحِبّوا يِـدْرُسـوا.	هُمَّ

Remember that the subjunctive verb appears after certain other verbs or phrases such as the following:

لازِم	مُمْكِن	بِدّنا	مِنْحِبّ
		بِدّكُم	بِتْحِبّوا
		بِدّهُم	بِتْحِبّي

Recall that the expression for "to want" in Levantine Arabic is not a verb and thus does not conjugate like a verb; rather it uses attached pronoun suffixes. The example below shows how this combination is used together:

I want to study.	بِدّي أَدْرُس	أنا
You want to study. (m.)	بِدّك تِـدْرُس.	أنتَ
You want to study. (f.)	بِدّك تِـدْرُسـي.	أنتِ
He wants to study.	بِدُّه يِـدْرُس.	هو
She wants to study.	بِدّها تِـدْرُس.	هي
We want to study.	بِدّنا نِـدْرُس.	اِحْنا
You want to study. (plural)	بِدّكُم تِـدْرُسـوا.	إنْتو
They want to study.	بِدّهُم يِـدْرُسـوا.	هُمَّ

Activity 10 Practicing grammar: Verbs in Modern Standard Arabic   نشاط ١٠   تدريب على القواعد: الافعال بالفصحى

In this activity you will practice identifying plural verb forms. The examples will feature Modern Standard Arabic, since they come from newspaper headlines.

Before reading   قبل القراءة

Working with a classmate, make a list of three familiar verbs referring to activities. Write the stem of each verb by itself, and then add the plural verb suffixes for Modern Standard Arabic to each one. Read the words aloud together. Follow the example below:

I draw		أَرْسُم
[verb stem]		رْسُم

we draw	نَرْسُم
you draw (plural)	تَرْسُمون
they draw	يَرْسُمون

Start reading ابدأوا القراءة

Now look at the following news headlines and search for any plural verbs. Make a list of the verbs on a separate sheet of paper and write next to each verb the pronoun that matches the conjugation: هم, نحن, or أنتم.

الشباب لا يقرأون... حقاً لا يقرأون[2]

هل تريدون حقا إصلاح التعليم؟[3]

جنون أم رياضة .. سباحون يلعبون الشطرنج وسط الثلج[4]

ماذا نأكل في العالم العربي؟[5]

"لينجارد": "روني" مثال يُحتذى به وجميع الشباب يريدون أن يصبحوا مثله[6]

الآلاف يشاهدون فيلم The Salesman في ساحات لندن تضامنا مع مخرجه الإيراني[7]

الشباب يحبون "سنابتشات" والكبار "فيسبوك"[8]

كل ما تريدون أن تعرفوه عن نجم "أرب أيدول" يعقوب شاهين[9]

هل هذا الفيديو لشباب يشربون القهوة أم أنه فيلم "رعب"؟[10]

"نحن نحب القراءة" تنظم فعالية للأطفال السبت المقبل[11]

After reading بعد القراءة

Write at least three headlines about your school using the three new verb conjugations.

نشاط ١١   محادثة: مع بعضنا البعض

Activity 11   Conversation: Together

In this activity, you will talk about what people in your family and social group like to do and what you do with them.

Before speaking قبل المحادثة

1. Listen again to ياسمين on the video call with her mother and review your notes with a classmate. Discuss in Arabic what each group of people likes to do together, using plural verb forms for هم:

يوسف وروزا   ياسمين ونادين   ياسمين وتغريد

2. To prepare for a conversation about your own family and friends circle, independently practice conjugating verbs to express what you like to do with different
   members of your family. Choose a few these sentence prompts (or create your
   own) and write down the verb forms you will use:

أنا وأخوي...	أنا وأخي...
أنا وأختي...	أنا وأختي...
أنا والعيلة...	أنا والعائلة...
أنا والأصحاب...	أنا والأصدقاء...

3. Practice speaking the questions you will use to ask your classmates about what
   they like to do with different groups. Review the example below and create at least
   two more possible questions of your own.

ماذا تُحِبّون أَنْ تَفْعَلوا أَنْتَ وَالأَصْدِقاء؟	شو بِتْحِبّوا تِعمَلوا إِنْت والأَصْحاب؟

Speaking   المحادثة

With a classmate, ask and answer questions about what they do with their friends and
various family members. Record simple notes on who does what using a table like the one
below. Try to find at least one activity that you have in common with your conversation
partner.

ماذا يفعلون؟	مَن؟
يشاهدون الأفلام	هي وأخوها

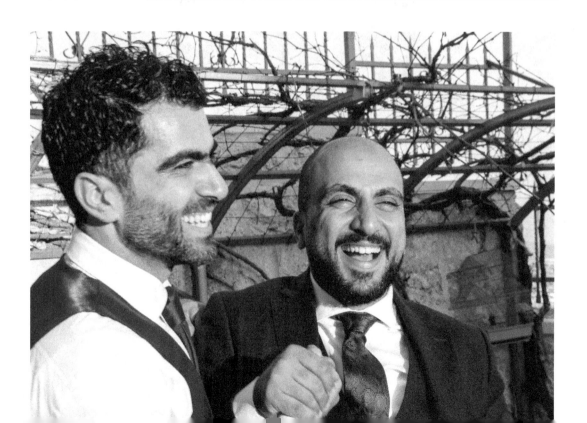

After speaking   بعد المحادثة

Review your notes and identify at least one activity you have in common with your classmate and one you do not. Talk with someone you haven't spoken with yet and report what
you have noticed.

Activity 12 Conversation: Twins   نشاط ١٢   محادثة: توأم

In this activity, you will join an imaginary family and find a classmate in an imaginary family
that matches yours.

Before speaking   قبل المحادثة

Review the following words that are used to form questions:

من وين وين شو	ما ماذا أين
كم إيمتى كيف	من أين كيف
	متى كم

   Your teacher will give you five statements about an imaginary family, which you will
pretend is your family. Come up with at least five questions that could be answered by
these statements, making sure you use the new pronouns and verb conjugations. Use a
variety of question words from above, and do not make yes-or-no questions!
   Remember, when you pose the question, you should use the verb form for "you all":

What do you all like to do?	شو بِتْحِبّوا تِعْمَلوا؟	ماذا تُحِبّون أَنْ تَفْعَلوا؟

And when you answer, you should use the verb form for "we," as in the following example:

We like to play soccer.	مِنْحِبّ نِلْعَب كُرة القَدَم.	نُحِبّ أَنْ نِلْعَب كُرة القَدَم.

Speaking   المحادثة

Walk around the classroom asking and answering questions to find the classmate who has
the same family as you. When you find the matching family, say:

I found you! *(m.)*	لَقَيتَك!	وَجَدْتُكَ!
I found you! *(f.)*	لَقَيتِك!	وَجَدْتُكِ!

Activity 13 Conversation: What do students from your school like?

نشاط ١٣   محادثة: ماذا يحبّ طلاب مدرستكم؟

A national publication is doing an article about your school to find out what students there like. In this activity, you will act as the reporter, first formulating questions and then posing them to a student representative.

Before speaking

قبل المحادثة

As the reporter, you will plan at least eight questions you would like to ask the student representative at your school. The questions should shed light on different topics such as hobbies, school life, and preferences of the students. Write your questions, and make sure to use all the question words in the word banks. Share your questions with a classmate to check that they are understandable.

من وين وين شو	أين ماذا ما
كم إيمتى كيف	من أين كيف
	متى كم هل

Speaking

المحادثة

Take turns being the reporter or the student representative. As the reporter, ask the student representative the questions you have prepared and take notes on their responses. As the student representative, remember that you need to answer on behalf of all the students and not just yourself, so be sure to use the "we" form when you answer.

After listening

بعد المحادثة

Now write a short article based on the responses you received. Make sure you introduce the school, note where it is located, and mention the name of the student representative with whom you spoke.

Activity 14 Practicing grammar: Picture bingo

نشاط ١٤   تدريب على الأفعال: بينغو بالصور

You and your classmate will take turns pulling a picture from an envelope provided to you by your teacher. Describe it using at least three sentences and even more if you can. In each sentence, include at least one verb conjugated for هم, نحن, أنتم. If the description you hear fits the picture on the handout distributed to you by your teacher, cross it off. If it does not, simply say:

I don't have the picture.	ما عِنْدي الصورة.	لَيْسَ عِنْدي الصورة.

Once you get three pictures in a row, across or diagonal, say:

عندي بينغو!

For example, if you pulled this picture, you could say the following about it:

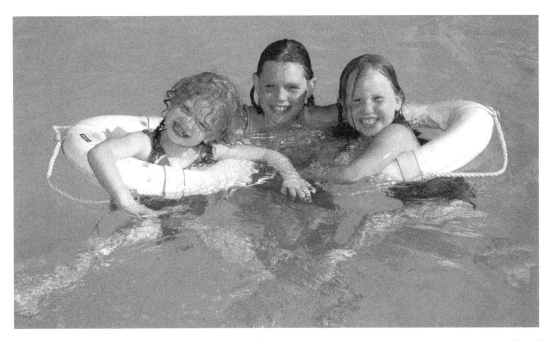

أنا وإخْواتي في الصورة. اِحْنا مْنِسْبَح ومْنِلْعَب في المَيّ. أخْتي رَنْدة عُمُرها ١١ سَنة وهِيّ قَصيرة وأخْتي تالة عُمُرها ١٦ سَنة وهِيّ طَويلة. هُمَّ كمان بيحِبّوا يروحوا عَلى السوق بَس أنا ما بَحِبّ السوق!	أنا وَأخْواتي في الصورة. نَحْنُ نَسْبَح وَنَلْعَب في الماء. أخْتي رَنْدة عُمْرُها ١١ سَنة وُهِيَ قَصيرة وَأُخْتي تالة عُمْرُها ١٦ سَنة وَهِيَ طَويلة. هُم أيْضاً يُحِبّون أنْ يَذْهَبوا إلى السوق وَلَكِن أنا لا أُحِبّ السوق!

Activity 15 Conversation: Survey   محادثة: استطلاع رأي   نشاط ١٥

You have been hired to gather information about how students spend their time with their friends and families. You will be assigned one question for which you must gather responses and then report this information.

Before speaking   قبل المحادثة

Look at the prompt given to you by your teacher. Formulate your question in Arabic. Remember to use the plural form of "you."

Speaking   المحادثة

As you gather your classmate's responses, record them on a sheet of paper. Don't forget to greet your classmates, answer their questions, and excuse yourself before moving on to another person.

Look at your findings. What are the overlaps? What trends do you notice? Share your responses with your class and then formulate some conclusions and comparisons using the sentence structure below as a model:

With family, the students like to . . .	مَع العَيلة، الطُّلّاب بيحِبّوا . . .	مَع العائِلة، الطُّلّاب يُحِبّون أنْ . . .
But with friends, they prefer to . . .	بَس مَع الأَصحاب، هُمَّ بيفَضّلوا . . .	وَلٰكِن مَع الأَصدِقاء، هُم يُفَضِّلون أنْ . . .

**Activity 16 Writing and conversation:
A family suitable for me**

نشاط ١٦   كتابة ومحادثة: عائلة مناسبة لي

Your family will be out of town to attend to some family business, and you need to find a host family to stay with during this period. In this drill, you will formulate questions to your classmates to find out if any of their families are a suitable match for you.

You have a meeting with some prospective families who want to host you in your family's absence. Write down at least five important questions on a separate sheet of paper you would like to ask them that will determine whether they might be a good match for you. Be sure to think about whether you will be asking one person, using أنتَ / أنتِ, or directing the question to multiple people, using أنتم.

Pretend your classmates are representing their own families. Interview them using the questions you came up with. Remember to use polite expressions and to introduce yourself and talk about your family a bit before you start with the questions.

Which of the families that you interviewed is the best fit for you? Why? Write a few sentences justifying your choice.

How often do you...?

الدرس التاسع عشر

كم مرّة...؟

LESSON NINETEEN GOALS

أهداف الدرس التاسع عشر

By the end of this lesson, you should be able to do the following:

- Tell how often you do different activities
- Tell whether you do activities with friends, family, or by yourself
- Write a letter to someone explaining how often you do things with your friends and how often you do them with your family

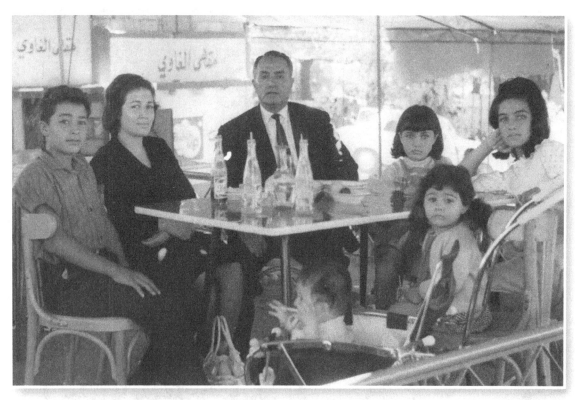

- How often do you do your favorite hobbies with friends or with family?
- How often do you do things by yourself?
- How does your culture influence who you spend time with?

HOW OFTEN DO YOU...?

Vocabulary

كم مرّة...؟
المفردات

المعنى	العاميّة الشاميّة	الفصحى
How many times...? How often...?	گَم مَرّة...؟	كَم مَرّة...؟
one time an instance	مَرّة	مَرّة
times instances	مَرّات	مَرّات
each, every, all	كُل	كُل
day	يوم	يَوْم
days	أَيّام	أَيّام
month	شَهْر	شَهْر
months	شُهور	شُهور
year	سَنة	سَنة
years	سِنين	سَنَوات
together	مع بَعْض	مَعاً
by myself	لَحالي	وَحْدي

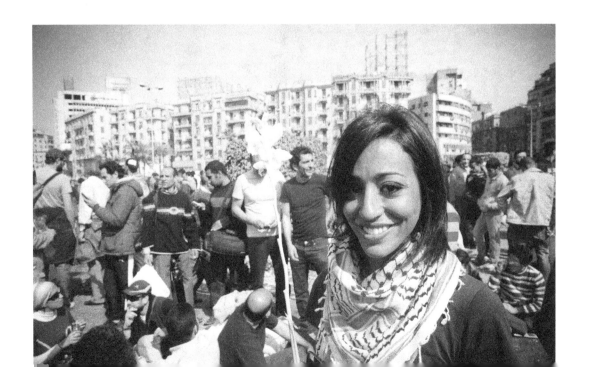

Activity 1   Listening: Ghada's calendar   استماع: تقويم غادة   نشاط ١

Here is a calendar of Ghada's activities in Cairo, Egypt:

شهر فبراير						
يوم السبت	يوم الجمعة	يوم الخميس	يوم الأربعاء	يوم الثلاثاء	يوم الاثنين	يوم الأحد
7 🏙️	6 🕌	5 🎨	4	3 ⚽	2 🎨	1
14	13 🕌	12 🎨	11 ⚽	10	9 🎨	8
21 🏛️	20 🕌	19 🎨	18	17	16 🎨	15
28 🏙️	27 🕌	26 🎨	25 💃	24 ⚽	23 🎨	22

Before listening   قبل الاستماع

1. Look at Ghada's calendar. What can you say about her schedule? In Arabic, write down or tell classmates anything you notice, using as many complete sentences as you can.

Listening   الاستماع

2. Number a separate sheet of paper from one to ten. You will listen to ten statements about Ghada's activities. As you hear each statement, mark whether the statement is true or false.

After listening 1   بعد الاستماع ١

3. Listen again and pause at each sentence marked "false." Can you give the correct information, either in a phrase or a complete sentence? Write it down on your paper and tell a classmate.

After listening 2   بعد الاستماع ٢

4. Create a calendar for the current month with your own activities on it, represented either in pictures or writing.

5. Use the calendar to play two truths and a lie with a classmate: Tell your classmate two true statements about what you are doing this month and one false statement. Your classmate must use your calendar to determine which of your statements is false.

Activity 2   Listening: "zuuruunii"   استماع: "زوروني"   نشاط ٢

One of the Arab world's most famous singers is فَيروز, an artist from Lebanon, and one of her most famous songs is called "زوروني."

Before listening   قبل الاستماع

What might the word زوروني mean? What word do you know that has the same root?

Listening   الاستماع

Search for the song "زوروني" on the internet. Listen to it and write down as many words from the song's chorus that you can.

After listening   بعد الاستماع

Share the words you were able to recognize with a classmate. What do you think the message of the song is? Who is someone in your life for whom the song's message applies?

Activity 3   Listening: Once, twice, three times?   استماع: مرة، مرتين، ثلاث مرات؟   نشاط ٣

In this activity, practice finding out how often people do different activities.

Before listening   قبل الاستماع

Practice formulating the phrases listed below using new and old vocabulary words, following the examples. Write them on a separate piece of paper.

One time	مرة مرة واحدة
Three times	ثلاث مرّات*

1. Two times
2. Four times
3. Every day
4. Every week
5. Every month
6. Every year
7. Every two days
8. Two times every day

*You may notice that you sometimes see the number three as ثلاثة and sometimes as ثلاث. These two forms have the same meaning. Numbers in Arabic follow agreement rules. Ask your teacher if you want to learn more, but you do not need to master these rules for now.

Listening الاستماع

Listen to the recording, and write how often the speaker does each activity:

1.

2.

3.

4.

5.

6.

7.

8.

After listening بعد الاستماع

Tell a classmate the following in Arabic:

- Something you do once per week
- Something you two twice each week
- Something you do three (or more) times each week
- Something you do every two days
- Something you do twice every day

نشاط ٤ قراءة: كم ساعة يقضي الأمريكيون في...؟ Activity 4 Reading: How many hours do Americans spend on . . .

Every year, the US Department of Labor surveys Americans to find out how much time they spend on common activities and reports the averages. In this activity, you will learn about how much time the average American was spending on different activities in 2019.

Before reading قبل القراءة

Read the following activities reported on the time-use survey. For each, draw a picture on a separate piece of paper representing what you think the word or phrase means. These words are similar to, but not exactly the same as, vocabulary words you previously studied.

- لعب الرياضة
- التسوّق
- مشاهدة التلفزيون
- الدراسة في المدرسة أو في البيت
- المحادثة على التلفون وقراءة الإيميلات

Reading 　　　　　　　　　　　　　　　　　　 القراءة

The table below lists in a random order the activities above along with the average amounts of time Americans spend on these activities. First, read through the column of average lengths of time. Then, match each activity with the amount of time you think Americans spend on it. To form matches, write on a separate sheet of paper the letter of each length of time next to the activity you think it matches with.

　　You may see or want to use the following words:

minute	دَقيقة	دَقيقة
minutes	دَقايِق	دَقائِق

النشاط	Average time Americans spend on the activity
١. لعب الرياضة	أ. ٦ ساعات و٤ دقائق كل أسبوع
٢. التسوّق	ب. ٥ ساعات و١٥ دقيقة كل أسبوع
٣. مشاهدة التلفزيون	ت. ٢٣ ساعة و٥٥ دقيقة كل أسبوع
٤. الدراسة في المدرسة أو في البيت	ث. ١١ ساعة و٥ دقائق كل أسبوع
٥. المحادثة على التلفون وقراءة الإيميلات	ج. يومان و١١١ ساعة و٣٠ دقيقة كل أسبوع

After reading 　　　　　　　　　　　　　 بعد القراءة

What are some surprising facts about how you spend your time?

1. Brainstorm some activities that you think you might spend a surprising amount of time on, compared to your classmates. Estimate how long you spend on each per day, per week, per month, or per year.
2. Make two side-by-side lists in Arabic, one with each activity you do and the other with the time you spend on each—but in a mixed-up order.
3. When you are done with your lists, share them with a classmate. Ask them to guess how much time you spend on each activity by drawing lines between the two lists.

Activity 5	Conversation and listening: How often do you go on Facebook?	محادثة واستماع: كم مرة تدخل في فيسبوك؟	نشاط ٥

In this activity, you'll practice talking about social media use in Arabic.

Before speaking and listening   قبل المحادثة والاستماع

What social media sites do people at your school use? Brainstorm as many as you can.
Make a list and try to figure out how you would write them in Arabic letters.

Listening   الاستماع

Watch the video of Hiba talking about which social media sites she uses. For each social
media site below, put a check ✔ if you hear Hiba mention it and an **X** if you don't. For the
ones that she mentions, write down how much she uses it.

١. بينتريست
٢. تويتر
٣. سنابتشات
٤. تومبلر
٥. فيسبوك
٦. إنستغرام
٧. تيك توك

Speaking   المحادثة

Ask another classmate how often they go onto each of the social media sites you came up
with. Use the model question below and record your classmate's answers next to each site
you listed in قبل المحادثة والاستماع.

كَم مَرّة بِتْفوت عَلى الفَيْسْبوك كُلّ يوم؟	كَم مَرّة تَدْخُل الفَيْسْبوك كُلّ يَوْم؟
كَم مَرّة بِتْفوتي عَلى الفَيْسْبوك كُلّ يوم؟	كَم مَرّة تَدْخُلين في الفَيْسْبوك كُلّ يَوْم؟

After listening and speaking   بعد الاستماع والمحادثة

Write at least three sentences comparing your social media use, your classmate's social
media use, and Hiba's social media use. Use ولكن or بس to compare and contrast different levels of use. Use the following sentence as a model:

أنا بَحِبّ أفوت عَلى الفَيْسْبوك ٧ مَرات كُلّ	أُحِبّ أَنْ أَدْخُل في الفَيْسْبوك ٧ مَرّات كُلّ
يوم بَس صاحْبي بيفَضِّل يفوت عَلى الفَيْسْبوك مَرّة واحْدة كُلّ يوم.	يَوْم وَلْكِن يُفَضِّل صَديقي أَنْ يَدْخُل في الفَيْسْبوك مَرّة واحِدة كُلّ يَوْم.

Activity 6   Listening: I don't have much   استماع: ما عندي وقت فراغ   نشاط ٦
              free time   كتير

In the video titled "ما عندي وقت فراغ كتير," you will see a conversation between توماس
and عصام about what they do in their free time.

Listening   الاستماع

Watch the video, then complete the following:

1. Write down or draw pictures of the activities توماس and عصام say they like.
2. Write down how often they do each activity (if mentioned).

Close listening   الاستماع الدقيق

العامِيّة differs not only from country to country but within countries and cities as well.
In the video, توماس uses some pronunciations that more prevalent in rural areas of Jordan,
while عصام uses some pronunciations that are more often heard in the capital city, Amman.

3. What difference do you hear between the way توماس and عصام pronounce words
   or phrases like وقت فراغ (0:23, 0:28) and قهوة (1:58, 2:01)?
4. What difference do you hear between the ways they pronounce the word كثير
   (0:21, 0:29)?

Activity 7   Reading and conversation: قراءة ومحادثة: كل عام وأنت   نشاط ٧
             May you be well every year!   بخير!

What do you say to people on their birthday? On a religious holiday you celebrate?
On Father's Day or Mother's Day?

Before reading   قبل القراءة

In Arabic, you can use the same greeting on all holidays, both religious and non-religious:

May you be well every year!	كُلّ عام وَأَنْت بِخَير!

This phrase has a synonym for year:

سَنة	عام

Sometimes you will hear varieties of this phrase, as follows:

- كُلّ سَنة وَأَنتَ سالِم!
- كُلّ سَنة وَأَنتِ سالِمة!
- كُلّ سَنة وَأَنتَ طَيِّب!
- كُلّ سَنة وَأَنتِ طَيِّبة!

Practice using these phrases with a classmate.

Reading   القراءة

As demonstrated by the examples below, Arabic speakers often share holiday messages
on social media using different variations of these phrases.

1. For each post: Who might post it on social media? To whom might it be sent? Think of characters from movies or television or people in real life (assuming that they would want to use an Arabic card, of course).
2. What words in the text support your idea about who could give this card and who could receive it? Write some of the key words you used to make your decision.
3. Guess the meaning of the following words or phrases from context:

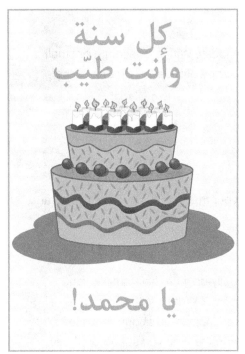

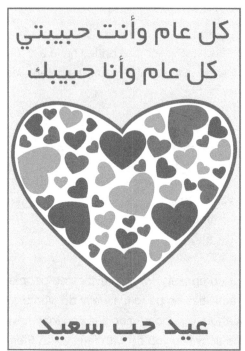

After reading 1   بعد القراءة ١

As you have seen in the various greeting cards and social media posts in this unit, it is common to play on the phrase كل سنة وأنت سالم or كل عام وأنت بخير to celebrate different occasions on social media. Create a post of your own playing off of this phrase that you could share on social media on a specific holiday, then share it with a classmate (or on your own social media profile).

After reading 2   بعد القراءة ٢

On the internet, find out which celebrities have a birthday today. With a classmate or small group, create a short skit in which you wish celebrities a happy birthday using one of the phrases above.

| Activity 8   Conversation: Do you do that with family or with friends? | محادثة: هل تفعل ذلك مع العائلة أو أم مع الأصدقاء؟   نشاط ٨ |

Some of what you choose to do with your family or with your friends is informed by cultural norms in your community.

Before speaking   قبل المحادثة

1. In your community, what activities do people usually do with their families, and what activities do people usually do with their friends? Write a list in Arabic.
2. Think about other communities you may have lived in, learned about, or visited. Are the activities you do with family and friends and the time you spend on those activities the same as in other communities?

Speaking   المحادثة

3. Pick one activity and ask your classmates how often they do this activity with their family and how often they do it with their friends (each day, week, month, or year).

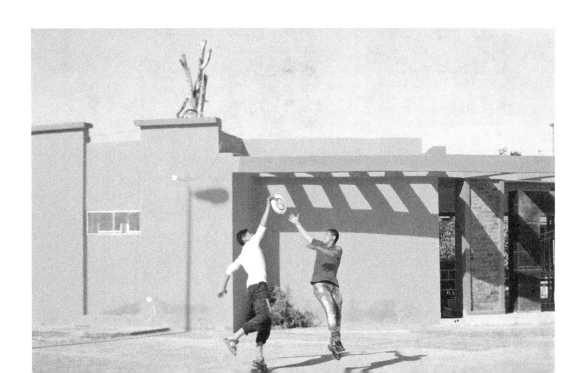

Use the sentence below as a model for how to ask these questions:

كَم مَرّة كُلّ أسبوع بِتْروح عَلى المول مَع عَيلْتَك؟	كَم مَرّة كُلّ أُسْبوع تَذْهَب إلى مَرْكَز التَّسَوُّق مَع عائِلَتِكَ؟
كَم مَرّة كُلّ أُسبوع بِتْروحي عَلى المول مَع عَيلْتِك؟	كَم مَرّة كل أُسْبوع تَذْهَبِين إلى مَرْكَز التَّسَوُّق مَع عائِلَتِكِ؟

As you talk with your classmates, keep track of their answers in a chart like this on a separate piece of paper:

مع الأصدقاء	مع العائلة	الاسم

4. What is the overall trend you notice from the answers above? In Arabic, summarize your conclusion in one or two sentences, then present your finding to your classmates.
5. Take notes as you listen to your classmates. Which activities are done more frequently with family? Which are done more frequently with friends?

Culture: Spending time with family   الثقافة: قضاء الوقت مع العائلة

Look back at the previous activity and the class discussion around it and write a reflection about the following:

*   In your community or family, what are some important activities in which you are expected to participate? How often do they take place? What are your family's expectations about how much time you spend with them?
*   What are some responsibilities you have toward your family now, and what are some you expect to have later in life? At what age would your family stop supporting you financially? At what age might you help support your parents or other family members financially?

Broadly speaking, many sociologists consider the basic unit of American society to be the individual, whereas the basic unit of Arab societies (and societies across Asia, Africa, and Latin America) is the family. Many Arab middle and high school students are expected to spend more time with their families than their American counterparts. In many Arab families, one day of the weekend is dedicated to visiting and spending time with immediate and extended family members.

In the Arab world, the dominant social expectations and economic realities mean that young adults commonly live at home with their parents after graduating high school, during

their university education (if their university is nearby), and until they get married in their twenties or thirties. Many young Arabs appreciate living at home and see having tightly knit families as a strength of their culture. The traditional expectation is that parents will house and take care of their children until marriage and that the kids will reciprocate by housing their elderly parents, if need be, later in life. In your family or community, what is considered an appropriate age to begin living away from home? Where are elderly community members expected to live and who is expected to care for them?

| Activity 9 | Reading, conversation, and writing: Do you want to live with my family? | نشاط ٩ | قراءة ومحادثة وكتابة: هل تريد أن تسكن مع عائلتي؟ |

Imagine that you are going to live with another family on a study abroad trip for a month.

Before reading   قبل القراءة

What are some things that you would hope to do with your host family? How often would you want to do them? Create a chart similar to the one below on a separate piece of paper:

كم مرة؟	النشاط

   Ahmed is a Jordanian student whose family loves to host foreign students on an exchange trip to Jordan. He has penned a letter for Arabic learners like you in hopes you will choose to live with him and his family. Notice that you can read this letter in الفصحى or العاميّة الشاميّة. Arabic speakers might write an email to someone they don't know in either variety. Their choice of register would likely depend upon multiple factors, such as their (and their addressee's) level of formal education, the impression they wish to make, and their own personal preferences.

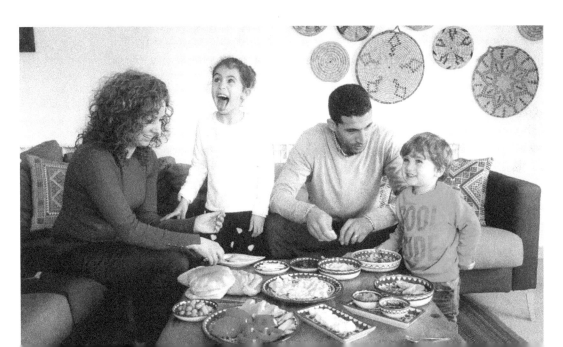

Reading

Keep track of the activities the writer does and how often he does them, then mark whether you consider this a positive or negative reason for living with this family. Create a chart on a separate piece of paper similar to the chart below:

إيجابيّ 👍 أم سلبيّ 👎؟	كم مرة؟	النشاط

What other information can you find in the letter that would influence your decision to choose this family as your host family (or not)?

أهلاً!

تحية طيّبة وبعد. أتمنّى أن تكونوا بأحسن صحّة وحال.

اسمي أحمد جمال حليلة وأنا طالب في المدرسة الثانويّة. أسكن في مدينة عمّان في الأردنّ. عائلتي كبيرة وتتكوّن من أخ وأختين أكبر منّي وأختين أصغر منّي. عائلتي خفيفة الدمّ ولطيفة جدّاً. أيضاً عندي كثير من الأصدقاء في المدرسة.

عندي هوايات كثيرة فأقرأ كل يوم عادةً وأحبّ أيضاً أن ألعب ألعاب الفيديو ثلاث أو أربع مرّات كلّ أسبوع. ألعبها مع أصدقائي وأحياناً مع أخي الكبير. لا أحبّ أن ألعب الرياضة فأفضّل أن أشاهد الرياضة في التلفزيون. أشاهد كرة القدم كلّ أسبوع مع أبي.

هل تحبّون أن تستمعوا إلى الموسيقى؟ أيّ موسيقى تحبّون؟ أفضّل موسيقى "هيب هوب" من أمريكا وأستمع إليها كلّ يوم. أحبّ الموسيقى العربيّة أيضاً ولكن لا أحبّ أن أستمع إليها كلّ يوم، ربما مرّة أو مرّتين كلّ شهر. تحب أمّي الموسيقى العربيّة كثيراً.

أحبّ أيضا أن أذهب إلى المدرسة لأرى أصدقائي، ولكن لا أحبّ أن أدرس وأعمل الواجب. أعمل الواجب ربما مرّة كلّ سنة، ههههههههههه. أنا وعائلتي نذهب إلى المطاعم أو المقاهي قليلاً، ليس كثيراً. نذهب مرّة كلّ شهر أو شهرين. يحبّ أبي أن يلتقي بأصدقائه في المقهى ويذهب هناك مرّة أو مرّتين كلّ أسبوع.

حسناً، خبّروني عن أنفسكم. ماذا تحبّون أن تفعلوا في وقت الفراغ، وماذا تحبّ عائلتكم؟ أتطلع للقائكم بالأردنّ قريباً إن شاء الله!

صديقكم أحمد

مرحبا!

كيفكم؟ شو أخباركم؟ بتمنّى تكونوا بأحسن صحّة وحال.

اسمي أحمد جمال حليلة وأنا طالب بالمدرسة الثانويّة. أنا ساكن بمدينة عمّان بالأردنّ. عائلتي كبيرة بتتكوّن من أخ وأختين أكبر منّي أختين أصغر منّي. عيلتي خفيفة الدمّ وكثير لطيفة. كمان عندي كثير أصحاب بالمدرسة.

عندي هوايات كثيرة فبقرا كلّ يوم عادةً، وكمان بحبّ ألعب ألعاب الفيديو ثلاث أو أربع مرّات كلّ أسبوع. بحبّ ألعبها مع أصحابي وأحياناً مع أخي الكبير. ما بحبّ ألعب الرياضة بس بحب أتفرّج على الرياضة بالتلفزيون. بتفرّج على كرة القدم كلّ أسبوع مع أبوي.

بتحبّوا تسمعوا موسيقى؟ أيّ موسيقى بتحبّوا؟ أنا بفضّل موسيقى "هيب هوب" من أمريكا وبسمعها كلّ يوم. بحبّ الموسيقى العربيّة كمان بس ما بحبّ أسمعها كلّ يوم، ممكن مرّة أو مرّتين كلّ شهر. أمّي كثير بتحبّ الموسيقى العربيّة.

بحبّ أروح على المدرسة عشان أشوف أصحابي، بس ما بحبّ أدرس وأعمل الواجب. بعمل الواجب ممكن مرّة كلّ سنة، هههههههه.

أنا وعيلتي ما كثير منحبّ نروح على مطعم أو قهوة. منحبّ نروح مرّة كل شهر أو كلّ شهرين. أبوي بحبّ يطلع مع أصحابه على القهوة كثير وبروح على كافيه مرّة أو مرّتين كلّ أسبوع.

يلا، خبّروني عن حالكم. شو بتحبّوا وشو بتحبّ عيلتكم؟ إن شاء الله أشوفكم بالأردنّ عن قريب!

صاحبكم أحمد

Speaking

المحادثة

How many people in your class would want to live with the family described in the previous activity, and how many would not? Ask as many classmates as you can, and be sure to write down at least one reason. On a separate piece of paper, create a chart similar to the chart below:

السَبَب Reason	يُريد أم لا يُريد؟	الاسم

Writing

الكتابة

Write an email in reply to Ahmed explaining whether or not you would be a good fit for his family as an exchange student. Be sure to do the following in your email:

- Describe your family and tell who is in it.
- Tell what activities you like to do and how often you like to do them.

- Use كمان or أيضاً to tell what activities Ahmed and his family do that your family also does.
- Use ولكن or بس to tell some activities your family does, or does not do, that Ahmed's family does.
- Refer back to Activity 7 in Lesson Sixteen for the stylistic elements of an informal email.

Unit Four Vocabulary

مفردات الوحدة الرابعة

LESSON FIFTEEN

الدرس الخامس عشر

Core vocabulary

المفردات الأساسيّة

المعنى	العاميّة الشاميّة	الفصحى
Where . . . ?	وَين...؟	أَيْنَ...؟
book	كْتاب	كِتاب
notebook	دَفْتَر	دَفْتَر
Which ____?	أيّ ____؟	أيّ ____؟
On/In which ____?	بِأيّ ____؟	في أيّ ____؟
page	صَفْحة	صَفْحة
activity	نَشاط	نَشاط
number	رَقْم	رَقْم
lesson	دَرْس	دَرْس
professor teacher	أُسْتاذ / أُسْتاذة	أُسْتاذ / أُسْتاذة
teacher *(usually in a school setting)*	مُعَلِّم / مُعَلِّمة	مُعَلِّم / مُعَلِّمة
student	طالِب / طالِبة	طالِب / طالِبة
students *(all-male or mixed group)*	طُلّاب	طُلّاب

المعنى	العاميّة الشاميّة	الفصحى
students *(all-female group)*	طالِبات	طالِبات
present *(in class)*	موْجود / موْجودة	موْجود / مَوْجودة
absent	غايِب / غايْبة	غائِب / غائِبة
class	صَفّ	صَفّ

Extra vocabulary   المفردات الإضافيّة

Is Ahmed there?	أَحْمَد موْجود؟	هَل أَحْمَد مَوْجود؟
Is Samira there?	سَميرة موْجودة؟	هَل سَميرة مَوْجودة؟

LESSON SIXTEEN   **الدرس السادس عشر**

Core vocabulary   المفردات الأساسية

المعنى	العاميّة الشاميّة	الفصحى
family	عَيلة	عائلة
mother	أُمّ إمّ	أُمّ
father	أَب	أَب
husband	جوز	زَوْج
wife	مَرة	زَوْجة
partner *(m.)*	شَريك	شَريك
partner *(f.)*	شَريكة	شَريكة
brother	أَخ	أَخ
brothers	إخْوان	إخْوة
sister	أُخْت إخْت	أُخْت
sisters	إخْوات	أَخَوات

المعنى	العاميّة الشاميّة	الفصحى
I have	عِنْدي	عِنْدي
I don't have	ما عِنْدي	لَيْسَ عِنْدي
you have (m.)	عِنْدَك	عِنْدَك
you have (f.)	عِنْدِك	عِنْدَك
he has	عِنْدُه	عِنْدَهُ
she has	عِنْدَها	عِنْدَها
Do you have . . . ? (m.)	عِنْدَك...؟	هَل عِنْدَك...؟
Do you have . . . ? (f.)	عِنْدِك...؟	هَل عِنْدَكِ...؟
with	مَعَ	مَعَ
friend (m.)	صاحِب	صَديق
friend (f.)	صاحْبة	صَديقة
friends (all-male or mixed-gender)	أَصْحاب	أَصْدِقاء
friends (all-female)	صاحْبات	صَديقات
beloved dear boyfriend	حَبيب	حَبيب
beloved dear girlfriend	حَبيبة	حَبيبة

Extra Vocabulary   المفردات الإضافيّة

How many siblings do you have? (m.)	كَم أخ وأُخْت عِنْدَك؟	كَم أخاً وأُخْتاً عِنْدَك؟
How many siblings do you have? (f.)	كَم أخ وأُخْت عِنْدِك؟	كَم أخاً وأُخْتاً عِنْدَكِ؟
holiday	عيد	عيد
I met . . .	تْعَرَّفِت عَلى...	تَعَرَّفْتُ عَلى...

LESSON SEVENTEEN
Core vocabulary

الدرس السابع عشر
المفردات الأساسية

المعنى	العاميّة الشاميّة	الفصحى
old a grown-up *(when describing things, this word means "big")*	كْبير (بالسِّنّ)	كَبير (في السِّنّ)
young a child *(when describing things, this word means "small")*	صْغير (بالسِّنّ)	صَغير (في السِّنّ)
tall *(when describing things, this word can also mean "long")*	طَويل	طَويل
short	قَصير	قَصير
friendly nice	لَطيف	لَطيف
handsome beautiful	حِلْو	جَميل
smart	ذَكي	ذَكِيّ
pleasant fun to be around *(literally: "light of blood")*	خَفيف الدَّمّ	خَفيف الدَّمّ
unpleasant not fun to be around *(literally: "heavy of blood")*	ثْقيل الدَّمّ	ثَقيل الدَّمّ
crazy insane	مَجْنون	مَجْنون
very tall	طَويل كثير	طَويل جِدّاً
very	كثير	جِدّاً
(he) is not …	مِش	لَيْسَ
(she) is not …	مِش	لَيْسَتْ

المعنى	العاميّة الشاميّة	الفصحى
(I) am not . . .	مِش	لَسْتُ
older than bigger than	أَكْبَر مِن	أَكْبَر مِن
younger than smaller than	أَصْغَر مِن	أَصْغَر مِن
taller than	أَطْوَل مِن	أَطْوَل مِن
shorter than	أَقْصَر مِن	أَقْصَر مِن
nicer than	أَلْطَف مِن	أَلْطَف مِن
more beautiful than	أَحْلى مِن	أَجْمَل مِن
smarter than	أَذْكى مِن	أَذْكى مِن
my name	اِسْمي	اِسْمي
your name (m.)	اِسْمَك	اِسْمُكَ
your name (f.)	اِسْمِك	اِسْمُكِ
his name	اِسْمُهْ	اسمُهُ
her name	اِسْمْها	اسمُها
my	‍ـي	‍ـي
your (m.)	‍ـَك	‍ـُكَ
your (f.)	‍ـِك	‍ـُكِ
his	‍ـُهْ	‍ـُهُ
her	‍ـها	‍ـُها

Extra vocabulary

المفردات الإضافيّة

المعنى	العاميّة الشاميّة	الفصحى
That's it!	هاذا هُوِّ!	هٰذا هُوَ!
Bravo!	عَلَيك! يا عَيني عَلَيكِ!	عَلَيك! يا عَيْني عَلَيكِ!

الفصحى	العاميّة الشاميّة	المعنى
أُريد أَنْ أزور بُرْج إيفل.	بِدّي أزور بُرْج إيفل.	I want to visit the Eiffel Tower.
___ أَكْبَر مِن ___ بِـ...	___ أَكْبَر مِن ___ بِـ...	___ is older than ___ by . . .
___ أَصْغَر مِن ___ بِـ...	___ أَصْغَر مِن ___ بِـ...	___ is younger than ___ by . . .
كَثير	كْثير	a lot
قَليل	شْوَي	a little
سَنة	سَنة	one year
سَنَتَين	سَنْتَين	two years
ثَلاث سَنوات	ثَلاث سْنين	three years
جَدّ	جِدّ	grandfather
جَدّة	سِتّ	grandmother
اِبْني	اِبْني	my son
بِنْتي	بِنْتي	my daughter
هٰذا مُناسِب!	هاذا مُناسِب!	This is appropriate!
هٰذا لَيْسَ مُناسِباً!	هاذا مِش مُناسِب!	This is not appropriate!

LESSON EIGHTEEN

الدرس الثامن عشر

Core vocabulary

المفردات الأساسية

الفصحى	العاميّة الشاميّة	المعنى
عِشْرون عِشْرين	عِشْرين	20
واحِد وَعِشْرون واحِد وَعِشْرين	واحِد وعِشْرين	21
اِثْنان وَعِشْرون اِثْنَيْن وَعِشْرين	اِثْنَين وعِشْرين	22

المعنى	العاميّة الشاميّة	الفصحى
23	ثَلاثة وعِشرين	ثَلاثة وَعِشرون ثَلاثة وَعِشرين
30	ثَلاثين	ثَلاثون ثَلاثين
40	أَرْبَعين	أَرْبَعون أَرْبَعين
50	خَمْسين	خَمْسون خَمْسين
60	سِتّين	سِتّون سِتّين
70	سَبْعين	سَبْعون سَبْعين
80	ثمانين	ثَمانون ثَمانين
90	تِسْعين	تِسْعون تِسْعين
100	مِيّة	مِئة (مائة)
we	اِحْنا	نَحْنُ
you (plural)	إِنْتو	أَنْتُم
they	هُمَّ	هُم

Extra vocabulary   المفردات الإضافيّة

المعنى	العاميّة الشاميّة	الفصحى
The temperature in Boston is 50 degrees Fahrenheit.	الحَرارة في بوسطن 50 دَرَجة فَهْرِنْهايْت.	الحَرارة في بوسطن 50 دَرَجة فَهْرِنْهايْت.
My birthday is in month ____ [number].	عيد ميلادي في شَهْر ____.	عيد ميلادي في شَهْر ____.
I found you! (m.)	لَقيتَك!	وَجَدْتُكَ!

المعنى	العاميّة الشاميّة	الفصحى
I found you! *(f.)*	لَقَيتِك!	وَجَدْتُك!
With family, the students like to . . .	مَع العَيلة، الطُّلّاب بِيحِبّوا...	مَع العائلة، الطُّلّاب يُحِبّون أنْ...
But with friends, they prefer to . . .	بَس مَع الأَصحاب، هُمَّ بيفَضّلوا...	ولٰكِن مَع الأَصْدِقاء، هُم يُفَضّلون أنْ...

LESSON NINETEEN

Core vocabulary

الدرس التاسع عشر
المفردات الأساسية

المعنى	العاميّة الشاميّة	الفصحى
How many times . . . ? How often . . . ?	كَم مَرّة...؟	كَم مَرّة...؟
one time an instance	مَرّة	مَرّة
times instances	مَرّات	مَرّات
each, every, all	كُل	كُل
day	يوم	يَوْم
days	أَيّام	أَيّام
month	شَهِر	شَهْر
months	شُهور	شُهور
year	سَنة	سَنة
years	سِنين	سَنَوات
together	مع بَعْض	مَعاً
by myself	لَحالي	وَحْدي

Extra vocabulary   المفردات الإضافيّة

minute	دَقيقة	دَقيقة
minutes	دَقائِق	دَقائِق
May you be well every year!	كُلّ عام وَأنْت بِخَيْر!	كُلّ عام وأَنْت بِخَيْر!

Sources

LESSON 4

Activity 12

Note 1: Source: http://www.migrationpolicy.org/programs/data-hub/charts/largest
-immigrant-groups-over-time

LESSON 12

Activity 2

Note 1: Data drawn from the following sources: https://www.oecd-ilibrary.org/education
/does-homework-perpetuate-inequities-in-education5jxrhqhtx2xt-en and https://www
.kff.org/wp-content/uploads/2013/01/8010.pdf

Activity 4

Note 2: http://www.wamda.com/2011/12/who-s-shopping-online-in-the-arab-world-

Activity 7

Note 3: http://sabq.org/1tbfde

Activity 11

Note 4: http://www.bloomberg.com/bw/articles/2014-06-24/on-tv-at-least-world-cup
-soccer-is-americas-second-most-popular-sport

Activity 14

Note 5: http://www.bbc.co.uk/arabic/scienceandtech/2015/01
/150113healthpersonalitycomputers

Note 6: http://almesryoon.comرونالدو-ضمنت-صفحة-في-كتاب-عظماء-كرة-القدم

Note 7: http://www.al-sharq.com/news/details/300253#.VLWuSCvF9Q4

Note 8: http://www.alfajertv.com/cocktail/3895904.html

Note 9: http://www.almasryalyoum.com/news/details/628052

Note 10: http://www.aljazeera.net/news/miscellaneous/2015/1/8/فلسطيني-يسبح-بجليد
-هدى-تضامنا-مع-غزة-وسوريا

Note 11: http://www.almasryalyoum.com/news/details/628673. Headline edited slightly.

Note 12: http://www.alnilin.com/news-action-show-id-123260.htm

Note 13: http://www.alkhaleej.ae/sports/page/d284a8b4-ed07-4771-9f9f-040dce1944fe

Note 14: http://www.almasryalyoum.com/news/details/628826

LESSON 13

Activity 1

Note 1: Text adapted from: https://www.addustour.com/articles/978063-أوقات-الفراغ-لدى
-المواطنين-كيف-يستغلونها؟

Activity 8

Note 2: Average usages based on http://www.marketresearchworld.net/index.php?option
=comcontent&task=view&id=102

LESSON 14

Activity 7

Note 1: Inspired by http://ar.hotels.com/ho172396/brj-al-rb-jmyra-dby-alamarat-al-rbyt
-almthdt/

Activity 15

Note 2: Information extracted from: http://www.safrah.com/showthread.php?t=84

LESSON 17

Activity 3

Note 1: All ads are adapted from ads on www.jordanzawaj.com

LESSON 18

Activity 5

Note 1: Information from: http://elaph.com/Web/Economics/2016/3/1078242.html

Note Zainab Mohammed and Salwa Akhnoush were not used because their dates of birth
were not available.

Activity 10

Note 2: http://newspaper.annahar.com/article/117931-الشباب-لا-يقرأون-حقا-لا-يقرأون

Note 3: http://www.aljazeera.net/knowledgegate/books/2008/8/29/هل-تريدون-حقا-إصلاح
-التعليم

Note 4: http://mubasher.aljazeera.net/news/جنون-أم-رياضة-سباحون-يلعبون-الشطرنج-وسط-الثلج

Note 5: http://www.aljazeera.net/programs/economyandpeople/2017/2/4/ماذا-نأكل-في-العالم-العربي

Note 6: http://www.btolat.com/News-59773

Note 7: http://www.filfan.com/news/details/63962

Note 8: http://www.aljazeera.net/news/scienceandtechnology/2015/3/30/دراسة-الشباب-يحبون-سنابتشات-والكبار

Note 9: http://khbrpress.com/post/96900القميص-الأبيضldquo-هذه-قصةrdquoو-كل-ما-تريدون-أن-تrdquoتسلم

Note 10: http://www.mbc.net/ar/news/life/articles/cafe.html

Note 11: https://addustour.com/articles/939786نحن-نحب-القراءة-تنظم-فعالية-للأطفال-السبت-المقبل

Art Credits

All photographs not attributed were taken by Sarah Standish, Richard Cozzens, or Rana Abdul-Aziz or are in the public domain.

All illustrations and maps are by Clinton Reno unless otherwise attributed, © 2022 Georgetown University Press.

INTRODUCTION

Woman, p. xiv: Adobe Stock user Cookie Studio. Used with permission.
Seeds, p. xiv: Adobe Stock user artrachen. Used with permission.
Bird, p. xv: Adobe Stock user Tom. Used with permission.

LESSON 1

High school students, p. 3: Muayad Khdear, © 2022 Qatar Foundation International. Used with permission.

LESSON 2

Men shaking hands, p. 9: Muayad Khdear, © 2022 Qatar Foundation International. Used with permission.
Two men at a table, p. 11: © 2022 Qatar Foundation International. Used with permission.
Two men greeting with a kiss, p. 12: Muayad Khdear, © 2022 Qatar Foundation International. Used with permission.
Woman greeting another woman at the door, p. 13: © 2022 Qatar Foundation International. Used with permission.
Two women greeting with a kiss, p. 14: Muayad Khdear, © 2022 Qatar Foundation International. Used with permission.
Oud, p. 15: Wikimedia user Céréales Killer. Creative Commons license: Attribution-ShareAlike 3.0 Unported (CC By-SA 3.0).
Two men hugging, p. 18: © 2022 Qatar Foundation International. Used with permission.
Two women talking in a hallway, p. 21: © 2022 Qatar Foundation International. Used with permission.

LESSON 3

Family greeting a visitor, p. 23: © 2022 Qatar Foundation International. Used with permission.

Woman talking to the camera, p. 26: © 2022 Qatar Foundation International. Used with permission.

Two women in a store, p. 27: © 2022 Qatar Foundation International. Used with permission.

Two students, p. 28: Muayad Khdear, © 2022 Qatar Foundation International. Used with permission.

One figure pointing to another, p. 29: Illustration by Christopher W. Totten, © 2022 Georgetown University Press.

Figure pointing to themselves, p. 29: Illustration by Christopher W. Totten, © 2022 Georgetown University Press.

Three people sitting in an event hall, p. 29: © Maliha Rahman. Used with permission.

Police car, p. 31: Wikimedia user High Contrast. Creative Commons license: Attribution 3.0 Germany (CC BY 3.0 DE).

Men taking a selfie, p. 34: Flickr user Land Rover MENA. Creative Commons license: Attribution 2.0 Generic (CC BY 2.0).

Two people sitting outside, p. 35: © 2022 Qatar Foundation International. Used with permission.

Two men sitting at a table, p. 36: © 2022 Qatar Foundation International. Used with permission.

Three women outside, p. 37: Muayad Khdear, © 2022 Qatar Foundation International. Used with permission.

LESSON 4

Two men, p. 39: Flickr user Ali Almazawi. Creative Commons license: Attribution-NoDerivs 2.0 Generic (CC BY-ND 2.0).

Four girls making peace signs, p. 41: Muayad Khdear, © 2022 Qatar Foundation International. Used with permission.

Four boys sitting, p. 44: Muayad Khdear, © 2022 Qatar Foundation International. Used with permission.

Two figures pointing to a third, p. 45: Illustration by Christopher W. Totten, © 2022 Georgetown University Press.

Two men sitting, p. 47: Muayad Khdear, © 2022 Qatar Foundation International. Used with permission.

Students studying, p. 51: © 2022 Qatar Foundation International. Used with permission.

LESSON 5

Arabic iPhone keypad, p. 55: Clara Totten, © 2022 Georgetown University Press.

Woman in an office chair talking to a man, p. 62: © 2022 Qatar Foundation International. Used with permission.

Two women talking in a hallway, pg. 63: © 2022 Qatar Foundation International. Used with permission.

Group of women looking at a phone, p. 65: Muayad Khdear, © 2022 Qatar Foundation International. Used with permission.

Three people in a store, p. 68: © 2022 Qatar Foundation International. Used with permission.

LESSON 6

Man raising his hand, p. 81: UC Davis College of Engineering. Creative Commons license: Attribution 2.0 Generic (CC BY 2.0).

Boys around a water fountain, p. 82: Middle East Children's Alliance. Creative Commons license: Attribution 2.0 Generic (CC BY 2.0).

Signs on a wall, p. 82: Flickr user Emanuello Brigant. Creative Commons license: Attribution 2.0 Generic (CC BY 2.0).

LESSON 7

Two women looking at a cell phone, p. 85: Muayad Khdear, © 2022 Qatar Foundation International. Used with permission.

Two women eating lunch, p. 89: Muayad Khdear, © 2022 Qatar Foundation International. Used with permission.

Family in a park, p. 94: Muayad Khdear, © 2022 Qatar Foundation International. Used with permission.

Men jumping, p. 95: Illustration by Christopher W. Totten, © 2022 Georgetown University Press.

Woman doing a zaghrouta, p. 95: Illustration by Christopher W. Totten, © 2022 Georgetown University Press.

Cartoon with three men, p. 98: © مُحَمّد عَبْداللّطيف. Used with permission.

Museum of Islamic Art, p. 101: Flickr user Jimmy Baikovicius. Creative Commons license: Attribution-ShareAlike 2.0 Generic (CC BY-SA 2.0).

LESSON 8

Man waiting at a table, p. 103: © 2022 Qatar Foundation International. Used with permission.

People praying in a mosque, p. 114: AMISOM Public Information. Public domain.

Doha city skyline, p. 115: © 2022 Qatar Foundation International. Used with permission.

Students taking a group selfie: p. 119: Muayad Khdear, © 2022 Qatar Foundation International. Used with permission.

LESSON 9

People seated to eat a meal, p. 123: © 2022 Qatar Foundation International. Used with permission.

Man and a woman talking on a bench, p. 128: Muayad Khdear, © 2022 Qatar Foundation International. Used with permission.

Taxi parking, p. 137: Muayad Khdear, © 2022 Qatar Foundation International. Used with permission.

LESSON 10

Coffee cup and pot on a tray, p. 139: Muayad Khdear, © 2022 Qatar Foundation International. Used with permission.

Green drink and tea, p. 142: Flickr user Marco Ooi. Creative Commons license: Attribution-ShareAlike 2.0 Generic (CC BY-SA 2.0).

Vietnamese coffee and a glass of ice, p. 142: Flickr user Ron Dollete. Creative Commons license: Attribution-No Derivs 2.0 Generic (CC BY-ND 2.0).

Cup and coffee pot, p. 142: Flickr user Alper Çuğun. Creative Commons license: Attribution 2.0 Generic (CC BY 2.0).

Starbucks mug, p. 142: Flickr user Libby Arnold. Creative Commons license: Attribution 2.0 Generic (CC BY 2.0).

French tea setting, p. 142: Flickr user Jason Tong. Creative Commons license: Attribution 2.0 Generic (CC BY 2.0).

Espresso mug, p. 142: Flickr user cyclonebill. Creative Commons license: Attribution-ShareAlike 2.0 Generic (CC BY-SA 2.0).

Man pouring from a ladle, p. 142: Flickr user Will De Freitas. Creative Commons license: Attribution-NoDerivs 2.0 Generic (CC BY-ND 2.0).

Man pouring tea, p. 142: Flickr user Katie Bordner. Creative Commons license: Attribution 2.0 Generic (CC BY 2.0).

Bubble tea, p. 142: Flick user snowpea&bokchoi. Creative Commons license: Attribution 2.0 Generic (CC BY 2.0).

Group of men having tea, p. 145: Muayad Khdear, © 2022 Qatar Foundation International. Used with permission.

Outdoor market, p. 148: Muayad Khdear, © 2022 Qatar Foundation International. Used with permission.

Small cup of coffee, p. 149: Muayad Khdear, © 2022 Qatar Foundation International. Used with permission.

Someone making coffee, p. 151: © 2022 Qatar Foundation International. Used with permission.

Coffee serving tray, p. 152: © 2022 Qatar Foundation International. Used with permission.

Someone serving tea, p. 153: Muayad Khdear, © 2022 Qatar Foundation International. Used with permission.

Three people drinking coffee, p. 155: Muayad Khdear, © 2022 Qatar Foundation International. Used with permission.

Man in red with tray, p. 156: Muayad Khdear, © 2022 Qatar Foundation International. Used with permission.

LESSON 11

Students looking at a map, p. 169: © 2022 Qatar Foundation International. Used with permission.

Boys in class, p. 170: Flickr user Russell Watkins/ DFID. Creative Commons license: Attribution 2.0 Generic (CC BY 2.0).

LESSON 12

Soccer players, p. 173: Flickr user AK Bijuraj. Creative Commons license: Attribution 2.0 Generic (CC BY 2.0).

Spray paint artists, p. 174: © 2022 Qatar Foundation International. Used with permission.

Two men sitting outside, p. 175: © 2022 Qatar Foundation International. Used with permission.

Souq, p. 183: Flickr user M. Higuera. Creative Commons license: Attribution 2.0 Generic (CC BY 2.0).

Men painting calligraphy, p. 185: © 2022 Qatar Foundation International. Used with permission.

People relaxing at a mosque, p. 186: Flickr user Abdulla Al Muhairi. Creative Commons license: Attribution 2.0 Generic (CC BY 2.0).

Qatari women's equestrian team, p. 190: Doha Stadium Plus Qatar. Creative Commons license: Attribution 2.0 Generic (CC BY 2.0).

Two boys playing soccer, p. 191: Flickr user James. Creative Commons license: Attribution 2.0 Generic (CC BY 2.0).

Soccer team, p. 194: Doha Stadium plus Qatar. Creative Commons license: Attribution 2.0 Generic (CC BY 2.0).

Lebanon versus Syria basketball game, p. 196: Doha Stadium plus Qatar. Creative Commons license: Attribution 2.0 Generic (CC BY 2.0).

LESSON 13

Two girls reading, p. 203: UNESCO. Creative Commons license: Attribution-ShareAlike 3.0 IGO (CC BY-SA 3.0 IGO).

Group of young adults sitting, p. 204: Muayad Khdear, © 2022 Qatar Foundation International. Used with permission.

Woman lifting weights, p. 208: Muayad Khdear, © 2022 Qatar Foundation International. Used with permission.

People playing a game, p. 210: Muayad Khdear, © 2022 Qatar Foundation International. Used with permission.

Dominoes, p. 210: Flickr user Michael Bentley. Creative Commons license: Attribution 2.0 Generic (CC BY 2.0).

Students painting a sidewalk, p. 213: Al Ahliyya Amman University. Creative Commons license: Attribution-ShareAlike 2.0 Generic (CC BY-SA 2.0).

LESSON 14

Colorful building, p. 225: Muayad Khdear, © 2022 Qatar Foundation International. Used with permission.

Traffic circle, p. 228: Muayad Khdear, © 2022 Qatar Foundation International. Used with permission.

Fruit sellers, p. 232: Muayad Khdear, © 2022 Qatar Foundation International. Used with permission.

Family eating dinner, p. 238: Muayad Khdear, © 2022 Qatar Foundation International. Used with permission.

Bags of tea for sale, p. 246: Muayad Khdear, © 2022 Qatar Foundation International. Used with permission.

Men playing musical instruments, p. 248: Flickr user Hernán Piñera. Creative Commons license: Attribution-ShareAlike 2.0 Generic (CC BY-SA 2.0).

Man in his shop in a souq, p. 248: Flickr user Khalid Almasoud. Creative Commons license: Attribution-NonCommercial 2.0 Generic (CC BY-NC 2.0). Used with permission.

Two students, p. 253: Muayad Khdear, © 2022 Qatar Foundation International. Used with permission.

LESSON 15

School children, p. 263: Flickr user Cluster Munition Coalition. Creative Commons license: Attribution 2.0 Generic (CC BY 2.0).

Children's books, p. 264: Flickr user Dennis Jarvis. Creative Commons license: Attribution-ShareAlike 2.0 Generic (CC BY-SA 2.0).

LESSON 16

Two women in front of the sea, p. 271: Flickr user Patrick Gaudin for Voyages Provence. Creative Commons license: Attribution 2.0 Generic (CC BY 2.0).

Berber family, p. 273: Flickr user ReflectedSerendipity. Creative Commons license: Attribution-ShareAlike 2.0 Generic (CC BY-SA 2.0).

Family sitting outside on grass, p. 273: Muayad Khdear, © 2022 Qatar Foundation International. Used with permission.

Family on the street with balloons, p. 274: Flickr user Land Rover MENA. Creative Commons license: Attribution 2.0 Generic (CC BY 2.0).

Crowd and a family, p. 275: © 2022 Qatar Foundation International. Used with permission.

Family sitting in a living room, p. 278. © 2022 Qatar Foundation International. Used with permission.

Goup of women, p. 289: Flickr user Patrick Gaudin. Creative Commons license: Attribution 2.0 Generic (CC BY 2.0).

Two women on a park bench, p. 292: Muayad Khdear, © 2022 Qatar Foundation International. Used with permission.

LESSON 17

People posing on the stairs, p. 297: Flickr user Patrick Gaudin. Creative Commons license: Attribution 2.0 Generic (CC BY 2.0).

Students standing together, p. 298: Muayad Khdear, © 2022 Qatar Foundation International. Used with permission.

Group of students looking at a book, p. 308: © 2022 Qatar Foundation International. Used with permission.

Great Pyramid of Giza, p. 312: Flickr user Jerome Bon. Creative Commons license: Attribution 2.0 Generic (CC BY 2.0).

Tokyo Tower, p. 313: Flickr user Perry Li. Creative Commons license: Attribution-ShareAlike 2.0 Generic (CC BY-SA 2.0).

Burj Khalifa, p. 313: Flickr user Colin Capelle. Creative Commons license: Attribution 2.0 Generic (CC BY 2.0).

Abraj al-Bayt, p. 313: Flickr user Abdulla Al Muhairi. Creative Commons license: Attribution 2.0 Generic (CC BY 2.0).

One World Trade Center, p. 313: Flickr user R. Boed. Creative Commons license: Attribution 2.0 Generic (CC BY 2.0).

Willis Tower in Chicago, p. 313: Flickr user Francisco Antunes. Creative Commons license: Attribution 2.0 Generic (CC BY 2.0).

Empire State Buiding, p. 313: Flickr user Tom Thai. Creative Commons license: Attribution 2.0 Generic (CC BY 2.0).

Eifel Tower, p. 313: Flickr user James Diedrick. Creative Commons license: Attribution 2.0 Generic (CC BY 2.0).

Space Needle, p. 313: Flickr user Jonathan Miske. Creative Commons license: Attribution-ShareAlike 2.0 Generic (CC BY-SA 2.0).

Fairuz on stage, p. 315: Creative Commons license: Attribution-ShareAlike 3.0 Unported (CC BY-SA 3.0).

Elissa singing, p. 315: Flickr user Ahmed Zayer. Creative Commons license: Attribution 2.0 Generic (CC BY 2.0).

Kazem singing, p. 316: Wikimedia user Y. Momani. Public domain.

Wael Kfoury on stage, p. 316: Flickr user Dianna Farroukh. Creative Commons license: Attribution 2.0 Generic (CC BY 2.0).

Damascus from a distance, p. 322: Flickr user upyernoz. Creative Commons license: Attribution 2.0 Generic (CC BY 2.0).

Women posing together, p. 325: Muayad Khdear, © 2022 Qatar Foundation International. Used with permission.

LESSON 18

Family of various ages, p. 327: © Souhad Zendah. Used with Permission

Doha cityscape, p. 329: © 2022 Qatar Foundation International. Used with permission.

Couple at a wedding, p. 332: Flickr user Ikmal H. Noordin. Creative Commons license: Attribution 2.0 Generic (CC BY 2.0).

Woman in sunglasses, p. 334: Muayad Khdear, © 2022 Qatar Foundation International. Used with permission.

Wedding party, p. 337: © Maliha Rahman. Used with permission.

Two men laughing, p. 345: Muayad Khdear © 2022 Qatar Foundation International. Used with permission.

Girls in a pool, p. 348: Flickr user Chascar. Creative Commons license: Attribution 2.0 Generic (CC BY 2.0).

LESSON 19

Family photograph in black and white, p. 351. © Rana Abdul-Aziz.

Young woman at Tahrir Square, p. 352: Flickr user Al Jazeera English. Creative Commons license: Attribution-ShareAlike 2.0 Generic (CC BY-SA 2.0).

Boys playing frisbee, p. 360: © 2022 Qatar Foundation International. Used with permission.

Family eating, p. 362: Muayad Khdear © 2022 Qatar Foundation International. Used with permission.

Grammar Index

فهرست القواعد

About the Authors

Sarah Standish was the founding teacher of the first high school Arabic program in the state of Oregon and also served as deputy director at OneWorld Now! in Seattle, Washington. She is the author of *Culture Smart! Syria*.

Richard Cozzens is a preceptor in Arabic at Harvard University and has served as the director of the STARTALK Arabic Summer Academy in Boston, Massachusetts. He has taught Arabic to high school and university students since 2008.

Rana Abdul-Aziz is a senior lecturer and the Arabic language coordinator at Tufts University. She has been teaching Arabic at various institutions and training new Arabic teachers for more than fifteen years.